LIBRARY OF RELIGIOUS BIOGRAPHY

Edited by Mark A. Noll, Nathan O. Hatch, and Allen C. Guelzo

THE LIBRARY OF RELIGIOUS BIOGRAPHY is a series of original biographies on important religious figures throughout American and British history.

The authors are well-known historians, each a recognized authority in the period of religious history in which his or her subject lived and worked. Grounded in solid research of both published and archival sources, these volumes link the lives of their subjects — not always thought of as "religious" persons — to the broader cultural contexts and religious issues that surrounded them.

Marked by careful scholarship yet free of academic jargon, the books in this series are well-written narratives meant to be *read* and *enjoyed* as well as studied.

LIBRARY OF RELIGIOUS BIOGRAPHY

William Ewart Gladstone: Faith and Politics in Victorian Britain
David Bebbington

Aimee Semple McPherson: Everybody's Sister • *Edith L. Blumhofer*

Her Heart Can See: The Life and Hymns of Fanny J. Crosby
Edith L. Blumhofer

Abraham Kuyper: Modern Calvinist, Christian Democrat • *James D. Bratt*

Orestes A. Brownson: American Religious Weathervane
Patrick W. Carey

Thomas Merton and the Monastic Vision • *Lawrence S. Cunningham*

Billy Sunday and the Redemption of Urban America • *Lyle W. Dorsett*

The Kingdom Is Always but Coming: A Life of Walter Rauschenbusch
Christopher H. Evans

Liberty of Conscience: Roger Williams in America • *Edwin S. Gaustad*

Sworn on the Altar of God: A Religious Biography of Thomas Jefferson
Edwin S. Gaustad

Abraham Lincoln: Redeemer President • *Allen C. Guelzo*

Charles G. Finney and the Spirit of American Evangelicalism
Charles E. Hambrick-Stowe

Francis Schaeffer and the Shaping of Evangelical America
Barry Hankins

Harriet Beecher Stowe: A Spiritual Life • *Nancy Koester*

Emily Dickinson and the Art of Belief • *Roger Lundin*

A Short Life of Jonathan Edwards • *George M. Marsden*

The Puritan as Yankee: A Life of Horace Bushnell • *Robert Bruce Mullin*

Prophetess of Health: A Study of Ellen G. White • *Ronald L. Numbers*

Blaise Pascal: Reasons of the Heart • *Marvin R. O'Connell*

Occupy Until I Come: A. T. Pierson and the Evangelization of the World
Dana L. Robert

God's Strange Work: William Miller and the End of the World
David L. Rowe

The Divine Dramatist: George Whitefield and the
Rise of Modern Evangelicalism • *Harry S. Stout*

Assist Me to Proclaim: The Life and Hymns of Charles Wesley
John R. Tyson

Harriet Beecher Stowe

A Spiritual Life

Nancy Koester

WILLIAM B. EERDMANS PUBLISHING COMPANY

GRAND RAPIDS, MICHIGAN / CAMBRIDGE, U.K.

Wm. B. Eerdmans Publishing Co.
2140 Oak Industrial Drive N.E., Grand Rapids, Michigan 49505 /
P.O. Box 163, Cambridge CB3 9PU U.K.

Printed in the United States of America

20 19 18 17 16 15 14   7 6 5 4 3 2 1

Library of Congress Cataloging-in-Publication Data

Koester, Nancy, 1954-
Harriet Beecher Stowe: a spiritual life / Nancy Koester.
pages   cm.   — (Library of Religious Biography)
Includes bibliographical references and index.
ISBN 978-0-8028-3304-4 (pbk.: alk. paper)
1. Stowe, Harriet Beecher, 1811-1896.
2. Women authors, American — 19th century— Biography.
3. Abolitionists — United States — Biography.   I. Title.

PS2956.K64   2013
813′.3 — dc23
[B]

2013027100

www.eerdmans.com

Contents

Contents

Acknowledgments

The book tells the story of the life of Harriet Beecher Stowe as a Christian author who drew inspiration from her faith. It is written by a historian of Christianity in America who seeks to foreground the role of faith in Stowe's life, and to see Stowe in the context of the times in which she lived. It is therefore a work that draws from scholars across several disciplines. The work of many scholars has enriched this book, with special thanks to Mark Noll, Vincent Harding, Joan Hedrick, and Bruce Kirkham.

Librarians and archivists helped make this book possible. I am especially grateful to staff of the New York Public Library, the University of Virginia, the Cincinnati Historical Society and the Public Library of Cincinnati, the Bowdoin College Special Collections, the Rutherford B. Hayes Presidential Library, and Princeton University. Special thanks are due to Beth Burgess at the Harriet Beecher Stowe Center in Hartford. Kate Skrebutenas at Princeton Seminary Library and Karen Alexander at Luther Seminary in St. Paul gave expert help with interlibrary loans. I have relied on the work of Bruce Kirkham, who spent decades compiling a searchable database of Stowe's correspondence, available at the Stowe Center in Hartford, and Stephen Railton, whose multimedia archive "Uncle Tom's Cabin & American Culture" is an Internet goldmine.

Harriet Beecher Stowe drew inspiration from the "Communion of Saints," the Church in every time and place. In that spirit, I express my gratitude to St. Anthony Park Lutheran Church in St. Paul, Minnesota, and to Sacred Harp Singers, who still fill the air with hymns Stowe knew and loved. The spiritual direction community helped me to listen more deeply for the movement of God in my own life, and this in turn made me more aware of the spiritual journey of Harriet Beecher Stowe.

Eerdmans gave me the opportunity to write this book and helped bring it to fruition. Reinder van Til first raised the idea of writing a volume on Harriet Beecher Stowe. I am grateful to David Bratt, my editor, who knew just when to be patient and when to give me a push. I thank him for his editorial skill, his good advice, and all the things he did behind the scenes to make this book happen.

Friends and family read part or all the manuscript in its various stages. Thanks are due to Claudia, Kristi, Emily, and Chuck, for telling me what they *really* thought. Most of all I thank my husband Craig, my live-in Bible scholar and best friend, who always believed I would finish this work, and who walked the long tow path with me.

This book is lovingly dedicated to my mother, Margaret, a pastor's daughter and pastor's wife who raised five children by the grace of God.

Introduction

January 1, 1863, was to be a New Year's Day like no other. Abraham Lincoln was to sign the Emancipation Proclamation, declaring all slaves in states still in rebellion against the United States to be "thenceforth and forever free." It would give new purpose to the war and show the world that the Union cause and the end of slavery went hand in hand. All across the North, crowds waited for word that Lincoln had indeed signed. Until that news came, the jubilation was on hold. The word from Washington City would come in coded clicks transmitted on wires stretched across the country — the telegraph. The news might come at any instant, but instead the hours dragged by. Some people murmured that perhaps Lincoln changed his mind because of the Union defeat at Fredericksburg.

Finally, as night fell, runners from a telegraph office brought the message: Lincoln signed! In Boston's packed Music Hall the news uncorked a tumult of joy. Amidst the whistling, cheering, and stomping someone shouted, "Harriet Beecher Stowe! Harriet Beecher Stowe!" The crowd took up the chant. She was there that night, up in the balcony, and now she made her way forward, a small, middle-aged woman, her skirts and bonnet crushed in the press of the crowd. They knew — everyone knew — that Stowe had helped bring freedom to the slaves.

She did so with a story that swept readers by the tens of thousands into the antislavery movement. Before her antislavery novel *Uncle Tom's Cabin* ran as a magazine serial in 1851 and appeared as a book in 1852, most Northerners accepted slavery or tried to look the other way. Those who actively opposed slavery were a small minority, and these "abolitionists" were regarded as crackpots and fanatics. But after *Uncle Tom's Cabin* appeared, public opinion in the North changed. The release of Stowe's book was a historic event. In the South, Stowe's book was banned. Hostile reviewers called Stowe a traitor to her race, the devil in petticoats, a slanderer whose book was sure to start a war. Of course the war would have come without *Uncle Tom's Cabin,* and slavery would have ended. But somehow in the providence of God, Stowe believed, her story had done its work. Now she stood in Boston's Music Hall on the night of January 1, 1863, and wept for joy.

As the celebration rolled on, Stowe receded into the crowd. Perhaps she thought of her son Fred, a soldier in the Union Army — what price would he pay for the cause of freedom? That night her beloved father, Lyman Beecher, was slipping away, his once brilliant mind now so feeble that he would never know, would never hear Emancipation proclaimed. Perhaps Stowe thought of her meeting with Lincoln in the White House the previous November. Like other abolitionists, Stowe was frustrated that the president was taking so long to strike directly at slavery, and she wanted to make sure that he was serious about Emancipation. But now she trusted that Lincoln had his reasons and would keep his word.

That the Proclamation was a war measure, and therefore limited and temporary, none knew better than Lincoln. "We are like whalers who have long been on a chase," Lincoln later said; with the Emancipation Proclamation "we have at last got the harpoon into the monster, but we must now look how we steer, or with one 'flop' of his tail he will send us all to eternity."[1] It would take a Constitutional amendment to end slavery once and for all — along with the surrender of the Southern armies. Long before the war began, abolitionists were attacking slavery. But the shafts they hurled seemed to glance off without making a dent. Remarkably, what struck deep in the conscience of the North (which was, after all, complicit in slavery) was a novel written by a woman.

In those days women were expected to remain silent on public issues. They could not vote and had few legal rights. Colleges did not admit female students when Harriet was growing up. Women could not enter the professions except to teach for very low pay (which Harriet did). They were barred from speaking in public, except to groups of women and children. Churches did not allow women to preach. But with her pen Stowe shaped public opinion. Her first novel, *Uncle Tom's Cabin,* was the best seller of the century, second only to the Bible.

Stowe was a prolific writer, producing books, magazine articles, devotional works, poems, and children's stories. After doing battle with slavery she turned her attention to another conflict, a spiritual one, with the religion of her father Lyman Beecher. His New England Calvinism helped to fire her moral indignation against slavery and gave her the audacity to call a nation to repentance. But that same faith also inflicted deep wounds on her, and she began her quest to find some other way to be a Christian. Her struggles to free herself from New England Calvinism, while honoring her father and following Jesus, form the heart of some of her best fiction. Like Jacob wrestling with the angel, she cried, "I will not let you go until you bless me."

Stowe believed strongly in Jesus, and her Christian faith was central to her life and work. She knew moments of glory and dark nights of the soul, long periods of plodding and flashes of inspiration. Over the course of her lifetime, her spiritual quest changed. But it never ended, and it never failed to shape her life.

CHAPTER ONE

This Old House

Harriet Elizabeth Beecher was born on June 14, 1811, the sixth living child of Lyman and Roxana Beecher. Babies were "no longer a novelty" in the family, so each new arrival had to find a place among "the wants and clamors of older children,"[1] Harriet later recalled. The house was full of the wants and clamors of adults too, for Lyman Beecher was the minister of the local Congregational church in Litchfield, Connecticut. His parishioners often came to the Beecher home, and clergy passing through town would have dinner and stay overnight with the Beechers. To make ends meet, the Beechers often took in boarders. In such a busy household, the children had to be "washed and dressed and catechized, got to school at regular hours in the morning, and [sent] to bed inflexibly at the earliest possible hour of the night."[2]

Beecher children were given chores to do according to their age and capability. The vegetable garden had to be weeded and fruit picked in season, the chickens fed, eggs gathered, the cow milked and horses tended. The older boys caught fish in nearby streams or hunted for small game, while the girls picked berries to make into jams and jellies. Bread was baked at home; even the yeast had to be cultured or "caught" from the air. Water was collected in rain barrels or pumped by hand. Kindling was split and stacked by the stone hearth and the bare wood kitchen floor was scrubbed with sand to keep it clean. Sewing machines were not yet available, so every stitch of clothing and bedding was done by hand. Most people made their own candles, soap, and brooms, or traded for goods in kind.

Travel was slow in 1811 in the days before railroads, though in

1

Harriet's childhood the first steamboats began chugging along the Ohio and Mississippi Rivers. Work began on the Erie Canal when Harriet was six years old, and when she was seventeen, the first telegraph message was sent in the United States. The world of Harriet's childhood was not all that different from that of her parents' generation.

Harriet's father, Lyman Beecher, was born in 1775, a premature baby so small no one thought he would live. His mother survived only a few days after giving birth, and the women attending the birth said it would be a mercy if the baby died too, since the father would not be able to take care of him. So the women wrapped the child and set him aside while they tended the mother. But Lyman Beecher defied expectations and laid hold on life. He was given into the care of an aunt and uncle, who raised him on their farm near Guilford, Connecticut. But Lyman had little interest in farming; instead he wanted to go to school.

Beecher was converted under the preaching of Timothy Dwight at Yale College, where he committed his life to "the Church of God, my country, and the world given to Christ." He saw himself as "harnessed to the Chariot of Christ, whose wheels of fire" were rolling onward, "high and dreadful to his foes, and glorious to his friends. I could not stop."[3] If the Lord's chariot got mired in mud, or if Lyman Beecher collapsed in harness, then his family needed to climb out and push.

As a young man Beecher vowed "never to marry a weak woman." He needed a wife with "sense" and "strength to lean upon." He found a woman who was strong and sensible, but from a higher class than Beecher himself. Roxana Foote was the granddaughter of a general who served under George Washington. Roxana was a cultivated young woman who could sing, speak French, and paint miniature portraits on ivory. She enjoyed mathematics and studied chemistry; indeed, "the whole circle in which she moved was one of uncommon intelligence, vivacity, and wit." Lyman called Roxana his better half "both intellectually and morally." Best of all, she possessed a "restful and peace-giving" temperament that allowed her to rise above every trial. Lyman saw in Roxana "those qualities . . . [which were] indispensable to my happiness."[4]

But Roxana's family was too worldly for Lyman Beecher. They exchanged Christmas gifts and read novels! Roxana even devised a bookstand so that she could read novels while spinning flax. More troubling was the fact that Roxana and her family were Episcopalians. Lyman Beecher would be a Congregationalist minister, but Episcopalians did not recognize Congregationalists as "real" clergy. Episcopalians recognized as valid only one form of ministry: ordination (holy orders) by the laying on of hands, from a bishop who stood in apostolic succession. Without this particular rite, Lyman Beecher could not be a *real* minister in the eyes of Episcopalians. Fortunately Roxana was willing to bend on this point.

For his part, Lyman Beecher saw conversion as the only way to become a Christian. And now he was in love with a woman who saw no need for conversion, since she was baptized and raised in the faith. That issue — how one becomes a Christian — would be very significant in the life of Harriet Beecher Stowe.

Lyman and Roxana wrote to each other about this when they were courting. Lyman urged Roxana to bewail her sins and seek conversion. But Roxana "could not remember a time when she was anything less than deeply in love with God."[5] Lyman tried to convict Roxana of her sinful, depraved nature, so that she could repent and be saved. And Roxana became so introspective that her family feared Lyman was driving her to distraction.

He probably was. Lyman decided that if Roxana possessed a particular virtue, then he would be satisfied that she was really a Christian. That virtue was "benevolence" (also called "disinterestedness") — pure love, free from all taint of self-interest. Since all people are sinners, true benevolence must be God's gift. Of course, it is hard to know if one's love is completely free from self-interest. New England theologians came up with a litmus test: a person who is truly benevolent must be *sincerely willing even to be damned for the glory of God.*

Lyman therefore asked Roxana if she would be willing to be damned for the glory of God. She replied that she was *not* willing to be forsaken by God, and that God would not be glorified by the damnation of her soul or anyone else's. And Lyman answered, "Oh, Roxana, what a fool I've been!" Lyman was not about to give her up; but what if that meant he did not love God supremely?[6] The question troubled him, but not enough to make him end the courtship.

When Lyman Beecher completed his studies at Yale, he was licensed to preach and then ordained to serve a church in East Hampton on Long Island. In addition he was to serve a nearby settlement of free blacks and the Indian village of Montauk.[7]

All That and Heaven Too?

In the fall of 1799, Lyman married Roxana and brought her to East Hampton. Roxana's sister Mary came along. Except for one long street with a windmill at each end, wagon ruts sufficed for roads. There were no stores, and anything not made locally was brought in by boat. Few trees grew there, so Beecher planted an orchard. "All here is the unvaried calm of a frog pond, without the music of it," Mary wrote. "A kind of torpor and apathy seems to prevail over the face of things, as standing water begins to turn green."[8]

The artistic Roxana wanted to have something beautiful in her home. She wove a rug and painted a floral design on it using pigments she had ground and mixed herself. No other family in East Hampton possessed a rug. When an old deacon called on the Beechers, he hardly dared to tread on it. "D'ye think ye can have all that an' Heaven too?"[9] the old man wondered aloud.

Their first child, Catharine, was born in 1800, followed by William in 1802, Edward in 1803, Mary in 1805 and George in 1809. Roxana managed the household and cared for the children with her sister Mary's help. Back then, even people of modest means hired help for chopping wood, hauling water, washing clothes, and cooking. Two black cooks, Zillah and Rachel, worked for the Beechers not as slaves, but as indentured servants.

Lyman Beecher gave his all to ministry. Almost every night of the week he preached and taught at one of the three points of his parish.[10] What he saw in the Montauk village alarmed him: rum sellers exploited the Indians to the point of degradation. Later Beecher helped launch a major campaign against drunkenness.

But the first social issue he tackled was dueling. In this polite form of murder, gentlemen could defend their honor against insult and injury. Duels were fought under agreed-upon rules, using pistols or swords. As long as the duel was properly conducted, killing another man was legal. The practice had critics, but in 1804 dueling became a national scandal when Aaron Burr (Vice President of the United States) shot and killed Alexander Hamilton (Secretary of the Treasury) in a duel at Weehawken, New Jersey.

From his pulpit Lyman Beecher thundered that dueling was a sin, and said clergy should refuse Holy Communion to duelists and deny them a Christian burial. Duelists, said Beecher, should not be allowed to vote. A nation that allows dueling must repent — or face the awful judgment of God. The sermon was published and Lyman Beecher's name began to spread beyond Long Island.

After years of trying, Beecher stirred up a revival in East Hampton. God has a moral government, he declared, and we are accountable to it. Everyone is responsible to become a citizen of God's government (through conversion) and then live accordingly. Many of Beecher's flock were converted.[11] Then Beecher preached on God's moral government at a synod meeting in Newark and published his sermon: "The Government of God Desirable." Beecher's blend of divine power and personal freedom appealed to Americans born after the Revolution, which cast off imposed rule and created a new government.

Encouraged by his success, Beecher drove himself hard. He suffered a breakdown (then called a "state of nervous prostration") from which it took a year to recover. Then he stepped back into harness to pull the chariot of the Lord once again.

In the winter of 1809 a sixth child was born to the Beechers. They named her Harriet, after one of Roxana's sisters. But the baby contracted whooping cough and Roxana stayed up "night after night, taking care of the child till she was exhausted," Lyman later recalled. He told Roxana to get some rest while he watched over the child. But when Roxana woke up, little Harriet was dead. Roxana "was so resigned that she seemed almost happy," Lyman wrote. Though the loss of this child hurt her deeply, she accepted it as God's will. "After the child was laid out, she looked so very beautiful that [Roxana] took her pencil and sketched her likeness on ivory."[12]

The Beecher family was hard pressed to make ends meet. Lyman's salary of $400 a year would not stretch far enough to feed and clothe his family. Roxana and her sister Mary earned a little money by keeping school in their home and boarding four students. But the congregation balked when Beecher asked for a raise. Some disliked his revival preaching and wanted him to leave. Others insisted Beecher must live within his means. In their minds, the congregation was not ungenerous; East Hampton even had a custom that "one fourth of the whales stranded on the beach were always presented to the minister as a portion of his salary."[13] Whale oil was precious, but it would take more than a cut of blubber to lubricate the Beechers' budget. Lyman informed the congregation that unless they paid his debts and raised his salary to $500 per year *plus firewood,* he would re-sign on grounds of inadequate support.[14]

Then in January of 1810, Beecher received an invitation to preach at a Congregational church in Litchfield, Connecticut. After he did so, the congregation offered him $800 per year plus firewood — twice what Beecher made in East Hampton. Litchfield seemed like an excellent place for a rising young minister. Stagecoach lines connected it to New York and Boston, as well as to Hartford and Albany.[15] Here were several thriving businesses and trades, a law school, and a girls' academy. The town was "a delightful village on a fruitful hill" with "a population both enlightened and respectable." Its broad streets were "shaded by splendid elms" and graced by "many spacious and beautiful colonial houses."[16]

So it was that in 1810 the Beechers left Long Island for Litchfield with five children. Roxana's sister, Mary, came too. Her companionship and willing hands greatly eased Roxana's burden. And the children loved Mary like a second mother; Catharine called Aunt Mary "the poetry of my childhood." But Mary had suffered a tragedy. At the age of seventeen she married a wealthy merchant and sailed with him to Jamaica. Once on his plantation she discovered that he already had a family by a slave woman. "What she saw and heard of slavery filled her with constant horror and loathing," the family recalled. Mary returned to New England alone, and the Beechers embraced her as one of the family. Despite her sorrow, Mary charmed everyone with kindness and sympathetic feeling. Mary wrote that it was her "matchless sister" Roxana "who stepped between me and the grave and gave me back life with all its charms." Roxana's kindness restored Mary's life.[17]

In the winter of 1811 Roxana was pregnant again. In a letter to her sister-in-law Esther Beecher, Roxana said that the weather was cold and the firewood running low; Rev. Beecher was away on ministerial business. A houseguest needed food and a bed. There was an accident in the kitchen: one of the hired girls accidentally cut her finger off! Two of the children were sick. There was no time for reading, so Roxana resolved to be content with the knowledge she already had plus what she could glean from the conversation of others.[18]

Time would soon become still more precious: that June Roxana bore another daughter. This one also was called Harriet, the name being important in the family. The new little Harriet was the first Beecher child to be born in Litchfield.

Harriet's earliest memories were of summer evenings in their town in the Berkshires, with "golden sunsets, and moonlight nights . . . the doors and windows of the houses stood innocently open all night for the moon to shine in."[19] Litchfield winters, on the other hand, were severe. Snow drifted high, and "ice and sleet storms" had "sublime power and magnitude."[20] On winter nights she would lie curled up under the blankets with her sisters while gusts of wind rattled the windows and moaned in the chimneys. A big storm could make the old house groan like a ship on the high seas. And there were other sounds. In the walls lived rats that defied all attempts to eradicate them. So loud was their "gnawing and sawing" that it seemed "as if they had set up a carpenter's shop." Harriet fancied that "whole detachments of rats rolled in an avalanche down the walls with the corn they had been stealing."

The old house in Litchfield lived forever in Harriet's memory. Near the end of her life, Harriet wrote a semi-autobiographical novel about a little girl whose old house was "a silent influence, every day fashioning the sensitive, imaginative little soul that was growing up in its own sphere of loneliness there."[21] As a child Harriet could feel alone, even with so many people around. She became an observer, quietly storing things up in her mind.

Harriet was only two years old when her Aunt Mary died of tuberculosis. In those days the disease was called "consumption" because it seemed to consume its victims.[22] A sufferer might have vague symptoms — "hectic fevers" and spells of weakness — that would come and go for months. But once the victim began to cough up blood, the skin took on a ghostly pallor and the cheeks flushed alarmingly red, signaling that death was near.

As Mary lay dying, the family kept vigil at her bedside. Harriet's father sat with Mary in her last hours. She asked him to sing a favorite hymn: "Jesus can make a dying bed feel soft as downy pillows are; while on his breast I lean my head, and breathe my life out sweetly there." Then Lyman "took her up, and held her in my arms sitting in the rocking-chair" to ease her breathing. "'Oh!' said she, 'how distressed I am!'" Lyman "comforted her by telling her it would be over in a few minutes. And it was."[23] She died in his arms. Harriet was too young to remember Aunt Mary clearly, but the family told and re-told Aunt Mary's story. At a very young age Harriet learned that slavery broke Aunt Mary's heart. Aunt Mary's death was a severe blow — especially to Roxana, who now had to manage the household alone.

The Paterfamilias

Around this time Lyman Beecher launched his campaign against alcohol abuse. "America could not be great without being good," he believed, and so he must make society better. Moderate use of alcohol was not the issue. As a student at Yale, Lyman used to run a small grocery store which sold beer. Every year at the minister's wood spell (when parishioners hauled in a year's supply of wood) Lyman and Roxana served "flip" (spiced beer and rum) along with doughnuts. This was not unusual in New England, where libations flowed at community events.

Ministers were fond of spirits too. When Beecher was installed as a minister in Litchfield, "the innkeeper who entertained participating clergy" billed the First Ecclesiastical Society for seventeen bottles of wine, four bottles of "Branday," five bottles of spirits, one bottle of bitters, one bowl of punch, but only one "bole of lemonade."[24] When Beecher attended ordinations of new ministers he saw that visiting clergy had a drink "on arriving, before the service, and after the service." In the festivities following the ordination, men of the cloth drank "ardent spirits" to the point of "hilarity." Ministers were spilling drinks and lining up for more as if they were in a grog shop.[25] It disturbed Beecher that instead of setting an example, his fellow clergy were overindulging.

Beecher gathered some ministers to look into the problem. They said nothing could be done — which made him all the more determined to do something. He would start voluntary associations[26] to prevent drunkenness. He would preach a series of temperance sermons and get them published. Beecher became one of the founders of the temperance movement, and as his reputation grew, he was often away preaching, teaching, and meeting with other ministers.

When he was at home, Beecher loved being the paterfamilias. He would carry the children on his back, chase them around the house, or roll on the floor with the babies and toddlers. He used to play his fiddle; "Go to the Devil and Shake Yourself" was one of his favorite tunes. Sometimes he would dance a jig in his stocking feet — never mind that Roxana had to darn his socks. But he could be stern also. Catharine recalled her father's ideal form of discipline: the first time a child willfully disobeyed, Lyman would whip the culprit's bottom with a switch — harder than necessary so as not to have to do it again. Yet Lyman preferred to guide each child "with his eye" or a stern word.

Every fall Lyman took the older children nut gathering, out into the woods where chestnut trees grew high up on a rock ledge. Beecher would climb up, hang out over the ledge and shake the nuts loose, where the children waiting below could gather them. "Was there a tree [that father] could not climb — a chestnut, or walnut, or butternut, however exalted in fastness of the rock, that he could not shake down?" Harriet wrote. "No Highland follower ever gloried more in the physical prowess of his chief"[27] than the Beecher children did in their father.

Lyman Beecher's absent-mindedness was legendary. Once after gathering eggs from the hens, he came inside with his pockets full and sat down with a crunch. The children shrieked with glee to see the yokes and whites dripping through their father's trousers and onto the floor. Beecher was an avid fisherman, and once on his way to church he spied a fine trout swimming in the brook. He kept a pole stashed nearby and stopped to angle for the fish. He caught it, put it in his coat pocket, and proceeded to church. After church he came home and hung up the coat. A day or so later, a powerful smell drew every nose to Lyman's coat. Roxana's reaction was not recorded.

Roxana was a patient woman who was devoted to her husband. She had brought into the marriage a little sum of money which Lyman used to enlarge their house in Litchfield. To the downstairs a large parlor was added. Here visiting ministers could discuss church business amid clouds of tobacco smoke. Above the parlor on the second floor, four new bedrooms were built. Here the boarders stayed — "as many as eleven girls from Miss Pierce's school [and] several young men studying for the ministry."[28] The topmost part of the addition was Lyman's new attic study, where he could escape from his large family and write sermons in peace.

In June 1821 Lyman bought a used upright piano in Hartford. He had it tuned before it was padded, crated, and loaded into a horse-drawn wagon. Then came the hard part: moving it to Litchfield over thirty-two miles of rough dirt road, around sharp curves and up steep hills. After perhaps two days in transit, the wagon pulled up at the Beecher house. As the children watched, the instrument was unpacked and carried into the new parlor. Lyman was "in a state of entire suspense [to see] whether the tuning had stood." He set up the piano while the family watched in "in breathless expectation." A few chords were played and behold: most of the strings had held their pitch. Lyman quickly tuned the rest. Harriet would always remember the day the piano arrived: "The ark of the covenant was not brought into the tabernacle with more gladness," she recalled, "than this magical instrument into our abode."[29]

Now the family could hold "musical soirees" with flute and piano. "Father soon learned to accompany the piano with his violin in various psalm tunes and Scotch airs." These concerts did not "attain to the height of artistic perfection," Harriet admitted, but they "filled the house with gladness."[30] When older children were not practicing, the younger ones plinked away at the keys. Students from the Litchfield Academy (next door to the Beechers) used to give recitals in the Beecher parlor.

The Beechers were a musical family. All the children learned to sing as soon as they could talk. English folk songs, Scottish ballads, and popular ditties had their place; but hymns were loved best of all. The Beechers sang hymns in harmony with vigor and knew every verse by heart. There was a hymn for every purpose under heaven. Hymns steeled the soul: "Should earth against my soul engage, and fiery darts be hurled, then I can smile at Satan's rage and face a frowning world." They imparted hope: "There is a land of pure delight, where saints immortal reign. Infinite day excludes the night and pleasures banish pain." They lifted souls to worship: "My thoughts address his throne when morning brings the light. I'll seek his blessings every noon and pay my vows at night." And of course, hymns prepared the way for the sermon. "Send some message from Thy word, that may joy and peace afford; let Thy Spirit now impart full salvation to each heart."[31] The Beechers loved to "make the air vocal" with hymns.

They also loved to discuss theology — or at least Lyman did. He passed theology around the dinner table like bread and butter, and discussed it while doing chores. He went away to meetings where ministers waxed theological, and came home in a state of high excitement. At a very young age, the children acquired a theological vocabulary and learned to use it.

Renovations

To Beecher, theology was a set of tools for renovating New England Calvinism. Renovating the old house where Puritans once dwelt was a lifelong project for Beecher and his clergy brethren. New England Calvinism had a deep cellar and a steep roof with gables. It had been added onto and remodeled a time or two. It was the ultimate fixer-upper. The renovations carried on despite arguments among the clergy-carpenters. Some wanted merely to repaint the walls. Others wanted to knock down the walls. Some had already moved out and were calling others to leave. Still others stayed put and claimed they could retrofit this old house to the way it used to be. But what did that mean? Should it be John Winthrop's Calvinism, or that of Jonathan Edwards, or Cotton Mather?

Lyman Beecher's children grew up with the renovation of New England Calvinism in progress. It was as though they could hear the screech of nails being pulled from old boards and pounded into new ones; the rasping of saws; and the occasional breaking of glass. Harriet and her siblings breathed in a lot of sawdust and on occasion saw their father get injured on the job.

That old Puritan house was founded on a covenant (a sacred agreement) between God and his chosen people. God revealed his glory in the work of salvation, choosing sinners by divine decree. Humans had no choice in the matter — in fact, it was a mercy that God chose to save *anyone*. But then came the Enlightenment and the Revolution, bringing government by the consent of the people. If the people could choose their government, couldn't they also shape their destiny in religious matters?

So Lyman needed to begin with the foundation. The Puritans built their house on the rock of God's sovereignty (which was arbitrary and hidden). Lyman thought it should rest squarely on God's moral government (which was reasonable, since God never demands more than we can actually do.) Likewise, if God wants a moral society, then people *can* improve society. Reforms were the way to build a godly nation, under the moral government of God. Thus did Beecher and his colleagues provide "a restatement of the Puritan theory of the national covenant."[32] With the new foundation, Beecher expected the house would stand for years to come.

Beecher had plans for the front door too. In the old Puritan house, the door opened only to those elected by the sovereign God. Once in, always in: that was the "perseverance of the saints." But the old door opened only to the elect. Lyman would fix that, so that the door swung open to every convert. As a revivalist he preached many a soul over that threshold of repentance, through the door of conversion. Yet once inside, converts couldn't just sit around; they had to make themselves useful. They needed to keep the place up, bring in new converts, and clear away all vice. As for the windows, they were designed to let the glory of God shine in. Lyman proposed to open those windows to the breeze of human moral agency.

Lyman Beecher was a theological handyman. He followed (more or less) a blueprint drawn up by Nathaniel William Taylor, his friend and professor at Yale Divinity School. Taylor claimed to preserve the essentials of Calvinism, but he thought that old-style Calvinism, by denying human ability, gave people an excuse to be lazy. Taylor tried to motivate people to change themselves and society, by using the human freedom granted to them under the moral government of God. Likewise Beecher preached a "moral government . . . [which] includes a lawgiver, accountable subjects, and laws intelligibly revealed and maintained by rewards and punishments."[33]

Beecher followed Taylor's blueprint where possible. But like most good carpenters, he also knew how to improvise. Beecher "combined brilliance with a lack of concern for theological precision,"[34] according to George Marsden. Beecher did his best to apply Taylor's ideas to the practical concerns of revival, education, and reform. Beecher and Taylor were trying to make room for human ability without diminishing God's sovereignty. They "wanted revivals, good works and a moral society." Under God's moral government, "true godliness always blended personal holiness and responsible public morality,"[35] writes Mark Noll. For this Lyman Beecher labored day and night.

His wife Roxana had labors of another sort. Henry was born in 1813 and Charles in 1815, bringing the number of Beecher children to eight. Many years later in one of her novels, Harriet wrote a scene in which a minister's wife gives birth to yet another child. The minister puts aside the Lord's work to sit with his wife in her travail. When it is over, the minister kisses his wife and baby. *Now* he can get back to work on "an important treatise . . . to reconcile the decrees of God with the free agency of man." The baby's "entrance into this world had interrupted" the minister for some hours. But "the sermon was a perfect success I am told, and nobody that heard it ever had a moment's further trouble on that subject."[36]

I Shall Not Be with You Long

With so much responsibility for managing the home, Roxana's strength was wearing out. One evening Lyman and Roxana went to call on a parishioner who lived two or three miles away. It was a "fine winter night, not very cold, excellent sleighing, and a full moon," Lyman recalled. On the way home Roxana said, "I do not think I shall be with you long." When Lyman asked why, she replied, "I have had a vision of heaven and its blessedness."[37] Roxana had consumption, the same disease that took her sister Mary. Harriet was very young at the time, but she was allowed "to go once a day into her [mother's] room, where she sat bolstered up in bed." All her life Harriet would remember that "very fair face with a bright red spot on each cheek and her quiet smile."[38]

Roxana's spirit blazed brighter as her body failed. She told Lyman that he must find another wife to fill her place. And she prayed that "her children might be trained up for God."[39] She hoped her daughters would become godly wives and mothers, of course, but Roxana's expressed wish for her sons was that they would all become ministers. This became the family's Great Commission. As Roxana slipped away, Lyman wept and spoke her benediction: "You are now come unto Mount Zion, unto the city of the living God, to the heavenly Jerusalem, and to an innumerable company of angels" (Hebrews 12:22-24). It had been one of Roxana's favorite verses. For years afterward the children repeated it to each other. They "*must* attain" this vision, Harriet wrote, though they "scarcely knew how."[40]

Harriet's mother died on September 25, 1816, at the age of forty-one. She left a brood of children ranging in age from sixteen to nine months old. A family friend who was present heard the children wailing around their mother's deathbed and wondered: what was to become of them all? Harriet was five years old. She later remembered "the mourning dresses, the tears of the older children, the walking to the burial-ground, and somebody's speaking at the grave. Then all was closed." The little children "asked where [Mother] had gone and would she never come back. They told us at one time that she had been laid in the ground, and at another that she had gone to heaven." A few days later, Harriet's little brother Henry was found digging in the ground "with great zeal and earnestness." Asked what he was doing, Henry replied, "I'm going to heaven to find mamma."[41] For the rest of his life, Henry Ward Beecher would need more love than anyone could give.

Harriet would always remember finding comfort in the arms of a black washerwoman named Candace. Not long after Harriet's mother died, Candace was in the kitchen, perhaps boiling a kettle of water. It was time for family devotions, but Candace drew Harriet toward her and held the little girl close till family prayers were over. Then, Harriet recalled, "she kissed my hand, and I felt her tears drop on it. There was something about her feeling that struck me with awe. She scarcely spoke a word, but gave me to understand that she was paying homage to my mother's memory."

Lyman Beecher felt the death of his wife as "an overwhelming stroke." Looking back, Beecher said that after Roxana's death he was like "a child suddenly shut out alone in the dark." He threw himself into church work and rallied people to this or that cause while he struggled with an "overwhelming emptiness."

Roxana quickly achieved sainthood in the Beecher family. "If ever there was a perfect mind as respects submission, it was hers," Lyman said. There was no selfishness in her, "and if there ever was any such thing in the world as disinterestedness, she had it."[42] In life and death, Roxana proved that she was indeed one of God's elect. Therefore Lyman invoked her memory "in every scene of family joy or sorrow," Harriet recalled. "When father wished to make an appeal to our hearts which he knew we could not resist, he spoke of mother."[43] The children believed that their mother was watching over them, and that she could somehow impart blessings from heaven.

As the eldest child, Catharine tried to take care of her brothers and sisters. But it soon became clear that more help was needed. Charles, the baby, was temporarily placed with a neighbor while Harriet was taken to her grandmother's house in Connecticut. Aunt Harriet Foote accompanied her niece on the sixty-mile journey from Litchfield to Nutplains, the Foote family farm.

It was dark when they finally arrived. Aunt Harriet brought her young niece into "a large parlor where a cheerful wood fire was crackling." Grandmother Foote was waiting. The "old lady . . . held me close and wept silently," Harriet remembered. How comforting it must have been to be embraced by her mother's own mother. At Nutplains, Roxana seemed close by. "We saw her paintings, her needle-work, and heard a thousand little sayings and doings of her daily life."[44]

Grandmother Foote's house was full of treasures from around the world, brought back by Harriet's seafaring Uncle Samuel. Best of all Harriet loved the Oriental curtains which surrounded her bed. She awoke to fanciful scenes in a tropical forest, where brightly colored birds poised to seize strange insects. Little summer houses were decked with bells, and servants stood ready to strike the bells with their little hammers. Presiding over it all were the pipe-smoking Mandarins, wise and ageless. Harriet had a vivid imagination and loved scenes and stories of all kinds. Her Uncle George Foote read to her the ballads of Sir Walter Scott and the poems of Robert Burns,[45] just as Aunt Mary had.

It was Aunt Harriet who made life at Nutplains challenging for her young namesake. "Aunt" was a "vigorous English woman of the old school" who believed that little girls must "speak softly and prettily." They must "never tear their clothes, they must sew and knit at regular hours . . . go to church on Sunday and make all the responses, and [then] come home and be catechized."[46]

Aunt Harriet was a staunch Episcopalian. If she had the misfortune to be in Litchfield on a Sunday, she would march past Lyman's Congregational "meeting house" on her way to the Episcopal "church," a *real* church whose minister was ordained by the laying on of hands in apostolic succession. Aunt Harriet thought it possible that many people who were not Episcopalians "would be saved at last, but they were resting entirely on *uncovenanted mercy.*"[47]

With her niece Harriet at Nutplains, Aunt Harriet faced a dilemma: should her young namesake learn the Episcopal or the Westminster Catechism? She decided that young Harriet should learn *both.* The Westminster Catechism began with the weighty question, "What is the chief end of man?" No wonder then that young Harriet preferred the opening question of the Episcopal Catechism: "What is your name?" Aunt Harriet so disliked Calvinism that she reversed her decision and decided Niece could learn *that other* catechism when she returned home.[48]

Grandmother Foote did all she could to soften Harriet's stay at Nutplains. She "took my part in every childish grief," Harriet recalled.

The old woman never scolded when the little girl tore her dress, broke a needle, or wandered by the river when she "should have been sewing." Grandmother seemed "blind to all my faults,"[49] Harriet remembered. Grandmother Foote remained loyal to England and its Church long after the Revolution. She used the Book of Common Prayer daily, and said it grieved her that churches in America no longer prayed for the King and Queen. Decades later Harriet evoked these shades of the past to write her novels about New England.

Meanwhile, back in Litchfield, chaos reigned in the Beecher house. Lyman sent for reinforcements: his half-sister and his stepmother, Harriet's Aunt Esther and her Grandma Beecher. The two women came and took charge. They scrubbed the house from attic to cellar. They washed, mended, and sorted all the clothing and linens. Grandma Beecher was "a fine specimen of the Puritan character of the strictest pattern," Catharine remembered. "She was naturally kind, generous and sympathizing . . . [but] strict with herself and with all around." Indeed, thought Catharine, Aunt Esther's "habits of extreme neatness and order" ill suited her to "assume the management of such a household as ours." Roxana had made allowances for Lyman's foibles, but Aunt Esther and Grandma Beecher ran a tight ship: not even Lyman's attic study escaped their scrubbing. So the beleaguered man took refuge in "the barn, the garden, and the orchard," where the "inflexible rule"[50] of his mother and sister did not reach.

The Beecher women pinched pennies. They had to, since Lyman was no respecter of budgets. Since coming to Litchfield he had piled up $2,800 in debts — a large sum then. Judge Tapping Reeve of Litchfield took up a subscription to rescue Rev. Beecher from "pecuniary embarrassment."[51] Members of Lyman's church did what they could to help. After Roxana's death they brought food aplenty and made sure the "wood spell" was generous that year. They even brought mourning clothes for the family, it being the custom for mourners to wear black for up to a year after a loved one's death.

The first Thanksgiving without Roxana was poignant. The family, minus small children temporarily in the care of others, gathered around a table laden with food brought by parishioners. But no one felt like feasting. Lyman Beecher was unable to pray. Grandma Beecher and Aunt Esther waited with the older children "while great tears stole down [Lyman's] cheeks amid the sighs and tears of all around." When at last Lyman spoke his prayer, it seemed "as if the gentle spirit we mourned was near, shedding peace and comfort from her wings."[52]

In due time, Harriet was brought back to her family in Litchfield. She was there when Beecher brought home a new wife in the fall of 1817. Lyman had met Harriet Porter in Boston while he was in town to preach at an ordination. The lonely widower "swept her into an engagement . . . and rushed her into a marriage her parents thought hasty rather than ill-considered."[53] Miss Porter must have found Rev. Beecher very persuasive indeed.

She Never Made a Mistake

Though he was the son of a blacksmith, for the second time Lyman Beecher "captured a wife from a patrician family."[54] Harriet Porter came from an elite family in Maine. Her father was a doctor and her relatives included a state governor, a U.S. senator, and a congressman. Lyman's new bride was a "beautiful person" with "elegant manners" whose "sense of rectitude, order, and propriety was exquisite." She had the grace and dignity expected of a minister's wife. "She never made a mistake," Lyman said.[55]

Or did she? On some days she may have wondered what had possessed her to marry a poor clergyman with eight children. She was twenty-seven at the time, verging on spinsterhood by the standards of the day. If she wanted to marry, she had better do it. Yet there was more to her decision. Harriet Porter believed that a minister is a messenger from God, whose happiness "is to be regarded, his comfort to be promoted in every possible way. To be an instrument of good to such [a man] is also honorable . . . above the distinctions which usually give pre-eminence in this life."[56] In short, a minister's wife had a holy calling.

The wedding took place in Portland, Maine. The younger children knew only that their father was away and would be home soon. Young Harriet was sleeping in the nursery with Henry and Charles, her two younger brothers. "We heard father's voice in the entry, and started up in our little beds, crying out as he entered our room, 'Why, here's pa!' A cheerful voice called out from behind him, 'And here's ma!'" Harriet got her first glimpse of her new stepmother. She saw a fair young woman "with bright blue eyes, and soft auburn hair bound round with a black velvet bandeau." The little children clamored to get up and be dressed, but were told to go back to bed; they would see more of their new mother in the morning. Harriet later wrote that the next day

> we looked at her with awe. She seemed to us so fair, so delicate, so elegant, we were almost afraid to go near her. We must have been rough, red-cheeked, hearty country children, honest, obedient and bashful. . . . I remember I used to feel breezy, rough and rude in her presence. We felt a little in awe of her, as if she were a strange princess, rather than our own mamma; but her voice was very sweet, her ways of moving and speaking very graceful, and she took us up in her lap and let us play with her beautiful hands, which seemed wonderful things, made of pearl, and ornamented with strange rings.[57]

Now that Lyman Beecher had a wife, Grandma Beecher and Aunt Esther could depart in peace. But Lyman's second wife was a bit too high-strung for the task that lay before her. Harriet later said that her stepmother "had little sympathy with the ordinary feelings of childhood." The new Mrs. Beecher took seriously her religious duty toward Lyman's children. Every Sunday night she took them into her bedroom to "read and talk and pray with them." She "gave an impression of religion as being like herself, calm, solemn, inflexible, mysteriously sad and rigorously exacting," Harriet recalled.[58]

The first child of Lyman and Harriet Porter Beecher died of scarlet fever. Mrs. Beecher suffered with depression, but went on to have three more children, all healthy. All told, eleven of Lyman Beecher's children lived to adulthood; most became ministers and teachers, writers and reformers. It was said that Lyman Beecher "fathered more brains than any man in America." He expected great things from his children — and taught them to expect great things of themselves.

CHAPTER TWO

Your Daughter, Sir!

Harriet Beecher was an odd little girl. She flitted about the house like an owl — solemn, yet comical. She loved to play make-believe, so if one of the family cats died, Harriet got to be chief mourner at the feline funeral staged by the children. Harriet "makes just as many wry faces, is just as odd, and loves to be laughed at as much as ever,"[1] her older sister Catharine said.

Harriet loved stories and quickly learned to read. Alas, there were no children's books in the Beecher home. Lyman Beecher took a dim view of fiction. It was waste of time — perhaps even a bad influence. Lyman Beecher's opinion was not unusual in a time when many devout Christians believed that novels "raise false ideas in the mind, and . . . destroy the taste for history, philosophy, and other branches of useful science."[2] Though she grew up to be a famous novelist, Harriet began her life in a home without fiction[3] and had to make up her own stories.

As a child Harriet used to climb the stairs to her father's attic study, in search of something to read. What she found was daunting: "Bell's Sermons, Bogue's Essays, Bonnet's Inquiry, Toplady on Predestination, Horsley's Tracts . . . and . . . The State of the Clergy during the French Revolution," which "had horrible stories in it stranger than fiction." Yet she searched "wistfully, day after day."

In his attic study Beecher used to store old sermons and pamphlets in barrels. Peering into one of these, Harriet saw a mother cat nursing her kittens; the cat had given birth atop "An Appeal on the Unlawfulness of a Man's Marrying His Wife's Sister." In another barrel Harriet discovered "an ancient volume of *The Arabian Nights.*" Once she found pages of *"Don Quixote* scattered among sermons, essays and reviews." Any scrap of fiction seemed to her "an enchanted island [rising] out of an ocean of mud."[4]

In the attic study Harriet found two books she came to love. One was Cotton Mather's 1702 *Magnalia Christi Americana.* It told of New England Puritans as God's chosen flock, the people of his particular providence. Mather could be stuffy, but sometimes he told thrilling tales of sailors who survived shipwreck or settlers who escaped from captivity among the Indians. Reading the *Magnalia* made Harriet feel that "the very ground she trod on was consecrated by some special dealing of providence."[5] All her life, Harriet believed that "God maintains an active presence in the world and in the lives of his people."[6]

The book Harriet loved best was *Pilgrim's Progress,* John Bunyan's 1678 allegory of the Christian life. The work was second only to the Bible in the Beecher home, and the children knew every scene and character by heart. Later in life, it was not unusual for them to see the world through Bunyan's eyes. For example: near the beginning of *Pilgrim's Progress,* Christian's heavy burden falls from his back and rolls into the tomb of Christ. In 1863 Stowe said slavery was "the burden of our national guilt." Thanks to Emancipation, it "rolled off & I hope has fallen into a sepulcher from which no [devil] ever so intent on mischief shall ever fish it up."[7]

Real Genius and Real Culture

Lyman Beecher thought his children should read only sacred literature. But after reading one of Sir Walter Scott's novels for himself, he changed his mind. "Great was the light and joy," Harriet recalled, "when father spoke *ex cathedra*" and permitted the reading of Scott's novels. "I have always disapproved of novels as trash," Lyman said, "but in these is real genius and real culture, and you may read them."[8] Harriet was then about twelve years old.

Without delay the Beecher children plunged into *Ivanhoe.* They spent many hours discussing it — not idly, of course, but over chores. Every fall the orchard bore apples and quinces. These were picked and brought in bushel baskets to the kitchen. As the children peeled, cored, and chopped the fruit, their father quizzed them on scenes and characters from Scott's novels. Those who remembered the most earned their father's praise.[9] The prepared fruit was set to boil in an "immense brass kettle" hanging in the hearth. Next it was poured off into a large barrel and set in a cool place to freeze. All winter long, big chunks of cider-sauce were broken off, thawed and served up with memories of Scott's stories. Many years later Harriet toured Scotland and visited the home of her childhood literary hero.

Another writer to make an early impression was the English romantic poet Lord Byron. So popular were his works that even the prim Aunt Esther kept "a stray volume of Lord's Byron's poetry" in her room. One day Aunt Esther, to appease her niece's "craving for something to read," handed Harriet a copy of *The Corsair* (a pirate story based partly on Byron's life). All her life Harriet remembered how reading it "astonished and electrified" her. Harriet "kept calling to Aunt Esther to hear the wonderful things . . . in it, and to ask her what it could mean."[10] Aunt Esther replied vaguely that this was just "Byron's way," but something about Byron made Aunt Esther uneasy.

Harriet once overheard her father speaking, in hushed tones, of "Byron's separation from his wife." The poet was in his thirties when he died in Greece in 1824. Slowly the news crossed the sea. One day Harriet's father told her, "my dear, Byron is — *gone*." Stowe recalled her father's "sorrowful countenance, as if announcing the death of someone very interesting to him." Rev. Beecher sighed, "Oh, I'm sorry Byron is dead. I did hope he would have lived to do something for Christ. What a harp he might have swept!"

That afternoon Harriet went up to Chestnut Hill to pick strawberries. But soon she put aside her basket and "lay down among the daisies." She looked up at the sky and pondered that "great eternity into which Byron had entered, and wondered how it might be with his soul."[11] The next Sunday in church, Lyman Beecher warned his flock that no degree of brilliance could preserve the works of wicked people. He concluded his sermon with "a most eloquent lamentation on the wasted life and misused powers of the great poet."[12] Had Rev. Beecher known more about Byron, he would have made his sermon blaze hotter. Many years later, when Harriet met Byron's widow in London, she was shocked to find out that Lord Byron had committed adultery and incest. He seemed to think himself exempt from normal rules of morality, due to his genius with words. But words, Harriet learned as a child, should be used to tell the truth, to give love and encouragement.

21

Words that came in letters written by a loved one's hand were especially prized. Lyman Beecher wrote many letters, since he was often
away from home. As the children grew up, they all become prolific letter writers. The letters were read aloud to gathered family, and sent on
as circulars ("round robin" letters). The Beechers saved letters, and
many of them were later published. And they wrote about everything
from tulip bulbs to sanctification. They wrote about slavery and what
should be done about it.

Lyman Beecher wrote for an audience wider than his family, as
many of his sermons and articles were published. "Father was never
satisfied with his writings," Harriet's oldest sister Catharine recalled,
"till he had read them over to mother and Aunt Mary or Aunt Esther.
By this intellectual companionship our house became in reality a
school of the highest kind, in which he was all the while exerting a
powerful influence on the mind and character of his children."[13] Harriet absorbed it all.

Writing for entertainment was encouraged among the Beechers.
Catharine enjoyed composing light verse to be "presented and read,
and circulated" among "appreciative circles of Litchfield." To write
for the pleasure of friends "had a charm of its own, un-invaded by
sneering criticism," Stowe recalled, and this "added to the interest of
the Litchfield society."[14] Throughout her long life, Harriet loved to
read her own stories aloud to family and friends.

As an adult, she wrote many stories that looked back at her childhood, and the character building that went on in her family. "Everyone must do his little part in the battle of life," she recalled, and "nobody was pretty enough or good enough to be kept merely for
ornamental purposes." Satan finds mischief for idle hands. So hands
must be busy: little girls were set to the grinding of salt or spices with
a mortar and pestle; they had to learn how to brown coffee beans to an
"exact and beautiful shade." Harriet did not mind the kitchen chores.
Sewing was another matter; indeed, "darning socks and stitching
wristbands and 'scratching' gathers" were forms of penance.[15] When
Harriet was nine or ten years old visiting her relatives in Nutplains,
Connecticut, Catharine wrote, "[you must] learn to stand and sit
straight . . . and to sew and knit well, and if you don't learn while you
are with Aunt Harriet, I am afraid you never will."[16]

Girls were supposed to be happy indoors, but Harriet loved to
ramble outside. She would run through the tall meadow grass and

white daisies until she came to a "clear gurgling stream" that she could cross on "mossy stepping-stones." She would gaze into the deep pools, watching the "slim, straight pickerel." She roamed the banks picking "pink and white azalea" and "honeysuckle apples" and "crimson wintergreen berries."[17]

Lyman Beecher often took his sons hunting and fishing. Harriet would watch from the window as they tramped off. The house grew very still without the "laughing, wrestling boys [and their] singing and shouting." Harriet was usually given some sewing to do while the boys were gone, perhaps a sheet that needed re-hemming — the dullest job ever! Somehow the day passed. After dark father and sons "burst into the kitchen with long strings of perch, pickerel and bullheads." Beecher himself cleaned and cooked the fish, for "to his latest day he held the opinion that no feminine hand could broil or fry fish with that perfection of skill which belonged to himself alone, as king of woodcraft and woodland cookery."

Harriet's father also loved gardening. Each year he vied with his friend, Professor Taylor, to see who could grow the earliest cucumbers. Lyman had a scheme. In the fall when his parishioners brought wood, he would get them to pile it over the cucumber patch to keep the ground from freezing. Early in the spring Lyman and the boys would move the woodpile so the cucumbers could be planted in the soft ground. The mountain of logs must be "cut, split, and carried into the woodhouse . . . and it required a miracle of generalship to get it done," Harriet recalled.

Sawing logs and splitting wood was boy's work, so Harriet donned a little black coat to make herself look boyish. "Casting needle and thread to the wind," she ran outside and began to carry the kindling and sweep up the woodchips. "The axes rung, and the chips flew, and the jokes and stories flew faster." Harriet was the "sole little girl among so many boys." She heard her father say that he "wished Harriet was a boy, [for] she would do more than any of them." This was high praise. It took a day and a half to finish moving the woodpile. As a reward, Lyman took the boys fishing and this time he let Harriet come along.

Rev. Beecher used to coach his sons in debate. He would "raise a point of theology . . . and ask the opinion of one of his boys," and play devil's advocate to make his sons practice their logic. Sometimes Lyman would stop and explain, "the argument lies so, my son; do that, and you'll trip me up."[18] Harriet was listening.

23

"Harriet is a great genius," Lyman wrote to one of Harriet's uncles. "I would give a hundred dollars if she was a boy & Henry a girl — she is odd — as she is intelligent and studious." Beecher went on to report that Henry was "learning some bad things from bad boys — but on the whole a lovely child — Charles is as intelligent as ever & falls down 20 times a day — he will doubtless be a great man."[19]

The Church of God

The Beecher children attended church several times a week. The Congregational church was an extension of their home, since their father held sway in both. In Litchfield, Beecher's was *the* church, despite the presence of a small Episcopal church and a few Methodists who as yet had no church building.[20]

Beecher's church was in the center of town on what is now Litchfield's village green. The building had two stories, with double rows of rectangular windows and a larger arched window in the middle. A tall, slender steeple pointed to the glory of God; and the clock, bell, and weathervane indicated the duties of man.[21]

The interior of the church was "divided into large square pew boxes" for the families who worshipped there. Above was the singer's gallery, curving like a horseshoe around the back and sides. Up in this gallery sat "blushing girls . . . and the confident young men" trying to attract the girls' attention during the sermon.

When it came time for the anthem, Harriet and her siblings would turn around in their pew box. Looking up, they could see the song master in the center gallery. They could hear him sing out the pitches for each part "preparatory to their general *set to.*" Then the song master beat time fast enough to "astonish the zephyrs" and the anthem soared. The glory of the song master's art, Stowe recalled, was to lead "those good old billowy compositions called fugueing tunes." Each vocal part raced "around one after another, each singing a different set of words, till at length, by some inexplicable magic," they converged "and sail[ed] smoothly out into a rolling sea of harmony!" With awe young Harriet heard "treble, tenor, counter and bass . . . roaring and foaming." Just when the psalm seemed about to go "to pieces among the breakers," the music would emerge "whole and uninjured from the storm."[22]

But the sermon was central to worship. Harriet spent so many hours staring at her father's pulpit that for the rest of her life she recalled its every detail. Above the pulpit was a turnip-shaped canopy, hanging from an iron rod. The canopy was an acoustic device meant to direct the preacher's voice outward to the congregation. The side panels of the pulpit were decorated with carved tulips, painted red. The front panel had a grape vine motif, with "exactly triangular bunches of grapes alternating at exact intervals with exactly triangular leaves." These symbols called to mind the Trinity, the Lord's Supper, or perhaps Jesus' words, "I am the vine, you are the branches, abide in me."

To abide in Christ was to keep the Sabbath. Work and play, travel and trade stopped — worship was the one thing needful. Isaac Watts, whose hymns were beloved in New England, said it well: "Sweet is the day of sacred rest, No mortal care shall fill my breast; Oh, may my heart in tune be found, Like David's harp of solemn sound."[23]

It was no day of rest for Lyman Beecher. He preached three times each Sunday — a different sermon at each service. "I always commenced by investigations of Christian doctrines, duty, and experience with the teachings of the Bible," Beecher explained. These he "considered as a system of moral government, legal and evangelical, in the hand of a Mediator, administered by his word and Spirit, over a world of rebel, free, and accountable subjects."[24] The younger children did not understand. To them it seemed as though their father spoke "in Choctaw."[25] Mercifully, mothers and little children were excused from the evening service. Rev. Beecher would come home on Sunday night to find his youngest progeny tucked in bed.

Harriet slept securely knowing that her kind and powerful father would return soon. Perhaps as she drifted off, she imagined him standing in his pulpit with its strange canopy. As a child, she used to wonder what the canopy was for and what would happen to her father if it fell down on his head.

One day in 1818 the canopy fell, symbolically, when the state of Connecticut disestablished the Congregational Church, which had been the official state church since Puritan times. Its clergy (called the Standing Order) enjoyed special privileges *and* an amplified voice that ministers of other churches lacked.

Lyman Beecher fought hard to defend the established church in Connecticut. Politically he was a Federalist, favoring a strong national government and stable social institutions. The Federalists and Congregationalists were natural allies, since both "identified society's well-being with that of its prosperous citizens."[26] Opposing them was the Democratic-Republican Party of Thomas Jefferson, derisively called the "Toleration Party." Jefferson's party championed religious freedom; it accepted deists and Sabbath breakers and joined forces with Baptists and others who resisted paying taxes to support a state church. Thanks to the Bill of Rights, the federal government did not have a state church. It was only a matter of time before each of the states followed suit.

September 15, 1817, was Election Day. When the results were tallied, someone ran to the Beecher home with the dire news: "The Democrats have beaten us all to pieces!" And in the Beecher home "a perfect wail arose." Oliver Wolcott Jr. (the "toleration candidate") won the governorship by a landslide. The Democrats also won "both houses of the assembly . . . [and] immediately called for a constitutional convention." The new constitution disestablished the Congregationalists and made all sects voluntary.[27]

This was a crisis for Lyman Beecher. "They slung us out like a stone from a sling," he later said. The day after the election, Harriet's father was the picture of gloom. He was slumped in an old rush-bottomed chair, "his head drooping on his breast, and his arms hanging down." Catharine asked her father what was on his mind. "THE CHURCH OF GOD," he intoned. For months after disestablishment, Beecher was lost in "fear, fog and depression." He suffered dyspepsia. He lost his voice and was unable to preach or teach. He sought refuge in the garden, or his library, or fishing in a nearby trout stream.

Yet Beecher was resilient. He could change his mind. And he later hailed disestablishment as "the best thing that ever happened to the State of Connecticut." He came to see it as a blessing, saying that it "cut the churches loose from dependence on state support." "It threw them wholly on their own resources and on God." From now on clergy were "obliged to develop all our own energy."[28] And Lyman Beecher seemed to have the energy of ten normal people.

Disestablishment was like a continental divide that Beecher had to cross. It changed the trajectory of his career and made a strong impression on his children. A half-century later Harriet praised the "wise and strong Connecticut clergy" who gracefully laid aside "a species of power they could no longer wield." As a result, they gained "a kind of power that could never be taken from them." She added that "when the theocracy had passed away, they spent no time lamenting it."[29] But her father *did* spend time lamenting it. He never gave up his vision of a godly society.

What changed was his strategy. After disestablishment, Beecher recognized that the way to shape society was through "voluntary efforts, societies, missions and revivals"[30] Collectively dubbed "the benevolent empire," these efforts aimed to bring social reform through moral influence.[31] Beecher once said that "The great aim of the Christian Church in its relation to the present life is not only to renew the individual man, but also to reform human society."[32] To which all of his children would eventually say Amen.

The Litchfield Female Academy

Christian schools were part of this benevolent empire, and Rev. Beecher saw to it that his children got the best education available. Happily, the Beechers lived next to the Litchfield Female Academy — one of the finest girls' schools in the nation. Harriet attended the Litchfield Female Academy when female education was on the rise. Her education was better than what her older sisters got (at the same school). And what the Beecher girls got exceeded what their mother learned in school and far surpassed what their grandmothers were taught.

Harriet Beecher Stowe was a lifelong promoter of female education, so a brief sketch of its history belongs in her story. Before the American Revolution, only girls born to wealth got an advanced education. This consisted of "ornamentals," such as fine needlework, drawing, and painting. To attract a husband of suitable rank, girls might also learn conversational French, music, and dancing. The overall goal of female education was to prepare young women to bring refinement to their homes.

The Revolution brought change to many things, including what girls were taught. If girls were to help the new nation succeed, they must be trained to provide virtuous citizens. Girls therefore needed basic academic skills and a strong sense of civic virtue. In short, girls had to be prepared for "Republican motherhood." This was not only for the daughters of the wealthy, but for those born to "middling" families.

Harriet was born in a time when female education was expanding. "Between 1790 and 1830," writes historian Mary Kelley, "182 academies and at least 14 seminaries were established exclusively for women in the North and South."[33] So Harriet Beecher was on the cusp of a wave of educated women who became "prominent reformers . . . abolitionists and leaders of the woman's rights movement."[34]

Harriet started at the Litchfield Female Academy in 1819[35] when she was about eight years old. Most of the other students were older, coming from out of town and boarding with families in Litchfield.[36] But since the Beechers lived close by, Harriet could start young and live at home.

Lyman Beecher did not have to pay tuition,[37] but he led worship services at the school and taught basic Christian doctrine. Thus the school was in some ways an extension of the church. Some of Harriet's brothers also attended the Litchfield Female Academy — and why not, since the instruction was good, the location convenient, and the tuition free. All of Lyman's sons went on to college. Colleges accepted only male students, and women's colleges did not yet exist.[38]

The Litchfield Female Academy was founded by Sarah Pierce in 1792, in her own home. The school flourished and moved into larger quarters. It became "one of the first major educational institutions for women in the United States" and served 3,000 students over the course of forty-one years.[39] Sarah Pierce said she wanted her school to "vindicate the quality of female intellect." She also sought to mold character so that each of her students would have "a kind heart, controlled by the head and subservient to authority."[40] Such girls would one day become "the moral and spiritual guardians of society."[41]

Miss Pierce was completely dedicated to her teaching and never married. Her portrait[42] shows her in plain, dark dress, a white collar and lace cap framing her face. She has the no-nonsense gaze of a veteran teacher, yet her eyes hold a gleam of mischief. Catharine recalled Miss Pierce's sense of "humor and fun," which came out in the plays she wrote for the girls to perform. These plays imparted moral lessons based on the Bible;[43] mere frivolous play-acting had no place in her school.

Miss Pierce had her students read works by women writers such as Hannah More and Maria Edgeworth.[44] She also taught geography and history and compiled her own history textbook. Decades later Harriet wrote to Miss Pierce asking for two copies of her history "compend" and thanking her for her "early care of my life."[45] Harriet also felt lifelong gratitude to John Brace, the teacher Miss Pierce hired to expand the curriculum at the Litchfield Female Academy. Harriet described John Brace as "one of the most stimulating instructors" she ever knew.[46] He kindled the love of learning and believed that girls should study the same subjects as boys. Brace taught English literature as well as "advanced courses in mathematics, the sciences, moral philosophy."[47] Informally he gave instruction in Greek and Latin; but only by request,[48] since classical languages were thought to be for boys only.

Half a century later in her novel *Oldtown Folks,* Harriet Beecher Stowe paid homage to John Brace. She based her fictional teacher Mr. Rossiter on Brace. Rossiter taught "by the sheer force of moral and intellectual influences," Stowe wrote. He had no need to use the switch, but ruled through the "sparing [use] of praise." That praise was as rare as rubies, so the whole school strove to earn it. Mr. Rossiter challenged his students to think independently: "Your heads may not be the best in the world . . . but they are the best God has given you, and you must use them for yourselves."[49] In Stowe's fictional account, boys and girls studied together and learned the same subjects on equal terms.

Not so, however, in the real Litchfield Female Academy. It was assumed that boys would go on to college and girls would marry. The older girls were given opportunities to mix with eligible young men, and there were several in Litchfield, thanks to the law school there. Under Miss Pierce's watchful eye, older girls were allowed to promenade through the town arm-in-arm with their male escorts. To the music of flutes, "young people passed and re-passed through the broad and shaded street to and from . . . Prospect Hill."[50] Many a match was made in this way.

Harriet was too young for courting, but what bothered her more was that she was too young to study composition. So she eavesdropped on the lessons given to older girls sitting in front of her. Sarah Pierce's Academy had one large room for instruction. Seating was by rank. Mr. Brace and Miss Pierce (or sometimes an advanced student helper) circulated throughout the classroom giving lessons and hearing students recite what they had learned. Memorization was thought to be the best way to "exercise the minds" of students.[51] At any given time, up to one hundred students could be seen — and heard — writing and speaking their lessons while the teachers made their rounds.

"Much of the training and inspiration of my early days," Harriet later recalled, "consisted not in the things that I was supposed to be studying, but in hearing, while seated unnoticed at my desk, the conversation of Mr. Brace with the older classes."[52] One day she heard Mr. Brace say, "The main requisite" for composition "is to have something which one feels interested to say." Her whole life long, Harriet had things she felt interested to say, things she was sure others would want to read.

Her first composition was on "The Difference between the Natural and the Moral Sublime." So pleased was John Brace with Harriet's work that he asked her to write a composition for the school's public exhibition — a high honor for a nine-year-old!

The public exhibition was a big event in Litchfield, like a school open house but with much more pressure on the students. In the weeks before the exhibition, girls vied for a place in the spelling, arithmetic, or geography contest. Music was practiced, and needlework, drawings, and paintings were prepared for display.

But the high point was the "public performance of compositions written [beforehand] by students."[53] Mr. Brace had chosen Harriet Beecher to write an essay on this question: "Can the Immortality of the Soul be Proved by the Light of Nature?" It was a theme calculated to stretch young minds "to the higher regions of thought," Stowe recalled.[54] This had been discussed by students at the Academy long before the exhibition. Many girls took the classic Enlightenment view that Nature *can* prove the immortality of the soul; and that the Scriptures neither add to nor contradict Nature. Harriet disagreed: she believed that only divine revelation[55] discloses the immortality of the soul.

Harriet was nervous on the day of the exhibition, but at least she would not have to read her own composition. That would be done by John Brace or some other leading citizen, since girls were not supposed to speak before mixed audiences. "The hall was crowded with the literati of Litchfield," Harriet recalled. "Before them all the compositions were read aloud. When mine was read, I noticed that father, who was sitting on high by Mr. Brace, brightened and looked interested, and at the close I heard him say, 'Who wrote that composition?' '*Your daughter, sir!*' was the answer. It was the proudest moment of my life. There was no mistaking father's face when he was pleased, and to have interested *him* was beyond all juvenile triumphs."[56]

More than a half century later, Harriet's son Charles found her essay from the Litchfield exhibition. It was "carefully preserved, and on the old yellow sheets the cramped childish handwriting is still distinctly legible."[57] It was Harriet's first success as a writer, and she kept it all her life.

Knowledge and virtue were prized at Sarah Pierce's school, and so was true religion. Beecher's message of Christian conversion and moral agency "permeated every aspect of life at the Litchfield Female Academy."[58] Students had to attend several worship services on Sunday. They wrote journals in which they summarized sermons and confessed their failings, and these journals were checked weekly. On Sunday evenings the girls held their own Bible studies and prayer meetings. Girls who boarded locally attended devotions with their host families, who reported to Miss Pierce on each girl's piety and conduct. Thus no matter where a girl was — at school, church, or boarding house — she was encouraged to "seize the moment and choose Jesus."[59]

Periodically revivals were held at the Litchfield Female Academy. Classroom routines were set aside to make room for preaching and soul searching. Girls unsure of their own salvation prayed for conversion, and the already converted prayed that their wavering friends might find grace. If any girl left Litchfield Academy unsaved it was not for want of trying, for "Sarah Pierce and John Pierce Brace based their educational efforts upon their deeply-held Christian belief in individual conversion and salvation."[60] Brace was himself converted under Lyman Beecher's preaching. "My understanding was first convinced," Brace said, "and then my heart affected."[61]

Pierce, Brace, and Beecher were enlightened evangelicals. They wanted students at the Academy to develop their minds, experience conversion, and go on to work "for the religious Awakening of American society as a whole."[62] It was assumed that girls would marry and work from their homes, but in time benevolent societies and reform movements came to be seen as extensions of the home. As for women who remained single, they might one day become teachers like Miss Pierce.

Handling Edge Tools

Catharine Beecher did not start out to follow in Miss Pierce's footsteps and become a serious schoolteacher. Indeed, Harriet remembered Catharine as "a constant stream of mirthfulness" in "a great household inspired by the spirit of cheerfulness and hilarity."[63] Catharine attracted a suitor: Alexander Fisher, a professor of natural philosophy at Yale. Though still in his twenties, Fisher was "a brilliant scientific thinker" as well as a student of theology and music.[64] Fisher read Catharine's poetry in *The Christian Spectator,* but the poems were signed only "C.D.D." A little sleuthing revealed the author's identity. Then Fisher visited Litchfield early in 1821 and attended Rev. Beecher's church, where he was introduced to Catharine and invited to Sunday dinner at the Beechers' home.

Within a year, the pair had formed a "settled connection." However, Fisher had long desired to visit European universities and decided to do so before getting married. The separation would be hard, but Catharine could look forward to becoming the wife of a distinguished professor. She would have her own "home in the beautiful rural city of New Haven, in cultured literary society," Harriet later wrote, just "an hour or two [away] from father and home."[65]

Fisher crossed the Atlantic aboard the *Albion,* but he never set foot in Europe. Off the coast of Ireland, the *Albion* was caught in a gale. The rudder broke and the ship crashed on the rocks near Kinsale Point. More than a month later, Lyman was attending a ministers' conference in New Haven when news reached him of the shipwreck. It was his sad duty to inform Catharine: "It is all but certain that Professor Fisher is no more."

She was devastated. Her fiancé and her future had sunk to the bottom of the sea. And now Catharine feared that if Fisher died unconverted, he was doomed to hell. Lyman wrote to Catharine and told her she had a choice: she could cast her thoughts toward the battered coast of Ireland (where there was no hope) *or* she could repent of her sins and set her heart on things eternal. Lyman hoped the crisis would induce Catharine's conversion. But Catharine did not want to resign all to God. Besides, if her beloved was not in heaven she did not want to be separated from him for all eternity.

Heartbroken, Catharine went to Franklin, Massachusetts, for a long visit with Fisher's parents. She spent many hours reading his personal papers — as if they could somehow bring her closer to him. But instead of consolation, she found that Fisher had despaired of his own salvation.

Attending church with Fisher's parents, Catharine heard the preaching of Rev. Nathaniel Emmons. That was harrowing, since Emmons preached eternal punishment for the unconverted. Emmons offered no more comfort to Catharine than the cliffs of Ireland gave to the passengers of the *Albion*,[66] Harriet said years later.

Catharine felt as if her soul were drowning. She exchanged many letters with her father, but if she hoped he would throw her a rope she was quite mistaken. Sometimes her brother Edward (now safely converted) joined in the correspondence. And both Lyman and Edward pressed Catharine to renounce her sins and seek conversion. According to Catharine's biographer, "Lyman and Edward made it impossible for Catharine to express any feelings of personal loss for Fisher's death." Instead "they made the theme of her loss their own and used it against her."[67]

Catharine was grieving, but her father diagnosed her problem as unbelief and pushed conversion as the only cure. For a while Catharine tried to work herself into a state of repentance (a first step toward conversion). But she felt no remorse. She tried to work up remorse and it would not come. Then Catharine began to challenge her father's views and to defend herself. Lyman Beecher was impressed: he told his son Edward that Catharine "is now . . . handling edge-tools with powerful grasp."

Catharine was using those edge tools of theological argument to cut loose from her father's beliefs. How could a just and merciful God *require* her to convert, and condemn her if she proved *unable* to do so? There must be "something terribly wrong," Catharine decided, some "dreadful mistake made somewhere."[68]

In the end Catharine went her own way. She decided that God saves those who lead moral lives, with or without conversion. Therefore Alexander Fisher was not doomed to hell, and neither was she. She further decided that if she could not find solace in spiritual things, she must find comfort from the world. Now "Catharine had won the right to define her own religious and emotional life and to inhabit her own moral universe," wrote Catharine's biographer. "She had turned the rites of submission into a ritual of endurance."[69]

Catharine needed to move on with her life. "As to my future employment I wish to consult you," she wrote her father. She saw no "extensive sphere of usefulness for a single woman but that which can be found in the limits of a school-room." She knew she had coasted through the Litchfield Female Academy, but after Fisher's death she found out that her intellect was keener than supposed. While studying Fisher's books and papers, she discovered that she could understand — and even enjoy — chemistry, philosophy, and algebra. She realized that she could teach these subjects to girls.

Catharine had heard that a good female school was needed in Hartford. She proposed starting one. Lyman Beecher liked the idea, but he advised his eldest daughter not to begin unless she could put all her strength and talent into it. A half-hearted effort "will not answer," he warned. She was a Beecher, so she must not conduct a merely average school; it must "be of a higher order." Catharine "had best not begin" unless she meant to put all her "talents and strength into it."[70] Catharine promised to do so. And so Lyman Beecher went to Hartford in March 1823 to drum up some support for Catharine's school and to round up a few young "scholars" to enroll. Before long, Harriet would become a pupil at the Hartford Female Seminary. Under Catharine's watchful eye, Harriet would grow up into a teacher who dreamed of being a writer.

CHAPTER THREE

On the Waves

In 1823, when Catharine started the Hartford Female Seminary, Harriet was still at home with her parents in Litchfield. There she attended Miss Pierce's school and babysat for her little half-sister Isabella. But Catharine had plans for Harriet. She meant to take charge of Harriet's education and train her as a teacher.

Catharine started her school with seven students and kept school in a rented room above a harness shop. From such humble beginnings the Hartford Female Seminary would become an "outstanding academy for girls" and a "force in American education for more than sixty years."[1] And Harriet Beecher played a part in that story.

When Harriet joined Catharine in Hartford in 1824, she was a dreamy girl who longed to be a poet. Catharine said no, Harriet was not to waste time on such flummery. Instead Harriet had to "discipline her mind by the study of 'Butler's Analogy.'" (*The Analogy of Religion, Natural and Revealed, to the Constitution and Course of Nature*, by the Anglican Bishop Joseph Butler, was first published in 1736.) Butler argued that science poses no threat to Christianity, since nature and scripture have the same divine author. Butler's *Analogy* was esteemed in American schools, and Catharine needed someone to teach it.

So Harriet hiked up her skirts and waded in. Soon she was teaching *Analogy* to girls her own age, if just barely keeping her own head above water. But Harriet was not inspired. She later poked fun at Butler's "outrageous style of parentheses and foggification."[2]

Harriet found her inspiration elsewhere. Her favorite book at this time in her life was *Saints' Everlasting Rest*. Written by seventeenth-century Puritan Richard Baxter, it called for active devotion to the glory of God.³ Reading it moved Harriet so deeply that she wished the streets "might sink beneath me if only I might find myself in heaven."⁴ But she lacked the one thing the book told her was needful: a conversion experience.

In the summer of 1825 Harriet was back in Litchfield, where her father was preaching revival. Her siblings Charles and Edward were "visibly affected," and Mary, twenty years old, "finally committed her life to Christ."⁵ At fourteen, Harriet still had time to convert; yet she felt awkward in church on the "sacramental" (Communion) Sunday, when only the saved could receive the bread and wine. It was a painful reminder to Harriet of her unconverted state.

A dutiful preacher's daughter, Harriet tried to work up the proper feelings of remorse, but nature worked against her. As Harriet walked to church through the morning dew, the birds, flowers, and rippling brooks all gave her a sense of lightness and joy. Her mood again darkened upon entering the church where she saw the communion table covered with a white linen cloth and set with bread and communion cups. She sighed and thought to herself, "[T]here won't be anything for me to-day, it is all for these grown-up Christians."

That Sunday Beecher preached on John 15:15: "Behold, I call you no longer servants, but friends." All her life Harriet would recall her father's message of Jesus as a soul friend for every human being. Lyman "spoke in direct, simple, and tender language of the great love of Christ and his care for the soul . . . patient with our errors, compassionate with our weaknesses, and sympathetic for our sorrows. [Christ] was ever near us, enlightening our ignorance, guiding our wanderings, comforting our sorrows with a love unwearied by faults, un-chilled by ingratitude, till at last He should present us faultless before the throne of His glory with exceeding joy."

Harriet was a small, bookish girl, surrounded by people and yet alone. Jesus was the friend she needed. Her father gave the invitation: "Come, then, and trust your soul to this faithful friend." Harriet longed to accept, but she knew she was supposed to feel remorse for her sins — and she didn't. Then it came to her that "if I needed conviction of sin, [Jesus] was able to give me this also. I would trust him for the whole." Her soul filled with joy. She walked home feeling as though all nature praised God.

When Lyman came home from church, Harriet followed him to his attic study. "Father," she told him, "I have given myself to Jesus, and He has taken me." Lyman embraced his daughter and she felt his tears falling on her head. "Is it so?" he asked tenderly. "Then has a new flower blossomed in the kingdom this day."[6] Now Harriet was converted. She could receive communion and her father could rejoice that another of his lambs had safely entered the fold.

But Catharine was skeptical about Harriet's conversion. It seemed so easy! How could her little sister traipse so lightly into the Kingdom, when Catharine had agonized and never felt converted? How could a lamb "come into the fold without first being chased all over the lot by the shepherd"? Harriet found religion "easy and delightful," but for Catharine it was "mostly a way of darkness and heaviness."[7] Catharine would not be the only one to question Harriet's conversion. And Harriet's newfound status as a full member of her father's church was not to last long.

A Fire in My Bones

Lyman Beecher was ready to leave Litchfield. During the fifteen years he had been there, his salary had remained flat while his family grew. Now the older sons were going to college and their education had to be paid for. *All* of his sons (eventually six) were expected to go to college and then study theology to prepare for the ministry. If Catharine's school prospered, perhaps she would help put her brothers through school.[8]

Lyman was a man of the cloth, but that cloth was threadbare. His horse and wagon were shabby and his children dressed in clothes patched and "turned" (remade) from older clothes. The house needed painting and the fences needed mending. Beecher still felt called to pull the chariot of the Lord, but Litchfield was feeling like a rut.

Boston beckoned Beecher and roused his fighting spirit. That former citadel of Puritanism was now infiltrated by Unitarians who denied the Trinity. As many as eighty churches in the Boston area had "gone over" to the Unitarians; likewise Harvard College. Beecher was alarmed and wanted to do something about it.

He was not alone. "New England Calvinism for more than forty years was fixated upon the Unitarian peril," writes Mark Noll. Seminaries and journals sprang up to defend Calvinism from "infidelity." Unitarians enjoyed "intellectual influence far out of proportion to their actual numbers" because they appealed to the educated and wealthy.[9] For years Beecher had watched from the sidelines as Unitarianism spread. "'It was a fire in my bones,' he said; 'my mind was all the time heating — heating — heating.'"[10] In Boston Beecher could be a David slinging stones at Goliath.

Three of Boston's embattled Congregational churches devised a plan. They would start a new congregation: the Hanover Street Church. It would hold revivals and grow, perhaps even win back some Unitarians. It would be a staging area for moral reform societies. So the right minister must be found. That man was none other than Lyman Beecher, revival preacher and champion of reform.[11]

When Beecher got the letter from Hanover Street Church, he knew his moment had come. Now he had a chance "to restore the social influence of evangelical religion"[12] in Boston and in America. Many years later, when Harriet commented on her father's move to Boston, she said that the Unitarians had nothing to unite them but rejection of Calvinism. "Enthusiasm cannot long be kept up simply by not believing," she wrote. Sooner or later people needed a "positive and definite faith"[13] — and Lyman Beecher was the man to offer it.

The younger Harriet was more matter-of-fact. "Papa has received a call to Boston," she wrote to her grandmother. He has accepted "because he could not support his family in Litchfield. . . . Papa's salary is to be $2,000 and a $500 settlement [for moving expenses]."[14] Children seldom like being uprooted even for a higher standard of living. One of the Beecher children — perhaps Catharine — mourned for the old house and orchard, the woods and hills, lakes and streams once "full of the feelings of youth."[15]

The Beechers left Litchfield in 1826. By that time, several of Harriet's older siblings were already on their own. William was in Boston working in a hardware store, his path to the ministry temporarily blocked by lack of conversion. Edward had gone to Yale College and then Andover Seminary to study theology. Catharine and Mary were teaching in Hartford, where George was also in school.

Harriet was now fifteen, and her father wanted her to move to Boston, at least for a while. She was grouped with the younger children, including Henry (twelve), Charles (ten), Isabella (four), and Thomas (two). James, the last of Lyman's children, would be born in Boston. Aunt Esther had been in Hartford keeping house for Catharine, but now she went to Boston to help establish Lyman's new household.

Their new home was to be at 18 Shaefe Street in Boston's North End, a once-fashionable neighborhood now in decline. Grand houses decayed and many were torn down to make room for tenements crowded with German and Irish immigrants.[16] For the Beechers, however, this was still hallowed ground. Nearby was the Copps Hill burying ground, where Puritan worthies like Cotton Mather awaited the resurrection, blissfully unaware that Unitarians were preaching from their pulpits. Harriet long remembered her father leading the family prayers in Boston, beseeching Jesus to come and rebuild the church and gather his scattered flock. Harriet would look back on her father's time in Boston as "the most active, glowing and successful period of his life. It was the high noon of his manhood, the flood-tide of his powers."[17] Beecher was fifty-one years old and primed to defend the faith once delivered to the saints.

But Boston had changed a great deal since Puritan times. Its population leaped from 43,000 in 1820 to 61,000 by 1830. New mills and factories made cloth from Southern cotton. Harbors bristled with the masts of ships from around the world. Rowdy sailors frequented the grog shops and brothels. On the high end of the scale was Harvard College, an elite group of authors and publishers, a theater community (though many disapproved of the theater) and many venerable churches. While the Congregationalists and Unitarians fought over the old institutions, other groups — Roman Catholics, Baptists, Quakers, Universalists, Swedenborgians, Restorationists, and even a few Lutherans — were diversifying Boston.

And so Beecher felt great pressure to prove himself. He must show the Hanover Street Church that they had called the right man to revive Congregationalism in Boston. Beecher's stress soon manifested itself with a flare-up of dyspepsia. Sharp, stabbing stomach pain brought him to the floor. He lay in front of the fireplace, groaning that he was about to die. "Well," his wife replied, "you have said this before, and have gotten over it."

With prayer, exercise, and a very careful diet, Beecher rallied.[18] In the backyard he set up parallel bars, a single bar, and a rope ladder. There Harriet watched her father perform gymnastic feats for visiting ministers. He also split and sawed wood and lifted dumbbells. In the basement Beecher kept a huge pile of heavy sand, which he would shovel "from one side of the basement to the other"[19] to work off his nervous energy.

Beecher's church was an important place for Harriet when she was in Boston. The Hanover Street Church looked like a fortress, with walls of rough granite and a bell tower like a castle keep.[20] The building's design reflected the church's mission, which was to defend Boston from Unitarian takeover, according to historian Vincent Harding. On the inside the church looked like a lecture hall or theater, with a thrust pulpit to enhance preaching and seating meant to encourage congregational singing.[21] Below were offices for benevolent societies, such as the "American Board of Commissioners for Foreign Missions."

Sunday was the high point of the week for the Beechers. Early in the morning Lyman went to his study and swung his dumbbells a bit to limber up his muscles. Then he scribbled sermon notes on paper small enough to fit into the palm of his hand. When the church bells began to ring, Harriet and the other children would shout up the stairs: *Father, you must get to church.* With the peal of the last bell fading, Beecher threw on his coat and thundered down the stairs. As he headed for the door, "female hands" fluttered over him, adjusting his coat collar and cravat. Someone found a pin to fasten his sermon notes together. He dropped the notes in his hat and put his hat on his head. Then, "hooking wife or daughter like a satchel on his arm," he dashed through the cobbled streets to the church. At the church doors, the faithful parted to let the preacher through. Every eye followed Beecher as he strode up the aisle to the pulpit.

Beecher thought sermons should get results. He would start with a proposition, and then develop it with scripture and illustrations. Then he pushed for a response. "Will you do it? Will you change? *Will* you?" Businessmen liked Beecher's direct approach, and joined the church because of it.[22] Harriet watched closely. One day she too would challenge people to change their minds and hearts, to feel right and live right.

I Am a Strange, Inconsistent Being

Back in Hartford, Catharine's school soon outgrew its room above the harness shop. It moved to the basement of North Church, into a larger classroom equipped with heating stove. Games and exercise were held in a field outdoors. Catharine was now living in a rented house with Mary and other Beecher siblings who rotated through Hartford. Harriet knew she had a place there too, when the time came.

Her place in the church, however, was now in question. She no longer belonged in Litchfield, and since she would be returning to Hartford it did not make sense for her to join her father's church in Boston. So Lyman told Harriet to join the First Church [Congregational] of Hartford. Beecher knew the pastor there: Joel Hawes was on the board of trustees for Hartford Female Seminary. Dutifully, Harriet went to see him. To her dismay, Hawes doubted the authenticity of Harriet's conversion, perhaps because of her youth. He informed her that only the saved could join First Church and receive the Lord's Supper. To relax this policy would result in "an unregenerate membership" which would not "cleave to an evangelical creed, or tolerate an orthodox ministry."[23] So he needed to find out if Harriet's conversion was genuine.

He began the interrogation. "Harriet, do you feel that if the universe should be destroyed (awful pause) you could be happy with God alone?" Meekly she answered, "Yes, sir." Rev. Hawes pressed on: "You realize, I trust . . . in some measure at least, the deceitfulness of your heart, and that in punishment for your sins God might justly leave you to make yourself miserable as you have made yourself sinful?" Harriet was shaking as she replied, "Yes, sir." Harriet was dismissed with a benediction which did nothing to calm her troubled heart.

Harriet wrote to her older brother Edward, who was her confidant. She said that her religious feelings were fading like a mirage. Her sins were taking away her happiness, and all because of her pride. Long after her interview with Hawes, Harriet dreaded sharing any "private religious feelings. If anyone questions me, my first impulse is to conceal all I can."[24] Harriet doubted her faith and feared she would waste her life. She recalled with sadness that day in Litchfield when a gentle tide of grace had lifted her into her father's arms; now the tide had turned, leaving her stranded.

An opportunity came for Harriet to prove her sincerity: Catharine decided to hold a revival at Hartford Female Seminary. Catharine remained unconverted, so it may seem strange that she wanted a revival at her school. Yet she saw her father's revivals as being socially beneficial, and she wished to enhance her role as a moral leader in Hartford. Harriet would do all she could to promote the revival, and perhaps this would show Rev. Hawes that she, Harriet, was indeed a converted Christian mature enough to receive the Lord's Supper.

Catharine knew how to start a revival. She held prayer sessions at her school and preached informally to her students and fellow teachers. (It was acceptable for a woman to preach informally — that is, not from a pulpit — and to an all-female audience; women were not supposed to address a "promiscuous assembly" of males and females.) Catharine made her students pray regularly and keep a diary on their spiritual condition; she counseled them on their spiritual progress. In the evenings Catharine held prayer meetings at her house. Soon several girls converted, while others renewed their Christian commitments.[25]

Harriet attended Catharine's prayer meetings faithfully and wrote letters of spiritual counsel. In one of these, Harriet said many people see Jesus "as a Friend to whom they can go with all their *great* trials — of whom they can ask direction in all cases of *great* emergency — but they do not think of bringing to him every little trouble or of asking his direction in every little duty." But no concern is too small for the God who can count the hairs on human heads and guide the fall of a sparrow. Christians can ask for God's guidance in everything and cultivate a constant awareness of God's presence.[26] Twenty-five years or so later, Harriet Beecher Stowe published a devotional essay called "Earthly Care a Heavenly Discipline."[27] By that time Stowe was a woman with all the earthly cares of a family and a rising outrage against slavery. Her "Earthly Care" essay was consistent with what she wrote as a teenager back in Hartford: when troubles make it hard for Christians to feel God's presence, they can embrace trials, pray about them, and learn to depend on God.

Harriet Beecher sought to grow spiritually, even as Catharine strove to rise professionally. Having successfully launched a revival at her school, Catharine wanted to spread it into the town. This was a delicate matter back in the day when women were not supposed to be teaching or preaching to men. Those who did so were shunned as radicals. Catharine did not wish to hurt her standing in the community by crossing those lines.

So she held a special assembly at the Hartford Female Seminary. She set aside a week for her students to "labor for the salvation of their fellow men." Catharine declared that this week[28] would show whether the revival could spread to the churches and homes of Hartford. The girls were to do nothing publicly, but they could, by private example and secret prayer, influence the families they boarded with and the churches they attended. Catharine invited women from several churches to special prayer meetings. And "by the summer of 1826 all the Congregational churches were engaged" in the revival.

Now the time was ripe for a full-scale revival, so Catharine invited her father to come to Hartford and preach. He declined, warning that too much religious intensity might harm Catharine's spiritual health and that of her students. Beecher warned his daughter against taking upon herself the "overpowering weight of responsibility and care" involved in a revival.[29] Beecher may have thought that females should not be stirring up revivals, or that Catharine's emotional health was fragile, or both.

Let down by her father, Catharine now turned to Rev. Hawes. He was, after all, the leader of "religious exercises" at her school every Monday[30] and a member of the board of directors of her school. But no, Hawes was leaving for Northampton "to assist in the great revival there and to gain *the spirit of a revival.*" Spirit of revival indeed! Why was Northhampton more important than Hartford? She "felt like crying all day" when Hawes left town.[31] *Two* ministers — one of them her own father — had refused to harvest the seeds she had planted. But when Hawes returned from Northampton, he preached to young *men* in Hartford. According to Hawes's biography, *his* Hartford revival was a particular success. Catharine Beecher's name is not mentioned.

Still, Catharine benefited from the revival. Parents were happy that their daughters were converted, and some even increased their giving to the school. As for Harriet, although she had helped to cultivate the revival, she still felt spiritually bruised. She missed her father. Perhaps, with fewer children under his roof, he would have more time for her. So Harriet went back to Boston for a while, where she "was much more with [Father] and associated in companionship of thought and feeling for a longer period than any other of my experience."[32]

But she was still troubled. She felt like the raven in Noah's flood, sent out from the ark and flying to and fro with no sign of land. Boston wasn't home. Harriet was not close to her stepmother. She was close to her younger brother Henry, but he was away at school during the day. Harriet had no friends in Boston; her old friends were back in Litchfield, and her new schoolmates were in Hartford. She was an adolescent uprooted from her childhood home, questioning her faith, and missing her mother.

"I don't know as I'm fit for anything," Harriet lamented in a letter to Catharine. She wished she could die young. "You don't know how perfectly wretched I often feel: so useless, so weak, so destitute of all energy. Mamma often tells me that I am a strange, inconsistent being." Sometimes Harriet "could not sleep, and . . . groaned and cried until midnight, while in the daytime I tried to appear cheerful and succeeded so well that Papa reproved me for laughing so much." Harriet was absent-minded and "made strange mistakes, and then they all laughed at me, and I laughed too, though I felt as though I should go distracted."[33]

That letter convinced Catharine that Harriet needed to return to Hartford. "Harriet will have young society here all the time," Catharine wrote her father, "and I think cheerful and amusing friends will do much for her." Besides, Hartford Female Seminary needed an art teacher, and Harriet could be trained to fill that role. Lyman agreed, and Harriet went back to Hartford.[34]

Several months later, back in Boston between school terms, Harriet probably heard her father talk about Charles Grandison Finney, an upstart preacher known for his sensational revivals. Finney had set out to be a lawyer until a dramatic conversion moved him (as he said) to plead the Lord's cause. Under Finney's preaching, sinners fell down shrieking and groaning. Finney raised them up and told them to fight sin anywhere they found it — even the sin of slavery. Thanks to "new measures" (techniques) borrowed from the Methodists and Baptists, Finney enjoyed spectacular success. But more conventional preachers condemned Finney's revivals as crude and uncouth. Revivals were getting a bad name, at the very time Beecher sought to win elite Unitarians back to Christ! Beecher warned Finney: don't even think of coming to Massachusetts, or "I'll meet you at the State line, call out all the artillerymen, and fight every inch of the way to Boston, and then I'll fight you there."

Hoping to curb Finney and his brand of revivalism, Beecher helped organize a meeting of Presbyterian ministers in New Lebanon, New York, in July 1827. There they heard Finney out. The results were mixed, but Beecher changed his mind about Finney and so did several other ministers. Later, Beecher invited Finney to preach for six months in Boston in hopes that Finney could convert the Unitarians.[35] Little did Lyman Beecher dream that his career would be almost ruined by a Finney convert.

God Has Given Me Talents

Harriet's older brother Edward came to Boston to serve Park Street Church, dubbed "Brimstone Corner" because it was so militantly orthodox.[36] Lyman helped Edward get the position, and in return Edward was expected to help his father fight the Unitarians.[37] But Edward lacked his father's zest for combat; instead he loved theological speculation and admired the writings of the Unitarian William Ellery Channing. Edward's gentle, thoughtful personality drew Harriet to confide in him. "Little things have great power over me," she confessed. "And if I meet with the least thing that crosses my feelings, I am often rendered unhappy for days and weeks." She wished she could stop caring what others thought of her: "I believe there never was a person more dependent on the good and evil opinions of those around than I am." She concluded that the "desire to be loved forms, I fear, the great motive for all my actions."[38] And that was a problem, since Harriet was taught to see selfishness as the greatest sin, and benevolence (unselfish love) as the greatest ideal. It pained her to fall short.

Harriet and Edward debated theology in their letters. Edward took the modern view: people create religion, starting from their feelings and moving toward God. Edward ventured that human feelings may even affect God's happiness. If religion begins with our feelings, then we are responsible for working up the right feelings.

Harriet disagreed. Experience told her that the harder she tried to work up religious feelings, the more lost she felt. God is greater than our own feelings, she insisted. That gave her hope when she lacked the proper feelings. She thought that by starting with human feelings, Edward merely shifted spiritual burdens without lifting them.

What Harriet wanted most was for Jesus to be her trusted friend, just as her father had preached that Sunday back in Litchfield. "I sometimes wish that the Savior were visibly present in this world," she told Edward, so that "I might go to Him for the solution of some of my difficulties." She wondered if God loves sinners before they come to him. If so, then she could tell "those who are in deep distress, 'God is interested in you; He feels for you and loves you.'"

Harriet told Edward she felt God might be calling her to become a writer. Edward replied that literature can be a "snare." "Perhaps, but was this always true?" Harriet rejoined. Through the fog of adolescence she glimpsed her path. "I do not mean to live in vain," she vowed. God "has given me talents, and I will lay them at His feet, well satisfied. All my powers He can enlarge. He made my mind, and He can teach me to cultivate and exert its faculties."

In the fall of 1827 Harriet returned to Hartford and prepared herself to be a full-time teacher. That winter she took lessons in drawing and painting; she studied French and hoped to learn Italian. She was teaching Latin and tutoring two students in Virgil. "I am very comfortable and happy," she wrote her grandmother Foote. She wondered if her mother's death had caused the sadness that burdened her for so long. Now she could feel that sadness lifting. In its place came a desire to do something "my dear mother loved and admired." Her mother had loved to paint, so Harriet would learn that skill and "cherish it for her sake."[39]

All this time Catharine strove to improve her school. She came to dislike the "blab school" method in which students recited lessons from memory. Recitation was standard practice, but Catharine wondered "how much was clearly understood, or how much was mere memorization of words."[40] She also disliked the one-room-schoolhouse in which students of all levels and ages worked in the same space. All was "confusion, haste and imperfection" and "nothing was done as it should be." She longed to try new methods.

For that she needed a new school building — large enough to accommodate 150 students and several teachers. Her dream school would have several small rooms and a large room for lectures, assemblies, and study hall. This would allow Catharine to divide the students by age or ability. Catharine's scheme met with resistance from some of the board members, who thought her plans "absurd." Undaunted, Catharine persuaded several "intelligent and influential women" (whose husbands were on the board), and the wives in turn persuaded their husbands. Thus "by February of 1827 [Catharine] had raised nearly five thousand dollars through the sale of stock subscriptions, and in the fall of that year her seminary opened in its own handsome neoclassical building."[41] Inside it had everything Catharine desired; and outside an elegant façade with pillars that bespoke a temple of learning.

Catharine could now try some new things. She believed that teachers thrived when teaching what they know and love best. Boys in college learned from experts, so why shouldn't girls have teachers like that? Soon Hartford Female Seminary had eight teachers, each with a special area of expertise.[42] Every teacher could choose one of the "best and brightest scholars in her classes" to assist her. Girls selected for this responsibility often went on to become full-fledged teachers themselves. Catharine could now also group the students according to ability, so that none would be "hurried forward" and none kept back "for the sake of others, as is the common fault of large classes."[43] Finally she encouraged physical education, believing that the mind works better if the body has exercise.

Harriet could teach several subjects, but her specialty was composition. She most likely began by imitating her former teacher John Brace[44] and went on to develop her own approach. First, students had to learn vocabulary from literature that Harriet gave them. The girls would write each new word, what it meant, and how it was used. Then they used the new words in sentences.

The next step was to write an essay. And to do that, they would need a basic structure. Harriet would select a model piece of writing and outline its structure. Then each student created her own outline (called a "skeleton") for the teacher to correct. Based on that corrected outline the girls proceeded to write their essays. Thus the scholars at Hartford Female Seminary learned the craft of writing, unaware that they would one day be able to look back and say they had learned from one of the most famous authors in American history.

Harriet knew she was swimming against cultural currents. Many people assumed that the female intellect was limited and that girls lacked the mental capacity to reach the heights of abstract thought. Harriet Beecher disagreed. If something was hard to understand, the problem could be that the men who wrote the books simply were not good writers.

She raised that point in a satirical piece called "Modern Uses of Language"[45] written for the *Levee Gazette* (a handwritten magazine of Hartford Female Seminary). Why do intelligent men write unintelligibly? she asked. Perhaps they do not take the trouble to write clearly. And that is not the reader's fault. Take for example, the Common Sense philosophers; their works occupy the summit of learning, yet their meaning is often obscure. Or take Coleridge's *Aids to Reflection*. How often Harriet's students tried to read it, only to lament, "What an insignificant insect I am! I thought I could read the English language, but I was mistaken! Not one word . . . can I understand!" And then

Harriet said with mock piety, "What a great mind the man must have to say things so incomprehensibly!" Well! How naïve of these girls to expect language to reveal ideas, Harriet teased, when in fact too many authors used language "first, to *conceal* ideas" and, second, to conceal the *lack* of ideas.[46] Harriet Beecher used satire to teach her students to write clearly, and to respect their own intellects.

Harriet gave herself completely to the Hartford Female Seminary. In the fall of 1828, she was living with Catharine and two other teachers. "I am a *real school ma'am*," Harriet told a friend. "I do not mean that I am very grave, very precise, very learned, *or* very conceited — but simply that my school duties take up all my time." She didn't have much time to socialize or even to read for pleasure and felt "obliged to sacrifice my own private feelings in many things." But she was happy. She found in teaching a "form of *pleasure* — certainly this is more than I deserve."[47]

There were other pleasures, too. Early in the morning Catharine and Harriet often went horseback riding. There were weekly socials at the school, featuring music, games, and a chance to socialize with young men.

Even a place as serious as the Hartford Female Seminary had the occasional prankster, like Sarah Willis, who loved drawing others into mischief. Willis later became a popular writer under the pen name "Fanny Fern." Long after school girl days were over, Harriet Beecher Stowe wrote a letter to Willis's husband, James Parton (also a well-known literary figure).

> I believe you have claim on a certain naughty girl once called Sarah Willis. . . . I grieve to say one night [at the Hartford Female Seminary] she stole a pie . . . and did feloniously excite unto sedition & rebellion some five or six other girls — eating said pie between eleven & twelve o'clock in defiance of the laws of the school & in breach of the peace — ask her if it isn't so — & if she remembers curling her hair with leaves from her geometry [book]? — Perhaps she has long been penitent — *perhaps* — but ah me, when I read Fanny Fern's articles I detect sparks of the old witchcraft. . . . That's Sarah Willis I know.[48]

Harriet's last sibling was born in the fall of 1828, and she went to Boston to see him. Her infant half-brother James, Harriet said, looked like every other baby "except [for] a very large pair of blue eyes and an uncommonly fair complexion," charms that were "no sort of use or advantage to a man or boy."[49] From Boston Harriet went to Groton, where her brother George was studying. She was alarmed to find him in a state of depression. She thought he should not be left alone, so she wanted to stay. But Catharine and Lyman insisted that she return to Hartford.

Now in her late teens, Harriet still corresponded with her older brother Edward. They often discussed the Bible and theology. Like Edward, Harriet believed that God loves "his guilty, afflicted creatures." She believed "that God is such a being as you represent Him to be, and in the New Testament I find in the character of Jesus Christ a revelation of God as merciful and compassionate; in fact, just such a God as I need." Still, many Bible texts troubled her, for example the Old Testament book of Job, in which a righteous man suffers one calamity after another. If God is always loving (as Edward said) why do the righteous suffer? How could Edward explain God confronting Job out of the whirlwind "with a display of [divine] power and justice"?

Harriet pondered sin and salvation. If we cannot help being sinners, then why do we blame ourselves for being sinful? Rev. Hawes (who had made Harriet miserable as well as sinful) used to pray: *We have nothing to offer in extenuation of our sins.* Harriet now felt strong enough to disagree with Hawes. Indeed Harriet felt we have something to offer. We can take charge of our lives. And if it is not in our power to change our lives, why should we wallow in guilt? If a drunkard cannot help himself, why should we blame him for his conduct? Either we are responsible for our actions or we are not. Like Catharine, Harriet sensed something "dreadfully wrong" with punishing people for things they cannot change.

Both Edward and Lyman Beecher approached salvation as though it were a spiritual combination lock, requiring deft permutations. But Harriet sought one simple key: the grace of God. She found it in the atonement (Christ's death on the cross). Here was "undeserved mercy." She did not claim to understand it. She admitted that the Bible has many "difficulties." And yet it "holds out the hope that in a future world all shall be made plain. . . . So you see I am, as Mr. Hawes says, 'on the waves' and all I can do is to take the word of God that He does do right and there I rest."[50] She hoped that her long unhappiness was over, "and that I have found in Him who died for me all, and more than all, I could desire." She looked to Jesus as her "best friend," with whom she enjoyed "close and near communion." To him she confided every joy and sorrow; to him she looked "for direction and guidance."

In Hartford she took up her first social cause: the fate of the Cherokee Indians. The Cherokee lived in the region where northern Georgia, western North Carolina, and eastern Tennessee converge. Missionaries told the Cherokee that the best way to remain on their lands was to adopt white ways. Cherokee therefore signed treaties with the United States government, became farmers, and built roads, schools, and churches. But the pressure from white settlers increased nonetheless. Settlers (and the men they elected to represent them) clamored for the Indians to be removed. Christian missionaries defended the Cherokee, but Andrew Jackson was elected President in 1828, and the "old Indian fighter" swore to remove all Indians from the path of white settlement.

Opposition came mostly from "Protestant clergy and women"[51] who condemned Indian Removal as morally wrong. A Christian nation must keep its promises, they said, and breaking treaties would forever stain America's honor. Fighting on behalf of the Cherokee was the lawyer Jeremiah Evarts, an evangelical Christian, friend of Lyman Beecher, and the Secretary of the American Board of Commissioners for Foreign Missions. Evarts lobbied Congressmen, organized rallies, made speeches, and published articles to win support for the Cherokee.[52]

Women should be involved in the campaign, Evarts thought. So he approached Catharine Beecher (perhaps at Lyman's suggestion). It was a delicate matter, since in that time it was feared that women could not speak out on public issues without "unsexing" themselves. And yet it was also believed that women had pure emotions and could truly feel for the distressed.

Catharine agreed that women had a moral duty to plead with "the National Government to protect the Indians."[53] So she launched a petition drive — discreetly, of course. First, she wrote an anonymous letter on behalf of the Cherokee. Then she found a printer to typeset the letter and print it in bulk. At this point, the students and teachers of the Hartford Female Seminary (including Harriet) got involved, sending Catharine's letter to friends and family. It spread throughout New England and beyond. Women responded by writing petitions and gathering signatures, which were then sent to Congress. One such document from Hallowell, Maine, stated that "we are unwilling that the church, the schools, and the domestic altar should be thrown down before the avaricious god of power." It was the first time so many women publicly expressed their views. One historian wrote that "Catharine Beecher's petition drive against Removal set a pattern that would be followed by the antislavery movement in years to come."[54]

But the petitions were ignored. Gold was discovered on Cherokee land in the late 1820s, and that decided the issue. In 1831 the state of Georgia declared Cherokee laws and government to be null and void. In *Cherokee Nation v. Georgia,* the Supreme Court declared native tribes "domestic dependent nations," and as such they could not appeal to the Supreme Court.[55] The Cherokee were marched first to Tennessee and then 800 miles west to "Indian Territory." Indian Removal began in 1831 with the Choctaw, continuing with several tribes until the Cherokee "trail of tears" in the winter of 1838.

That Catharine opposed Cherokee removal was a testament to her leadership and moral courage. But she began to overreach. She had started the Hartford Female Seminary with a simple goal: to offer a quality education for girls. Over time, she envisioned an elite school that would train girls in religion and social refinement — as well as academics. Catharine wanted her students to influence society through moral example. She decided she must have someone to take charge of the religious and moral instruction at the school. She pinned her hopes on Zilpha Grant, the co-principal at Ipswich Academy. Catharine offered $1,000 per year but Grant declined the position as "too worldly."[56] Catharine was devastated. She also wanted an endowment to secure the financial future of the school. She saw no reason why a girls' school should not enjoy secure funding, just as the best colleges for boys had.[57] But the trustees and donors balked; they thought Catharine had asked for too much.

And that was not all. Catharine also wanted to build a dormitory. The current arrangement was for the students to board with local families; when the school day ended, the girls dispersed to host families in Hartford. Catharine wanted a dormitory because it would empower her to form the "consciences" and direct the "moral characters" of her students.[58] But parents were reluctant to give Catharine more control, and host families wanted the income from student boarders. Catharine felt blocked everywhere she turned.

Fatigued and frustrated, Catharine finally broke down. She described herself as "utterly prostrated and unable to perform any school duty without extreme pain and such confusion of thought as seemed like approaching insanity." Catharine took refuge with her father in Boston — leaving eighteen-year-old Harriet in charge of the Hartford Female Seminary.

Faced with the daunting prospect of running the school, Harriet gathered the students and teachers to explain how the school would be run in Catharine's absence. Together, students and teachers would conduct "an experiment in democracy." Everyone would be a responsible citizen. Each teacher was put in charge of a group of students, and each group had particular duties. She did not want Catharine to rush back; everyone wanted her to have the rest she needed. Harriet reported to her sister that the teachers "sat up till eleven o'clock finishing our Cherokee letters," and that public meetings and petitions were "getting up in New York and other places." Also, four students asked to make "a public profession of religion."

Harriet was warming to her new role. "Your absence is doing me good," she wrote, "for I never before felt such confidence to go forward and act, and the other teachers feel the same." Harriet felt willing "to devote my whole life to this institution, as I never did before." She felt equal to "anything, even to standing up with a good face for an hour's lecture." She told Catharine, "if you come home I fear, to speak classically, that I shall 'draw in my horns.'"[59]

Harriet did not have to draw in her horns very far, for Catharine returned to Hartford in the winter of 1830 weak and frail. Emotional distress and attacks of sciatica (nerve pain in the lower back and legs) plagued her. Living with other teachers was too stressful, so Catharine and Harriet moved in with their sister, Mary Beecher Perkins. In September of 1831 Catharine resigned from the Hartford Female Seminary.

A New Sphere of Usefulness

Thanks to their father, Catharine and Harriet could look forward to "a new sphere of usefulness": Lyman Beecher was moving to the West. A start-up Presbyterian seminary in Ohio invited him to be its president. There was a great sense of urgency: if New England Calvinists wished to put their stamp on the West, there was no time to lose. Irish Catholics and Methodists were already settling in Ohio, Indiana, and Illinois — as were many Southerners. As one historian explains, "Settlers moved faster than church organizations, and the Reformed denominations lacked sufficient trained pastors for the new areas."[60] Lyman Beecher would be the man to train those pastors. As Beecher himself put it, the church needed one of its "best generals" to "occupy the very seat of Western warfare while the enemy is coming in like a flood." That "seat of warfare" was Cincinnati, then called the gateway to the West.

The proposed school was to be called Lane Seminary. It had sixty acres, a board of trustees, and a charter, but no buildings and no funds to pay faculty. Then someone pledged $20,000 — a hefty sum in those days. The donor was Arthur Tappan, a wealthy New York merchant who bankrolled many evangelical projects.

Tappan's donation was conditional upon Lyman Beecher becoming Lane's first president. The board concurred: "Dr. Beecher, of Boston," was "the most prominent, popular, and powerful preacher in our nation" and would "immediately give character, elevation, and success to our seminary." So the Lane trustees elected Lyman Beecher as seminary president and professor of theology. When agents from Lane visited Beecher and informed him of their decision, Lyman recalled it as "the greatest thought that ever entered my soul; it filled it, and displaced everything else."[61]

Lyman wrote to Catharine that "the moral destiny of our nation, and of all our institutions and hopes, and the world's hopes, turns on the character of the West." Beecher felt compelled to go "to Cincinnati . . . to spend the remnant of my days in that great conflict." Beecher saw this as a turning point for evangelical Christianity in America: "If we gain the West, all is safe; if we lose it, all is lost." There was something in it for Catharine, too. Her father said, "If I go, it will be part of my plan that *you* go . . . and probably all my sons and all my daughters who are willing to go."[62] And that, of course, included Harriet.

But Beecher had only served his Boston church for five years when Lane Seminary started courting him. So he could not appear too eager to move. It would be prudent to visit Cincinnati and speak in person with trustees. So in the spring of 1832, Lyman Beecher and Catharine traveled west. Catharine sent glowing descriptions of Cincinnati to Harriet. The Ohio River town was surrounded with "a constant succession and variety of hills of all shapes and sizes, forming an extensive amphitheater," Catharine reported. Above the town was the hamlet of Walnut Hills, where Lane Seminary would rise amid "fine groves of trees." Cincinnati was a "New England city in all its habits, and its inhabitants are more than half from New England." Catharine saw a golden future in the West, and she thought Harriet needed to be part of it. "The folks here are very anxious to have a school on our plan," Catharine said. In the West lay a great "field of usefulness and influence"[63] for their father . . . and rich gleanings for his daughters Catharine and Harriet.

CHAPTER FOUR

We Mean to Turn Over the West

In September 1832, Harriet Beecher left New England and moved with her family to Ohio. She was twenty-one years old, with no suitors to tie her down. Harriet's stepmother and Aunt Esther made the journey, as did Catharine, George, and their young half-siblings Isabella, Thomas, and James. Henry and Charles were in college but would soon join the family in Ohio, while several of Harriet's older siblings were already on their own.[1]

Before turning westward, Lyman stopped in several eastern cities to raise funds for Lane Seminary. "Father goes here, there and everywhere — begging, borrowing and spoiling the Egyptians," Harriet wrote, "delighted with past successes, and confident in the future,"[2] although in Philadelphia Beecher did "not succeed very well in opening purses." With the fundraising and speechmaking concluded, the Beechers boarded a westbound stagecoach. And it came to pass, Harriet wrote, that "Noah, and his wife, and his sons, and his daughters, with cattle and creeping things, all dropped down in the front parlor of this tavern, about thirty miles from Philadelphia." As they traveled, they passed the time singing. "Jubilee" was a favorite hymn, giving voice to their new calling in the West:

> Hark! the jubilee is sounding,
> Oh the joyful news is come;
> Free salvation is proclaimed
> In and through God's only Son.
> Now we have the invitation
> To the meek and lowly Lamb,

55

Glory, honor and salvation;
Christ, the Lord, is come to reign.[3]

As they "made the air vocal" with song, the Beechers also made the land moral with print. Harriet's brother George had brought along bundles of tracts to be handed out along the way, "*peppering* the land with moral influence."[4] Tracts were cheap and plentiful, thanks to new printing and papermaking technologies. In 1825 the American Tract Society was formed to produce tracts, pamphlets, and small books. These were distributed by traveling "colporteurs," a role George Beecher took upon himself during the family's journey west.

But as the Beechers crossed the Allegheny Mountains, the trip bogged down. It took eight days of toil up and down steep grades, and those who could do so probably climbed down from the coach and walked to spare the horses. After they reached Wheeling, they planned to take a steamboat all the way to Cincinnati — until they heard that cholera had broken out in Cincinnati. Four hundred people were reported dead, and boats on the Ohio River carried cholera sufferers.[5]

So the Beechers dallied in Wheeling. Never one to waste an opportunity, Lyman arranged to preach eleven times. The theological climate was different than back east. Here Beecher seemed to have no antagonists — people listened so willingly! The family hoped that Cincinnati would be just as receptive.

Loath to risk exposing his family to cholera, Lyman Beecher hired a stagecoach to finish the journey. About one hundred miles west of Wheeling, they stopped at Granville. There a "protracted meeting" (revival) was in progress. Lyman and George each preached several times, converting forty-five souls. Then the Beechers continued west, their coach jolting toward Columbus over "corduroy road made of logs laid crosswise."

Cincinnati, Ohio

The Beechers arrived in Cincinnati on November 14, 1832. A delegation from Lane Seminary met them, and escorted them the last two miles uphill from town to the little hamlet of Walnut Hills (now part of Cincinnati).

Harriet Beecher soon wrote in glowing terms of her new home. "These high hills are covered with beautiful woods, and from the top of them you may see the city extending up and down the banks of the river, with all the bustle of business going on. It is laid out in fine streets and has many handsome houses and churches, while all around it are gardens and green fields, and the river is covered with flat boats and steam boats, passing up and down, or stopping at the wharf." It seemed to Harriet that Cincinnati, with its handsome public buildings, factories, and schools, might one day become one of the greatest cities in the world.[6]

There were other, less flattering descriptions of Cincinnati. Because of the meatpacking industry, the town was dubbed "Porkopolis," and pigs ran loose eating garbage and wallowing anywhere they could find a mud hole. In the slaughterhouse districts, blood flowed into the streets. German immigrants worked in the meat business and brewed oceans of beer. As a river town with a busy port, Cincinnati drew transients — including gamblers and thieves. Mobs formed quickly to smash windows, set fires,[7] and generally raise hell. But the greatest danger was cholera. It came like the angel of death in the summer and tapered off in the fall.

Although Ohio was a free state, slavery had a strong presence there. The slave state of Kentucky was, quite literally, a stone's throw away across the river from Cincinnati. Many white Ohioans had slaveholding relatives and friends. Even whites who disliked slavery had little choice but to accept it as part of life. When southerners came to Cincinnati on business or to see family, they could bring and keep their slaves with them for weeks or even months at a time (though the slaves might attempt to escape). Boats carrying slaves to be sold in the south routinely docked in Cincinnati.

Harriet saw "those floating palaces which plied between Cincinnati and New Orleans." In the cabin above, she later wrote, "were happy mothers, wives and husbands, brothers and sisters rejoicing in secure family affection, and on the deck below, miserable shattered fragments of black families, wives torn from husbands, children without mothers and mothers without children," not knowing where they were going except "down river." They would never hear from their families nor their families from them, "for slavery took care that slaves should write no letters."[8]

Runaway slaves crossed the Ohio River, seeking freedom. They would hide in Cincinnati and other river towns before making their way further north. Slave catchers scoured these towns for runaways. Cincinnati had a black population of about two thousand, mostly former slaves. Their living conditions varied, but the neighborhood known as Bucktown (or the Bottoms) was a "wretched basin of tenements and shanties drained by an odiferous stream that carried the bloody runoff from slaughter houses."[9]

In contrast Walnut Hills, where the Beechers lived, was a pleasant village on the hillside above Cincinnati. There Lane Seminary was located, and there the Beechers would live. A new house was being built for them, but it was not ready when the Beechers arrived. A grumpy Harriet described their temporary quarters as "inconvenient, ill-arranged, good for nothing." Their westward journey was over, and now waves of homesickness washed over Harriet. Weeks went by with no word from home. Finally a letter arrived from Harriet's sister Mary back in Hartford. Harriet snatched the letter and bounded upstairs to read it all by herself.

She wrote back immediately. Four-year-old James, Harriet reported, was seen "with his arm over the neck of a great hog . . . and the other day he actually got upon the back of one and rode some distance."[10] Then she told Mary of her longings for their New England home. "Never was there such an abundance of meditation on our native land, on the joys of friendship, and pains of separation," she sighed.

Things improved that winter when the Beechers moved into the new seminary president's house. It was a two-story brick house, L-shaped with generous windows and a double porch. The wide front door led to a spacious hall for receiving guests, with Lyman's study conveniently off to one side. The downstairs had a large front parlor, a back parlor, and a dining room; at the back of the house were the kitchen and service areas. Upstairs were several bedrooms for the family and guests.

Outside in the back yard, the vegetable garden slept beneath the snow. Stands of oak and beech trees graced the property. There were several small outbuildings, including the "necessary house" and a stable where the Beechers could keep their milk cow and a spotted horse named Charley. "Charley horse" would pull the family buggy down the hill to Cincinnati and back up again — sometimes making several trips a day. Charley was a progressive horse, for he "believed in going ahead, whether uphill or down." Aunt Esther and Mrs. Beecher managed the house, garden, and livestock and hired help for kitchen chores and laundry.

Later Harriet remembered the house at Lane Seminary as "a kind of moral heaven." It resounded with laughter, prayer, and song. Here learned folk discussed the issues of the day. The very air seemed "replete with moral oxygen — full charged with intellectual electricity."[11] The house still stands today, the last remnant of Lane Seminary.

The Young Writer

During that first winter in Cincinnati, Harriet finished her first book — a textbook she had started writing back East. *Primary Geography* was published by Corey and Fairbank of Cincinnati in May 1833, bringing Harriet the tidy sum of $187.[12] Harriet shared the credit with Catharine, under the byline "C & H Beecher." The first advertisement for the book named "Catharine Beecher" as sole author.[13] After all, Catharine may have thought, the book was written by *her* sister for *her* school.

But this was Harriet's work, written in a chatty and confiding tone to engage her readers. She taught the basics of geography and, just as important, she gave the students a moral compass. According to Mary Kelley, a historian of female education, geography primers were intended to build a common worldview, just as "Noah Webster's dictionaries and spellers" built a common language. This worldview "prepared women to read . . . newspapers, periodicals, almanacs, histories, and novels"[14] that shaped American culture.

Harriet wanted her students to know the religion of each country or region, and why it mattered. In Christian nations, she said, girls are educated and treated like human beings with souls. However, "In all these countries where the Bible is unknown, females are despised and cruelly treated. There is no such thing as a school for females in any of them." Where the Bible is unknown, she wrote, women are treated as "slaves or dogs." Countries which are not Christian have "no charitable societies, to take care of women and orphan children, nor any of the benevolent institutions of Christian lands."[15] The way in which any culture treats women and children, she thought, is a fair test of how advanced it is.

Catharine Beecher's Western Female Institute opened in May

1833 at Sycamore and Fourth Street in Cincinnati with about forty students. Local businessmen gave money for desks, carpet and curtains, blackboards, and a piano. The school year was divided into three fourteen-week terms. The cost was eighteen dollars per term, including books.[16] Harriet and Catharine moved to lodgings near the school; the Beecher house in Walnut Hills was their retreat when school was not in session.

The Beecher sisters hoped to expand the Western Female Institute by adding a primary school for girls and boys. However, their dream was much bigger: "we mean to turn over [cultivate] the West," Harriet told a friend, "by means of *model schools* in this its capital."[17] These model schools would impart knowledge and shape character.

Catharine and Harriet could not do all this alone, so Catharine recruited two young women with teaching experience from the Hartford Female Seminary.[18] Catharine and Harriet became co-principals, but it was not an equal partnership. Harriet was stuck with much of the administrative work, leaving Catharine free to travel and promote the school and her vision for female education.

Harriet shared that vision. "Teaching will never be rightly done till it passes into *female* hands," Harriet told a friend back east. Women possess the "tact, versatility, talent and piety" and know how to use "patience, longsuffering, gentleness" required of good teachers. Some men have these qualities, said Harriet, but the classroom would not satisfy them. Men needed a more "thrilling call of action" and could find it in the ministry or foreign missions. Besides, "men must have salaries that can support a wife and family." Women cannot be ministers, Harriet said, but they can be teachers. If society does not value women's work highly enough, a dedicated teacher will still strive to do her best.

Catharine promised that Harriet would have time to write. But instead Harriet found all her time "taken up in the labor of our new school, or wasted in the fatigue and lassitude following such labor." Oh, how she hated meetings, wasting time on trifles like "quills and paper [left] on the floor; forming classes; drinking in the entry (cold water, mind you); giving leave to speak; recess bells, etc, etc." Harriet feared that she was "sinking into deadness."[19]

But rather than succumb to self-pity, she looked for ways to improve herself. An opening came when she and Catharine were invited to join the Semi-Colon Club — a literary society comprised of doctors and lawyers, professors and clergy, and businessmen. Lyman Beecher belonged, and so did Harriet's uncle, Samuel Foote, the former sea captain. Foote was now a wealthy merchant with a mansion in the fashionable part of town. His house was a "center of hospitality and cultural activity" in Cincinnati and a favorite meeting place for the Semi-Colons. Another member of the group was Salmon P. Chase, who later became governor of Ohio, served in Lincoln's cabinet, and was appointed chief justice of the United States. Professor Calvin Stowe of Lane Seminary belonged to the Semi-Colons, and came with his wife Eliza. Thanks to "the more liberal attitude prevailing in the West," the Semi-Colon Club admitted women.

The Semi-Colon Club was not about extravagant clothing and lavish meals. Rather, "the prime desideratum was rational amusement." Before each meeting, members wrote something to be read aloud and then discussed. To make it more fun, authors withheld their names, and their works were read aloud by a member such as William Greene, a lawyer with a "stately manner and stentorian voice."[20] After each reading, the group responded with praise and criticism. Sometimes they made a game of guessing the author's identity.

Members could write about almost anything. Topics ranged "from immortality to cranberry sauce, from Adam and Eve to old Dr Beecher," one member recalled. Scholarly folk in the group tried to refrain from lecturing; instead they made "light, fanciful offerings."[21] Humor and satire abounded, with much teasing about "matrimony, old maids and bachelors."

This was Harriet's big chance to improve her writing. She was bashful and unused to criticism, but the Semi-Colon Club encouraged her to write "for distinguished guests" and to get their honest opinion of her work.[22] And it brought out Harriet's playful side. Once she wrote a comical letter and claimed she received it in the mail. She smudged and smoked the paper to make it look worn, had it postmarked and sealed and addressed to herself. Another time she penned a set of comical rules barring the Semi-Colon Club from teasing old bachelors and old maids.

After all, Catharine was considered an old maid school teacher, and Harriet appeared to be going the same way. A contemporary described the Beecher sisters as "scarcely redeemed from homeliness" by the "expression of intelligence which lights them up, and fairly sparkles in the bluish grey eyes."[23] Another person said Harriet was "not distinguished for conversation, but when she did speak, she showed something of the peculiar strength and humor of her mind. Her sister, Miss Catharine Beecher, was a far more easy and fluent conversationalist."[24]

The Semi-Colon Club set the stage for Harriet's first published story. When one of Harriet's pieces was read aloud in the group, fellow-member and editor James Hall "chased down the identity of the author." Hall urged Harriet to enter her piece in his magazine, *Western Monthly,* in a contest for a fifty dollar prize. Harriet won the prize and her story, "A New England Sketch," was published in April 1834. It was her "first signed fictional piece."[25] The club helped to draw Harriet out of her shell, revealing her as a "bright and happy girl, running over with genius and sympathy." Years later, people who had known her in Cincinnati proudly remembered that the author of *Uncle Tom's Cabin* began her writing career[26] in the Semi-Colon Club.

Put on Your Bonnet and Go with Me

Harriet also sharpened her pen on church politics. In the spring of 1833 she wrote a satirical sketch of a presbytery meeting in Cincinnati. Harriet had a stake in this meeting, for it concerned her brother George, and whether or not he would be granted a preaching license. The outcome was a bit dicey, since Lyman Beecher already had foes in Ohio. The old school Presbyterians saw all Beechers as heretics; therefore they would try to stop George from getting a preaching license. "It would be much easier for the inquisitors to confound a stripling" like George, wrote one historian, "than a seasoned wrangler" like Lyman Beecher.[27]

The presbytery Harriet attended was but a minor skirmish in a much larger battle for control of Presbyterianism in America. On the Beecher side were the "New Schoolers." They embraced revivalism which gave sinners a voluntary relationship with God. They generally opposed slavery. On the other side were the "Old Schoolers." They held to a "hard literal interpretation" of the Bible and the Presbyterian confessions, which proclaimed "man's utter and absolute natural and moral inability to obey God's commands." The Old Schoolers generally supported slavery. Cincinnati's Old School faction was led by Joshua Wilson, who stood for "Calvinistic fatalism."[28]

The meeting was held at Second Presbyterian, Lyman Beecher's church. Harriet came with her new friend Eliza Stowe (whose husband Calvin was to be formally admitted to the presbytery that day). Aunt Esther came too. Women sat off to the side and did not speak. To a friend, Harriet wrote an irreverent account of the proceedings. The abbreviated version below suggests her sense of humor and deep family loyalty.

You never went to a Presbytery? Well, put on your bonnet, and go with me. . . . Inside the church the moderator calls the meeting to order. They proceed to business. They are to examine a candidate. The candidate is Mr. George Beecher, a New School man. . . . Dr. Wilson sits in the front, with his great ivory headed-cane leaning on the pew beside him, holding his copy of the Confession of faith as though it were the ultimate weapon. He is a tall, grave looking man, of strong and rather harsh features, very pale, with a severe seriousness of face, and with great formality and precision in every turn and motion. George Beecher sits opposite, on the pulpit stairs facing the assembly.

Dr. Wilson begins the inquisition: "Mr. Beecher, what is matter and what is mind, and what is Mechanics, and Optics, and Hydrostatics, and what is Mental Philosophy and what is Moral Philosophy, and what is right and wrong, and what is truth, and what is virtue, and what are the powers of the mind, and what is intellect, susceptibilities, and will and conscience" — *and everything else, world without end, amen! Wilson now relaxes into a smile which seems like a melting snowdrift. George answers as best he can.*

The trial moves on to theology. Now you may see the brethren bending forward, and shuffling, and looking wise. Over in the pew opposite to us are students of Lane Seminary, with attentive eyes.

Now one of Lyman's New School allies questions George. This is Mr. Gallagher, a shrewd man with a good sense of humor and real poetic feeling. Gallagher asks easy, open-ended questions on the broad truths of Christianity.

Next comes the fiery trial: any of the brethren can question the candidate. "Mr. Beecher, do you believe in the doctrine of election? What about the imputation of Adam's sin? Mr. Beecher, do you believe infants are sinners as soon as they are born? . . . Do you believe that men are able of themselves to obey the commandments of God? Mr. Beecher do you believe men are active or passive in regeneration? Mr. Beecher,

*do you make any distinction between regeneration and conversion? Mr.
Beecher, do you think that men are punished for the guilt of Adam's first
sin? Do you believe in imputed righteousness?"*

*George swings bravely at each question, with eyes flashing and
hands going, turning first to right and then to left, asking for clarifica-
tion, saying "yes sir, no sir, I should think so sir." One minister accuses
George of saying that "God has no right to require men to do what they
are not able to do. Now sir, this is an awful error. . . ." Aunt Esther and I
exchange glances with a very unsuitable degree of merriment.*

*On the second day of the presbytery, the church is packed. Lyman
Beecher rises to speak for a final time: George Beecher, he says, agrees
with the Confession of faith. The New School men are not intimidated.
Then Joshua Wilson declares: George Beecher is not a Christian . . . and
will never see the gates of eternal bliss.*[29]

In the end, the Presbytery granted George's preaching license.
Joshua Wilson lost this battle, but he would return to fight another day.

In the summer of 1833 a former student invited Harriet to visit
her home in Washington, Kentucky. It was Harriet's first and only
known visit to a plantation with slaves. Local lore has Harriet visiting
several plantations; even making return trips to the area. In one apocryphal story, Harriet Beecher witnessed a slave auction. All we know
for certain is that Harriet visited the home of a student "whose parents owned slaves." Later she used her memories of this visit to create
the fictional setting of the Shelby Plantation, where *Uncle Tom's Cabin*
begins.

Traveling with Harriet was Mary Dutton, who also taught at the
Western Female Institute. Dutton later said that Harriet "did not
seem to notice anything in particular that happened" during the visit.
Harriet "sat much of the time as though abstracted in thought. When
the negroes did funny things and cut up capers, she did not seem to
pay the slightest attention to them."[30] When Dutton read *Uncle Tom's
Cabin* some twenty years after that visit to Kentucky, she "recognized
scene after scene of that visit portrayed with the most minute fidelity,
and knew at once where the material for that portion of the story had
been gathered."[31]

In the summer of 1834 Harriet again traveled with Mary Dutton.
This time, they were headed for New England to visit family. The two
young women took a stagecoach to Toledo and then a steamboat

across Lake Erie. They stopped to do some sightseeing at Niagara Falls, where Harriet stood in awe before the thundering waters. The view seemed "unearthly" to Harriet, "like the strange dim images in the Revelation. I thought of the great white throne, the rainbow around it . . . [the] beautiful water rising like moonlight, falling as the soul sinks when it dies, to rise refined, spiritualized and pure. . . . I felt as if I could have *gone over* with the waters; there would be no fear in it. I felt the rock tremble under me with a sort of joy."[32]

The thrill of Niagara gave way to tedium: 288 slow miles on a canal boat, towed by mules from Buffalo to Albany. It must have been a relief to board a stagecoach for Amherst, where Harriet's brother Henry was graduating from college. She was the only family member to attend his graduation. There was nothing to suggest that he would one day be famous. Henry used to joke that he "stood next to the head of his class" only when "they were all arranged in a circle."[33]

Harriet was visiting relatives, perhaps in Hartford, when a letter came from her stepmother in Cincinnati. Bad news: another wave of cholera! The sickness reached Walnut Hills and Lane Seminary, where it claimed the life of Harriet's new friend Eliza Stowe. Cholera can be swift and cruel: severe diarrhea can dehydrate the victim, leading to a state of shock before death. Harriet's stepmother reported that doctors were summoned to Eliza's bedside but could do nothing. Eliza's husband Calvin did what he could: he read the Twenty-Third Psalm to Eliza, to comfort her. Before Eliza died, she had a vision of "joy unspeakable and full of glory"[34] as her loved ones prayed and sang around her deathbed. The beautiful and witty Eliza died at age twenty-five, leaving Professor Calvin Stowe alone with no children. Calvin came often to the Beecher home in Walnut Hills, seeking solace from those who had known and loved his wife. When Harriet returned to Cincinnati, she befriended the lonely widower.

The Lane Rebellion

Around this time Henry and Charles Beecher joined the family in Walnut Hills and enrolled at Lane Seminary. If they thought this was their father's school, they were in for a rude awakening. There was a crisis at Lane when a group of students tried to take over the school in the name of abolition. The struggle at Lane has been dubbed "the Lane debates," or "the Lane Rebellion." It nearly destroyed Lyman Beecher's career and affected his family at Walnut Hills for many years to come.

The turmoil at Lane was a sign of the times: the anti-slavery movement was becoming more militant. In 1831 (a few years before the Lane Rebellion) Nat Turner led slaves to rise up and murder sixty whites in Southampton County, Virginia. In revenge, white southerners killed about two hundred blacks and demanded stricter laws to enforce slavery. That same year in Boston, William Lloyd Garrison founded the *Liberator,* demanding immediate abolition of slavery. In 1833, the American Anti-Slavery Society was founded. At the time, many Americans saw the *Liberator* and the AASS as threats to the social order. Lyman Beecher thought slavery was wrong, but he feared that radical abolitionism would only make the slaveholders defensive. So Beecher favored gradual, voluntary emancipation, and the colonization of former slaves in Africa. But radical abolitionists began to see moderates like Beecher as impediments to reform.

Beecher was caught unprepared by the rising conflict over slavery; his priorities were elsewhere. He had come to Lane Seminary to spread evangelical Calvinism in the West. He was fighting Old School Presbyterians and worried about the rising tide of Catholic immigrants. He was blindsided when abolitionists — who saw Lane's strategic potential for training abolitionist clergy and hiding fugitive slaves escaping north via the Underground Railroad — tried to take over his school.

Meanwhile back east, money was talking. Arthur Tappan — the wealthy businessman who brokered Beecher's appointment as Lane's president — embraced radical abolitionism. He wished to see Lane Seminary follow suit. And he became impatient with Beecher's tepid stance on slavery. Tappan now supported the man who became the ringleader of the Lane Rebellion: Theodore Dwight Weld. A convert of Charles Finney (Beecher's old rival), Weld was fearless in front of hostile crowds. He looked like a prophet: he seldom bothered to shave, and his long hair stuck out in all directions like the quills of a porcupine.

Weld was thirty when he came to Lane Seminary in 1833. He was already an experienced organizer and accomplished public speaker. He brought several disciples who enrolled at Lane with him. "Weld was a genius," Lyman Beecher admitted years later. "In the estimation of the class, he was president. He took the lead of the whole institution. The young men had, many of them, been under his care, and they thought he was a god."[35] Beecher described the Lane students as "a noble class of young men, uncommonly strong, a little uncivilized, entirely radical, and terribly in earnest." So much did they esteem Weld that Beecher thought it "might prove difficult" to govern them "by ordinary college law." It did indeed prove difficult.

In the winter of 1834, Weld and other Lane students asked permission to hold a public debate on slavery. Similar debates had been staged elsewhere,[36] but the subject was flammable so the faculty delayed[37] until February. And when it finally happened, the format was not a debate, strictly speaking. It was a combination of lectures by experts and testimonies by those who had personal experience with slavery. Soon a revival spirit or "awakened fervor" took hold. For nine evenings the students argued about slavery and abolition. Then a vote was taken and most students took an anti-slavery stance. For the next nine sessions, the students debated what to do about slavery. Should slaves be freed immediately and stay in the United States (abolition)? Or should they be freed gradually and sent to West Africa (colonization)? Again the students voted. Abolition won and colonization lost. Among the newly awakened was George Beecher.[38]

Did Harriet Beecher witness the Lane debates? Historian Gilbert Barnes said so: "She heard the heartrending stories that the Southern students told of cruelty and wrong, and she heard Weld's moving plea for the abolition of slavery."[39] Solid evidence of her presence, however, is lacking. She may have been down in Cincinnati at the Western Female Institute. If so, she would have heard about the debates from her family.

The debates over, Weld moved quickly to organize Lane students into an anti-slavery society. Soon they were interacting with black people in town. Weld wrote to Arthur Tappan that "many of these former slaves were in constant terror of kidnappers and slave agents; most lived in pitiable conditions."[40] Blacks were shunned by whites unless there was menial work to be done. But now, Weld explained, Lane students had formed "a large and efficient organization for elevating the colored people of Cincinnati." Through education, Weld hoped to make Cincinnati a "spectacle of free black cultivation."[41] Arthur Tappan sent money and recruits to Weld.

Cincinnatians were alarmed to see seminary students fraternizing with blacks. Hate mail began arriving at Lane. The trustees of

Lane Seminary feared that a mob would burn down the seminary. They had reason to fear, for Cincinnati had a history of mob violence. "If you want to teach colored schools, I can fill your pockets with money," Beecher told Weld; "but if you will visit in colored families, and walk with them in the streets, you will be overwhelmed."[42]

In May 1834, two Lane students went to New York to attend an Anti-Slavery Society meeting. There the students gave the impression that Lane's faculty were abolitionists. Word got back to the Lane trustees, stoking their fears of mob violence. Beecher stayed calm. He knew that Ohio's Western Reserve College had had an anti-slavery abolitionist awakening in 1832, also led by Weld. It was the same pattern: convert students and faculty to abolition, form an abolitionist society, and send students out to work in the cause.[43] Western Reserve had weathered the storm, and Lane could, too.

So Beecher went back east in May of 1834[44] to attend meetings, to raise funds for Lane, and to visit family. The Board of Trustees was in charge of the school, but that did not stop Weld and his disciples from working among Cincinnati's black population. Infuriated, the trustees[45] appointed a committee to curb the students. The committee passed resolutions that, if approved by the board, would dissolve the Lane Anti-Slavery Society, impose a gag rule to prevent further discussion of slavery, allow the board to prohibit controversial behavior (i.e., fraternizing with blacks), and empower the board to dismiss any who "failed to comply with these regulations."[46] These were draconian measures. Back east, Beecher got letters urging him to rush back to Cincinnati and put out the flames. One person warned Beecher that Lane was "more to be dreaded than the cholera" and that "the spirit of insubordination"[47] must be quenched. But others wrote to beg Beecher to return and stand with the students against slavery.

By the time Beecher returned to Walnut Hills in October, the Board of Trustees had already passed rules to suppress the students. Beecher must now choose: he could oppose his own board, or condemn his own students. Beecher met with the other two professors, one of whom was Calvin Stowe. They would not oppose the board. Beecher did not condone slavery, but he did not want to sacrifice his school for the cause of radical abolition.

Most of the students felt betrayed by Beecher's lack of support. "Thirty eight of the fifty theological students" asked to be dismissed.

Also defecting were "more than fifty of the sixty"[48] preparatory students. Most of them eventually wound up at Oberlin Collegiate Institute (now Oberlin College) in northern Ohio. Weld continued his activism against slavery by compiling *American Slavery as It Is: Testimony of a Thousand Witnesses,* which Harriet used as a source for her own anti-slavery writings. And Charles Finney, Beecher's old rival and Weld's mentor, went to teach at Oberlin. Arthur Tappan stopped sending money to Lane and became a benefactor of Oberlin.

Out in Boston, William Lloyd Garrison, editor of the *Liberator,* denounced Lane Seminary as "a Bastille of Oppression — spiritual Inquisition" and printed 18,000 copies of this article to be "circulated by Arthur Tappan and other New York abolitionists." This would deter anti-slavery supporters from sending their sons to Lane Seminary.[49] But Beecher also had foes on the opposite side of the fence who saw him as a wild-eyed abolitionist.

Lyman Beecher tried to dismiss the whole affair as an "imbroglio." Lane would be better off without Weld and his followers, Beecher said, now that their departure had "purged out the old leaven."[50] In truth, Beecher was "strongly shaken," to the point where "some of his fairest hopes for the future and the nation were now being called into question."[51] Lyman said Weld and his followers were "he-goat men . . . butting everything in the line of their march which does not fall in or get out of the way . . . they are made up of vinegar, aqua fortis, and oil of vitriol, with brimstone, saltpeter and charcoal, to explode and scatter the corrosive matter."[52] Beecher was so deeply wounded that Harriet must have felt his distress.

Then in the summer of 1835, Lyman faced two assaults at once: his second wife died of consumption while the Old School Presbyterians put him on trial for heresy. Mrs. Beecher died on July 7 and was buried "beneath four weeping willows"[53] in the same graveyard where Eliza Stowe was laid to rest. Ten days later, Lyman was acquitted of heresy. His children rallied to support him, holding a surprise family reunion in celebration of his sixtieth birthday. The battered patriarch came down the stairs one morning and beheld all eleven of his children gathered for the first time under one roof. The old man wept. And his children poured out their love over two days of feasting, praying, and singing.

The events at Lane Seminary tarnished Lyman Beecher's reputation among the leaders of the anti-slavery movement. Almost twenty years later, Harriet was still defending her father's actions at Lane. When Wendell Phillips accused Beecher of silencing the discussion of slavery at Lane,[54] Harriet said no, her father and Calvin Stowe were out of town when the crisis came to a head. They returned to a bad choice: either submit to the board's actions or renounce their positions at Lane. Beecher chose to "submit temporarily" to the board's actions in order to salvage "the enterprise at Lane Seminary." As a now-famous anti-slavery author, Harriet gave credit to her father's influence. It was not her father's fault that Lane Theological Seminary was hijacked by "vigorous, radical young men, headed by that brilliant, erratic genius, Theodore D. Weld." These men enrolled as theological students "under Dr. Beecher and Professor Stowe" but they meant to "make of the Seminary an anti-slavery fort."[55]

The Beechers had gone west to Ohio with such high hopes, only to have Lyman's career nearly destroyed by abolitionists. This might have been enough to convince Harriet that abolitionism was something to be avoided. Yet in Cincinnati she also saw and heard things that roused her indignation against slavery. One of the most compelling stories — one she later used in *Uncle Tom's Cabin* — seems to have been told by a white clergyman named John Rankin. In the fall of 1834, during the crisis at Lane, Lyman Beecher attended a meeting of clergy in Ripley, a river town some sixty miles east of Cincinnati. For company Beecher brought with him his daughter Harriet and the recently widowed Professor Stowe.[56] In Ripley, so the story goes, they visited the home of Rev. John Rankin. It perched on a bluff overlooking the town of Ripley and the Ohio River. At night Rankin used to set up a signal lamp to guide fugitive slaves to his home. He would hide them in his barn or cellar until it was safe for them to move on. Today the Rankin house is a historic site, where one can buy a copy of Rankin's memoir and read the story in his own words:

> A Kentucky slave mother having been harshly treated by her mistress, took her child in her arms and in the night started for Canada. She came to the house of an old Scotsman who lived on the Ohio River. She asked him what was best for her to do. My house being on top of a high hill he pointed to it and said, "A good man lives in that house. Go to it and you will be safe." The river was frozen over and a thaw had come so the water was running over the ice, which was just ready to break up. She waded across and went to my

house, went into the kitchen, made a fire and dried herself. Then she waked up two of my boys and they conveyed her to another depot that same night. The lakes being frozen over she could not get to Canada till spring. She passed the winter at Greenfield. Her husband, who was also a slave, followed her there. . . .[57]

Whether Harriet heard this story from Rev. Rankin's own lips or in some other way, she never forgot it. At the right time, she would tell it to the world. She would show that while white men argued, a brave mother carried her child across the frozen river to freedom.

CHAPTER FIVE

Nobody Knows Who

The courtship of Harriet Beecher and Calvin Stowe began during the time of mourning for Calvin's first wife. The bereaved professor found a companion in Harriet. Family and friends fanned the sparks, hoping the friendship would grow into a romance to end Calvin's loneliness and save Harriet from spinsterhood. The engagement was announced in the fall of 1835.

At twenty-four years of age, Harriet Beecher possessed character and wit in abundance, though no one described her as beautiful. She was small in stature with sparkling grey-blue eyes. Her nose was long and her cheekbones high, but dark curls framed her face, softening her features. Calvin Stowe was nine years older than Harriet, and his hair was already thinning. He had the light of intelligence in his eyes and consumed books as eagerly as food. Like Harriet, he came from New England Puritan stock. When it came to temperament, however, the two were quite different. Calvin was frugal, but Harriet trusted in the Lord — or someone else — to make ends meet. He was fastidious and fussy; she left a swirl of clutter behind her. Calvin fretted and stewed, and Harriet prayed and acted.

They were married in January 1836 at the Beecher home in Walnut Hills, with Rev. Lyman Beecher officiating. Just before the wedding, Harriet wrote to a friend from schoolgirl days:[1]

> Well, my dear G., about half an hour more and your old friend, companion, schoolmate, sister, etc. will cease to be Hatty Beecher and change into nobody knows who. . . . Well, my dear, I have been dreading and dreading the time, and lying awake all last week won-

dering how I should live through this overwhelming crisis, and lo! It has come and I feel *nothing at all.*

The wedding is to be altogether domestic; nobody present but my own brothers and sisters, my old colleague, Mary Dutton; and as there is a sufficiency of the ministry in our family we have not even to call in the foreign aid of a minister. Sister Katy [Catharine] is not here, so she will not witness my departure from her care and guidance to that of another. . . . Well, here comes Mr. S., so farewell, and for the last time I subscribe

Your own H.E.B.

One biographer thought Harriet's comment about "dreading and dreading the time" meant that she dreaded sex,[2] but more likely it was marriage she feared. Marriage was a leap of no return, and divorce was not an option. Even a happy marriage brought the perils of childbirth and the long, wearing years of child-rearing. Harriet's own mother died young, and so did her stepmother. Harriet had a tremendous will to write, but how she would find the time for it while raising a family she did not know.

Calvin knew that by marrying a Beecher, he was getting a highly intelligent and articulate mate. Beyond that he had no idea what he was in for. He could not have foreseen that she would become famous, be absent from home for long periods of time, and make more money than he did — all unusual for those times.

Calvin Stowe

Calvin Stowe was born in Natick, Massachusetts, in 1802. His father, a baker, died at the age of thirty-six, and his widowed mother went to live with her father. At an early age Calvin learned to read the Bible and *Pilgrim's Progress.* He attended a local school and then was apprenticed to a man who owned a paper mill. Calvin had to get up at three in the morning and "go to the mill to start the fires under the boiler" so that there would be steam "when the men came to work at six."[3] When things got slow at the mill, Calvin memorized Latin from a book given to him by an uncle. Sometimes Calvin was paid in new paper from the mill, which he traded for used books from a local deacon. Calvin's mother, seeing that her son had the makings of a scholar, somehow found the means (or a benefactor) to send him to a local academy.

In his late teens Calvin attended revival meetings and was converted. He met a Christian businessman who offered to pay for his education at Bowdoin College in Brunswick, Maine.[4] Calvin graduated at the head of his class in 1824 and stayed two more years as an instructor and librarian. He went from there to Andover Theological Seminary, where he studied under Moses Stuart, a biblical scholar who took the lead in bringing German methods of biblical study into American theological education.

Next Calvin went to Dartmouth College to teach Latin and Greek. He traveled to Dartmouth by stagecoach, rocking along through the drizzle for "two gloomy, dreary November days." On the way he read Goethe's *Faust,* the tale of a brilliant young man who sold his soul to the devil. The experience "perfectly dissolved" Calvin,[5] and German literature became one of his lifelong passions.

Calvin was married in 1829 to Eliza Tyler, the daughter of Dartmouth College president Bennet Tyler. A few years later Lyman Beecher met and recruited Professor Stowe to teach biblical literature at Lane Seminary. It must have been quite a sales pitch: Beecher told Stowe that Lane Seminary was destined to be *the* theological school of the West. Here Calvin's academic career would thrive. Beecher himself raised the funds to pay Stowe's salary. So in 1832, the same year that Harriet traveled west with her family, Calvin took his bride to Ohio, where she died when cholera swept through Cincinnati.

Though a birthright Calvinist, Stowe was strongly attracted to German theology. His intellectual hero was Friedrich Tholuck, a German theologian who combined modern scholarship with religious experience. Tholuck had been influenced by Friedrich Schleiermacher, the German "father of liberalism" who taught that all religion is *feeling.*

Calvin had to keep his interest in German theology to himself, lest orthodox Presbyterians — including Joshua Wilson, Beecher's arch foe — catch the scent of heresy. But Calvin could safely share his interests with Harriet. Later in life, Harriet said that Calvin did not use "the Bible as a carpenter does his nail-box, going to it only to find screws and nails to hold together the framework of a theological system"; instead her husband treated the books of the Bible "as divinely inspired compositions, yet truly and warmly human." He applied to the Bible "the same rules of reason and common sense which pertain to all human documents."[6]

Calvin's intellect was disciplined, but his imagination could run wild. He could fret himself into a depression, a process Harriet called "cultivating indigo." As a child Calvin believed that ghosts and spirits visited him — not just once or twice, but consistently over a period of years. He wrote up some of these experiences for the Semi-Colon Club.[7] Calvin loved telling weird folktales he'd heard as a child in New England. And now, after the death of his first wife, Calvin Stowe needed a companion.

The wedding of Calvin Stowe and Harriet Beecher was short and simple. Harriet felt they could forgo "conformity to [the] ordinary custom" of a honeymoon. Shortly after the wedding Calvin had to give a lecture in Columbus, and she went with him. Never mind the bad roads in winter — this was their "wedding excursion." When they returned, Harriet wrote to a friend that she and Calvin were sitting by their own fireside, "as domestic as any pair of tame fowl you ever saw." Harriet described herself as "tranquil, quiet, and happy."[8]

It would not last long, for soon Calvin was off to Europe. The trip had been in the offing for some time; Calvin had been commissioned to buy books for Lane Seminary's library. And the Ohio Legislature asked him to visit elementary schools in Germany and England and bring back a report that would help them to plan the state's educational system.[9]

Harriet planned to go with Calvin to the East Coast; when he sailed for Europe, she would return to Cincinnati. Then she found out she was pregnant and decided not to travel. She sent Calvin off with a letter and instructed him to open it when his ship was at sea. "Now, my dear," she wrote, ". . . you are gone where you are out of the reach of my care, advice and good management." She warned him against cultivating indigo and told him how to keep his spirits up. "Only think of all you expect to see: the great libraries and beautiful paintings, fine churches, and, above all, think of seeing Tholuck, your great Apollo." She could not resist sighing: "My dear, I wish I were a man in your place; if I wouldn't have a grand time!"

During Calvin's absence Harriet lived with her father in the seminary president's house in Walnut Hills. With Aunt Esther in charge of the household, Harriet could rest from housework. She would not be alone, since the three youngest of the Beecher children were home, and Henry and Charles were studying at Lane. Harriet wrote a daily journal for Calvin and sent him installments each month, as well as articles and stories.[10]

The Riot of 1836

Lyman Beecher went back east in the summer of 1836 and married his third wife. Lydia Jackson of Boston was a widow in her late forties, strong-willed and resourceful — just the type to manage Beecher's chaotic life. When sixty-one-year-old Lyman Beecher brought Lydia back to Cincinnati, he looked like a new man, with "shoes well shined, his coat brushed, and his cravat neatly tied," reported Catharine. She was "amused to see how spruce he looks."[11]

While Lyman Beecher was out of town and Calvin Stowe was in Europe, race riots convulsed Cincinnati. Trouble had been brewing since April when a scuffle between black and white boys escalated into a general melee. Homes of blacks were burned, and several people were killed before the state militia came to restore order.[12] In those days racial violence was often blamed on abolitionists: if only they would cease from troubling, all would be well.

Blame fell on James G. Birney, editor of an anti-slavery paper in town. Birney himself had once been a slaveholding southerner, but he freed his slaves and took up the abolitionist cause. He tried to start an anti-slavery paper in Kentucky, but mobs forced him across the river into Ohio. In Cincinnati he started a moderate anti-slavery paper called the *Philanthropist,* which had strong allies like Salmon P. Chase, whom Harriet knew from the Semi-Colon Club, and Gamaliel Bailey, who later became Harriet's editor.

Cincinnati merchants who traded with Southern planters wanted Birney silenced. They warned him to stop publishing or face consequences. But he kept on. On the night of July 12 a mob vandalized Birney's printing press. Birney "promptly patched up [his] equipment and went on with the next edition."[13] The mob held a public meeting to consider its next move.

Harriet's sympathies were with Birney. "The mob madness is certainly upon this city," she told Calvin, when even respectable citizens approve of mob violence. She hoped Birney would "stand his ground and assert his rights." At least now Birney had a fireproof office surrounded by high walls, Harriet reported. So he could possibly defend his printing office with "armed men." If she were a man she would go "and take good care of at least one window."

But Beechers were better at firing words than bullets. When the race riot broke out, Harriet's brother Henry was the temporary editor of the *Cincinnati Journal and Luminary* and Harriet was helping him. She told Calvin that Henry was writing "a most valiant editorial" to "wax . . . mighty in battle." Henry would "make a first-rate writer," she predicted. Her own writing she dismissed as "scribbling" in a "light, sketchy style." Calvin must not worry that she would get mixed up with public issues: "I thought, when I was writing last night, that I was, like a good wife, defending one of your principles in your absence, and wanted you to see how manfully I talked about it." If only her father were in town, Harriet said, he could preach a sermon to help restore order.[14]

Thus Harriet gave the men in her life the "deferential modesty"[15] expected of women. Yet she did something else: she wrote a letter for the *Cincinnati Journal and Luminary.* She kept it anonymous, for she knew that if she signed with a woman's name, few readers would take her letter seriously. She signed it "Franklin" after the printer patriot.

"Franklin" did not take a stand on slavery, but rather defended the freedom of the press and private property. Mob rule was like "a train of gunpowder, extending under every house in the city." It is one thing to demolish a few useless and ugly buildings, "but the same train of gunpowder runs under your house and mine." Therefore Cincinnatians must stand firmly for "the rights of property and free opinion."[16] Regardless of what one thought of slavery, to suppress Birney's paper was to threaten the constitutional freedom of all citizens, Franklin warned.

On July 21, 1836, the same day the Franklin letter appeared, an anti-Birney meeting was held at Lower Market Street. Told to stop the press or face the mob, Birney said he would keep publishing. On the night of July 31, a mob made its way to the office of the *Philanthropist* on Lower Main Street. They smashed the printing press, hauled the wreckage outside and threw it into the Ohio River, and then returned to destroy Birney's office. Next they went to the boarding house where Birney lodged. Blocking the doorway was Salmon P. Chase, "six foot two, with broad shoulders, a massive chest, and a determined set to his jaw."[17] At that point the mayor (who was with the mob as a "silent spectator") was heard to say, "Well, lads, you have done well so far. Now go home before you disgrace yourselves."

But the "lads" continued to disgrace themselves, spending Saturday night and part of Sunday wrecking homes of black people. The city authorized armed volunteers to patrol the streets; among them was Henry Ward Beecher. He left home each day with two loaded pistols — but he never fired a shot. As Harriet explained to Calvin, when the mob saw their fellow citizens turning against them, they "slunk into their dens and were still."[18]

Birney went into hiding during the riots, only to reappear and continue publishing the *Philanthropist* despite threats on his life.[19] After several months he sold the paper to his co-editor, Gamaliel Bailey. Birney went into politics and ran for president twice on the Liberty Party ticket. Bailey later went to Washington and started the *National Era,* the anti-slavery paper that would be the first to publish *Uncle Tom's Cabin.*

As anti-slavery publishing grew in the 1830s, mob violence (targeting anti-slavery presses and editors) also increased. Harriet told Calvin that mob violence "may make converts to abolitionism."[20] The mobs proved that freedom of the press would have difficulty coexisting with slavery.

I Am but a Mere Drudge

Harriet went into labor on the night of September 29, two months after the riots. A doctor attended her at home, and no sooner did she deliver one baby than a second labor began. Harriet was the mother of twins. The first she named Eliza Tyler Stowe, after Calvin's first wife. The second one she named Isabella Beecher Stowe.

The Beechers were ecstatic. Harriet made them "all jump & laugh & shout & cry & feel glad & sorry 'all under one.'" She could be forgiven for causing such a stir because she was "a genius, and therefore cannot be expected to walk in a beaten track."[21]

Calvin was still abroad, unaware that he was the father of twins. He had visited many schools for the Ohio State Legislature. And for Lane Seminary, he had bought some five thousand volumes — Greek and Roman literature, Early Church Fathers, Protestant reformers, encyclopedias, and poetry, as well as illustrations of art, architecture, and costumes of the ancient Near East.[22] Calvin's voyage home aboard the *Gladiator* took two months over stormy seas. Thanksgiving, Christmas, and New Year's Day he spent churning over the Atlantic.

When at last he reached New York, a letter informed him that Harriet had given birth to twins. Overjoyed, Calvin wrote to Harriet: they must name one of the twins after Harriet! "Eliza and Harriet! Eliza and Harriet! ELIZA AND HARRIET!"[23] Calvin would not memorialize his dead wife without honoring the living one. Harriet needed to use *her* name. Calvin made the long trip back to Cincinnati, eager to embrace his wife and daughters.

Harriet and Calvin had very little time together before becoming parents of twins. And then, just as they were adjusting to parenthood, the economy crashed. A bubble had been growing for years, as investors used credit (paper notes) to buy land and to finance turnpikes, canals, and railroads.[24] This credit was not sufficiently backed by specie (gold or silver). When too many people tried to redeem the paper notes for gold or silver, banks turned them away. All the banks in New York City stopped payment of gold and silver coins. Hundreds of banks closed and businesses went into freefall. The so-called Panic of 1837 lasted for several years.

Harriet and Calvin Stowe had little money to lose, but it seemed that everyone was hurt in some way by the panic. In Hartford, Harriet's brother-in-law could not pay his creditors, so his wife (Mary Beecher Perkins) had to sell her piano and all her best furniture.[25] In Cincinnati, Harriet's Uncle Foote went bankrupt and sold his mansion, causing the Semi-Colon Club to lose its favorite meeting place. The Semi-Colons "limped along" for a while "and then expired."[26] Lane Seminary was in dire financial straits: the Lane Rebellion had seriously wounded the school, and the financial panic only made things worse. Lyman Beecher's salary was deferred, and once more he found himself scrambling to pay his bills.

Lane Seminary had not yet kept its promise to Professor Stowe of a full-sized house. Living in a "a small brick cottage" with twins was making the family cramped and crabby: Calvin sputtered that his "miserable accommodation" amounted to "covenant-breaking . . . by the [Lane Seminary] board." Compared to the dwellings of other faculty, including Lyman Beecher, Calvin felt their little cottage was "degrading." Calvin said their poor housing caused "three fourths of my unhappiness since I returned from Europe."[27] What caused the remainder of his unhappiness he did not say.

While Calvin nursed his resentment, Harriet nursed the twins. Or tried to — she had difficulty breastfeeding, and hired a wet nurse. Still, she was so busy she could barely write a line or two on family letters. One of the twins was fat and well; the other was thin and sickly. Harriet said Calvin was "a very worthy man who tries to do his duty all round," but lecturing and attending faculty meetings by day and tending one baby or the other at night (while Harriet tended the other one) left Calvin sleep-deprived.

At least they had some domestic help, thanks to Anna Smith, a young woman from England hired by the Stowes in 1836. Domestic chores were arduous, and household help was so cheap that even middle class families could afford it. For more than eighteen years Anna helped Harriet with the cooking, cleaning, and childcare. According to scholar Joan Hedrick, Smith became more a sister to Harriet "than a domestic servant."[28] But three adults and two babies in one small house must have been cramped indeed.

Lane Seminary's promise of a larger house seemed to Harriet like a "mirage in the desert." After "fussing and fuming a while," Calvin and Harriet resolved to hole up "in our old lair, being thankful to God that we have a warm comfortable house." They had a new Olmstead stove, which heated their parlor, and had a newfangled device for making toast. Over tea and toast, the family would sit by the stove as Calvin read aloud fairy tales such as "Blue Beard" or "Puss in Boots" in German. Calvin found there was nothing like the sound of German to shake off "a fit of the blues."[29]

But Harriet found strength in Isaac Watts's hymn: "Through Every Age Eternal God, thou art our rest, our safe abode."[30] *Rest* would indeed seem a divine gift to a sleep-starved mother of twins! But women of every age had survived motherhood, and Harriet could, too.

Around this time Harriet's mother-in-law, Hepzibah Stowe, came from Massachusetts to spend some time with her new granddaughters. Having survived motherhood as a poor widow, Calvin's mother could not see why Harriet needed household help — especially when *she,* the mother-in-law, was there for an extended visit. According to Joan Hedrick, Anna Smith's salary of $1.25 per week, plus $3.00 per week for the twins' wet nurse, took about "20 percent of Calvin Stowe's annual salary."[31] Harriet's mother-in-law thought the expense unwarranted.

To Harriet's dismay, Calvin sided with his mother. "Poor thing," Catharine Beecher wrote to their sister Mary. "[Harriet] bears up wonderfully well, and I hope lives through this first tug of matrimonial warfare." Harriet told Catharine she would "not have any more *children, she knows for certain,* for one while. Though how she found this out I cannot say, but she seems quite confident about it."[32]

Harriet was mistaken, for the twins were barely fourteen months old when the next baby came. She named him Henry, after her closest brother. Now with three infants to care for, Harriet's life was a daily battle with chaos. Somehow she found time to write to her old friend Georgiana. She reported that Mina (the wet nurse) needed constant supervision. Calvin bought the groceries, but Harriet had to tell him what to buy. She had to oversee the meals and the laundry. She also needed to make clothes for the children, but when she picked up her scissors to "cut out some little dresses," Henry began to wail. She picked him up just as one of the twins dumped over her sewing box. The other twin sat "by the hearth chewing coals and scraping up ashes with great apparent relish." Grandmother Stowe soothed the baby, and Harriet returned to cutting out the cloth. Then the twins began to quarrel — "Number one pushes number two over. Number two screams: that frightens the baby and he joins in. I call number one a naughty girl, take the persecuted one in my arms, and endeavor to comfort her. . . . Meanwhile number one makes her way to the slop jar and forthwith proceeds to wash her apron in it. Grandmother catches her by one shoulder, drags her away, and sets the jar up out of her reach." Harriet lamented, "I am but a mere drudge with few ideas beyond babies and housekeeping. As for thoughts, reflections, and sentiments, good lack! good lack!"[33] She hoped she might "grow young again one of these days." She added bravely, "I will speak well" of married life.

Anti-Slavery Feeling

While Harriet was consumed with domestic cares, the issue of slavery was simmering. Harriet's oldest brother William, a Presbyterian minister in Putman, Ohio, took a public stand against slavery. Some of his church members took offense, but others applauded.

Harriet visited William in Putnam during her second pregnancy. She was present when a woman from the Female Anti-Slavery Society came to the house. Harriet described this group as "ultra" (extremist), yet she found anti-slavery feeling stirring inside her. "No one can have the system of slavery brought before him," she wrote, "without an irrepressible desire to *do* something . . . but what is there to be done?"[34]

While Harriet was in Putnam, she got a letter from Calvin informing her that the Presbyterians were splitting. In 1837, when the Presbyterian General Assembly met in Philadelphia, the "Old School" Presbyterians leveraged enough power to expel most of their opponents, the "New School" Presbyterians, from the denomination. "In one blow 553 churches, 509 ministers and between sixty and a hundred thousand members were lopped from the rolls,"[35] according to historian Sidney Ahlstrom. Among the disinherited ministers were several Beechers.

The trouble had been brewing for a long time — at least since 1801. In that year the Presbyterians and the Congregationalists agreed on the Plan of Union, a strategy for cooperating in church-planting in the West. The plan provided for free exchange of ministers and members among the two denominations. Four western synods had been formed under the Plan of Union. These synods were strongholds of New School Presbyterians and had many anti-slavery pastors. The Old Schoolers, stronger in the South, tended to support slavery. By 1837 the differences could no longer be housed in the same church, the Old Schoolers decided.

Harriet heard plenty of commentary on the schism. Calvin predicted it would "make more abolitionists than anything that has been done yet."[36] Many years later, Lyman Beecher said that "the South finally took the Old School side." The schism "was a cruel thing — it was a cursed thing, and 'twas slavery that did it."[37] Things were not quite that simple, of course. Scholars debate the role of slavery in the split, and even after the schism the New School "failed to live up to its alleged radicalism,"[38] for fear of alienating the southern members it still had.

While the Presbyterians split up in the city of brotherly love, the American Anti-Slavery Society was also meeting in Philadelphia. The AASS was scheduled to meet in Pennsylvania Hall, but a mob burned down the building. When the group reconvened in another building, the mob torched that one too. "The Philadelphia Fire department, which had merely let Pennsylvania Hall burn, tried to extinguish the second blaze, but the mob cut the hoses,"[39] wrote one historian.

Mobs roiled Illinois, resulting in the murder of Elijah Lovejoy in Alton in 1837. Lovejoy was a Presbyterian minister who, in addition to serving his congregation, edited an anti-slavery paper called the *Observer*. Lovejoy's press was destroyed three times and threats were made against his life. His anti-slavery views were moderate: he neither called for immediate abolition nor encouraged slaves to run away.[40] Harriet's older brother Edward (president of Illinois College in Jacksonville) was a friend of Lovejoy's.

Edward went to Alton to help Lovejoy convene the Illinois Anti-Slavery Society. Many Presbyterian and Congregationalist ministers attended. But Alton was just across the river from slave-holding Missouri, and there was strong pro-slavery feeling in town. Lovejoy's activism seemed likely to bring on a pro-slavery backlash. Several town meetings were held to defuse the tension, but things only got worse. At one of these meetings Lovejoy was told to stop his paper and leave town if he wished to remain alive. He replied, "You can crush me if you will, but I shall die at my post, for I cannot and will not forsake it."[41] Then he wept for his family and what they might face if he got killed. At that very time, Lovejoy's new printing press was being shipped to Alton aboard the *Missouri Fulton*. Late that night, the press was unloaded under cover of darkness and locked in a warehouse by the river. Edward Beecher and others stayed in town to protect Lovejoy and his new press.

The next morning, Edward met with Lovejoy and his wife for prayer in their home. The press seemed secure, and Edward, believing the crisis was over, left for Jacksonville. That night Lovejoy and his supporters were guarding the press when a large drunken mob came to the warehouse and attempted to set it on fire. Lovejoy ran out, armed to defend himself and his press. He was shot five times. The mob roared in triumph and surged into the warehouse to destroy the press.[42] Back in Cincinnati, Harriet and her family heard of Lovejoy's death and feared that Edward might also have been killed. They were relieved to learn that Edward was safe in Jacksonville, yet they remained deeply shaken. A Presbyterian minister had been murdered in a *free* state for taking a *moderate* stand against slavery.

Northerners were outraged. "If Lovejoy's death cannot rouse us," Edward wrote, "nothing can. We are gone." Edward declared the gospel of Jesus Christ to be at risk. "Until this question [of slavery] is decided no man can tell what the gospel is," wrote Edward. If the gospel

83

"rebukes" slavery "as it does all other sins," then the church must now take a public stand against it.[43] By this time, Edward, Charles, and William were taking a public stand against slavery. Harriet and Henry were not far behind.

Catharine disliked slavery, but felt inhibited by her views on the role of women. Catharine believed women could change society only through moral suasion — which they could use only in the privacy of their homes. Catharine Beecher's ideal woman would transcend politics.[44] If women gave speeches or joined anti-slavery societies, she said, mobs would subject them to "sneers and ridicule in public places," which would not help slaves.

Angelina Grimke disagreed with Catharine, and made bold to speak out. Grimke was southern-born and rejected both slavery and the silencing of women. She was planning a speaking tour in the North to get women to form abolition societies. Angelina and her sister Sarah were also speaking out on women's rights, which they connected with abolition. Years before, Catharine and Harriet had met Angelina Grimke in Hartford, but now Catharine and the Grimkes debated (in print) the role of women in the anti-slavery movement. In 1837 Catharine published her *Essay on Slavery and Abolitionism, with Reference to the Duty of American Females.*[45] Sooner or later, Harriet would have to decide whether to step over what Catharine considered respectable boundaries for women.

Things were not going well for Catharine. The Western Female Institute was tottering. The bad economy didn't help, but the deeper problem was that Catharine managed to offend many of her supporters. Cincinnatians resented Catharine's East Coast snobbery and chafed at her frequent travels, which left others to run the school. Harriet was no longer at the Western Female Institute, having quit teaching when she got married.

The school closed in 1837. When accounts were settled, Catharine "quite ruthlessly appropriated all the money [from the school] for herself and left Mary Dutton and Harriet to bear the financial losses,"[46] wrote Catharine's biographer. Harriet lost $200 and Dutton $500 — large sums in those days. Harriet and Calvin had no money to spare. Harriet later scolded Catharine: "I had very serious doubts about your ability to carry [the school] through . . . and told you often and fully, to draw back before we committed ourselves."[47]

I Do It for the Pay

Now that Harriet was out from under Catharine's tutelage, her desire to write faced an even bigger challenge: motherhood. Harriet wanted to buy writing time, which became easier when her mother-in-law returned to New England. "I have [earned] enough by my writing," she told a friend, "to add to my establishment a stout German girl who does my housework." True, the new girl was "fresh caught" from Germany and needed much "shaping."[48] But if the new girl could do basic housework, then Anna Smith could manage the children and Harriet could have three hours a day for writing. "If you see my name coming out everywhere, you may be sure of one thing, that I *do* it for *the pay,*" Harriet told her friend. As a single woman she had spent her time studying, teaching, and writing, so she could not be satisfied to be "a mere domestic slave." Besides, her children were better off when their mother was happy. "I am certain as yet that I am not only more comfortable, but my house affairs and my children are in better keeping than when I was pressed and worried and teased in trying to do more than I could . . . [when I was] shut up in my nursery."

At last Lane Seminary fulfilled its promise and provided a bigger house for the Stowes, conveniently located near the seminary campus. It was spacious and had a yard where Harriet could grow calla lilies, geraniums, and roses. Later she would look back on these days of raising flowers and young children as among the happiest of her life.[49]

Money was still tight, however. Lane Seminary struggled to survive, and as a result Calvin's pay was getting squeezed to the point where, in 1843, he made only $600 per year — half of what he was promised. All the more reason for Harriet to write! Lyman Beecher was not receiving his full salary, either; he "was forced to ask personal help from his children and friends" to pay his bills.[50] In 1838 Harriet described her father's school as "in debt & embarrassed." Donors defaulted on their pledges. Enrollment stayed stubbornly low. Students from the East found it cheaper to stay closer to home, and there were few seminary students "to be found in this ungodly west — [we] must retrench,"[51] Harriet sighed.

In the lean years, Lyman Beecher would go out to beg for money and to recruit students. Drawing on biblical imagery, Calvin said that his father-in-law was giving a banquet to which nobody came, so the seminary president had to go to the "highways and hedges, and compel them to come in." If Lyman Beecher "could not clamber over an obstacle, he would go around it or dig through it. . . . [I]n every tight place he would say, 'Come, let us get by this pinch, and then we'll have plain sailing.'" Calvin never believed it, so Lyman finally "changed his pitch and began to say, 'Come, Stowe, let us get by this pinch, and then we'll get ready for the next.'"[52] Which made Harriet more determined to write for pay.

One summer, the Ohio River ran so low that people could wade across it. At the same time, Lane Seminary seemed to be drying up too. For a while Calvin Stowe and Lyman Beecher were the only faculty, and Lane had no students for its incoming class. Beecher would not give up. "I went to Marietta College," he recalled. "There I secured four or five [students] . . . went down to Louisville . . . got one student there. . . . Then I went to Jacksonville, and there I found six." Returning to Walnut Hills, Beecher found his son-in-law "sick abed, and all discouraged." Calvin groaned that it was all over; they might as well give up and go back east — and the sooner, the better. "'Stowe,' said Beecher, 'I've brought ye twelve students. You've got no faith, and I've got nothing but faith. Get up and wash, and eat bread, and prepare to have a good class.'" Another student arrived, bringing the total to thirteen; the next year they had thirty-five.[53] By 1844 Lane was finally able to pay Calvin's full salary.

The Stowes needed the money Harriet could make from writing, so she continued to hire help. For a time they paid a "colored girl from Kentucky" to help with domestic chores. The Stowes thought this person was legally free, "having been brought into the State [Ohio] and left there by her mistress."[54] Then one day Calvin heard that "the girl's master was in town looking for her" to force her back into slavery. Alarmed, the Stowes hid their "help" until well past dark. Then Calvin and Harriet's brother Henry put the fugitive in a carriage and drove by backroads to the home of a Mr. Van Zandt. A former slave owner, Van Zandt had freed his slaves and moved to Ohio, and was now helping fugitives make their way further north. Van Zandt sheltered and fed the Stowes' hired girl and then helped her on to the next safe hideout. Harriet later used the incident for *Uncle Tom's Cabin,* changing the name Van Zandt to Van Tromp.[55]

The original Van Zandt paid dearly for obeying his conscience. In 1846 he was sued for concealing and harboring a fugitive slave, in defiance of the Fugitive Slave Law of 1793. The case went all the way to the

Supreme Court, which found Van Zandt guilty as charged. He was fined so heavily that he was financially ruined and died a broken man.[56]

During the Cincinnati years, Harriet and Calvin also hired a cook named Eliza Buck, a former slave. Buck was of mixed-race descent and "of good family," and she was a skilled seamstress. But when her white owners needed money, they sold her to a plantation in Louisiana where slaves were routinely whipped. Eliza would sneak out at night to bathe the torn flesh of the victims. Then Eliza was sold to a man in Kentucky. He became the father of her "quadroon" (one-quarter black, three-quarters white) children. Harriet kept a "family school" in her home and taught Eliza's children along with her own. Eliza Buck referred to the father of her children as "my husband," but he never married her, and he probably had a white wife. Stowe never forgot Eliza's "humble apology, 'You know, Mrs. Stowe, slave women cannot help themselves,'"[57] which was a polite way of saying that if a white master demands sex, the female slave must comply. The more Harriet learned what slave women endured, the more horrified she became.

Meanwhile her own family was growing. Harriet may have had one or more miscarriages, and during one pregnancy she suffered from "a severe neuralgic complaint" in her eyes. In May 1840 Frederick William was born, the Stowes' second son and fourth child. Harriet was confined to her room, and even the smallest amount of daylight caused her great pain.[58] Except for a few business letters, Harriet was unable to write for an entire year.

While Harriet fought to get her strength back, another riot erupted in Cincinnati. This time blacks chose a leader and armed themselves. As many as 300 black men were hauled off to jail, and their homes were searched for weapons. With black defenders locked up, white rioters ran wild. A witness recalled the "howls, and yells, and screams, and oaths and vulgarities" of the mob, which "dragged the press of the *Philanthropist* down Main street and threw it into the river." The mob attacked "an abolitionist book depository," a bakery owned by a white man suspected of helping fugitives, an African American church, and black homes and businesses. The *Daily Cincinnati Gazette* reported "complete anarchy." Ohio Governor Thomas Crown deputized citizens and called in police and military companies. The mob raged until sheer exhaustion stopped it. Many blacks gave up on Cincinnati and moved to Canada.[59] Above the town in Walnut Hills, Lane Seminary was spared. And "Franklin" was silent.

CHAPTER SIX

A Deep, Immortal Longing

Harriet Beecher Stowe wondered if she would accomplish anything. She was thirty years old, she wrote to an aunt,[1] and time
was slipping by. If ever she were to make her mark on the world, she
felt it would be by writing.

For the time being, magazine articles were her medium, and the
New York Evangelist was a good outlet for her work. At first it served as
the venue for some of her lighter pieces, but by 1839 she was ready to
write about social issues, beginning with "The Drunkard Reclaimed."[2]
She also tried literary criticism — commenting, for example, on works
of Charles Dickens. But even there her social-reform impulses shone
through. Dickens, she wrote, did "a real service to humanity" by calling
attention to the "oppressed, the neglected, and forgotten, the sinning
and suffering." But she thought his work lacked a strong Christian
foundation. For one thing, in Dickens's novels Christians were made
to seem dull and hypocritical. His most lovable characters — such as
Oliver Twist — seemed unchurched. But how could Oliver have grown
up among thieves and prostitutes, yet retained such a fine personal
character, Stowe wondered. She saw Dickens as morally inconsistent:
he thought slavery was wrong, yet he accepted drunkenness as a matter of course. But both were forms of bondage! Stowe concluded that
Dickens lacked "profound habits or capacity of reflections on moral
subjects."[3] Stowe saw Dickens's popularity as a "literary epidemic"
that could not last long.

Several years later, in 1845, the *New York Evangelist* printed
Stowe's first piece on slavery: "Immediate Emancipation." It told of a
man who realizes his slave is also a human being, and therefore de-

cides to free him. Stowe wanted to show that slaveholders were not evil people; rather, the *system* of slavery was evil. The "moral of our story," Stowe said, is that "a man who has had the misfortune to be born and bred a slaveholder, may be enlightened, generous, humane, and capable of the most disinterested regard to the welfare of his slaves."[4]

"Disinterested" was a loaded word. In 1765 Jonathan Edwards wrote *The Nature of True Virtue,* making "disinterested benevolence" the gold standard of Christian character for American Calvinists. To be *dis*interested was to seek the well-being of others even at one's own expense. But how could slaveholders be disinterested (impartial) about slavery, when it served their interests? It was unthinkable for slaveholders to practice disinterested benevolence — and free their slaves — without changing their whole perspective. Without a spiritual awakening, slaveholders would not voluntarily free their slaves. Could Stowe write something to ignite that awakening?

You Must Be a Literary Woman

For the time being, her goal was to help pay the family bills. She earned some cash by writing for "gift annuals" such as *The Christian Souvenir, The Christian Keepsake and Missionary Annual,* and *The Religious Souvenir for Christmas and New Years Presents.* These offered poems, stories, and pictures for "traditional English holidays."[5]

A greater challenge was to write for *Godey's Lady's Book,* one of the most popular magazines of that era. *Godey's* printed the work of topnotch writers such as Lydia Sigourney, Nathaniel Hawthorne, Ralph Waldo Emerson, Catharine Maria Sedgwick, and Edgar Allan Poe. *Godey's* also offered needlework patterns, fashion plates, printed music, and advice on childrearing and homemaking.

The editor of *Godey's* was Sarah Josepha Hale. Much like Catharine Beecher, Hale saw women as intellectually equal to men, yet belonging in the home. Hale wanted *Godey's* to "mark the progress of female improvement, and to cherish the effusions of female intellect."[6] However, *Godey's* primly sidestepped controversy, remaining silent on slavery and women's rights. Stowe wrote several pieces for *Godey's,* boosting her reputation as a magazine article writer.

By the spring of 1842, Stowe had enough stories and sketches to gather into a book. She traveled to New York to finalize a publishing agreement with Harper and Brothers. As always, any trip out east included time to visit relatives, which extended her leave from home. Calvin missed Harriet; in a letter he playfully reminded her of Richard Baxter, the English Puritan who used to lie in bed with his wife "and sing psalms together for their mutual edification." He was sure "some of our *discourses in sheets*" were just as "agreeable and edifying. I wish we could have another this very night."[7]

To his everlasting credit, Calvin encouraged Harriet to write. "You must be a *literary woman.* It is so written in the book of fate," he declared. "Make all your calculations accordingly, get a good stock of health, brush up your mind." In those days female authors often used a pseudonym, or initials so that their work would not be dismissed for being written by a woman. But Calvin said Harriet should use her own name, "Harriet Beecher Stowe, which is a name euphonious, flowing, and full of meaning." Quoting Proverbs, he predicted that Harriet would bring honor to him "in the gate" — that is, where the public gathers — and that her "children would rise up and call her blessed."

Harriet expected payment for her book "sometime this winter or spring," she told Calvin. "The terms they offer me are very low but I shall make something on it." Next time, she would ask for better terms. "On the whole, my dear, if I wish to be a literary lady, I have, I think, as good a chance of making profit by it as any one I know of." But how to be both mother and writer she did not know. Children need "a mother's whole attention. Can I lawfully divide my attention by literary efforts?" She was not sure, but she knew that to be a writer she must "have a room to myself, which shall be *my* room."[8]

"It is just as I told you in my last letter," Calvin replied. "God has written it in his book that you must be a literary woman, and who are we that we should contend against God?" So Harriet should set her mind "to spend the rest of your life with your pen." Calvin knew his own needs, too, and expected Harriet to meet them. "And now, my dear wife, I want you to come home as quick as you can. The fact is I cannot live without you and if I were not so prodigious poor I would come for you at once." And he praised her lavishly: "Who else has so much talent with so little self-conceit . . . so much tongue with so little scold; so much sweetness with so little softness; so much of so many things and so little of so many other things?"[9]

Calvin's letters were sweet and encouraging, reflecting a tender relationship. But when Harriet examined her relationship with God, she felt dissatisfied. She yearned to glimpse an "eternal weight of glory, beyond all comparison" (2 Cor. 4:17). She hoped that the hardships of their life in Cincinnati — including illness, childbearing, low pay, plagues, and riots — were but "slight momentary afflictions" on the way to something higher.

Harriet felt that for years she and Calvin had been toiling in "a hard place because of religious motives." Truth be told, they both longed to be "somewhere else" where life was easier. She had to admit that they felt trapped, which meant that they were not really serving God unselfishly. "What have we done and suffered for Christ?"[10]

And now they were getting older, but no closer to God. "Why look at it — Life is half gone! — What have we done?" She told Calvin, "I think of dying, [and] I say 'not yet oh Lord. I have not finished the work thou hast given me to do.' My heart is not yet wholly renewed — my pride not yet subdued [and] Christ not wholly formed in me."

That sounded like perfectionism, which Harriet knew was dangerous. So she told Calvin that she did "not believe in *perfection* in this life — but I do believe, & my thoughts have turned much to it this week, in a baptism of the spirit — a second conversion that is to the Christian as real an advance, as his first regeneration." This was to be "sought and strived and prayed for." What she wanted was spiritual renewal for herself and for Calvin. "What is the use of dragging through life lame, sick and halt, when Jesus has promised to make us whole if we will ask? We have not yet half used the power of prayer, we have not yet taken the almighty hand that is held out to us, we have not yet put forth our utmost energy."

Harriet wanted a new start. She was returning to Ohio, but not — she hoped — to the same old rut. "Now by the grace of God I am resolved to come home & live for God, it is time to prepare to die — the lamp has not long to burn — the hour is flying — all things are sliding away & eternity is coming." Wanting Calvin to share her fervor, she exhorted, "Will you dear husband join with me in simplicity & earnestness to lead a new life. . . . Now let us try once more, let us first give ourselves wholly to Christ to know him, the power of his death" and "his sufferings."

Whether or not Calvin shared Harriet's desire for spiritual renewal, he wanted his wife back. And she took her time. In those times of arduous travel, if people went somewhere, they usually stayed long enough to make the effort worthwhile. Harriet was away from Cincinnati for half a year contacting publishers and visiting family.[11] Meanwhile Aunt Esther nursed the Stowe children through several illnesses.

Soon after Harriet returned to Cincinnati, she suffered "a mysterious nervous malady that caused her to [temporarily] lose the use of her arms." Catharine had similar symptoms, perhaps the result of mercury poisoning from the "blue pills" prescribed for common ailments. Harriet wrote that "Dr. Drake gave me enough blue pills to last one life time, in consequence whereof I have been four or five times saturated."[12] On top of all this, typhoid broke out at Lane Seminary and sick students were sent to the homes of faculty to be nursed back to health. Harriet's spiritual longings would once more be tested by poor health and endless chores.

Stowe's first book of stories and sketches appeared in 1843. She called it *The May Flower or, Sketches of the Descendents of the Pilgrims.* As Stowe told her readers, the "may flower" is a hardy plant which blooms in early spring, at the edges of snow banks and on granite ledges. It was an "emblem of that faith, hope and piety, by which our fathers were supported in dreary and barren enterprises, and which drew their life and fragrance from heaven more than earth."[13]

Life Is Short

Fortunately Stowe found inspiration in the past, since there was no future left. That was according to William Miller, who set October 22, 1844, as the date for Christ's return. Miller, a Baptist minister, got this date by matching biblical prophecy with historic events and making some calculations. Huge crowds came to hear him speak on the end times. When Miller came to Cincinnati in the summer of 1844,[14] more than four thousand people turned out to hear him. His followers (called Millerites) sold their property and left their unbelieving churches behind, so as to be ready when Christ came in the clouds with power and great glory. When he did not come at the appointed time, the Millerites suffered the "Great Disappointment."

Stowe could hardly have missed the Millerites, but it seems unlikely that she was influenced by them — despite what her letters to Calvin said about time running out. Calvin himself wrote a pamphlet debunking Miller's claims,[15] and Harriet was not likely to embrace a theology that her husband rejected. Harriet's father preached revival and reform to prepare the way for Christ's return; Christians were supposed to obey God's moral government and re-make the world, not withdraw from it.

Harriet's urgency came, rather, from a keen awareness that life is short. Her own mother did not have a long life, and Harriet did not expect one, either. But when the world suddenly ended for Harriet's brother George, the Beechers were deeply shaken.

Perhaps they should have seen it coming, for George Beecher was a highly sensitive person. As an adolescent, George experienced spiritual pain and bliss beyond the usual when his father held revivals. As a student at Yale, "nervous dread" sometimes washed over him and he had difficulty sleeping. At other times, however, George could soar, as on the Beechers' westward trek, when George reveled in singing hymns and distributing tracts. In Cincinnati, George's licensure trial was high drama, and he rose to the occasion. He then served his first church in Batavia, New York, where he married Sarah Buckingham, daughter of a well-to-do family in his parish. After their first child died in infancy, George took a leave of absence.

George was drawn to reform movements. He joined an anti-slavery society in 1836, "the first Beecher to take so radical a stand."[16] He imbibed the Oberlin Perfectionism[17] of Charles Finney, which proclaimed human ability to meet God's demands for complete selflessness and absolute benevolence. Since Christians *can* reach this state of perfection, they *must* strive for it. And George Beecher did strive.

George's perfectionism troubled the Beecher family. For one thing, it was bad theology (Calvinists believe that sinful human beings cannot save themselves). And it was dangerous, especially for an emotionally fragile person like George, who needed perfectionism like a drowning man needs a sack of bricks.

Family members cautioned George against perfectionism in one of their "circular" letters. Harriet's brother Charles warned that the more perfect you think you are, the more likely you are to be deceived. Henry approved of George's decision to delay publishing on the subject of perfection. Harriet sidestepped "metaphysics" and asked George how to grow dahlias. Then she mused upon soil and growing conditions, hinting that George should not set himself up for failure. George responded: "I am quite amused with the sympathy of all my brothers, and their fatherly advice touching perfectionism, as if I were on the verge of a great precipice; but I trust in Him that is able to keep me from falling."[18]

Now George and his wife Sarah were in Chillicothe, Ohio, where George served a congregation. They had a healthy baby son, a newly built house, and a flourishing garden. George invited all the Beechers to a family gathering in his home. Catharine arrived first. Early in the next morning, George went out into his orchard. When a servant girl went to call George for breakfast, she found him lying dead with part of the top of his head blown off. Catharine was present when the body was borne back to the house. Word spread quickly that George had shot himself, though the coroner pronounced George's death accidental.

That George's death was a suicide was unthinkable to the Beechers. Their explanation was that George's wife Sarah was afraid of firearms and George hardly ever used a gun. George loved his garden and orchard, and when birds were pecking at his cherry trees, he tried to scare them off. The first round from the double-barreled, muzzle-loading shotgun fired well — but just as George was blowing the smoke away, the second shot went off prematurely.[19] But not everything fit neatly into that scenario. On the evening before he died, George told his congregation of his "eagerness to join Christ in heaven," adding that this would be the last thing many of them would hear him say.[20] And indeed it was.

Lyman Beecher missed the funeral. He was out East on business when someone showed him the obituary. News of his son's death hit like a body blow, taking his breath away. Only when the tears began to flow did his gasps subside. He went to his "place of letters" and found a letter from Catharine, which opened "deeper sluices of sorrow," he later recalled. The grieving father returned to his room "sighing and bathed in tears, subsiding and anon bursting out again." Soon after this, he wrote to console George's widow, Sarah: "God was preparing [George] for more esteemed usefulness in a higher, nobler sphere; and, though we see not exactly what it is, we may confide in him who reigns above that there is no mistake."[21] There *could* be no mistake. Henry also wrote to Sarah,[22] saying that George was "translated to heaven where he would enjoy a wider sphere of usefulness." And now George was Sarah's guardian angel, to console her through this life and finally to conduct her to heaven.

After the funeral, Harriet also wrote a letter to console family members. In it, she faced death honestly. She said George could not hear the cries of his family, for the grave means absolute silence. Death separates us completely from our loved ones. There is no communication between the living and the dead, and even the fondest earthly love ends in "a coffin and a grave." She saw death and grief as "the deepest and most powerful argument for the religion of Christ. . . . Take from us Christ and what he taught, and what have we here? . . . But give HIM to us, and even the most stricken heart can rise under the blow, yea, even triumph. 'Thy brother shall rise again.'" That is Jesus' promise to all Christians. She ended her letter with an exhortation to fight the good fight as soldiers of Christ, until they all would meet at Jesus' feet, never to be parted again.[23]

Later Harriet admitted that George's death shook her "like an earthquake" and set off "indistinct terrors." Feeling "alone [and] unsupported," she asked, *Where is God?* She found that self-examination only made things worse, for the more truthful she was, the more she despaired. For a time she thought "I am not a Christian," for "my will is, at best, only in a small degree subjected to [God's]." This ideal of subjecting one's will perfectly to God, and the notion of degrees of subjection, is itself a kind of perfectionism — a habit of mind Harriet might have recognized as dangerous.

After George's death Harriet gave birth to a baby girl and named her Georgiana. Again she had trouble nursing, but could scarcely afford to pay a wet nurse. "Our straits for money this year," Harriet wrote, "are unparalleled even in our annals"[24] — which was saying a lot. Meanwhile, Harriet persisted in flirting with perfectionism. In her 1845 article, "The Interior Life"[25] she touted the ideal of "sinless rest" in which "our will must be identical" with God's will. Even if this sinless rest is beyond reach, the hope of it may change our lives, Harriet told readers of the *New York Evangelist.*

But in the same year Harriet published this article, she wrote to her brother Thomas in a different spiritual key. She told him that she saw a "deep, immortal longing" in human beings. This longing points to something more than — indeed *other* than — our daily experience. We are homesick for a place we have never seen, wrote Harriet; we long to return to a place we have never been. "In sensitive souls this restlessness can intensify to the point of torment," she wrote, no doubt thinking of George. "All this points to some higher and better life than we can now experience."[26]

95

"Now, here is my creed," Stowe continued. God made us to be happy — not by ourselves, but happy only in "a deep, absorbing, sympathizing union" with our Maker. Such a union "makes God's will the soul's will, God's joy our joy." We were created to share in God's will and joy. As Augustine said, "O God, Thou hast made us for Thyself, and we are restless until we find our rest in Thee."

And yet people try to run away from God. To them, divine power is like a storm at sea that moves "with blind, inflexible certainty" despite the "struggles, resistance, and agony of those who stand in its way. . . . Old ocean lifts one scornful, hissing wave, stops every sense, strangles, bears [us] off, and dashes [us] like a weed upon the strand."[27] In nature God's will appears as raw, blind power.

The Bible reveals a different side of God, Harriet wrote. Scripture shows us "a Father," who cares for "the happiness of each individual as minutely . . . as for the sublime whole." God invites us, "Love me, and I will love thee,' choose with me, sympathize with me, and all my power, and all my wealth, and my glory are thine!" The soul's union with God is like a marriage in which God "makes a whole gift of Himself, and all that He has, to each individual, as far as they can comprehend or use it." God can satisfy our deepest longings if we but surrender to his will.

She confided to her brother Thomas that she fell far short of her own spiritual ideals. God, she said, dwells in "hopeless heights of unattainable excellence." Note the words *hopeless* and *unattainable.* What happens when earnest souls reach for perfection and fail? Satan mocks them and dares them to try harder. But the harder they try, the more they despair. Harriet came to see her own spiritual striving as a "vain experiment." She identified with the story of Jesus' disciples, who spent all night fishing but came up with empty nets. Then Jesus told them to take their boat out into the deep water and let down their nets. "Master," they replied, "*we have toiled all night and have taken nothing.* Nevertheless, *at thy word* we will let down the net" (Luke 5:5). Soon their nets were so filled with fish they could scarcely haul in the catch.

Since Stowe's own efforts led nowhere, "the word of Christ" must now be her hope. She said that she found life in Christ's promise: "I . . . and my Father . . . will come unto [the Christian] and *make our abode with him*" (John 14:23). And again: "Abide in me, and I in you" (John 15:4). Harriet told Thomas that when she quit striving and relied on God's word, "*All* changed." Rather than swimming upstream with all her might, she felt swept along. "The will of Christ seems to me the steady pulse of my being. I go because I cannot help it." Now that she had stopped trying, she could feel God's glory and presence: "I seem to see the full blaze of the Shekinah everywhere," she wrote.

Yet Harriet could plummet like a falcon from heaven to earth with breathtaking speed. On June 16, 1845, when Calvin was at a ministers' conference in Detroit, she wrote,

> MY DEAR HUSBAND, It is a dark, sloppy, rainy, muddy disagreeable day, and I have been working hard (for me) all day in the kitchen, washing dishes, looking into closets, and seeing a great deal of that dark side of domestic life. . . . I am sick of the smell of sour milk, and sour meat, and sour everything, and then the clothes *will* not dry, and no wet thing does, and everything smells moldy; and altogether I feel as if I never wanted to eat again.

She told Calvin she was getting thin — "ethereal" — as she put it. She lacked energy and suffered "a distress of the brain" (perhaps severe headaches). When these spells came on, the household "had no mainspring." Little Georgiana was so "nervous, cross and fretful, night and day" that Anna Smith could do little else besides care for her. And the other children were "like other little sons and daughters of Adam, full of all kinds of absurdity and folly." Then pulling herself up from this nosedive, Harriet added, "Yet I do rejoice in my God and know in whom I believe, and only pray that the fire may consume the dross; as the gold, that is imperishable. No real evil can happen to me, so I fear nothing for the future, and only suffer in the present tense."

But the present tense was getting harder as Harriet became run down, perhaps even suffering chronic fatigue. The Stowes thought Harriet needed a leave of absence to recover her health and strength — but how to pay for it? "If God wills I go. He can easily find means," Harriet told Calvin. "Money, I suppose, is as plenty with Him now as it always has been, and if He sees it is really best He will doubtless help me."[28]

Later that summer Calvin and Harriet traveled east, leaving the children in the care of Anna Smith. Calvin was to raise funds for Lane Seminary while Harriet got some rest in the home of her sister Mary in Hartford. But there Harriet came down with a severe illness. A doctor came and went, leaving medicine but little hope.

Lyman Beecher was also in Hartford at the time. He thought Harriet had cholera: she suffered "spasms, burning, and cramps, and the stamp of death [was] on her face." Lyman took Harriet's hands and began to rub them vigorously. She was given brandy and other home remedies. When she began to sing "in a wandering way" Lyman thought she was dying. He would not leave Mary's house, but spent the night on the settee in the dining room, which was "hot as an oven and thronged with mosquitoes." All night Lyman Beecher lay awake listening for "every noise and movement" in the house,[29] wondering if his daughter would live or die. Harriet was better in the morning, though it took days for her to feel stronger. Hearing of a "water-cure" sanitarium at Brattleboro, Vermont,[30] she wondered if she should check herself in.

When the Stowes returned to Cincinnati, Harriet's health seemed worse. Calvin tried to help. "My husband," she wrote, "has developed wonderfully as house-father and nurse. You would laugh to see him in his spectacles gravely marching the little troop in their nightgowns up to bed, tagging after them, as he says, like an old hen after a flock of ducks." But Harriet's health did not improve.

The Water Cure

Finally Harriet and Calvin decided she should try the water cure in Brattleboro, Vermont, "if she ever hoped to regain her health."[31] It would take several months and cost something like an extended stay at "a mountain or seaside hotel."[32] Harriet felt that if God wanted her to go, God would make it possible. Alarmed by Harriet's decline and aware of Calvin's low pay, friends and family raised the money. The day Harriet left, Calvin wrote to tell her that two letters with fifty dollar donations and several others with lesser amounts were waiting for him at the post office.

Harriet left Cincinnati in March 1846. She visited family in the East. In May she checked into the water cure at Brattleboro, and stayed until March 1847. Catharine Beecher was with Harriet for part of that time, giving the sisters a chance to mend their relationship after the strains from the closing of Catharine's school.

Brattleboro was Harriet's immersion into the holistic health movement of her day. In the nineteenth century over two hundred water cure establishments opened, mostly in the East.[33] These health spas aimed to work *with* nature to heal the body (or prevent illness) instead of attacking the body with drugs. The water cures promoted fresh air, exercise, and community. And instead of the grease-laden foods so common back then, the water cures served whole grains, fruits, and vegetables, with meat used sparingly if at all. At the water cure, women shed their tight corsets and heavy skirts in favor of loose clothes that allowed them to exercise freely.

All this was good, but water was the most important thing — clear, cold water, and plenty of it. Patients were to drink water, and soak, shower, and bathe in it. One famous treatment was the wet-sheet pack. The patient would lie on a wet sheet, "which had been dipped in cold water, wrung out, and placed on top of four blankets. The patient was wrapped first in the wet sheet and then in each blanket in turn. Every body part was covered except the face." More blankets could be put on and hot water bottles could be used at the feet and the armpits until the patient "burst into perspiration."[34] Then the person would be unwrapped and plunged into cold or tepid water. Or water would be poured over them, the colder the better. This was done to drive sickness out of the body so that health could take over. It was something like taking a sauna and then plunging into a cold lake. Another treatment was the pummeling shower, in which freezing cold water was poured down from a great height upon a patient. There were also cold baths and wave pools.

Water treatments did no harm, and may have done some good. Certainly they were better than some of the standard medical practices in early America, such as bloodletting by cutting veins or applying leeches. In Stowe's lifetime the practice of bloodletting was going away, but "massive doses of harsh, frequently dangerous medication" such as mercury to "produce purging and sweating"[35] were common. Water cure establishments let people stay for weeks or months to get all the toxins out of their systems.

The water cures had male and female patients, but women found the philosophy of hydrotherapy especially appealing. Instead of treating women's reproductive cycles as a disease, water cures treated them as normal and natural. The water cure spas taught women to take charge of their own health through exercise, diet, and dress. The call to self-reliance inspired women, and female practitioners of hydrotherapy were among the first women to enter a health-care profession.[36]

Harriet was not pampered at Brattleboro. "For this week," she wrote, "I have gone before breakfast to the wave-bath and let all the waves and billows roll over me till every limb ached with cold." Then she walked vigorously to warm up, and came back to breakfast with a hearty appetite. "Brown bread and milk are luxuries indeed, and the only fear is that I may eat too much." At eleven she walked in a driving rain to her shower, which may have been at a natural cliff. There cold water was poured on her from eighteen feet above, for ten minutes. Then she walked back in the rain. After lunch she might "roll ninepins" or go for a walk, take "a sitz bath, and another walk till six."[37]

The water cure was a magnet for reformers of all types. Vegetarians, temperance workers, feminists, and anti-slavery advocates flocked to the water cures as "the central link in a national reform network."[38] Devotees of spiritualism and phrenology came too.

Religion was part of the experience, for "the newly cured often reacted with the enthusiasm of the religious convert." One woman testified: "I feel as though I had been born again; your system has been my salvation. . . ." Fervently she prayed that "the system of truth which you are ably advocating, and so successfully practicing may soon extend to the uttermost parts of the earth."[39] In addition to revival and evangelism, the water cure had a ritual element. Water was revered for its healing powers, calling to mind baptism by immersion, spiritual rebirth, and cleansing.[40] Stowe in her old age said that her time at Brattleboro raised her from "the borders of the grave" to "full health." She took the cure and "returned home *well*."[41]

Women also found at water cures a respite from pregnancy and motherhood.[42] Stowe had five children when she went to Brattleboro, and she would bear two more. A time out probably did her as much good as all the wet sheet packs and pummeling showers. A woman with children at home could hardly justify a long absence — unless her health demanded it. Women were expected to put family first, but at the water cure they were told "to focus on their own needs rather than the needs of others."[43]

Harriet *did* feel guilty, of course. "My dear husband," she wrote, "I have been thinking of all your trials, and I really pity you in having such a wife." She feared she had been more a hindrance than a help to him, and she asked God to restore her health so she could "do something for you and my family." She missed her children: "they will never know how I love them."

Meanwhile back in Cincinnati, Calvin was thinking over their past life. He told Harriet that that all their failures stemmed from lack of order and system in their home, and what they really needed was to get organized. No, Harriet replied; they should focus on shaping their children's characters, especially the three oldest. "Oh that God would give me these five years in full possession of my mind and body, that I may train my children as they should be trained,"[44] Stowe prayed. She simply *had* to regain her health.

Harriet heard the gospel of wellness at Brattleboro, and she now preached it to Calvin. "Ministers think there is no way to serve Christ but to overdraw on their physical capital for four or five years . . . and then have nothing to give" but to be a burden for Jesus to bear. Clergy burnout, it seems, is not new.

Harriet advised Calvin to take a long walk before breakfast and get some fresh air. He must not remain shut up in the hot, stuffy room he used for a study. "Above all, do *amuse* yourself." She prodded him to spend a social evening with one of the other professors or even with her father, maybe even organize some dancing cotillions. "Bless me! What a profane set everybody would think you were, and yet you are the people . . . most solemnly in need of it. I wish you could be with me in Brattleboro and coast down hill on a sled, go sliding and snowballing by moonlight! I would snowball every bit of the *hypo* out of you!" Besides, if Calvin did not take care of himself, she would have to come home before she was really and truly well, and then their separation would be in vain.

In January, Calvin sent Harriet a dark, moody letter. "My dear Soul," Harriet teased, "Why didn't you engage the two tombstones, one for you and one for me?" Calvin's problem, Harriet said, was that he always put things in a negative light. Harriet could sympathize up to a point for she herself had been "heartsick" for some three weeks, wanting nothing more than to "get home and die . . . but," she admitted, "I suppose I was never less prepared to do so."[45]

The Stowes were apart on their eleventh wedding anniversary. Harriet recalled that as a young wife awaiting motherhood, her heart was "full of love" for their children yet unborn. But now after years of "wearing, wasting days and nights," she had learned a bitter lesson:

she was wrong to make "family be my chief good."[46] Only God should have that place.

Harriet told Calvin that she would still choose him, but not blindly. From now on, she hoped to love more truly, more wisely. Perhaps her long absence would help them to understand each other and make a fresh start. Could Calvin apologize for all the times he'd criticized her unjustly? Could he cultivate gratitude for God's mercies? Could he break his habit of fault-finding? She knew Calvin wanted her to be happy, but somehow things had gotten off track.

Harriet traced the problem back to when Calvin's mother lived with them. The elder Mrs. Stowe "constantly pointed out my faults & kept up a perpetual state of complaint & irritation." She called Harriet "extravagant" for hiring household help. After that Harriet could see "two currents" in Calvin's mind, one positive and the other negative: "looking with a brooding & jealous eye on my faults — exaggerating them & predisposing to impatience." What did Calvin *think* it took to run a large household and cope with all the pregnancies and illnesses? In fact she was right to get help. When Calvin's "peculiarities" seemed "unreasonable," she simply did things her own way. Yes, she had her faults too. "I am constitutionally careless & too impetuous & impulsive," she confessed. "I often undertake more than I can perform & so come to mortifying failures." But these letters were clearing the air, so that when she came home, they could start over again.

Samuel Charles

In March 1847 Harriet left Brattleboro, healthy and strong. She visited relatives in the East and returned to Cincinnati in May. Her family greeted her with joy — Calvin especially — and she became pregnant right away.

In January of 1848, the Stowes' sixth child was born. They named him Samuel Charles — "Samuel in remembrance of the beautiful story of Samuel in the Old Testament — 'Long as he liveth he shall be lent to the Lord.'"[47] Harriet would always remember "Charley" as a "beautiful, loving, gladsome baby . . . full of life, strength and hope."[48] For once she had no trouble nursing her baby.

In Harriet's absence Calvin had gained weight and become depressed. At least Lane Seminary was paying his full salary, but for "fifteen years he had enjoyed no real vacation, and at forty-five" he felt that his job was a dead end. Calvin decided to try the water cure. He left for Vermont in June 1848 and stayed at Brattleboro for fifteen months. Time flew swiftly as Harriet cared for the children, ran the household, and even conducted a small school in her home.[49]

In January 1849 several cases of cholera broke out among "the poorer classes"[50] of Cincinnati. Cholera was thought to come from "miasma" (unhealthy vapors) in the air; no one knew it came from water-borne bacteria. Cincinnati's water was pumped from the Ohio River to reservoirs above the town, and then let down by gravity to customers below. People also got water from wells and rain barrels; this was probably safe, but downtown there were huge standing puddles where cholera could breed.

Late spring found the cholera spreading. On every street corner burned coal fires laced with lime and sulfur — thought to combat the miasma in the air. The fires did nothing to stop the disease, but they did spread foul smelling smoke and soot everywhere. Sick people who could afford treatment might be dosed with calomel (mercury), opium, and camphor, which probably only hastened their demise.

Harriet wrote to Calvin that the hearse drivers were so busy they hardly had time to un-harness their horses. "Furniture carts and common vehicles" were used to remove the dead. One Tuesday a hundred and sixteen people died. "That night the air was . . . peculiarly oppressive"; it seemed to "lie like lead on the brain and soul." Calvin should not come home, Harriet said, for if he got sick he would be no help at all. She and the children were fine, and Harriet hoped they would remain so.[51]

On June 30, the mayor called "a day of general fasting, humiliation and prayer." Those of more worldly persuasion filled Cincinnati's bars to overflowing; some stood drinking on the streets where coffins were stacked waiting for transport. A local paper reported hearse drivers racing on their way to graveyards: "more than once the coffin has been pitched out in the race and the dead uncovered."[52]

By July 3, Harriet told Calvin that the doctors in town were "nearly used up" from laboring night and day among the sick. Riverboats passed Cincinnati without stopping. More than one hundred people were dying each day, so that death was getting to be routine. "Gentlemen make themselves agreeable to the ladies," Harriet wrote, "by reciting the number of deaths in this house or that . . . [while] talk of funerals, cholera medicines, cholera dietetics, and chloride of lime form the ordinary staple of conversation. Serious people of course throw in moral reflections to their taste."[53] On the Fourth of July, revelers lit firecrackers as usual.

Then Charley began to get sick. Harriet was frightened: even "a slight illness seems like a death sentence." Harriet carried Charley to see a doctor, but there was nothing to be done. Harriet and Anna Smith tried water cure methods, wrapping Charley in a wet sheet to help him sweat off his fever. Charley rallied and scolded so loudly that he seemed to be recovering. "Never was crossness more admired in a baby," Harriet said. But their hopes were dashed when Charley began "gradually sinking." Now Harriet knew for certain that her baby had cholera. She told Calvin to stay put; he could not possibly reach Cincinnati in time. It was said that no one survived this kind of cholera, and Harriet dreaded losing her husband. She wanted him to stay in Brattleboro and "bear up" while Charley fought for his life.

On July 26, Harriet broke the bad news to Calvin. "At last it is over," she wrote, "and our dear little one is gone from us." Harriet sat upstairs writing the letter, while Charley lay in the room below, "shrouded, pale and cold." Harriet recalled the joy and consolation Charley had given her, and how she would "hold him to my bosom and feel the loneliness and sorrow pass out of me with the touch of his little warm hands." But when he got sick, try as she might, she could do "nothing" to relieve "his cruel suffering . . . but pray in my anguish that he might die soon." She added that "this heartbreak, this anguish, has been everywhere, and when it will end God alone knows."[54] Over the summer of 1849, as many as 4,000 people died of cholera in Cincinnati.[55]

Calvin came home in September bringing good news: Bowdoin College, in Brunswick, Maine, had invited him to be the Collins Professor of Natural and Revealed Religion. They would pay him $1,000 per year. Lane Seminary, loath to lose its biblical professor, made a counteroffer: $1500 per year plus housing. Calvin used Lane's offer to leverage an additional $500 from Bowdoin, which nevertheless did not offer housing. Still, Calvin's new job would sustain the Stowes in the genteel poverty they were used to. The move to Maine would not improve the Stowes' standard of living, but it would give them what they needed most: a fresh start in New England. It was time to go home.

CHAPTER SEVEN

If I Live

As Harriet and Calvin turned eastward, settlers swarmed west — to California where the gold rush was underway. Soon that far western territory had enough settlers to request admission to the Union as a free state. This alarmed Southern congressmen who saw that the balance of power in Congress would tip toward the North and the free states. A fragile political balance had been cobbled together, but something now must be done to prevent the house of cards from toppling.

Senator Henry Clay of Kentucky came to the rescue — or so it seemed at the time — with a bundle of legislation now known as the Compromise of 1850.[1] The series of trade-offs included California's admission to the Union as a free state, offset by a tough new Fugitive Slave Law that would guarantee southern rights to hold slaves as property — even when slaves escaped to the free states.

This was the lightning rod in the Compromise of 1850. The Fugitive Slave Law would require northerners to help capture runaway slaves. It would protect southern "property" in *every* state of the Union, not just the slave states. Critics of the Fugitive Slave Law pointed out that, in effect, it extended slavery throughout the entire country. From now on those caught helping fugitive slaves — even in the north — could be treated as criminals. As for former slaves living in the North, they could be captured and returned to slavery with no right to defend themselves. Fugitive slave laws had existed before 1850 but they were unevenly enforced; some northern states even had liberty of conscience laws protecting people who helped runaways. No more of that: the Compromise of 1850 brought a new sheriff to town.[2] Now those who worked on the Underground Railroad — a network of activists who helped fugitives flee northward to freedom — were served notice that their crimes would be punished.

Harriet Beecher Stowe was preparing to leave Cincinnati in the spring of 1850 when Senator William Seward of New York spoke against the Fugitive Slave bill. He told Congress that a law must be just to be legitimate; the proposed law was unjust, and therefore illegitimate. Seward "denied 'that the Constitution recognizes property in man' and asserted . . . [that] the nation's charter must heed 'a higher law.'"[3] People who felt bound to obey this higher law would feel it their duty to disobey the Fugitive Slave Law. Southern congressmen cried foul; Seward, they said, was encouraging fanatics to pick and choose which laws to obey, thus opening the door to "racial amalgamation, socialism, and women's rights."

Perhaps he was. Seward believed that "law derives its legitimacy from the dominant moral consensus," according to Gregg Crane. Governments cannot force people to change their moral convictions — but if the moral consensus changes, then people will change the laws. Thus "literary and cultural figures" could play a huge role in the slavery issue. By convincing the public that slavery was wrong, they could change public morality. Seward sensed that public sentiment was changing on the slavery question. Little did he know that the person who would do more than any other single individual to change public sentiment on the slavery issue was at that time a pregnant housewife, packing her bags to travel halfway across the country with three children in tow.[4]

Calvin Stowe would remain behind at Walnut Hills to teach another term at Lane Seminary and earn some much-needed income. Staying with Calvin were the smaller children, Frederick and Georgiana. Harriet would take the older children and proceed on to Brunswick, Maine, to get the Stowe household up and running before the baby came.

The Move to Maine

Harriet left Cincinnati in April 1850 on a steamboat bound for Pittsburgh. With her traveled the twins, Eliza and Hattie, Henry, and Aunt Esther. "An *Old Maid* at the head of a party of females," Aunt Esther wrote, "will be as efisicent [*sic*] to keep off all intruders as a half a dozen mastiffs."[5] As the steamboat chuffed its way eastward, with slaveholding Kentucky on the right and free Ohio on the left, passengers may have argued about the Fugitive Slave bill. From Pittsburgh Harriet and company took a canal boat pulled by horses or mules, and then a train to Philadelphia, with transfers to New York. They stayed a few days in Brooklyn with Harriet's brother Henry, who was now the pastor of Plymouth Congregational Church.

In Boston Harriet bought bedsteads and mattresses, tables and chairs, to be shipped to Brunswick. She had spent about $150 on furniture and $76 on travel and was now running short of cash. There was also the physical and emotional toll of travel. "I want you to reflect calmly," Harriet told Calvin, how rigorous all this transit was for a pregnant woman who needed "rest, repose, and quiet." She had pushed her way "through hurrying crowds, looking out for trunks, and bargaining" with drivers. The trip was "a very severe trial of my strength, to say nothing of the usual fatigues of traveling."

Stowe was tired from the trip, but being back in New England was like a tonic to her. She told Calvin that although *he* was not able to bear anything, *she* never doubted or despaired: "I am strong in spirit, and God who has been with me in so many straits will not forsake me now. I know Him well; He is my Father, and though I may be a blind and erring child, He will help me for all that." She had already done some networking with editors in her efforts to get work to help the Stowes pay their bills. With God's help, "we shall not sink, my dear Husband."[6]

Harriet and company took a night steamer to Bath, Maine. The full moon bathed the coastal islands in mystic light, but when a storm blew in the seas got so rough that many passengers got sick.[7] It was pouring rain when the boat finally landed in Bath, where Stowe boarded a train to Brunswick. There Harriet and company were greeted by Bowdoin College's Professor Upham and his wife. They told her that the college had found a rental house for the Stowes — a large frame house on Federal Street, convenient to the campus.[8] The house was somewhat run down, but the windows let in plenty of light and, best of all, it was a large dwelling. The rent was higher than expected but Harriet assured Calvin, "I mean to raise a sum myself" by "writing an extra piece or two."[9]

With the rattle of trains and the whistle of steam boats still in her ears, as she put it to a relative, Stowe had to get the household set up before the baby came. The sheets and carpets she ordered were delayed; she had to borrow sheets. The furniture frames were delivered and had to be upholstered. The upholsterer ran out of thread — where to get more? There was no soap to clean the windows; one of the twins needed to go buy some. A workman came to check on the cistern. A crate of household goods arrived and had to be unpacked. The man who came to lay the carpet needed supervision. A peddler needed payment immediately. The meat man arrived — what to buy for dinner? The bedstead screws were missing. "Mrs. Stowe, what about this? Mrs. Stowe, what about that?" was the cry everywhere she turned. And Calvin wasn't exactly helpful, writing from Cincinnati that "he is sick abed, and all but dead; don't ever expect to see his family again; wants to know how I shall manage, in case I am left a widow; knows we shall get in debt and never get out; wonders at my courage; thinks I am very sanguine; warns me to be prudent, as there won't be much to live on in case of his death, &c &c. I read the letter and poke it into the stove, and proceed."

When Calvin got to Brunswick with the younger children, Harriet was great with child. Charles Edward Stowe was born on July 8, 1850. For two blessed weeks Harriet and the baby had the care of a nurse. Then the nurse left and Harriet came down with a fever and severe breast pain (probably mastitis). Once more she had to hire a wet nurse. Soon Charley was thriving. He was so much like his brother Samuel Charles (who died in the 1849 cholera epidemic) that the two could almost have been twins.

Rowing against Wind and Tide

Around the time of her move to Maine, Stowe had corresponded with an editor who would change her life: Gamaliel Bailey. Bailey had been in Cincinnati during the Lane debates, and he worked alongside James Birney on the *Philanthropist*. Bailey went to Washington City (as the capital was then called) and in 1847 he began publishing a new anti-slavery paper, the *National Era*. It was a daunting task, for Washington was a southern city and the hub for southern politicians fighting to defend slavery. The domestic slave trade thrived there until the Compromise of 1850 banned it, but slavery remained a fixture in the nation's capital.

Bailey was a "reasonable, diplomatic" person, "moderate"[10] in his anti-slavery views. He made sure that the *National Era* ran articles for general readers, including those not yet committed to the anti-slavery movement. He refrained from making direct, personal attacks on slaveholders as some of the more strident abolitionist papers did. For three days in 1848 Bailey was threatened by a mob, but he managed to "weather an attack successfully."[11] Bailey wanted "the *National Era* to expose the scandal of slavery in American society" *as a whole,* and not as the province of politicians.[12]

Bailey's approach appealed to Stowe. Like him, she despised slavery as a system, but saw little to be gained by vilifying slaveholders. Better to show the effects of slavery more broadly, and try to persuade those who were wavering.

Stowe's first article for Bailey appeared in August 1850, entitled "The Freeman's Dream: a Parable."[13] Here Stowe applied Jesus' parable of the last judgment (Matthew 25) to slavery and the Fugitive Slave Law. Stowe's story opens on a fair summer evening, with a farmer who looks out over his lands, content with his prosperity. Then a poor black family approaches him. Hungry, weary, and pursued by slave catchers, they need shelter for just one night. The white farmer is not a bad man but he obeys "human laws" and turns the fugitives away. Soon he sees slave catchers approaching. From a distance the white farmer hears the cries of the captives being dragged away. That night the farmer dreams that he stands before God's throne. He hears an awful voice say: *Depart from me, ye accursed! For I was hungry and you did not feed me, a stranger and you did not welcome me.* In his dream the farmer also sees the "poor fugitive slaves" sheltered behind God's throne. The man awakes in terror. Refusing help to a slave, Stowe said, was tantamount to rejecting Christ and exposed a person to terrible judgment.

When this article was published, the Stowes could hardly afford the price of their subscription to the *National Era.*[14] Calvin was tired of scraping by on low pay. So, although he was expected to teach at Bowdoin in the fall of 1850, he accepted another term from Lane when they offered him better pay. He returned to Ohio to teach the November-March term. That left Harriet in Brunswick with a passel of children — and a burning desire to write.

Fortunately she was not alone. She had her sister Catharine, who was living with her for a time,[15] and Anna Smith, who at some point joined the family in Maine. The three women started a boarding school in their home. Catharine hoped to raise money for "a new furnace, fixtures, furniture, carpets, wood and coal." Harriet taught for an hour or two a day. In the evening she read aloud to the assembled household from the novels of Sir Walter Scott. As a child, Stowe had loved Scott. And now she was learning from him "how to put her sketches together" to include "all social levels," according to scholar Bruce Kirkham. During this time Stowe was also reading Charles Dickens with an eye for his domestic fiction that contained a social message.[16]

Harriet could scarcely find time to write a letter. During one attempt, she said she was "called off at least a dozen times; once for the fish-man, to buy a codfish; once to see a man who had brought me some barrels of apples; once to see a book-man." On and on went the list. Then she had to nurse the baby, and "make a chowder for dinner. . . . [N]othing but deadly determination enables me ever to write; it is rowing against wind and tide."[17]

Somehow Harriet managed to write a few light articles for pay. But that wasn't enough, for by this time her wrath burned against slavery and the Fugitive Slave Law. Newspapers reported on black people in northern states being captured and hauled south. Stowe got letters from her sister-in-law Isabella (Edward's wife) in Boston, telling of people who were wrenched from their families and forced back into slavery. "Now Hattie," Isabella wrote, "if I could use a pen as you can, I would write something that would make this whole nation feel what an accursed thing slavery is." Stowe read Isabella's letter aloud to her family, and when she came to the part urging her to "write something" about slavery, she "rose from her chair, crush[ed] the letter in her hand" and vowed "I will write something. I will if I live."[18]

Somebody had to do something! But not the Boston clergy, for Harriet heard that very few of them were willing to denounce the Fugitive Slave Law. Their silence was to Harriet "inconceivable, amazing — mournful." She remembered her Aunt Mary, who married a plantation owner and found out that he owned several of his own children as slaves. "I feel as Aunt Mary said," that "I could be willing to sink" into the sea with all this sin and misery if only that would end slavery. Stowe wished her father would come to Boston and preach on the Fugitive Slave Law, or that "some Martin Luther would arise to set this community right."[19] She felt compelled to write against slavery — yet blocked by domestic responsibilities. "As long as the baby sleeps with me nights," Stowe told her husband, "I cannot do much at anything — but I shall do it at last. I shall write that thing if I live."

The year 1851 began with a blizzard. Snow sifted in through the windows.[20] Fires had to be stoked constantly just to heat a few rooms in the Stowes' drafty old house. The children hated going up to their cold beds at night. Harriet told Calvin that it was "better to sleep in cold rooms"; she herself "was bred to such hardness from the cradle and so did not mind it."[21] She mentioned that she was writing a story for the *New York Evangelist* and one for the *National Era*.

That winter there was soul-chilling news. Slave catchers combed Boston and other northern cities looking for fugitives. One man, upon hearing that his former master was seeking to capture him, "set out for Canada in midwinter on foot, as he did not dare to take a public conveyance. He froze both his feet on the journey, and they had to be amputated,"[22] Harriet reported to Calvin.

One night in January Harriet's brother Henry was in the area giving lectures, and he stopped to visit her. They sat up till dawn discussing how to expose "the horrid cruelties" perpetrated on the black people. Harriet felt that her "heart was burning itself out with indignation & anguish." Henry said he was staging mock slave auctions at Plymouth Church in Brooklyn, in which the congregation would bid up enough money to buy a slave's freedom. His reputation as a preacher was growing, and he meant to use it to fight slavery. Then Harriet said she was doing something, too: "I have begun a story, trying to set forth the sufferings & wrongs of the slave." Henry encouraged her, vowing to spread her story "as thick as the leaves of Vallombrosa."[23]

Stowe would often look back on that winter night with Henry. It became for her one of those defining moments that sealed her resolve to fight slavery. As it turned out, Stowe would not need Henry's help to spread her story. But his moral support was for her a kind of covenant that she cherished for the rest of her life.

Henry's "Vallombrosa" lay in sunny Italy, but just then Harriet's world was locked in ice. With Calvin far away, she took their baby Charley to bed for warmth and company. She would lie awake listening to the wind, thinking of her "summer child" who died of cholera. She wept to think of slave children sold away from their mothers. She remembered the former slave she'd hired back in Cincinnati, who bore her master's children because she had no choice. Harriet asked herself just what it was that had moved them, back in Ohio, to help former slaves and even fugitives. She felt it was "the influence that we found in the church and by the altar."[24]

Sacrifices are made on an altar. And Stowe knew from her Bible that a sacrifice may be true worship — or it may be idolatry. Everything depended on what god was being worshipped. With this in mind Stowe wrote "The Two Altars" for the *Independent*.[25] It appeared in two installments. Part one depicted patriots in the American Revolution offering their lives on the altar of liberty in a sacrifice freely made. Part two depicted a scene from 1851. In a free state, a black family gathered for a meal. This peaceful scene was shattered when slave catchers came to take the black man away. That the man was a father and husband providing for his family made no difference. He must be "sacrificed — on the altar of the Union . . . bound to the horns of the glorious American altar," Stowe wrote sarcastically. Alas, without these human sacrifices, the Union would not survive.

This was idolatry, Stowe told readers. In a private letter Harriet wrote, "This Union! Some unions I think are better broken than kept," if they are "cemented on such terms."[26] Frederick Douglass used similar language. When a black man was captured in Boston, dragged as a prisoner to Savannah and whipped in the public square, Douglass called the captive "a living sacrifice to appease the slave god of the American Union."[27]

The Man That Was a Thing

Stowe wrote to her editor at the *National Era*. She worried that he was "overstocked with contributors" and would need nothing more from her. She sent him a couple of light domestic sketches. Gamaliel Bailey wrote back to Harriet, encouraging her to write more and enclosing a draft for one hundred dollars.[28] Several weeks later Stowe told Bailey that she was working on a story to

> give the lights and shadows of the "patriarchal institution," written either from observation, incidents which have occurred in the sphere of my personal knowledge, or in the knowledge of my friends. I shall show the *best side* of the thing, and something *faintly approaching the worst.*

Up to this year I have always felt that I had no particular call to meddle with this subject, and I dreaded to expose even my own mind to the full force of its exciting power. But I feel now that the time has come when even a woman or a child who can speak a word for freedom and humanity is bound to speak. The Carthagenian women in the last peril of their state cut off their hair for bowstrings to give to the defenders of their country; and such peril and shame as now hangs over this country is worse than Roman slavery, and I hope every woman who can write will not be silent. . . .[29]

Stowe was well aware that women were expected to remain silent on public issues like slavery, and that speaking out would expose her to ridicule. But so great was her moral indignation that she was ready to "sacrifice . . . her womanhood" and become a "warrior"[30] in a righteous cause. The few women who had done so were shunned as fanatics. So be it; now Harriet Beecher Stowe would join them.

Bailey advertised Stowe's story as *Uncle Tom's Cabin: Or, the Man That Was a Thing.* The first installment appeared in the *National Era* on June 5, 1851, with the subtitle *Life Among the Lowly.* Neither Stowe nor Bailey knew how big the story would be.

Just when Stowe began writing *Uncle Tom's Cabin* is debatable, since Stowe herself gave different versions of the story. Some twenty-five years after the fact, she wrote that "the first part of the book ever committed to writing was the death of Uncle Tom." She said the scene came to her in February 1851 at the college church in Brunswick. During the worship service she saw a vision "like the unrolling of a picture" of a black man being beaten to death. The scene was so vivid that Stowe wanted to cry aloud. The vision came into her "mind as by the rushing of a mighty wind." When church was over, Stowe rushed home and wrote down what she had seen. Then she gathered her family and read it aloud to them. The younger children began to cry and one of them said, "Oh, mamma, slavery is the most cruel thing in the world."[31]

Literary scholars point out that if Stowe had her vision in February, it could not have been the first part of the book, since her correspondence indicates that by that time she was *already* writing the book. Elsewhere Stowe said she was inspired to write the death of Tom in 1852 in Andover, when the novel was nearing completion.[32] No matter when, where, or how she wrote it, the death scene of Uncle Tom was a powerful icon — an icon of a black Christ. It is one thing to analyze an icon, and another to contemplate it. In the religious tradition of contemplation, what matters is that this image brings the viewer into the presence of God.

Stowe later said that *Uncle Tom's Cabin* was not so much "composed by her" as "imposed upon her." Indeed the "scenes, incidents, conversations" poured into her mind "with a vividness and importunity that would not be denied. The book insisted upon getting itself into being."[33] Near the end of her life, when her mind was failing, Stowe told an admirer not to praise her for writing *Uncle Tom's Cabin.* "God wrote it," she said. Critics later jibed that God could not have written a book so full of literary flaws. But icons are not supposed to be flawless works of art, and they are not written for critics.

Stowe was about forty years old when she wrote *Uncle Tom's Cabin.* She brought to the work her keen mind and vivid imagination, her Christian faith and her passion for a godly society. Her use of scripture will be explored in the next chapter, but here we note some other sources she used in writing *Uncle Tom's Cabin.*[34] These include her own observations from the years in Cincinnati, the firsthand testimony of others, newspaper clippings, and advertisements for runaway slaves. She used anti-slavery writings, especially *American Slavery As It Is: The Testimony of a Thousand Witnesses* by Theodore Dwight Weld (1839). Stowe used Weld for details of the "vicious whippings" and other cruelties inflicted on slaves, notes scholar Bruce Kirkham. Years later Stowe said that she "slept with *American Slavery* under her pillow" when she was writing *Uncle Tom's Cabin.*[35]

Much scholarly work has gone into Stowe's use of slave narratives — with particular attention to the sources for Stowe's fictional character Uncle Tom. The narrative of a former slave named Josiah Henson *(The Life of Josiah Henson, Formerly a Slave, now an Inhabitant of Canada, as Narrated by Himself)* first appeared in 1847. Henson later claimed to be the original Uncle Tom. But attempts to pin down exactly how Stowe used Henson's narrative have had "nebulous" results.[36] After *Uncle Tom's Cabin* was published in 1852, Stowe met Henson. At his request she wrote an introduction for an updated version of his autobiography. Henson's revisions pulled his own narrative closer to Stowe's Uncle Tom.[37]

After painstaking research, scholar Bruce Kirkham concluded that Stowe began with her own material. And "when she needed more background or wished to add a scene, she went to a printed source."

Kirkham cites a letter "probably written in 1852" in which Stowe describes where she got the idea for Uncle Tom. In Cincinnati, she hired a black cook whose husband was a slave in Kentucky. On her cook's behalf, Stowe used to write letters to this husband. He was entrusted with his master's business and the care of his horses. Sometimes he was even allowed to visit his wife in Ohio. "She tried to persuade him to run away," Stowe said, but he refused: "Master *trusts* me & I cannot." For three years in a row the master promised to free this slave at Christmas, but "never kept his promise." Several years later, Stowe again described this same cook and her husband. She wrote, "This was the first suggestion of the character [of Uncle Tom] — other incidents were added by reading the life of [Josiah] Henson in Canada."[38] In that case, Stowe conceived the idea for Tom from the cook's husband and later used Henson's story to supplement her own.

Stowe's approach to race in *Uncle Tom's Cabin* has also been much debated. She seems to have subscribed to a point of view later called "romantic racialism."[39] It attempted to describe racial differences without assuming the superiority of one race over another. Stowe scholar Joan Hedrick notes that this view of race was taught by Alexander Kinmot, a social theorist who wrote *Twelve Lectures on the Natural History of Man* (1839) and lectured in Cincinnati, where Stowe may have heard him in person. Kinmot taught that each race has its own distinctive traits. Africans, he said, are naturally more emotional and intuitive than whites, and therefore more receptive to religion. Kinmot saw black people as morally superior to whites even though he saw whites as more advanced intellectually. Thus, as Robert Levine put it, "Stowe celebrated blacks in *Uncle Tom's Cabin*" for what she saw as their naturally Christian ways — "domestic, noncompetitive, relatively passive."[40]

Stowe's approach to race was progressive for 1851. Yet it limited her ideas of black character, as scholar Sarah Robbins points out. For example, Stowe endows two of her fictional mixed-race characters with strong independent personalities. But her Tom character (who is of completely African descent) makes no attempt to escape and never uses violence even to protect himself. This more docile behavior and Tom's "natural affinity" toward religion Stowe ascribed to Tom's pure African nature.[41] "The negro is naturally more impressible to religious sentiment than the white," said one of Stowe's white characters in *Uncle Tom's Cabin*.[42]

Later, Stowe's approach was rejected because it reinforced stereotypes of black submissiveness and white superiority.[43] Indeed, this aspect of *Uncle Tom's Cabin* does not stand the test of time. Yet Stowe's approach to race was progressive in her day, and some people criticized her for it — including Charles Dickens. In a letter to Stowe on July 17, 1852,[44] Dickens praised *Uncle Tom's Cabin* and agreed with her that slavery was wrong. But the great English author challenged Stowe's views on race. "If I might suggest a fault . . . it would be that you go too far and seek to prove too much." Dickens saw no "warrant for making out the African race to be a great race, or for supposing the future destinies of the world to lie in that direction; and I think this extreme championship likely to repel some useful sympathy and support."

What exactly did Dickens mean by "extreme championship" of Africans? Was it perhaps Stowe's view that God intended Africa to play a central role in "the great drama of human improvement"? Someday, "life will awake there [in Africa] with a gorgeousness and splendor of which our cold western tribes have faintly conceived," Stowe wrote. This awakening would spring from what Stowe saw as the African character of gentleness, simplicity, docility, trust, and capacity for forgiveness. Stowe saw in Africa the potential home for the "highest form of *Christian life*." In her providential view of history, "God chastens whom he loves." God has chosen Africa in "the furnace of affliction" to make it "the highest and noblest . . . for the first shall be last, and the last first."[45] This must have sounded absurd to Dickens, for whom England was the apex of civilization. But Stowe thought Africa would one day become the new center of "Christian life."

Race mattered to Stowe, but to her the essence of humanity was something deeper. What makes us truly human in any race or time or place, she thought, is our capacity to be in relationship: first with God, and then with other people. Stowe saw that slavery perverts *every* relationship, not only for slaves but also for masters, whites that did not own slaves, and for free blacks — for everyone lived in a society defined by slavery.

Slavery was poison for relationships. It put the master in the place of God, which was idolatry. Black marriages were broken up, and white marriages were corrupted by infidelity. Worst of all, slavery made motherhood — which Stowe regarded as the most sacred human bond — into agony by selling children away from their mothers. Writing as a mother and as a Christian, Stowe exposed slavery as the great home wrecker. It destroyed and scattered black families, and gave whites the power to exploit, humiliate, and demean their fellow human beings.

White children absorbed the toxins of slavery from a very young age, and Stowe offered *Uncle Tom's Cabin* as a potent cure. Stowe knew that many families were reading her story aloud to their children as it ran serially in the *National Era*. So at the end of her tale, Stowe addressed children directly: "remember and pity the poor and oppressed," she told them, and "never, if you can help it, let a colored child be kept out of school, or treated with neglect and contempt, because of his color."[46]

Harriet was under relentless pressure as she wrote her story for the *National Era*. For nearly a year, deadlines ruled her life. The goal was to get one chapter per week into print (with some variation depending on circumstances). Stowe rarely missed a deadline, but if she did, Bailey printed an apology.[47] Each installment took several days to reach Bailey in Washington by mail.

Once the manuscript left her hands, she had no opportunity to review proofs. And so a legend grew that *Uncle Tom's Cabin* was "dashed off at a white heat with scarcely a revision." But according to Bruce Kirkham, Stowe did "considerable rewriting" on her chapters before sending them to the *Era*. And "between the publication of the story in the *Era* and its appearance in novel form" she made more revisions, some of them extensive.[48]

Stowe moved around while writing her book. The first chapters she wrote in Brunswick; some were written while visiting her brother Edward in Boston; and the last chapters were written in Andover, Massachusetts. Her story was coming out with unstoppable force, no matter how chaotic her circumstances.

A Brunswick neighbor described Harriet's "insane devotion" to the writing of *Uncle Tom's Cabin*. "As soon as she had swallowed her breakfast she would hurry down to the village and write, write, write, till the dinner bell sounded. Then [she would] hurry home, eat, and [go] right back and write till tea time." Professor Stowe's wife surely seemed an odd duck, heedless of her appearance with "her frizzy hair tossing in an unkempt disheveled mass upon her neck and shoulders, and her clothes hanging loosely about her form, as if they got there by accident."[49] The neighbor clucked disapprovingly that Stowe was too absorbed in her writing to take care of her own children.

A Family Affair

Fortunately, Stowe had help during the writing process. Her half-sister Isabella gave of her time to copy some of Harriet's manuscripts. Aunt Esther showed up to make the household run smoothly. Anna Smith was on hand to care for and play with the children, taking them sledding down the snowy hills of Brunswick. Harriet told her father that Catharine "has agreed to give me a year of her time" to teach the Stowe children and some cousins.[50] In September 1851, Catharine told sister Mary Beecher Perkins of their joint effort to "'get Uncle Tom out of the way' before winter began." For a while Harriet worked in Calvin's study at Appleton Hall at Bowdoin. "There was no other way to keep [Harriet] out of family cares and quietly at work and since this plan is adopted she goes ahead finely,"[51] Catharine explained.

The men of the family supported her too. Lyman Beecher stayed with the Stowes in Brunswick during the summer of 1851. Lyman did not help Harriet directly, but his mere presence made her determined to follow his motto: "trust God and do right." Henry Ward Beecher's nighttime covenant with Harriet continued to inspire her. Another brother, Edward, had long been a foe of slavery, and it was Edward's wife, Isabella, who famously urged Harriet to "write something." At some point in the process, Stowe visited Edward and Isabella in Boston. She could write undisturbed in Edward's study and then read her new draft aloud to his family.[52] In Boston she could also visit the American Anti-Slavery Society office to do research on slavery.[53]

She got help of another kind from her brother Charles, the only Beecher who had actually lived in the South. Back in 1839 Charles had gone to New Orleans, where he dreamed of becoming a church musician. He ended up working for a bank, traveling to collect unpaid bills. He rode the countryside on horseback or went "by boat through the bayous of Louisiana."[54] Charles saw a huge gap between the poor whites who lived hardscrabble lives and the opulent lifestyle of the planter class.[55] Charles found most planters to be "generous people" known for their southern hospitality. But despite their apparent wealth, many plantation owners were deep in debt. If they needed to raise money quickly, they sold slaves. Some planters told Charles they could make more money by "using their slaves up" and buying more, than by treating their slaves humanely. Charles met a plantation foreman whose fist was "like an oak burl"; this man made Charles feel his fist which he claimed grew hard from "knockin' down niggers." Here was the prototype for Stowe's arch-villain, Simon Legree.[56]

Harriet asked Charles to spend time with her and tell her all he had seen. So Charles took a leave of absence from his church in Newark, and in his absence Lyman Beecher filled his pulpit.[57] Around this time Charles published a sermon against the Fugitive Slave Law entitled "The Duty of Disobedience to Wicked Laws" — which promptly got him expelled from his ministerial association.[58]

Through it all, Calvin was Harriet's anchor. Like an anchor he was often out of sight, teaching at Lane Seminary in Ohio to support the family. But even when Calvin was away, their marriage grounded Harriet in a relationship of mutual trust. It was Calvin who had urged her to be "a literary woman." Calvin welcomed the income that Harriet made, but he was still the main breadwinner of the family. The Stowes had suffered for his scholarly career, and he was determined to rise if he ever got the chance.

That chance came when Calvin was in Ohio. Bowdoin College had loaned him to Lane Seminary when a *third* school, Andover Theological Seminary,[59] made him an offer. If he would come to Massachusetts and be Andover's professor of sacred literature, he could earn a good salary plus housing. Calvin accepted — on condition that Andover give him time to extricate himself from Bowdoin. After toiling so long in penury, Calvin Stowe now had three schools courting him. A writer for the New York *Independent* wondered how far Professor Stowe "approximates the faculty of omnipresence." He was going to need it, to serve two seminaries and one college simultaneously.[60]

Alas, Calvin had put Harriet in an awkward spot. *He* was far away in Ohio, but *she* was left to face friends at Bowdoin who were let down by Calvin's decision. She spent long hours conciliating Professor and Mrs. Upham — those good people who had gone out of their way to welcome her to Brunswick. Harriet wrote a scolding letter to Calvin. True, he was "*legally* free to leave" Bowdoin. But "You & Father have always asserted in my hearing that a man who enters a certain field of labor should not leave it till he has 'done a work' — i.e. perfected something that will not all go back & be lost by his leaving."[61] She urged Calvin to turn Andover down. *She* could earn enough money by writing to supplement Calvin's meager salary.

But Calvin's mind was made up. At long last he had a position that paid well, where he could stay till retirement. Calvin tried to soften

Bowdoin's loss by shuttling back and forth between Brunswick and Andover, teaching now here, and now there, until he felt he had paid his dues. The upshot for Harriet was that she had to move her household yet again. But now her story was forcing its way out like a child being born. Early in 1852, she finished writing *Uncle Tom's Cabin.* It went forth into the world and took on a life of its own. And nothing would ever be the same again for Harriet Beecher Stowe.

CHAPTER EIGHT

Uncle Tom's Cabin: *The Story of the Age*

UNCLE TOM'S CABIN.

BY MRS. HARRIET BEECHER STOWE.

For thrilling delineation of character, and power of description, this work is unrivalled. It has been denominated, and with truth, THE STORY OF THE AGE! . . . We look upon the writing of this book as providential . . . the best missionary God has yet sent into the field to plead for his poor and oppressed children at the South.

National Era, April 15, 1852[1]

Uncle Tom's Cabin opens in a parlor on a Kentucky plantation. The owner, Mr. Shelby, must pay some debts, and the quickest way to raise money is to sell some slaves. So Shelby is talking business with a slave trader, Mr. Haley, and the conversation turns to a particular slave named Tom. He is in the prime of life, strong, skilled, and trustworthy — thanks to his religion, which Haley says makes Tom even more "valeyable."[2] Mr. Shelby has a pang of conscience about selling such a loyal slave, but a master must not yield to such weakness. Business is business. A slave child enters the parlor, and Shelby orders the boy to dance and sing for the trader's amusement. Haley shrewdly appraises this child's market value. In comes the boy's mother, Eliza, searching for her son. Eliza is young, light-skinned, and beautiful. At once Haley sizes her up as a valuable item for the "fancy trade" (prostitution).

Eliza takes her son from the room, but through the closed door she hears what the men are planning. At first she cannot believe it. She has been the personal companion of Mrs. Shelby and she is now to be sold! Eliza is visited by her husband, George (a slave on another plantation, who becomes a significant character in the story). Eliza decides to flee north with her child. She leaves by night, stopping at Tom's cabin to tell him that he has been sold.

Now the story divides into two plots. Eliza takes her son Harry north to freedom, while Tom is taken south, deeper into slavery. Stowe moves back and forth between the two plots, keeping readers in suspense and sharpening the contrast between slavery and freedom. "Stowe imagines North America as a biblical landscape that reflects the geography of slavery," writes David Reynolds. "Canada represents Canaan or heaven, the Deep South becomes Sodom or hell, and the Ohio River the Jordan River across which slaves flee."[3]

The runaway Eliza must cross the frozen Ohio River before her pursuers overtake her. Clutching her child, she leaps and scrambles over the floating ice. She makes it to the other side, wet and freezing cold. Now desperate for a place to hide, she knocks on the door of strangers, and somehow they are moved to help her.

Eliza makes her way to a Quaker settlement and finds refuge with the Halliday family. There she is reunited with her husband George, who has also run away. The Quaker family is Stowe's domestic ideal, in which the races are equal and so are men and women (Mr. Halliday even commits the "anti-patriarchal" act of shaving). In this Quaker home, the runaway slave George "sat down on equal terms" at "a white man's table" for the first time in his life. As a slave George found it hard to believe in God. But here he receives "a living Gospel, breathed in living good will, preached by a thousand unconscious acts of love and good will."[4]

As the Quakers take the fugitives further north, armed slave catchers overtake them. George makes his "declaration of independence,"[5] and shoots one of the slave catchers. George is relieved that the slave catcher is only wounded, and helps him to a place where he will be cared for. Stowe asks her readers if there is any difference between the slave who fights for his freedom, and the patriots of the American Revolution.

After a few more adventures, George, Eliza, and Harry make it safely to Canada. There Stowe could have left them, happily ever after.

But she sends them to Africa as missionaries — thus seeming to endorse colonization as a solution to slavery.[6] This ending to the northern plot brought Stowe severe criticism from abolitionists, black and white.

It is the southern plot that bears the most weight in Stowe's story. In this journey into the depths of slavery, the central character is the slave named Tom. Sold away from his home and family on the Shelby plantation, he hopes in vain that his old master will buy him back someday. Tom is a noble human being who is treated like a "thing" or commodity in the domestic slave trade. (Stowe at first subtitled her story "The Man That Was a Thing," showing slavery as doomed by its own contradiction.) Stowe describes Tom as "a large, broad-chested, powerfully-made man of a full glossy black whose truly African features were characterized by an expression of steady good sense united with much kindliness and benevolence."[7] Benevolence, or true virtue, is selfless and pure. Tom is a man of God.

But he is also merchandise. He is loaded onto a steamboat bound for New Orleans. He and many other slaves are being shipped to the great slave market down south. Most of the slaves are confined in the lower part of the boat, while the white passengers travel in relative ease and comfort above. Tom has proved himself trustworthy (that is, he will not try to escape), so he is not chained. That proves fortunate, for when a little white girl slips and falls into the river Tom leaps overboard and saves her. The girl's name is Evangeline — Eva for short. She is traveling with her father Augustine St. Clare, a gentleman of New Orleans. Eva persuades her father to buy Tom, sparing him the ordeal of being sold at auction.

With the St. Clare family in New Orleans, Tom has the best situation any slave could hope for. He is treated well. He makes friends. "Generous hands concealed his chains with flowers,"[8] writes Stowe, but Tom remains a slave. He sorely misses his wife and children and longs for freedom. Tom rises in the St. Clare household like Joseph in Egypt, Stowe says. St. Clare gives Tom more and more responsibility and even considers setting Tom free.

Augustine St. Clare is one of Stowe's more complex characters. He is "indolent and careless with money"[9] but is a kind-hearted man who has never liked slavery and feels trapped in the system. He has a strong cynical streak and is not impressed when he hears white people use religion to support slavery. He sees that people are using religion only to justify slavery. St. Clare says he can be just as moral *without* religion as most people are *with* it. And yet he senses that Tom's faith is genuine. Early one morning when St. Clare goes down to the stables, he overhears Tom (whose quarters are above the stable) praying for him. Tom "put in for me," St. Clare says, "with a zeal that was quite apostolic." Indeed Tom "seemed to think there was decidedly room for improvement in me, and seemed very earnest that I should be converted."[10]

St. Clare does not have a happy marriage. As a young man he was prevented from marrying his true love, only to end up marrying Marie, a vain and self-absorbed woman who will not lift a finger to manage the household or to raise their daughter, Eva. So St. Clare has brought Miss Ophelia, his Yankee cousin, to live with the family and manage the household. Ophelia is a proper Yankee spinster raised on thrift and hard work. Ophelia dislikes slavery and says it makes white folks lazy. St. Clare agrees, but he challenges his cousin: the truth is, he says, Ophelia does not like *negroes* and does not want to be around them. (Stowe makes the point that northerners are usually just as prejudiced as southerners; it is only their circumstances that differ.) Ophelia thinks slaves are shiftless, but St. Clare points out that slavery has *made* them so.

St. Clare now conducts an experiment on his Yankee cousin. He gives her a present: a little slave girl named Topsy. St. Clare bought the waif out of pity, knowing she was good for nothing. Topsy had no kind of upbringing — she "just growed." She steals, lies, and capers her way through life with nary a pang of conscience. She is caught stealing from Ophelia and gets a whipping, which accomplishes nothing except to demonstrate that Ophelia cannot change slavery; rather, slavery will change *her*. Ophelia's experience shows that the system of slavery molds all who come into contact with it, regardless of their place of birth or good intentions. Whites may think they control slavery, but it controls them.

Meanwhile Tom has become close friends with little Eva St. Clare. Their friendship was risqué, for it involved a black man and a white girl. Stowe means to show that the love of Christ is not constrained by age, or sex, or race. These friends are living out Jesus' promise: "blessed are the pure in heart, for they shall see God." They delight to spend time together singing hymns and reading the Bible.

One day Eva reveals that she is going to die. Tom has been singing to her: "I see a band of spirits bright, that taste the glories there; They all are robed in spotless white, and conquering palms they bear." Eva says that she has seen those "spirits bright," and Tom believes her. Then she announces, "I'm going *there . . .* to the spirits bright . . . *I'm going, before long.*"[11] Eva is in the first stages of consumption.

The death of little Eva is one of the major events in *Uncle Tom's Cabin.* Modern readers find it hard to relate to, for it is long, drawn out, and sentimental to the point of being mawkish. But nineteenth-century readers found it riveting. The death of children from disease was tragically common in those days. Stowe knew from personal experience what passed through parents' hearts at such times, and how people would say that some children are too good for this earth. Losing them is heartbreaking, but these children go to heaven and impart blessings to those left behind.

There is yet a deeper level to the death of little Eva. In Stowe's system of belief, "dying is the supreme form of heroism," writes Jane Tompkins. Death is not defeat, but victory: "It brings an access of power, not a loss of it; it is not only the crowning achievement of life, it is life, and Stowe's entire presentation of little Eva is designed to dramatize this fact." Eva's spiritual power increases as her death draws near. She makes her father promise to set Tom free. The dying Eva loves even Topsy and accepts the slave girl's gift of flowers (never mind if they are stolen from the garden). "By giving Topsy her love, Eva initiates a process of redemption,"[12] writes Tompkins. Topsy becomes a Christian and Ophelia, for her part, begins to see Topsy as a person — not a problem to be solved or a will to be broken. Ophelia takes Topsy north to educate her and raise her like a daughter. So Eva's death imparts grace to the living.

But Augustine St. Clare is devastated by his daughter's death. He had promised her that he would free Tom, but he dies unexpectedly — before completing the paperwork necessary for Tom's freedom. Now the cruel Marie breaks up the household and sells off most of the slaves. Tom is worth money, and she will have it out of him.

Tom is sent to a slave warehouse in New Orleans and sold to the highest bidder: Simon Legree. "From the moment Tom saw him approaching, he felt an immediate and revolting horror at him."[13] Legree had a bullet shaped head and large, dirty hands which he boasted were good for "knocking down niggers." A Yankee by birth, Legree has bought a remote cotton plantation where he can be lord and master of his human property. He works his slaves to death and then buys more. There is no one to interfere.

A hopeless sense of abandonment engulfs the slaves on Legree's plantation. "I know the Lord ain't here," one slave tells Tom. Here Stowe turns to address her readers directly: "Is God HERE?" In a place of dire misrule of "unrebuked injustice," where is God? Tom can feel despair dragging him down like an undertow. One night, as he drifts off to sleep in the cramped and filthy cabin he shares with other slaves, he dreams that Eva is reading to him: "When thou passest through the waters, I will be with thee, and the rivers shall not overflow thee . . . for I am the Lord thy God, the Holy One of Israel, thy Savior."[14] It may have been a dream, says Stowe, or perhaps Tom really *has* heard Eva's voice.

Tom works hard on Legree's plantation, but when ordered to strike other slaves, he refuses. This is his spiritual warfare with Legree. "My soul an't yours, Mas'r! You haven't bought it, — ye can't buy it! It's been bought and paid for by the one that is able to keep it; . . . you can't harm me," Tom tells Legree.[15] And Legree vows to break Tom, body and soul. For Legree has bought Tom in order to make him an overseer. Tom is big and strong, and at the auction in New Orleans, Legree sized Tom up as one who could beat other slaves into submission and help enforce a reign of terror on the plantation. If only Tom would follow Legree's orders, he could avoid being beaten himself. Not only that, he would be given a ration of whiskey and invited to join the debauched parties at Legree's house. But Tom will not let Legree turn him into a beast. Tom secretly helps a weaker slave to pick her daily quota of cotton so that she will not get a beating. A suspicious Legree commands Tom to beat this woman anyway, and when Tom refuses, Legree orders two black overseers to beat Tom up.

That night, as Tom lies bruised and bleeding, he receives a visitor — Cassy, Legree's slave and concubine. Cassy brings water and dresses Tom's wounds. She advises Tom to do as he is told and avoid more beatings. "You are in the devil's hands," Cassy says. Legree "is the strongest, and you must give up!" Tom groans "O Lord! O Lord! How can I give up?" It's no use, Cassy insists; God never hears: "there isn't any God . . . or, if there is, he's taken sides against us. . . . Everything is pushing us into hell. Why shouldn't we go?" There is no law on Legree's plantation, Cassy says. Legree has taught all his slaves to be just as low and cruel to each other as he is to them. Tom may treat the other slaves kindly, but they will only turn against him the first chance they get. Tom hears Cassy out. Tom tells Cassy that he has lost everything — wife, children, and home — "I *can't* lose heaven too, no I can't get to be wicked, besides all!"[16]

Tom finds strength in scripture and the hymns he knows by heart. Legree hears Tom singing at work, and orders him to stop. "Join my church," Legree commands. Tom has only to worship Legree "and all will be well!" But like Jesus in the wilderness, Tom resists temptation. "The Lord may help me, or not help; but I'll hold to Him and believe Him to the last!"[17] Legree calls Tom a fool and departs breathing threats. Like Jesus in Gesthemane, Tom prays in anguish. He receives a vision of "one crowned with thorns, buffeted and bleeding." Seeing the "majestic patience" on Jesus' face, Tom stretches out his hands and falls on his knees. Then the vision changes and the sharp thorns encircling Jesus' head become "rays of glory." Jesus promises Tom, "He that overcometh shall sit down with me on my throne, even as I also overcame, and am set down with my Father on His throne." Tom surrenders his will to Jesus, "an unquestioning sacrifice to the Infinite." Legree owns Tom's body, but he will never own his soul.[18]

One night Cassy comes to Tom and asks him to help her kill Legree. She has gotten the master drunk on brandy, and she knows where to find an axe. No, Tom says, he must try to love his enemies. That is impossible, Cassy objects. Tom agrees: he does not have such love within himself. "But *He* gives it to us, and that's the *victory.* When we can love and pray over all and through all, the battle's past, and the victory's come — glory be to God." Here in a nutshell is Stowe's vision of the Christian life. But Tom does not expect everyone to follow this path. He urges Cassy to run away with Emmeline (a slave girl Legree has bought to replace his aging concubine). Cassy wants Tom to run away with them. Tom says no, he feels called to stay with the slaves on Legree's plantation[19] and minister to them.

Many slaves tried to escape Legree's plantation, only to be hunted down by dogs and men on horseback and brutally beaten. But Cassy is determined to get away from Legree, so she devises "the stratagem." Instead of running away, she and Emmeline will hide in the attic of Legree's house. When all the efforts to catch them have failed and the search is called off, Cassy and Emmeline will slip away. Cassy knows

Legree's weakness: he is terrified of ghosts and spirits. So Cassy stages a fake haunting in the attic, calculated to keep Legree away from the hiding place.

Legree suspects that Tom knows where Cassy and Emmeline are hiding. He threatens Tom: "do you know I've made up my mind to KILL you?" He commands Tom to betray his friends. Tom refuses. Then Legree orders two male slaves to beat Tom to death. Tom is strong and in his prime, so his death is slow and agonizing . . . like crucifixion. The dying Tom forgives Legree and prays for the slaves who are beating him, and forgives them. Astonished, they ask, "O Tom! Do tell us who is *Jesus,* anyhow?" He tells them that Jesus loves sinners and has the power to save them: "Oh Lord! Give me these two more souls, I pray!" are Tom's very last words. "That prayer was answered," Stowe says.[20] Tom's death is not in vain, for

> of old, there was One whose suffering changed an instrument of torture, degradation and shame, into a symbol of glory, honor and immortal life; and where His spirit is, neither degrading stripes, nor blood, nor insults, can make the Christian's last struggle less than glorious. . . . There stood by [Tom] ONE, — seen by him alone, — "like unto the Son of God."[21]

God does not abandon Tom in his suffering, but transforms him into the image of Christ. Stowe's Tom is noble, a Christ figure who dies so that others might live. Likewise Stowe saw Christ as a slave figure, the suffering servant. As historian Eugene Genovese writes, the suffering Christ was someone slave Christians identified with: "Time and again, the message of the black preachers turned precisely on the low earthly station of the Son of God." Jesus suffered like they suffered, understood them, and "offered them rest from their sufferings."[22]

Tom dies victorious. He never denies his Lord or betrays his fellow slaves. He prays for his enemies and even converts his tormenters. Tom's death sets in motion a chain of events in the plot, whereby the slaves on the Shelby plantation (Tom's old Kentucky home) are set free. Many of Stowe's fictional characters are changed because of the deaths of Tom and Eva.

Legions of Stowe's readers were also changed, converted to Christ and to anti-slavery at the same time.[23] They found, as Stowe said, that right feeling led to right action. After reading *Uncle Tom's Cabin,* thousands of northerners could not obey the Fugitive Slave Law, and it became difficult — if not impossible — to enforce it.

The Painter at Work

Stowe said she wrote *Uncle Tom's Cabin* to "awaken *sympathy and feeling* for the African race."[24] Just how did she do it? Her best strategy was to use pictures: graphic, moving pictures, sketched in words. Early in her writing process for *Uncle Tom's Cabin,* she told her editor Gamaliel Bailey: "My vocation is simply that of a painter, and my object will be to hold up in the most lifelike and graphic manner possible Slavery, its reverses, changes, and the negro character, which I have had ample opportunities for studying." Stowe had heard endless arguments about slavery, which never seemed to help the slaves. But "there is no arguing with *pictures,* and everybody is impressed by them, whether they mean to be or not."[25]

Casting slaves in leading roles was a bold stroke on Stowe's part, since in those days, if slaves appeared in fiction, they were stage props or status symbols for whites. But Stowe wanted her readers to see slaves as human beings in their own right. And this pointed up the fundamental contradiction of slavery — namely that a human being, by definition, cannot be owned. Slavery works only if some people are perceived as less human than others. Stowe therefore painted her black characters to show their humanity: their dignity and courage, their wit and drollery, their sorrow and despair and faith. To be sure, she was limited by her own assumptions about race. Yet her basic strategy worked.

Stowe painted pictures of white people too. A few were saintly — like little Eva or Rachel Halliday (a Quaker who helped slaves escape). But many were simply average. They were not terribly bad people, but they were so used to slavery that they accepted it as normal. Stowe tried hard *not* to show northern whites as morally superior to southern whites. She made the wicked Simon Legree a Yankee by birth. And even Miss Ophelia (a good Yankee Christian) was forced to confront her own deep-seated racial prejudice. Stowe wanted to show that slavery corrupted white people, regardless of their good intentions or where they were born.

Stowe wrote dialogs in which white people talked *about* slavery.

Then she juxtaposed their conversations with scenes from slave life, showing that while whites discussed slavery in abstract terms, black people were being sold, whipped, and torn away from their families. The whites talked as though they had all the time in the world, but at every moment slaves were sweating, bleeding, and dying. This contrast between idle talk and real suffering seared the consciences of readers. No doubt many of Stowe's readers had been party to the same idle discussions, but as they read *Uncle Tom's Cabin,* their consciences were pricked.

Slavery was a heavy subject. Lest her readers grow weary and cast the book aside, Stowe lightened her story with humor. Readers literally laughed and cried their way through *Uncle Tom's Cabin,* unable to stop turning the pages. Stowe credited much of the humor in her book to the "the never-failing wit and drollery of her former colored friends in Ohio."[26]

Early in the story Stowe stages a comic scene on the Shelby plantation. Mr. Haley the slave trader discovers that his new "property" Eliza has fled with her child. She is worth a lot of money and must be caught at once! But Mrs. Shelby, hearing of Eliza's escape, says, "Thank the Lord!" A slave named Andy hears it and understands that Mrs. Shelby *wants* Eliza to escape. So Andy, when told to get the horses ready to pursue Eliza, makes a great show of following orders. But he and his accomplice (a slave named Sam) manage to spook the horses, chase them all over the pasture and get them so lathered up that the pursuit of Eliza is delayed. Back in the barn, Sam and Andy "laughed to their hearts' content" while grooming Haley's winded horse. "Did yer see Misses [Shelby] up stairs at the winder? I seed her laughin." Once the horses are all "cotched" and groomed, Sam and Andy will get an "uncommon good" lunch. Later that day the two conspirators are sent off with Haley to help him find the right road, which they do as slowly as possible, to the exasperation of Haley and the amusement of the reader.

"A major source of strength of *Uncle Tom's Cabin* [was] its humor," noted Thomas Gossett. Not only did it keep readers engaged; humor helped them identify with the characters: "Humor was a way of establishing the reality of the characters of the novel, especially that of the blacks." It made the reader's sympathy with the black characters "less abstract and more personal."[27] Once that sympathy was awakened, hearts and minds could change.

Uncle Tom's Cabin was a life-changing experience for countless readers. It "is a great book," Ann Douglas wrote, "not because it is a great novel, but because it is a great revival sermon, aimed directly at the conversion of its hearers."[28] Stowe's strategy reaped many converts indeed.

Impassioned and Imaginative

We have already seen a number of religious themes — especially the Christ figures Eva and Tom, and the problem of abandonment, whether God is present where evil reigns. Another key religious theme in *Uncle Tom's Cabin* is slave Christianity. In her mind's eye Stowe said she saw Jesus reaching down to the slave and saying, "Fear not, for I have redeemed thee, I have called thee by thy name, thou art mine."[29] To "redeem" means to buy back. That would have powerful meaning to someone who is bought and sold. Stowe insists that only God can say to a human being, "thou art mine." Christian slaves tried to live as children of God, even while being treated as chattel.

Stowe was fascinated by slave religion and its power to help people transcend the most abject conditions. Near the beginning of the book Stowe paints a scene of slaves at worship in Tom's cabin on the Shelby plantation. After some socializing, the "meeting" begins with singing "at once wild and spirited." The slaves sing well-known hymns and tunes "of a wilder, more indefinite character, picked up at camp meetings." Like many whites who heard slaves singing, Stowe could never forget that sound. "The slaves' talent for improvisation," wrote historian Eugene Genovese, "as well as their deep religious conviction, drew expressions of wonder and admiration from almost everyone who heard them sing." One of these songs in the worship scene foreshadows Tom's story: "Die on the field of battle, die on the field of battle, die on the field of battle, glory in my soul."[30]

At Tom's cabin, the slaves sing their way over Jordan and into the Promised Land. This could mean freedom in the north, the afterlife, or a moment of transcendent joy here and now. "The several meanings of Heaven in the spirituals" must be seen as one, writes Genovese, since the slaves did not make "rigid separation of sacred and secular"[31] or divide time into categories. To dwell on heaven was to gain power for life in this world, as well as hope in the next. This life, with all its sorrow, is passing away. Even now God brings deliverance and allows a glimpse of divine glory. As the slaves worshipped and sang, "some laughed, and some cried, and some clapped hands, or shook hands rejoicingly [*sic*] with each other, as if they had fairly gained the other side of the river," Stowe wrote.

One senses that Stowe was drawn to this kind of worship. She explained that "the negro mind" was "impassioned and imaginative, always attach[ing] itself to hymns and expressions of a vivid and pictorial nature."[32] Of course that is racial stereotyping — but it also describes Stowe herself. *Her* mind was impassioned and imaginative, always attached itself to hymns and pictures, always working in a vivid and pictorial way.

In the worship scene at Tom's cabin, the high point is the reading of scripture. Since very few slaves could read, George Shelby, the master's son, is invited by the slaves to read aloud to them from the Bible. (This would not have been allowed on some plantations, but Mrs. Shelby wants the slaves to learn the Bible.) And so George reads "the last chapters of Revelation" which Stowe said the slaves knew and loved.

Stowe's readers would have known what the last chapters of Revelation are about. They tell of the Holy City, the New Jerusalem, coming down from heaven adorned like a bride with gold and pearls and gems. In the midst of the City stands the throne of God and the Lamb, whence flows the river of the water of life. In that heavenly City every tear is wiped away and there is no more crying or pain anymore. As George Shelby reads these things, the slaves cry out in joy and wonder, so that at times George's voice can scarcely be heard.

When it comes time to pray, all eyes look to Tom, who is respected as "a sort of minister among them." As Tom prays, "the language of Scripture"[33] comes naturally, flowing from some deep well within. Tom just prays "right up," with responses breaking out everywhere around him.

Stowe said nothing about sin and forgiveness in the worship at Tom's cabin. The omission was correct. "The slaves did not view their predicament as punishment for the collective sin of black people," writes Eugene Genovese. They had "little room" for a theology based on original sin. Thus "black theology largely ignored the one doctrine that might have reconciled the slaves to their bondage on a spiritual plane."[34] Whites used the concept of sin to preach against stealing, lying, and shirking, and thereby to control slave behavior.

Slaves saw through this. They did not embrace a religion of guilt, but one of liberation. The great African American intellectual W. E. B. Du Bois said that even in the deepest "sorrow songs" of slavery "there breathes a hope — a faith in the ultimate justice of things."[35] Genovese added that "the religion of the slaves . . . exhibited joy much as the religion of their African forebears had, [but] who in his right mind would say the same thing of the religion of the whites?"[36] Stowe voiced a similar frustration with white worship. Her white character St. Clare declines to go to church with his wife. "If I did go at all, I would go where Mammy goes; there's something to keep a fellow awake there, at least." St. Clare was bored by "the dead sea of your respectable churches."[37]

Visions also played a role in slave Christianity. On the Legree plantation, Tom had a vision of Jesus. Stowe then informed her readers that visionary states are "very common" among negroes. And who are *we* to say that the visions are not real? she asked. "If the poor forgotten slave believes that Jesus hath appeared and spoken to him, who shall contradict him?"[38] This too may sound like racial stereotyping, but Stowe herself seems to have had visionary experiences.

Both Sides Read the Same Bible

That Christians did not agree on what the Bible said about slavery Stowe was well aware. The Bible was supposed to be the highest moral authority. Yet when it came to slavery — the great moral issue of the era — Bible-quoting Christians seemed merely to cancel each other out. As historian Mark Noll has said, this was "a theological crisis."[39] Lincoln recognized it and spoke of it in his Second Inaugural Address: "both sides read the same Bible and pray to the same God, and each invokes His aid against the other." Early in the Civil War Lincoln wrote, "both [sides] *may* be, and one *must* be, wrong. God cannot be *for* and *against* the same thing at the same time."[40]

Christians used the Bible to argue for slavery and against it. Stowe wrote this into a minor scene in *Uncle Tom's Cabin*. On the riverboat bound for New Orleans two ministers are discussing slavery. The pro-slavery minister quotes, "Cursed be Canaan; a servant of servants shall he be" (Genesis 9:25 is from an obscure story where one of Noah's sons sees him drunk and naked. Enraged, Noah curses that son and condemns him to be a "servant of servants." This had nothing to do with Africa or with American slavery, but that did not stop people from quoting it to justify slavery.) Stowe hints that the minister who quotes "cursed be Canaan" is an ignorant bumpkin.

The second minister is cut from different cloth. He is compassionate and learned, and the biblical quote he applies to slavery is Luke 6:31, "do unto others as you would have them do unto you." He adds, "*that* is scripture, as much as 'Cursed be Canaan.'" But just when the lights should turn on, Stowe has a bystander lamely remark, "there's differences in parsons, an't there?"[41] Stowe's point: few people have the wherewithal to ask *how* the Bible is being used and *why* and *by whom*. All they can do is shrug and turn away.

But Stowe won't let her readers off the hook so easily. She shows that the problem is not that the Bible contradicts itself. The problem is that *slavery corrupts* Christians, and poisons the way they read the Bible.

"Religion!" Stowe has St. Clare exclaim. "Religion! Is what you hear at church, religion?" St. Clare is cynical because he has seen religion twisted every which way. "When I look for religion, I must look for something above me, not below me." St. Clare is a slaveholder, but he rolls his eyes at those who "put on a long face, and snuffle, and quote Scripture" to defend slavery as the will of God. The truth is simpler, St. Clare says. Slavery is not about scripture. It is about money. Suppose that the cotton market crashed and slavery ceased to be profitable. White southerners would quickly embrace "another version of the Scripture doctrine," says St. Clare. "A flood of light would pour into the church all at once, and . . . immediately it would be discovered that everything in the Bible and reason"[42] was opposed to slavery. If slavery did not make money, no one would bother quoting Scripture to defend it. In other words, those who defend slavery read the Bible through the eyes of self-interest. They convert the Bible to their own use, instead of letting the Bible convert them.

Who uses Scripture rightly? Those who follow Christ, like Tom and Eva. Instead of using the Scripture to lay burdens upon the backs of others, they carry the cross for others. Eva tells Tom, "I can understand why Jesus *wanted* to die for us." She said she would be "glad to die" if it could end all the misery caused by slavery.[43] If people obey God's call to bear burdens for others, to lay aside comfort and privilege on behalf of others, *then* Scripture is being used rightly.

One of Stowe's most important scenes about Scripture and slavery takes place in the northern plot. Eliza has just crossed the Ohio River and needs a place to hide. With Eliza for the moment "offstage," Stowe brings the reader to a warm, cozy parlor in Cincinnati: the home of a (fictional) U.S. Senator, John Bird of Ohio. He has just returned from Washington, where he has voted for the Fugitive Slave Law. His normally meek wife declares that *she* will not obey the law, even if *he* has voted for it. She says it is a wicked law and she vows to break it the first chance she gets — no idle threat with so many runaways crossing the river! Now, now, cajoles the Senator; the little wife must not let her feelings run away with her. She must abide by the law.

Mrs. Bird replies, "John, I don't know anything about politics, but I can read my Bible, and there I see that we must feed the hungry, clothe the naked, and comfort the desolate, and that Bible I mean to follow."[44] This is the classic "higher law" scenario, in which the Bible has a greater authority than any human law. The Senator and his wife now debate how Christians should respond to fugitive slaves — help them, ignore them, or turn them in. The debate is heated, but abstract. It is interrupted by a knock on the door.

There stands Eliza, wet and shivering, her child in her arms. This is the Senator's moment of truth. Will he help the runaway slave — and break the law he has just voted for? Stowe's readers want him to do the right thing and help Eliza. And he does. What has happened to the Senator? He has been awakened by "the real presence of distress."[45] It is as if Christ himself has appeared at the Senator's door in the guise of a runaway slave. And the Senator finds compassion welling up within him for "the least of these." Of this scene Michael Gilmore writes, "real presence alone can awaken readers or listeners out of their sleep of law and custom and rouse them to act in the name of conscience."[46] The real presence awakens Senator Bird's conscience and moves him to action. And that is exactly what Stowe wants her readers to experience. The Senator and his wife feed and clothe Eliza and her child and take them to a man who can help them to the next place on the journey to freedom.

Mrs. Bird already knows what to do but her husband, the Senator, must be converted. Then he will risk all to "follow the Bible."[47] Here too, one can tell right use of Scripture, because it leads one to become a servant, not to make *someone else* a slave.

The moral ideal here is benevolence: pure, unselfish love. Since human beings are sinful, true benevolence can only be a gift of grace. The ideal of benevolence in Calvinism can be seen in Jonathan Edwards's *The Nature of True Virtue,* and was basic to Lyman Beecher's New Divinity Calvinism. From her father Harriet also learned "Congregationalist habits of intensely scriptural piety" and the call to repent at once or face divine judgment. Later in her life Stowe moved away from her father's theology. But John Gatta is correct in saying that New England Calvinism was "artistically indispensable" to Stowe when she wrote *Uncle Tom's Cabin.*[48] And as Mark Noll has demonstrated, Calvinism was politically indispensable for the "religiously charged, public moral argument" against slavery in the years before the Civil War.[49]

The "intense scriptural piety" of the Beechers meant that Scripture was a living voice calling people to follow Jesus. It was not a *thing* to be used — any more than Tom was a *thing* to be bought and sold. Those who follow the Scriptures are gradually changed into the image of Christ — often through suffering. This is what happened to Tom and Eva in *Uncle Tom's Cabin.*

Tom could read his Bible a little bit (back on the Kentucky plantation the master's son was teaching Tom to read). Tom marked his favorite passages in the Bible and could slowly make out the words. More important, Tom had memorized large portions of Scripture that could never be taken from him.

As noted earlier, Tom and Eva loved to read the Scriptures together. And like the slaves in the opening worship scene, Eva was especially fond of Revelation and the prophets. Their "wondrous imagery . . . spoke of a glory to be revealed." Stowe said that Tom and Eva, "the old child and the young one, felt just alike about it." The Scriptures breathed "something wondrous yet to come, wherein their soul rejoiced, yet knew not why."[50] By reading the Bible aloud to each other, Tom and Eva enter into the presence of God. And as they do so, all human distinctions — black or white, slave or free, male or female — fall away.

After Eva's death, St. Clare reads to Tom from the Bible. He chooses a passage Tom marked heavily: the parable of the last judgment from Matthew 25. Stowe took the trouble to quote it in full in the text of *Uncle Tom's Cabin.* When St. Clare gets to the end, where people are judged according to how they have treated the poor, he feels as though he has seen himself in a mirror. Those who received a harsh judgment in the parable "seem to have been doing just what I have, — living good, easy, respectable lives, and not troubling themselves to inquire how many of their brethren were hungry or athirst, or sick, or in prison."[51] The Scripture was doing its work, afflicting the comfortable. Stowe also shows Scripture comforting the afflicted. Earlier we noted that when Tom feels abandoned by God on Legree's plantation, he hears Eva's voice read to him Isaiah 43:2, assuring him of God's presence.

But the devil can quote Scripture too, as Tom well knows. Legree told Tom that the Bible says *servants obey your masters.* Therefore Tom should obey when ordered to beat a fellow slave. Tom refuses, and Legree rants, "An't I yer master? Didn't I pay down twelve hundred dollars, cash, for all there is inside your old cussed black shell? An't yer mine, now, body and soul?" And Legree gives Tom "a violent kick with his heavy boot."[52] But Tom knows Legree is misusing Scripture. If a poor slave like Tom knows that, why then are some people so easily persuaded that Scripture supports slavery? The answer is self-interest. Even Legree can quote Scripture for gain, but the true child of God follows Scripture to the cross.

Scripture quotations abound in *Uncle Tom's Cabin.* Stowe scholar Stephen Railton tallies almost 100 biblical quotations and allusions.[53] The fictional characters who quote Scripture most often, according to Railton, are Tom, then Eva, and then the spiritual-but-not-religious Augustine St. Clare. As for the Quakers, they do not so much quote Scripture as live by it.

But in her authorial voice, Stowe invokes Scripture more than any of her fictional characters. In her "Concluding Remarks" she quotes the prophet Amos: the Day of the Lord will come! That is good news for the oppressed. But for the oppressors, it is as *"the day of vengeance."* Do we really know what we are praying for when we say "God's will be done on earth as it is in heaven"? God wills slavery to end. If we fail to end it, judgment will surely fall. "This is an age of the world," Stowe wrote, "when nations are trembling and convulsed." The world groans in travail. "And is America safe?" No, for America harbors a great injustice. Both North and South are "guilty before God; and the *Christian church* has a heavy account to answer." Time is running out. The sun is setting on the day of grace. Only "repentance, justice and mercy" can save the Union now. But those who protect "injustice and cruelty" will surely call down "the wrath of Almighty God!"[54]

CHAPTER NINE

I Grant I Am a Woman

Nobody knew *Uncle Tom's Cabin* would be the best seller of the century. While Stowe's story was running serially in *The National Era,* she sought a book publisher. Catharine Beecher suggested Phillips, Sampson & Company, but they feared "that an antislavery book by a woman would be a poor risk and might alienate a sizeable portion of their southern trade."[1] Then the Stowes tried John Jewett, who had published books by various Beechers. Jewett offered a ten percent royalty for *Uncle Tom's Cabin,* which the Stowes accepted. One friend told Calvin that *Uncle Tom's Cabin* might sell well enough for Harriet to buy a new dress from the proceeds.

On March 20, 1852, *Uncle Tom's Cabin* came out in two volumes. In just one week the entire print run of five thousand copies sold out. The next week, another five thousand sold out. After three months, the *New York Daily Times* reported Stowe's earnings to exceed $10,000 — more than any author had ever received from a book in that length of time.[2] Within one year *Uncle Tom's Cabin* had sold 300,000 copies in the U.S. and 1.5 million in Great Britain.

With sales of her book soaring, Stowe challenged Jewett: "Were you correct in persuading me & Mr. Stowe that a ten percent contract on books that sell as mine have is better for us than a *twenty percent one?*" Stowe said she had been "ignorant of business." But now "men of business" told her that Jewett could have and *should* have offered her twenty or even twenty-five percent in royalties.[3] But Jewett would not reconsider the terms of the contract. Catharine thought Jewett was "a scoundrel" and threatened to "make the matter public," wrote Stowe's younger sister Isabella. "What a pity that she will meddle so."[4]

Stowe could be a warrior, but she did not want to fight over royalties. "Great allowances can be made for Mr. Jewett," Stowe told her brother Edward. "He has made great efforts, he has given time thought & care to the sale of this book." Stowe considered herself "at liberty to decline future connections" with Jewett, adding that "peace of mind is worth more than money."[5]

The Defenders of Slavery Have Let Me Alone and Are Abusing You

And now she had other things to think about. Letters about *Uncle Tom's Cabin* surged into Stowe's home in Andover. Stowe could not get through all the mail without help. People wrote to praise her work and to tell their own stories about slavery, similar to — or worse than — the events in Stowe's fiction. Hate mail came too, calling Stowe a liar, a traitor to her race, and a disgrace to womanhood. Critics predicted that *Uncle Tom's Cabin* would incite a slave revolt, perhaps even a war. God would surely punish Harriet Beecher Stowe! Among the most chilling responses was the small package that arrived containing the severed ear of a slave.[6]

Then came printed reviews of *Uncle Tom's Cabin,* popping up in newspapers and magazines like dandelions in May. The *National Era* of course praised Stowe's book as "The Story of the Age," a "providential" work sent from God "to plead for his poor and oppressed children of the South."[7] New York's *Christian Inquirer* praised the theology of *Uncle Tom's Cabin,* in which "Life can triumph over Death" and "the power and presence of God" are real supports to the slave. Indeed, Stowe had made it "very possible to believe that the greatest triumphs of Christ and of his Gospel are still, as at first, taking place among the down-trodden and the wretched."[8]

There were hostile reviews, too. The *Southern Literary Messenger* charged Stowe with breaking God's commandment against bearing false witness.[9] The *New York Daily Times* mocked Stowe's treatment of slavery as so "fanciful that it should have been laid in some Oriental region, rather than amidst the sober and commonplace realities of the Plantation States."[10]

Many writers focused on Stowe's gender. Boston's *Morning Post* marveled "that a female . . . was capable" of such authorship. "One wonders, indeed, where a lady could pick up so much stuff, and how she could acquire such free and easy manners in disposing of it. Everything is fish that comes to her net, and she is equally at home with saint or sinner, black or white, high or low."[11] On the other hand, Henry Hughes of Mississippi had nothing but contempt for female authors. He condemned *Uncle Tom's Cabin* as "womanish & I am afraid absurdly unprincipled, written by a woman clearly."[12]

Some of the criticism was friendly fire from anti-slavery leaders. William Lloyd Garrison, editor of the *Liberator,* deeply regretted that Stowe "sent" some of her black characters to Africa as missionaries. Did Stowe mean to say that black people could never be equal to whites here in the U.S.? Garrison rejected colonization because blacks helped build this country and had earned the right to live here on equal terms with whites.[13] Garrison also criticized the character of Uncle Tom. He wondered if Stowe expected Christ-like behavior from blacks only. Was it black people *only* who must turn the other cheek and die praying for their oppressors? Was there to be one standard of behavior for blacks and another for whites? Garrison did not see blacks as more passive than whites; he thought that making blacks look docile was just another way of keeping them down. Still, he hailed *Uncle Tom's Cabin* for winning so many people to the anti-slavery cause. If the value of anti-slavery writing can be measured "by the abuse it brings," Garrison judged Stowe's book a success: "now all the defenders of slavery have let me alone and are abusing you."[14]

Many African Americans who responded to *Uncle Tom's Cabin* praised Stowe for striking a blow against slavery. However, some expressed dismay, if not outrage, at her apparent support of colonization in sending Eliza and George to Africa as missionaries. Critics charged that colonization was meant to keep America for whites only, and to deny blacks the fruit of their labors in building this country. William G. Allen, a black intellectual, wrote in 1852 of his "one regret" with regard to *Uncle Tom's Cabin:* "that the chapter favoring colonization was ever written."[15] Related to this was the charge that Stowe's black characters were too submissive — especially Tom. An African-Canadian paper, *Provincial Freeman,* said, "Uncle Tom must be killed, — George Harris exiled! Heaven for dead negroes! — Liberia for living mulattoes! Neither can live on the American Continent! Death or banishment is our doom, say the Slaveocrats, the Colonizationists, and, — [alas] — Mrs. Stowe!"[16]

The last wave of protest against Stowe's book was an armada of pro-slavery novels. Some thirty of these "anti-Tom" books appeared before the Civil War. They promoted "a crudely racist theory which condemns the blacks to a hopelessly inferior status."[17] Pro-slavery novelists "whitewashed" slavery to cover up the stain it made on the nation and on every home. Since Stowe charged that slavery ruined families, the anti-Tom novels showed happy homes where all was bright and cheerful. The plantation system, the anti-Tom writers claimed, gave the slaves work, food, and housing, and took care of those too old to work, while the northern factory owners provided nothing for their workers and let the aged starve. In 1853 John Page called his book *Uncle Robin in His Cabin in Virginia, and Tom without One in Boston.*

Harriet Wilson, a northern black writer, apparently felt that Stowe had not gone far enough in her protest. Wilson's 1859 novel showed what life was like for northern blacks. It moved "beyond *Uncle Tom's Cabin* toward a far more radical indictment of the endemic racial, gender, and class prejudices that infected the whole of American society, not just the slaveholding South," writes Joy Jordan-Lake.[18] Harriet Wilson's title still bristles: *Our Nig: or, Sketches from the Life of a Free Black, in a Two-Story White House, North. Showing that Slavery's Shadows Fall Even There. By "Our Nig."*

Of all the responses to *Uncle Tom's Cabin,* the most menacing one came from Presbyterian minister Joel Parker, who threatened to sue Stowe for damaging his reputation. Stowe had connected Parker's name with one of the worst scenes in her story. By means of an asterisk and his name at the bottom of a page, she exposed his support of slavery and condemned it.

The toxic footnote occurred in chapter 12, "Select Incident of Lawful Trade." At this point in the story, Tom is on the riverboat heading south for New Orleans, where most of the slaves will be sold. A few, however, are sold at various stops along the way. At one of these stops, the trader has a customer who wants to buy a slave child. When the mother finds out that her child has been sold, she is stricken with grief. That night, as the boat churns downriver, she jumps overboard and drowns. The next morning the trader finds out and enters the mother's name into his account book under "losses." He hopes that with a few good sales he can cover that loss. Slave trading has some unpleasant aspects, but the trader has *gotten used to it,* Stowe implies.

From the sidelines, Tom grieves for that slave mother and her child. Separating them was "unutterably horrible and cruel," Tom thinks. But then Stowe says sarcastically that Tom is just a "poor, ignorant black soul! . . . If he had only been instructed by certain ministers of Christianity," Tom might have accepted the sale as "an everyday incident of a lawful trade." Then Stowe says there are certain "ministers of Christianity" who see nothing wrong with the internal slave trade. For example, she knew of "an American divine" who said that slavery *"has no evils but such as are inseparable from any other relations in social and domestic life."* Whether the "relation" is that of husband to wife, or parent to child, or master to slave, a certain exercise of authority is necessary to maintain order. Then Stowe used a damning little asterisk to tell the world that this "American divine" was "Dr. Joel Parker."

Calvin warned Harriet to remove the footnote before her story came out as a book, but when the book appeared with the offense still in place, Parker exploded. He wrote to Calvin, scolding him for failing to control his wife. Then he wrote to Harriet charging her with "calumnious assault upon his Christian and ministerial character,"[19] for which he might take legal action against her.

Harriet replied coolly. She told Parker that she had seen — in print — his statement that slavery *"has no evils but such as are inseparable from any other relations in social and domestic life."* She had looked in vain for him to retract the statement. When he did not retract it, she concluded that he was in fact a supporter of slavery. So now the burden of proof was on him to publicly retract his statement. Stowe said she would "be sincerely glad to see you exonerated before the public."[20] If he could prove he was not a supporter of slavery, she would change the text of her book. Stowe's response was published in the New York *Tribune* on June 24, 1852.

Henry Ward Beecher jumped into the fray, writing letters to Parker and publishing articles defending his sister Harriet. In New York, two rival religious papers took sides: the anti-slavery *Independent* signed Stowe on as a regular contributor; the pro-slavery *Observer* dismissed Harriet and Henry as "liars, forgers, and heretics."[21]

Lyman Beecher's daughter was not about to back down. In a letter to the hostile *New York Observer* she quoted Shakespeare's *Julius Caesar:*

I grant I am a woman,
but withal
a woman well reputed,
Cato's daughter.
Think you I am no stronger than my sex,
Being so fathered?[22]

The *Observer* challenged Stowe to document that Parker (and other clergy) really believed that slavery was simply one more domestic institution. Harriet took up the challenge. "I am a daughter of a clergyman, wife to a clergyman, sister to six clergymen," she told the editor, "and I feel an interest of family honor in saying that the case is not so bad . . . with the American clergy" regarding slavery. But the case, she knew, was very bad indeed. Privately she told Henry that the *Observer* editor "has no kind of idea what he has brought upon himself."

Stowe sent her brothers on a fact-finding mission. Edward combed "declarations of synods, Presbyteries & ecclesiastical bodies of all denominations."[23] Henry scoured journals, including "back numbers of the *Princeton Repertory*." The Beecher brothers found in church records the hard evidence of clergy who defended slavery — at the expense of God's commandments. For example, adultery is forbidden, yet slave husbands and wives were sold apart from one another and forced to take other partners. Clergy were on record as supporting this. Murder is also against God's command. Yet some clergy were on record as supporting state laws that let masters scourge and even kill slaves with impunity. Some of the things the Beechers found would be almost funny, had they not been so tragic. For example, a South Carolina clergyman, Rev. Farman, Doctor of Divinity, died and his estate was broken up. Among the items for sale were: "a library . . . chiefly theological" and "27 Negroes, some of them very prime." What theology did the Rev. Dr. Farman read, to justify the sale of human beings?

Stowe sent this — and much more — evidence to the editor of the *New York Observer*. She reminded him that in the case of heresy, the rest of the church must clear itself "from complicity." This had not been done, so therefore the whole church must be complicit in the evil institution of slavery.[24]

The *New York Observer* did not print Stowe's letter.[25] So be it then, Stowe told Henry; "the world shall hear what atrocious things have been said in the name & authority of Christ by his church in this country."[26] The world did hear, in Stowe's next book.

She would write it from the campus of Andover Seminary, where Calvin had recently taken a professorship. The seminary had a house in mind for the Stowes, but Harriet had other ideas. There was a large building on the campus which had previously been used as a carpenter shop and a gymnasium. Harriet wanted it to be made over into a private dwelling, and the trustees agreed. The brown stone building had a simple, classical entrance and many windows graced by wooden shutters. It had a barn-style roof with dormer windows and two chimneys. The upstairs could accommodate the Stowes, visiting Beechers, and other guests, while the spacious downstairs could handle large social gatherings. She dubbed this house her "stone cabin."

Fact and Fiction

Stowe had fancied that, with *Uncle Tom's Cabin* finished, she could find peace and quiet in her study. There she would write a new novel set on Maine's rugged coast and people it with the quaint figures of her childhood. But first she felt she must answer those critics who charged that *Uncle Tom's Cabin* had no basis in fact. She would give them facts about slavery and show the world how brutal it truly was. She would include all the damning evidence her brothers found about slavery and the churches, too. She would use Weld's older documentary, *American Slavery As It Is,* and bring in newer evidence. She assembled all of this along with her own commentary. She called this book *A Key to Uncle Tom's Cabin* because it would open the world of truth on which her novel was based.

Stowe told a friend that *A Key* would "contain all the facts and documents" supporting *Uncle Tom's Cabin.* It would make public "an immense body" of "facts, reports, trials, legal documents, and testimony of people now living South, which will more than confirm every statement" in her novel. Stowe was horrified to discover that slavery was much worse than she had supposed: *Uncle Tom's Cabin* did not begin "to measure the depth of the abyss"[27] of slavery.

Her first step in writing *A Key* was to reread her novel through the eyes of her critics. Then, with their objections in mind, she documented events and characters from real life, which mirrored those in her fiction. But defending her novel was not enough. As one scholar put it, Stowe had to prove not only that "anti-slavery fictions *(Uncle Tom's Cabin)* are truths" but also "that pro-slavery facts are lies."[28]

Stowe identified several "facts" that were used to defend slavery: for example, the claim that southern laws prevented cruelty to slaves. Stowe documented horrific cases of brutality which went unpunished (or were only lightly reprimanded). She used actual laws and judicial verdicts to prove her point. Her evidence was so massive that it took up fifteen chapters, an entire section of her book. Of many court cases and decisions presented, that of *Souther vs. the Commonwealth [of Virginia]* in 1851 stands out. Here a man tortured his slave for twelve hours, "for chastisement." The slave died. The slaveholder was tried but not convicted, since he did not intend to kill the slave but merely to chastise him.[29]

A second pro-slavery "fact" was that public opinion protected slaves. But where, Stowe asked, does public opinion come from? It comes from education, formal and informal, that teaches people what to think. From the cradle, whites were taught that their race was superior. Whites were taught that blacks did not have the same emotions or the same capacity for physical pain. Therefore it was not cruel to punish slaves; indeed it was necessary to maintain order. Using the writings of southerners, Stowe had no difficulty showing that public opinion justified all manner of cruelty. Take for example the advertisements for runaway slaves. These ads identified fugitives by their scars, missing fingers, the brands in their flesh, or the limp in their walk — all marks of brutality. Such ads routinely ran alongside notices for auctions, farm implements, and the latest patent medicines, and public opinion accepted this as normal.

This was sin, Stowe said. Since the creation of the world, the great sin of humanity has been "to tread down, to vilify and crush the image of God, in the person of the poor and lowly." Slavery, Stowe wrote, was "the denial of humanity to man,"[30] and it was magnified by the absolute power of masters over slaves.[31] Stowe thought that no one, not even the kindest person, should hold absolute power over another, for power seduces us into treating our fellow human beings as *things* instead of people. And to treat human beings as objects is to violate God's moral law.[32] Christianity teaches that *all* human beings bear God's image. But, said Stowe, "public opinion" teaches otherwise.

A third pro-slavery "fact" was that Christianity and the Bible support American slavery. Stowe saw this claim as nothing but a religious fig leaf hiding the naked truth of self-interest. In a chapter entitled "The Influence of the American Church on Slavery," Stowe examined official documents from major Protestant denominations, North and South. For example, a South Carolina Presbytery declared that "the kingdom of our Lord is not of this world"; thus the church has no right to change any human institution. The Charleston Baptist association decreed that slavery was not a sin, for "the right of masters to dispose of the time of their slaves has been distinctly recognized by the Creator."[33] And a General Conference of Methodists in 1840 went on record supporting laws that forbade blacks the right to testify in court.[34] Stowe documented the "gag rules" used by church bodies in both regions to stifle any discussion of slavery at official church meetings. And all of them were simply kowtowing to moneyed interests.

Looking to the northern churches, Stowe found a ray of hope. In the late eighteenth and early nineteenth century, for example, the Methodists had condemned slavery as "contrary . . . to the conscience of true religion." But then the Methodists retreated, so as not to offend their southern constituents. By the 1830s, the Methodists had declared themselves "decidedly opposed to modern abolitionism."[35]

The use of the Bible and of church statements did not prove that Scripture condoned slavery, or that slavery was compatible with Christianity. What it proved was that slavery perverted Christians and skewed their use of the Bible. Relentlessly Stowe exposed the church's complicity in a slave system driven by greed. "Is not the doctrine that men may lawfully sell the members of Christ, his body, his flesh and bones, for purposes of gain, as really a heresy as the denial of the divinity of Christ?" Stowe demanded.

Masters taught their slaves that God wills them to "have nothing but poverty and toil in this world"; that if they disobey their masters, they will suffer both temporal punishment and eternal torment in hell. No wonder, said Stowe, that one slaveholder praised religion as more effective for keeping his slaves in line than a whole wagonload of whips.[36]

Christians who dared to speak the truth were persecuted like the prophets of old. So Stowe challenged Christians: put off cowardice and "seek the entire abolition of slavery." It was not enough merely to pass resolutions at a church meeting. Churches must get their members to *disobey* laws that support slavery. Christians should help black people with practical assistance, legal or illegal. Southerners should abolish slavery *and* Northerners should abolish the "system of caste"[37] which treated blacks as less than human.

Stowe was bold and confrontational in *A Key.* She dared her readers to watch the "mournful march of slave coffles [slaves chained together] . . . follow the bloody course of slave ships on your coast. What . . . does the Lamb of God think of all these things?" Then she exhorted Christians to show that they loved Jesus by embracing "the cause of his suffering poor." Everyone would be judged by their actions, or their failure to act. For Christ will say, "'I have been in the slave-prison — in the slave-coffle; I have been sold in your markets; I have toiled for naught in your fields; I have been smitten on the mouth in your courts of justice; I have been denied a hearing in my own Church, and ye cared not for it. Ye went, one to his farm, and another to his merchandise.' And if ye shall answer, *'When* Lord?' He shall say unto you, 'Inasmuch as ye have done it to the least of these my brethren, ye have done it unto me.'"[38]

Once more, Harriet slung a stone and hit the Goliath of slavery smack in the face. Southern reviewers struck back. "Mrs. Stowe," wrote one, "betrays a malignity so remarkable . . . that the petticoat lifts of itself, and we see the hoof of the beast under the table."[39] But they could not stop Americans from buying 90,000 copies of *A Key to Uncle Tom's Cabin* in its first month in print; eventually it sold 150,000[40] in the U.S. and did very well in England too.

Frederick Douglass was right when he said the "most unwise thing . . . ever done by slaveholders" was to call into question the truthfulness of *Uncle Tom's Cabin.* Stowe rose to their challenge and proved that in fact slavery was much worse than she had shown it in *Uncle Tom's Cabin.* "There has not been an exposure of slavery so terrible as *[A] Key to Uncle Tom's Cabin,*" Douglass said. He wanted everyone to read it, "and learn from it to hate slavery" intensely. Then Stowe's new book would become a key to "unlock the prison-house for the deliverance of millions who are now pining in chains, crying, 'HOW LONG! HOW LONG! O LORD GOD. . . . HOW LONG SHALL THESE THINGS BE?'"[41]

Preparing *A Key* was painful for Stowe. "I suffer exquisitely in writing these things," she lamented. "It may be truly said that I write with my heart's blood." She felt as though she were "forced by some awful oath to disclose in court some family disgrace."[42]

Harriet did find joy in her work when she saw a staged version of *Uncle Tom's Cabin* at Boston's National Theater. Francis Underwood, an editor and trusted friend, invited her to go. Underwood was sure Stowe had never in her life been to the theater, which her religious upbringing taught her to shun. But Underwood thought Stowe really must see her story brought to life on stage, so he secured box seats where "the authoress" would be shielded from view (she was, after all, a seminary professor's wife, and her attendance at a play could be criticized). Stowe "sat in the shade of the curtains of our box, and watched the play attentively," Underwood recalled. "I never saw such delight upon a human face" as when she saw her character "Topsy" brilliantly brought to life. Stowe "scarcely spoke during the evening; but her expression was eloquent, — smiles and tears succeeding each other through the whole."[43]

Will You Help?

After the publication of *Uncle Tom's Cabin,* black people often approached Stowe for help. Among the first to do so was Mrs. Edmondson, whom Stowe met at the home of her brother Henry Ward Beecher.[44] Edmondson was a slave in Washington City, but was given leave to travel north to raise money to free two of her children from slavery. Moved by the "depth of patient sorrow" she saw in the mother's eyes, Stowe agreed "at once" to make "the slave woman's cause her own." She promised to raise enough money to free two more of the children *and* Mrs. Edmondson. This required $1200 (roughly $34,500 in today's money). True to her word, Stowe solicited funds at anti-slavery bazaars in New York, Boston, and New Haven, as well as by mail and word of mouth. In a few weeks the entire sum was raised. Stowe stayed in touch with the family and later paid for the "Edmondson sisters [to] study at Oberlin."[45]

But Stowe did not help everyone who approached her. Take for example Harriet Jacobs, a former slave who asked for Stowe's help in publishing her memoir. Born a slave in North Carolina, Jacobs was sexually abused by her owner. Partly to protect herself, Jacobs took a white lover and had two children by him. But Jacobs's owner threatened to sell her children if she refused his advances. First Jacobs fled to a swamp, and then she hid in an attic crawl space in the house where her children lived. Her hiding space was cramped, but Jacobs could be near her children and see them secretly at night. For seven years she hid in the attic. Finally Jacobs escaped to New York, where she found work as a domestic servant. Friends arranged to buy her freedom and that of her children. And now she wanted to tell her life story.

Naturally Jacobs turned for help to the author of *Uncle Tom's Cabin.* Learning that Stowe was soon leaving for Europe, Jacobs asked if her daughter, Louisa, could go along (Jacobs would pay for Louisa's expenses). Through an intermediary (a Quaker activist named Amy Post) Jacobs contacted Stowe. Stowe was impressed with Jacobs's story and wanted to use it in *A Key,* but Jacobs wanted to tell her own story.[46] Stowe did not help Jacobs publish her story and refused to take her daughter to Europe, lest "such an experience . . . spoil her."[47] Eventually and without any help from Stowe, Jacobs did publish her memoir, *Incidents in the Life of a Slave Girl.* After the war, Jacobs and Stowe met, and Stowe gave Jacobs a signed copy of *Uncle Tom's Cabin.*[48]

Stowe's refusal to help Jacobs strikes a "discordant note" in her story.[49] Perhaps Stowe, pressured to finish *A Key* before leaving for Europe, was overextended and handled things poorly. Jacobs's request that Stowe take her daughter to Europe may have seemed importunate. Whatever the reason, Stowe failed to see Jacobs's right to tell her own story.

Around this time Stowe wrote to Frederick Douglass. She knew he had traveled abroad to meet with anti-slavery leaders and she wanted his advice. She told him she would soon depart for Britain, where she anticipated receiving monies to benefit "free colored people."[50] She wanted to discuss with Douglass how best to use these funds, and she invited him to her home. Arriving from Rochester, Douglass recalled being "received at her home with genuine cordiality." He observed "no contradiction between the author and her book." Stowe told Douglass of her "desire to have some monument rise after *Uncle Tom's Cabin,* which shall show that it produced more than a transient influence."

Douglass suggested an industrial college for black men. He envisioned black men supporting their families with skilled trades, preparing the way for their children and grandchildren to enter college and become professionals. Stowe asked Douglass to write his proposal, with supporting arguments, for her to show to benefactors abroad. She all but promised to underwrite the school, and Douglass was confident of her support.

While Stowe was in Europe, the founding meeting of the National Council of Colored People took place in Rochester, New York. There Douglass promoted the plan for the industrial college, thinking that he could count on funding from Stowe's European trip. While she was away and the pro-slavery press accused Stowe of raking in a personal fortune from British donations, Douglass defended her in print: the money, he promised, would be "sacredly devoted to the establishment of an industrial school for colored youth."[51] As things turned out, however, Stowe used the money she gathered for other projects on behalf of slaves and former slaves. Douglass gave Stowe the benefit of the doubt and said she acted "conscientiously." Still, she had put him in "an awkward position with the colored people of this country"[52] that wanted and needed the industrial school.

Another black leader to visit Stowe in Andover was Sojourner Truth. Truth asked Stowe to write an endorsement for a second edition of the *Narrative of Sojourner Truth.* Stowe did so, and according to Truth's biographer, "Stowe's puff surely boosted sales." Stowe gave a character reference with a strong religious endorsement, describing Truth as one gifted by a "separate revelation."[53]

Later, Harriet wrote about Sojourner for the *Atlantic Monthly.* But some ten years had passed since the two women had met, and factual errors crept into Stowe's article. (For example, Truth was not born in Africa, as Stowe said, but in New York State.) Stowe depicted Truth as a sort of African oracle ("The Libyan Sybil") rather than an American woman of grit and determination.[54] Yet Stowe's article did make many Americans aware of Sojourner Truth as a leader in the quest for black freedom and as a woman of deep faith. Truth had told Stowe about her conversion to Christ and sung the hymn, "There is a Holy City." The song describes the New Jerusalem, where saints dwell in light with "their great Redeemer." Those saints came through the great tribulation, and their example nerved Truth to face any trial.

> And what shall be my journey, How long I'll stay below
> Or what shall be my trials, Are not for me to know.
> In every day of trouble I'll raise my thoughts on high.
> I'll think of that bright temple And crowns above the sky.[55]

Truth sang this hymn with a fervor Stowe remembered for a decade. It was the song of the oppressed waiting and working for the glory of the Lord to be revealed.

Britain Beckons

A taste of that glory was being prepared in Great Britain, where the anti-slavery movement was primed to give Stowe a heroine's welcome. The first copies of *Uncle Tom's Cabin* to reach England were sent by Stowe (with cover letters introducing herself) to worthies such as Prince Albert, the Duke of Argyll, and the authors Macaulay and Dickens. The Earl of Shaftesbury wrote to Stowe that "none but a Christian believer could have produced such a book," which "impressed many thousands" with the cruelty and sin of slavery. Stowe responded with the news she and Calvin were soon departing for the British Isles. Female anti-slavery societies of Glasgow had asked the Stowes to come, she explained. Stowe was aware, from hostile British reviews, that moneyed interests in England were defending American slavery. But "*Christ* is certainly on our side," Stowe declared. "He *must at last prevail*" and slavery must end "'not by might, nor by power, but by His Spirit.'"[56]

Shaftesbury now wanted British women to speak out against slavery. It needed to be done in a socially acceptable way, so Shaftesbury wrote an anti-slavery letter for British women to sign. The letter and gathered signatures would be sent to women in the United States, showing female solidarity against slavery. The Shaftesbury letter was called "An Affectionate and Christian Address of Many Thousands of Women of Great Britain and Ireland to Their Sisters, the Women of the United States of America." It asked American women to judge slavery in the light of the Bible, "the inalienable rights of immortal souls," and Christianity. The signers agreed that all marriages should be honored, all families protected, and Christian education offered to all regardless of race. If these reforms could be made, slavery would surely die. The letter admitted England's guilt for American slavery: the mother country had "introduced" and even "compelled" its colonies to adopt slavery. The signers now exhorted American women to pray "for the removal of this affliction and disgrace from the Christian world."[57]

In the winter of 1853, while Stowe was working on *A Key to Uncle Tom's Cabin*, the Shaftesbury letter got enough signatures to fill twenty-six large leather-bound volumes. Elite women signed it, as did legions of middle- and working-class women, and even poor women who could barely scrawl their names. The text of the "Address" appeared in American newspapers.

Stowe received a letter from the author Eliza Cabot Follen, a New Englander then living in London with connections to British literati and reformers. Follen asked Stowe to introduce herself, and Stowe obliged with a short sketch of her life, knowing that Follen would circulate it among influential friends. Harriet described herself as "somewhat more than forty, about as thin and dry as a pinch of snuff; never very much to look at in my best days, and looking like a used-up article now."[58] She had married a man "rich in Greek and Hebrew, Latin and Arabic, and alas! Rich in nothing else." Their family had grown and Calvin's income had not, so Harriet started writing for pay. She had to hire help, and in this way she got to know former slaves. They told what it was like to be separated from their children and to be at the mercy of white men in all things. Harriet said she had also met fugitive slaves because "the underground railroad . . . ran through our house." Then, when Harriet's own child died from cholera, she learned "what a slave mother may feel when her child is torn away from her." She prayed that "the crushing of my own heart might enable me to work out some great good to others." The result was *Uncle Tom's Cabin*, proving that "God hath chosen 'the weak things of this world'" as instruments of his power. Harriet's letter to Follen exemplified Christian womanhood: modesty and hard work, faith in God through every trial, and compassion for the oppressed.

While these and other letters slowly crossed the Atlantic, British sales of *Uncle Tom's Cabin* soared. Almost overnight, "eighteen different London publishers" were selling forty editions of various price and quality.[59] *Uncle Tom's Cabin* was everywhere in Britain: it "peeps out from the apron, lies beneath the workman at his bench, and is found on every drawing room table," wrote one British reviewer. The book appealed to all classes. "In the palace, in the mansion, and the cottage, it has riveted attention. The sons of toil as well as the children of opulence have wept over its pages."[60] However, Stowe earned nothing from British sales, because she did not have a British publisher or a British copyright.

Like a crackling fire, *Uncle Tom's Cabin* leaped from the page to the stage: eleven English theaters produced it before the end of 1852, according to scholar Audrey Fisch. Stowe received no royalties from plays based on her book, nor could she control what happened to her plot and characters. Suddenly entrepreneurs were selling all manner of kitsch inspired by Stowe's story: porcelain figurines of Tom and Eva, songbooks, dolls, and games. Parents decorated nurseries with "wallpaper depicting Uncle Tom and Topsy in characteristic poses, or Eliza and Harry's famous escape."[61] These products were dubbed "Tomitudes" and reflected a popular craze called "Tom-mania," but Stowe herself earned nothing from them.

Great Britain was ripe for a huge bestseller. Literacy was on the rise, new printing methods made books affordable, and trains moved books quickly to be sold in bookstalls and shops. But what mattered most, in this case, was British anti-slavery sentiment. Stowe's timing was perfect, for "by the time Stowe's novel reached England, the British reading public had been reading about slavery regularly for several decades."[62] Tracts exposing the horrors of the slave trade were well known to British readers; so were slave narratives about life in captivity and daring escapes. Anti-slavery poetry, ballads, and hymns carried the message deeper into receptive hearts in a movement that "cut across lines of class, party and religion."[63] So it was that Stowe cast seeds on fertile ground.

The slave trade had been outlawed in the British Empire four years before Harriet Beecher was born. Harriet was a young mother in Cincinnati when Britain abolished slavery in its West Indian colonies. Then Great Britain worked, through diplomacy backed by the British Navy, to shut down the international slave trade. "By the 1850's, the only holdout that mattered was the United States," because only the U.S. Navy "could detain American ships."[64] The transatlantic slave trade was outlawed by the U.S. in 1807. But an illegal transatlantic slave trade operated out of New York and other northern ports, while the internal slave trade was legal and thriving in the South.

All of this mattered for Stowe's trip to England and how she was received there. From a British perspective, the fact that the United States still had slavery and a slave trade — legal and illegal — showed "British national superiority"[65] over the United States. To have an American author of British descent attacking slavery in the U.S. thrilled British readers. On her trip Stowe would have to steer around some anti-American currents flowing through the British anti-slavery movement. Fortunately, other American anti-slavery leaders had been to Britain before her and paved the way. But no one else had accomplished what Harriet achieved with *Uncle Tom's Cabin.* In Europe, she would be treated like an American idol.

Group portrait of Beecher family, 1859. Standing from left: Thomas, William, Edward, Charles, Henry. Seated from left: Isabella, Catharine, Lyman, Mary, Harriet. Not pictured: Harriet's brothers James (a missionary in China when photo was taken) and George (who died in 1843).   Schlesinger Library, Radcliffe Institute, Harvard University

Lane Seminary.

Lane Seminary in 1847
Ohio Historical Society

Woman and child on the auction block
New York Public Library

Ohio riverfront, Cincinnati, 1848. Runaway slaves crossed this river on their way north. Public Library of Cincinnati & Hamilton County

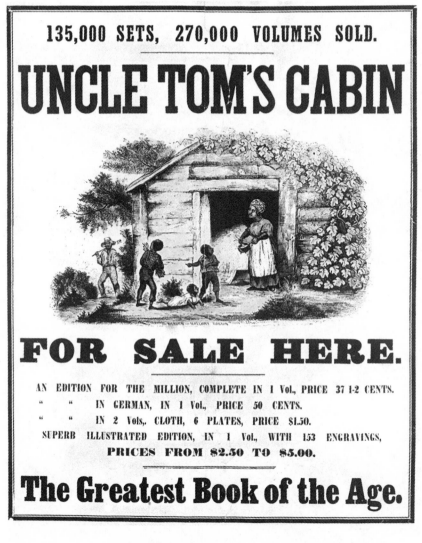

Advertisement for *Uncle Tom's Cabin*
Schlesinger Library, Radcliffe Institute, Harvard University

At Plymouth Church in Brooklyn, Henry Ward Beecher holds a mock auction to buy a slave's freedom.   New York Public Library

Prayer Meeting at Uncle Tom's Cabin. Illustration by George Cruikshank, from *Special Theatre Edition, Uncle Tom's Cabin* (New York: J. S. Ogilvie Publishing Company, n.d. [c. 1900])   Harriet Beecher Stowe Center, Hartford, Connecticut

**Harriet Beecher Stowe
and her brother
Henry Ward Beecher**
Schlesinger Library, Radcliffe
Institute, Harvard University

Calvin Stowe, 1850
George Eastman House

Stowe house in Hartford, 1870
Harriet Beecher Stowe Center, Hartford, Connecticut

The Stowes founded this church and school in Mandarin, Florida, shown here around 1872-1878. State Archives of Florida, *Florida Memory*

Stowe's home in Florida, lithograph c. 1882

State Archives of Florida, *Florida Memory*

Stowe in her front parlor in Hartford, 1886. Raphael's *Madonna* is on the wall behind her. Harriet Beecher Stowe Center, Hartford, Connecticut

CHAPTER TEN

Harriet Takes London

Before she wrote *Uncle Tom's Cabin,* Harriet Beecher Stowe could only dream of going to Europe. So when anti-slavery groups in Scotland offered to pay their travel expenses, the Stowes readily agreed. The official purpose of the trip was to strengthen ties between the American and British anti-slavery movements. Harriet would meet thousands of grateful readers and make some influential friends. She would also find a London publisher whose British copyright could protect sales of her future works abroad. And she would see cathedrals, art galleries, and historic sites. The trip would broaden her views and give new perspectives — at times disturbing ones — on her Calvinist heritage.

Harriet and Calvin Stowe sailed for Liverpool on April 1, 1853, on the *Canada,* a combination sail and steam ship. With them traveled Sarah Beecher (widow of Harriet's brother George), her twelve-year-old son, and her brother William.[1] A key member of the trip was Harriet's brother Charles, who kept track of train schedules, managed the engagement calendar, answered letters, and kept a diary which Harriet later used to write a book about the trip.

Once on the open sea, the *Canada* rolled "in the most graceful rises and pauses imaginable, like some voluptuous waltzer," Harriet recalled. The ship smelled of "the most mournful combination of grease, steam, onions, and dinners in general."[2] Passengers began to get seasick, and Harriet succumbed also. She tried to stay on deck where the fresh sea breeze could revive her, but sometimes she fled below to her berth to burrow like "an oyster in the mud." Later when seas and stomachs were calm, Harriet and company sat topside, behind the ship's red smoke stack, where they could shelter from the wind and watch for the occasional ship, porpoise, or whale spout to break the monotony.

Then the coast of Ireland appeared, low and green. Passengers got out their spyglasses and began to call out the names of places on the land. As the *Canada* approached St. George's Channel, Kinsale Point with its lighthouse came into view. Somewhere in these waters Catharine Beecher's fiancé had drowned in the wreck of the *Albion.* The tragedy had led Catharine to begin a school, setting a course for Harriet's young adulthood. It was a solemn thing for Harriet to see this place.

Soon the *Canada* passed northward between Ireland and Wales and entered the mouth of the Mersey River, where its passengers transferred to a steamboat that would take them to Liverpool. At the wharf a crowd was waiting to see the famous American author. Harriet and her traveling companions walked to their carriage, passing through "a long lane of people, bowing and looking very glad to see us."[3] People crowded around the carriage to catch a glimpse of Harriet. "What a pity they haven't something pretty to look at,"[4] Harriet told Calvin. After days of seasickness she felt like death warmed over. But the smiles of strangers boosted her spirits.[5] A rowdy boy pushed his way forward shouting, "I say I will see Mrs. Stowe!" The police removed him.

At their hotel in Liverpool, the Beecher-Stowe party delighted in fresh food and comfortable beds. Stowe's public duties began almost immediately, for two hundred ladies had gathered in Liverpool to greet her. They had collected funds for her use in the anti-slavery cause. Charles noted that his sister could look "demure" when "great folks get to saying fine things to her." He admired her "quiet simplicity" and saw "just a dash of fun and a tinge of puzzled feeling in her eye."[6]

Stowe was now famous, but she was silent before the crowds because women were not supposed to speak in public — except to address an all-female group. Even in the British anti-slavery slavery movement, only a few Quaker women dared speak to mixed groups. When Stowe visited England and Scotland, her husband spoke for her. Charles noted that London's House of Commons had a "nice little Oriental rookery (for doves, though) latticed off so that . . . ladies . . . could see and not be seen."[7] In other venues during their tour, Harriet was often seated in "a ladies gallery" off to one side, or in a balcony above.[8]

Scotland

The Beecher-Stowe party proceeded by train to Glasgow, where a huge anti-slavery convention was planned in their honor. When the Stowes entered the convention hall, a loud shout arose from two thousand people. As the visiting Americans made their way up to the gallery the crowd clapped and stomped and cheered. Looking down from the gallery, Charles saw multitudes waving white handkerchiefs like "*waves rising and the foam dashing up in spray.*" It seemed "as though the next moment they would rise bodily and fly up." Charles was proud of his sister: "Hatty is worthy of it all," he wrote, "through the grace of that Savior who lives in her and in whom she lives."[9] The anti-slavery meeting consisted mostly of speeches which went on for "seven mortal hours." Still, it was grand to sing the hymn "Old Hundred" in such a crowd. Firm in their "traditional Calvinist theology," the Scottish Presbyterians were stern opponents of slavery.[10] Here was Reformed theology, reformed society, and thunderous singing. The Stowes perhaps felt as if they had died and gone to heaven.

But Harriet was troubled by some things she saw in Scotland. While in Glasgow she visited the High Kirk of St. Mungo's — the only cathedral on the Scottish mainland to survive the Reformation somewhat intact. In Scotland the Reformation ignited an "iconoclastic crusade" which sought to destroy all art and ornamentation in the churches. Fortunately local tradesmen defended St. Mungo's and kept the iconoclasts out of the building, so the zealots attacked only the exterior of the church. They pulled down "idolatrous images of saints" from their niches and threw them into the brook. Now, three centuries later, harsh light glared through blank windows and Stowe yearned for "the many-colored, gorgeous mysticism of former times." Those old Scottish Calvinists were her theological kin, but now she felt cheated by their vandalism. Stowe commented that John Knox (who led the Scottish Reformation) was "very different from Luther, in that he had no conservative element in him, but warred equally against accessories and essentials."[11] Harriet's trip to Scotland showed her the destructive side of her own heritage.

If Stowe reckoned with the past on her trip, she also savored the present and looked to the future. During a carriage tour along the banks of the river Clyde, entire villages turned out to greet Harriet and her traveling companions. "The butcher came out of his stall, the baker from his shop, the miller, dusty with his flour, the blooming, comely young mother, with her baby in her arms, all smiling and bowing with that hearty, intelligent, friendly look, as if they knew we should be glad to see them," Stowe wrote. Just about everyone knew of *Uncle Tom's Cabin.* In the faces of these common people Stowe saw an affirmation of her hope that "a work of fiction so written to enlist the sympathies which are common to all classes" may do a great deal of good. Indeed fiction could become "a very great agency" for "doing good or evil."[12]

In Edinburgh the throngs were so vast that it was unsafe for Harriet and Calvin to walk out. The police had to cordon off the crowds and then part the multitudes so the Americans could get from the train station to their waiting carriage. There followed a whirl of social events, with the Edinburgh anti-slavery meeting as the highlight. After hours of speechmaking, a penny offering was taken to help the slaves. It came to some "1,000 sovereigns . . . or about $5,000," which was "presented on a massive silver salver."[13] The platter was Harriet's to keep, and the money was to be used to help the slaves.

From Edinburgh they went north, to Aberdeen and Dundee to attend anti-slavery events and socials. "At Aberdeen the railroad house was thronged," Charles wrote; "At Dundee the same. . . . At the church the multitudes filled the wide street as far as the eye could see. We drove in at the iron gates, and the police shut them behind us,"[14] to control the crowds.

Back in the United States, meanwhile, foes accused the Stowes of betraying America, by criticizing slavery abroad. A false report claimed that "the American flag was insulted, torn and mutilated"[15] at the Edinburgh anti-slavery meeting. But the Stowes believed that *slavery* was bad for America, and that the patriotic thing to do was to end slavery. Fortunately both Calvin Stowe and Charles Beecher were used to public speaking and could address the large anti-slavery meetings. Calvin denounced slavery as "a blight, a canker, a poison, in the very heart of our republic." Unless the nation could rid itself of slavery, "it will most assuredly be our ruin."[16] The Stowes could sense currents of anti-American feeling flowing through British anti-slavery zeal. It would take some finesse to navigate here.

Temperance meetings were easier, since they were less politically charged. Local temperance groups were constantly inviting Calvin and Charles to speak, and they obliged whenever possible. Charles wanted complete abstinence from alcohol, while Harriet and Calvin favored moderate use (temperance). "Wine, wine, wine," Charles complained to his diary. "I have seen more wine drunk in one week than for 10 years before. Even Stowe and Hatty and Sarah do not do as I wish they would. They take a little as *medicine.* They say they are sick and need it. . . . I mean to put a stop to it if I can."[17]

While Calvin and Charles addressed temperance meetings, Harriet and the others could sightsee in the Scottish countryside. They did not draw crowds if they went unannounced. Stowe was delighted to visit the grave of her literary hero, Sir Walter Scott, and tour his home. Unlike the plain-style homes of New England, Scott's Abbotsford House bristled with "gables, and pinnacles, and spires, and balconies, and buttresses."[18] Inside, the rooms were hung with fine paintings and rich draperies. Even the hallways and staircases were decked with stag's horns, crossed swords, and emblems of Scottish heraldry. What thrilled Harriet most was the library of Sir Walter Scott. Here were the very books Scott had loved, and the desk where he had written the novels she had read as a child.

Stowe and her companions also toured Melrose Abbey, immortalized in Scott's epic poem, "The Lay of the Last Minstrel." In medieval times Melrose Abbey had been the motherhouse of the Cistercian Order in Scotland. Now it lay in ruins. Reflecting on that place, Stowe wrote that "all the literature, art, and love of the beautiful, all the humanizing influences which held society together"[19] owed much to the monastic orders. She was gaining a greater appreciation for Catholicism.

The ruined monastery, with its graves and gargoyles, its saints and legends, stirred Stowe's imagination. She felt she must see Melrose Abbey by night:

If thou wouldst view Melrose aright,
go visit it by the pale moonlight . . .
when the distant Tweed is heard to rave
and the owlet to hoot o'er the dead man's grave.

Sir Walter Scott

Harriet and her fellow travelers went to their lodgings, but that night when the moon rose they returned to Melrose Abbey. They were not disappointed. They could hear the River Tweed "rave" in the darkness.

As the Americans gazed upon the ruins, two rooks burst into flight from beneath the crumbling arches, "rattling down some fragments of ruin as they went." Harriet said she "could not help fancying" that "these strange, goblin rooks were the spirits of old monks coming back to nestle and brood among their ancient cloisters!" Like a child on Halloween she dared the others to climb with her up the great abbey staircase to "get the full ghostliness" of the view from above. But as they mounted the crumbling steps a gust of mist and rain whooshed over them "like an army of spirits." Deliciously scared out of their wits, the party turned back and hastened to their rooms. All night long Harriet "dreamed of arches, and corbels, and gargoyles."[20]

One evening in Edinburgh, Charles, Harriet, and Sarah visited the Grayfriars Kirk. There, Scottish Presbyterians signed a National Covenant in 1638, in which they refused to conform to the Church of England. Some forty years later more than a thousand Covenanters were imprisoned in the churchyard of Grayfriars. Many died of starvation and exposure while awaiting trial. Standing at the memorial to these martyrs, Harriet felt deeply moved.

The Covenanters would rather die than accept the liturgy of the Church of England. Was that a cause worth dying for? Yes, Harriet thought, if the underlying issue was freedom. Her forebears need not be "right in all respects" in order for her to honor them. She admired them for sticking to principles "in a crisis."[21] The Covenanters believed in the freedom to worship according to conscience, and that the church should be free from government control. Stowe realized that modern trends (like broad-mindedness and the devaluation of theology) made modern people unable to see the heroism of these Calvinist martyrs. It was as though "a son, whom a mother had just borne from a burning dwelling," is embarrassed by his mother's "shrieks" and feels ashamed of "her disheveled hair and singed garments." We who enjoy freedom won for us by others, Stowe reflected, should at least respect those who died to win that freedom.

Harriet saw the heroism of the Scotch Calvinists, but she continued to see their excesses, too. In Aberdeen she visited a cathedral that had been richly decorated in medieval times. But reformers burned the wooden statues and defaced the granite ones. This cathedral once had a high altar of intricately carved wood, until a reform-minded minister ordered a carpenter to chop down the altar. When the carpenter hesitated, "the minister took the hatchet from his hand and gave the first blow." How pointless! People can make idols out of anything, even the hatchet that chops down the idols, Stowe said. Instead of aiming "an axe at the altar" the minister should have "aimed a sermon at the heart."[22] Harriet observed that "when human nature is denied beautiful idols, it will go after ugly ones." People are just as likely to elevate "coarse, bare, and disagreeable adjuncts of religion" as they are to venerate "beautiful and agreeable ones." Original sin is the human problem, and it remains after all the statues are torn down.

Visiting old churches and monasteries made Stowe aware of tensions within herself. On the one hand, she admired the courage of Calvinists who faced persecution. On the other hand, she deplored their iconoclasm, which destroyed so much beauty. Therefore she could "somewhat pardon" modern prejudice against them. She saw herself and her family and "all which is most precious to us" as "lineal descendents and heirs" of the Puritans[23] and their cousins the Scottish Presbyterians. At the same time, however, she felt drawn to the beauty and mystery of the medieval church. Could she somehow have it both ways?

After large meetings in the north of Scotland, Stowe and company passed through Edinburgh again. Some ladies visited Stowe and gave her a chalice carved from red agate and bearing 100 gold sovereigns for Harriet's own use. Charles marveled that in Calvin and Harriet's bathroom there was a furnace which could produce hot water for a bath any time of day or night. Oh, the wonders of the modern world!

On the day the Americans were to leave Scotland for England, they had to attend one more meeting with "about 300 ladies." After it was over, the carriage could hardly get through the crowd. When at last the Americans got to the train station, the doors were shut to keep the crowds at bay.[24]

England

Sarah Beecher, her son, and her brother proceeded on to London, but Harriet, Calvin, and Charles felt they must first visit Shakespeare's hometown. They arrived at Stratford upon Avon on a cold, rainy afternoon and checked into the White Lion, a tourist hotel with rooms named for Shakespeare's plays. Calvin and Harriet stayed in "Richard III." Charles wanted "All's Well That Ends Well" but had to settle for

"Hamlet."[25] That evening they visited Holy Trinity Church, where Shakespeare's remains are buried beneath a stone slab in the chancel. The Bard had chosen his own epitaph, and Harriet knew the words by heart:

> Good friend, for Jesu's sake forbear
> to dig the dust enclosed here.
> Blest be the man that spares these stones,
> and curst be he that moves my bones.

Harriet said she wished Shakespeare had chosen a more inspiring message. Still, gazing at the stone, she felt moved as though by "an emanation from the grave beneath." Later when they visited the house of Shakespeare's birth, she made the mistake of signing her name in the guestbook and, sure enough, curiosity seekers were soon following them on their Shakespeare pilgrimage.[26]

Harriet, Charles, and Calvin went on to Birmingham, where they stayed with Joseph Sturge, a Quaker pacifist and founder of the British and Foreign Anti-Slavery Society. Calvin went with Sturge to a Friends' meeting and heard Sybil Jones preach. The "lady preacher" told Calvin she had "a concern upon her mind" she would like to share personally with Harriet. A meeting was arranged, and there Jones warned Stowe not to let "flattery and applause" go to her head. Stowe should also beware of the "worldliness" of London. Indeed, Harriet was soon to enter the splendid palaces of London's elite.

After the trip, Stowe told readers about her meeting with Sybil Jones, and used the occasion to reflect more broadly on women as spiritual leaders. In every age of Christianity, she wrote, there have been women in religious vocations and even some in leadership roles. Indeed the Bible itself "always favors liberal development" and "countenances the idea" of women as religious leaders. But can such women retain their femininity? Stowe thought so. Quaker women like Sibyl Jones prove "that even public teaching, when performed under the influence of an overpowering devotional spirit, does not interfere with feminine propriety and modesty."[27]

Yet if Stowe thought women could ever be ministers, she didn't say so. She thought that "the number of women" with a genuine religious vocation "are comparatively few . . . they are exceptions." Yet she herself was an exception, for she wielded great influence as a writer.

Later in her life she would try speaking in public, but only when it was more socially acceptable.

Soon Harriet, Calvin, and Charles joined the rest of the group in London. Sarah Beecher informed them that they were all expected at the Lord Mayor's banquet, that very night! This annual gala honored England's judges and other luminaries, and there the Americans would meet London's elite. A carriage brought them to the Mayor's mansion, where the Americans passed through a large hall "supported by pillars" and "glittering with chandeliers." Harriet saw "servants with powdered heads and gold lave coats . . . hurrying to and fro in every direction, receiving company and announcing names."[28] Harriet "saw no big wigs" like the judges wore in court. The men wore black velvet and shirts ruffled with lace. All the ladies wore gowns with very full skirts; necks and shoulders were bared as required by fashion in high society.

At dinner, Harriet met Charles Dickens. He looked younger than she expected. A lifetime ago in Cincinnati, Stowe had written that Dickens lacked a sufficient moral compass. More recently, Dickens had reviewed *Uncle Tom's Cabin* and called it "noble but defective."[29] Now the two authors sat across the table from one another, with little chance to converse. Someone gave a toast to "Anglo-Saxon literature" and to the authors whose fiction awakened their countrymen "to the oppressed and suffering classes."[30] Many toasts was offered that night — to the annoyance of teetotaler Charles Beecher. At midnight the ladies went to the drawing room, where Stowe met Mrs. Dickens. She was "tall and [had] a fine, healthy color, and an air of frankness, cheerfulness and reliability," a fine specimen of English womanhood, Harriet noted approvingly.

As the Lord Mayor's dinner was breaking up, Harriet and Calvin were invited to go to the House of Commons, which was in session at that late hour. "With all my heart," Harriet replied. "If only I had another body to go into."[31] She and Calvin were not used to the late night hours of London, and so the whirl went on without them.

When reports of the Lord Mayor's dinner reached the States, the *Daily Dispatch*[32] of Richmond hissed that Stowe was a traitor abroad. "Mrs. Stowe has dined with . . . Mr. Charles Dickens" whose "atrocious slanders" displayed the "open hatred" both authors felt toward America. Harriet later wrote that the English accepted social criticism from their authors. "Mr. Dickens" exposed "all sorts of weak places in the

English fabric," yet no one attacked him "as the slanderer of his country." But the Americans "get into a passion" when their institutions are commented on.[33]

The high point of Stowe's stay in London — and perhaps of her entire trip — was a luncheon held in her honor at Stafford House. This was the London residence of the Duke and Duchess of Sutherland. It was so opulent that Queen Victoria, on visiting Stafford House, said to the Duchess, "I have come from my House to your Palace."[34]

Approaching the mansion, the Americans admired its grand marble columns. They entered through "vast halls with lofty ceilings" decorated with gold. They were escorted to a huge central room whose sweeping stairway dramatized the comings and goings of the rich and powerful. Every surface was adorned with paintings, statues, or immense gilded mirrors. Charles wrote in his diary that for the price of just one stick of furniture from this room, he could furnish his entire house! Still, he felt it was "appropriate that I should move in scenes as grand as these."[35] After all, he was a Beecher!

The queen was not present that day, but plenty of lords and ladies, dukes and duchesses were on hand. A bishop and even the archbishop of the Church of England attended, as did several members of Parliament and two future prime ministers (Palmerston and Gladstone). Quaker women were there, in honor of their work in the antislavery movement. The Friends' plain dark dresses must have looked stark in those opulent surroundings.

After a social hour the guests proceeded to a dining room, where they ate from plates of silver and spoons of gold. Then they ascended the grand stairs to the picture gallery, a huge, domed room where Stowe was given the seat of honor while the other guests formed a large circle around her. Speeches were made and dessert was served and then the company divided so that Harriet could speak to the women. The Duchess of Sutherland presented Harriet with a golden bracelet. Its links were shaped like slave shackles; some were engraved with the dates of slavery's ending in certain parts of the world and others were left blank, so that later on Stowe could engrave them with new dates commemorating the abolition of slavery in America. Then Stowe was presented with a copy of the "Affectionate Christian Address" that had been signed by half a million British women protesting slavery in America.[36]

On that day the Duchess of Sutherland was heard to say of Stowe, "what a good thing she is so simple."[37] Perhaps the Duchess meant "humble" or "unassuming." Harriet was not simple, but she may have been awestruck. Two days later, Stowe wrote to thank the Duchess for "a poetic dream" in a "fairy palace." When slavery ended in America, Stowe promised to have the date engraved on the gold bracelet. Perhaps Stowe remembered the Quaker preacher's warning, for she told the Duchess that "all a splendid world can offer is nothing compared to what He has laid up for those that love Him."[38]

While the Stowes were in London, many visitors sought Harriet out in her lodgings. Among them was Elizabeth Greenfield, a former slave and concert singer popularly known as "the Black Swan." Greenfield has been described as the best-known black concert artist of her time. In the U.S. she had to give separate concerts to blacks and whites, so she crossed the ocean to sing where there was no color barrier.

Greenfield sought Stowe out in London, to ask her help in finding concert venues. Greenfield sang Stephen Foster's "Old Folks at Home" while Charles accompanied her on the piano. Harriet and Charles were impressed by Greenfield's artistic expression. She had an amazing vocal range, but her lower voice had exquisite power and sweetness. Stowe was quite willing to use her own celebrity to help Greenfield.

A few days later the Duchesses of Sutherland and Argyle came to Stowe's lodgings to hear Greenfield. The Duchess of Sutherland was so impressed that she invited Greenfield to sing at the Stafford House — a high-profile London debut. Harriet no doubt enjoyed ordering a black silk concert dress for Greenfield to perform in.[39]

Two weeks later, Charles wrote that "the proudest and most brilliant of England's aristocracy" attended Greenfield's debut. The American vocalist was backed up by six professional singers. Sir George Smart (conductor of the Royal Philharmonic) accompanied the singers on a gilded grand piano placed on the landing of the grand staircase, which was banked with flowers. Greenfield performed brilliantly. Her voice was a "keen searching fire . . . so soft, so sweet, yet so regal, and cutting its way like a two-edged Damascus blade right to the heart."[40] After "rapturous encores" the "lords and ladies" spoke with Greenfield and shook her hand. This would not have happened in the States in those days — not even in the North, Stowe realized.

News of the concert at Stafford House crossed the Atlantic, with predictable results. The *Richmond Daily Dispatch* denounced "Stowe-ism and Black Swanism." Stowe did not act like a woman and Greenfield did not act like a Negro; they were freaks of nature, the editor sneered. But of course, the English had gone gaga over the midget Tom Thumb. How absurd for the Black Swan to ruffle "her ebony plumage" in a palace and be applauded by London's elite. It must be that the British, still smarting over the American Revolution, were just using Stowe and Greenfield to make Americans look ridiculous.[41]

Of course Greenfield's performance meant just the opposite to Stowe. Harriet grieved that "a race which might produce so much musical talent" was enslaved. If only Miss Greenfield could have had training "equal to her voice and ear no singer in any country could have surpassed her,"[42] Stowe thought. Apparently Queen Victoria felt the same way; Greenfield was later invited to sing for Her Royal Majesty at Buckingham Palace.

Stowe was a lover of music, but having grown up a Beecher, the form of public communication she knew best was the sermon. She knew what to listen for in preaching, and while in London she made sure to hear Rev. Baptist Noel. Noel was born to an elite family and had been an Anglican priest, but his evangelical faith had led him to seek baptism by immersion and to become a Baptist minister.[43] To leave the Church of England and become a "dissenter" meant a steep decline in status. Yet on hearing this "elegant and cultivated man" preaching in a bare chapel, Stowe felt "an emotion of reverence."[44]

Harriet said that she grew up "on the very battlefield of controversial theology" and was used to doctrinal disputes. Religious ideas were "guarded by definitions and thoroughly hammered on a logical anvil" in the pulpit. Preaching was used to trounce rivals, persuade skeptics, and save sinners. But Rev. Noel did none of those things. Instead he appealed to the essential goodness of human beings. He seemed to assume that everyone agreed with him, and needed only friendly persuasion to do right. What would "an American theological professor . . . think of such a sermon,"[45] Harriet wondered. Why, in just one sermon Noel covered the Christian virtues "faith, hope and charity." Whereas back home, Stowe teased, "we should have six sermons" on each of the virtues, "the nature of faith to begin with: on speculative faith, saving faith, practical faith, and the faith of miracles; then we should have the laws of faith, and the connection of faith with evidence, and the nature of evidence, and the different kinds of evidence, and so on." Everything was analyzed to death. Still, she saw

Calvinist preaching as "one of the strongest educational forces that forms the mind of our country."[46]

Fame and Infamy

Stowe was taken aback by the images of herself that she saw on display in bookshops and anti-slavery rallies. It looked to her as if "the Sphinx in the London Museum might have sat" for these pictures. No wonder that when people met her in person, they were relieved that she was not as bad-looking as her pictures. Stowe admired the people for "keeping up such a warm heart for such a Gorgon." Perhaps she should collect some of those ugly pictures to bring home. "There is a great variety of them, and they will be useful, like the Irishman's guideboard, which showed where the road did not go."[47] Stowe never claimed to be a beauty, but she sat for several artists, hoping for a result less "melancholy" than the ones she'd seen so far.

Meanwhile the British anti-slavery movement already had an icon. It originated long before Stowe was born, with a Quaker group. The image spread to America, and wherever anti-slavery groups gathered, it was displayed on banners and badges, ribbons and pins and placards. It showed a strong African man kneeling and lifting chained hands in supplication. Beneath the image ran the words, "Am I not a man and a brother?"

This was the personal seal of Thomas Clarkson, a pioneer in the crusade against slavery in the British Empire. Clarkson was no longer living when Stowe came to England, but she felt a bond with this evangelical Christian who fought slavery with his pen. Clarkson took on the nasty business of exposing the slave trade. In British ports he boarded slave ships where he saw — and smelled — the dark, airless holds where captive Africans had been packed like sardines. In Liverpool shop windows Clarkson saw the tools of the slave trade: branding irons, chains, handcuffs, and thumbscrews — even "instruments to open the mouth"[48] for force-feeding. Clarkson went to taverns and pubs to interview sailors and captains about life on board the slave ships. This was dangerous business; in 1787 he was nearly killed by sailors paid to assassinate him.[49] But he published his findings and shocked the nation. Thus did Clarkson work alongside William Wilberforce to abolish the slave trade in the British Empire.

Harriet and Charles therefore made a pilgrimage to Clarkson's home in Suffolk. "Playford Hall" was a medieval house, protected by high stone walls and a moat and drawbridge. But Clarkson's battle was against "principalities and powers, and the rulers of darkness of this world," Harriet wrote, quoting Ephesians 6:12. "As his great Master did before him," Clarkson prevailed "by faith, and prayer, and labor."

Clarkson was born to privilege and wealth, but slavery's fiercest foes also included plain folk or Quakers. Stowe wanted to mingle with them, so she attended a meeting of Quaker women in London. These women had resolved to boycott slave-grown cotton and sugar and to buy only goods made by free labor. Stowe described their "placid, amiable faces" in "plain Quaker bonnets." Perhaps she meant to offset the notion that female activists were ugly hags (or Gorgons, like the pictures she had seen of herself). So Stowe told her readers that "either a large number of very pretty women wear the Quaker dress, or it is quite becoming in its effect."[50] Stowe was trying to say that social activism does not "unsex" women at all. Stowe deeply admired the Quakers, as her flattering portrait of the Hallidays in *Uncle Tom's Cabin* showed. Quakers denied themselves many worldly pleasures; they did not attend the theater or go to a concert hall except to hear lectures on social reform.

Harriet, however, would much enjoy a concert of classical music. So Charles took his sister to Exeter Hall to hear the London Sacred Harmonic Society perform Haydn's oratorio *The Creation*. It was the first time Charles and Harriet had ever attended a concert of this scale — some 800 musicians in all. Before the performance, the conductor went up to the gallery where Harriet and Charles were seated and gave her a large copy of the musical score. The performance thrilled her: "I was never more animated," she wrote later.[51]

Stowe's published memoir omitted the scary part of the evening, but Charles's diary included it. When the concert ended, "a fearful crowd" began shouting "Mrs. Stowe, Mrs. Stowe." Amid the clapping and stomping, Charles also heard hissing. He thought some "southern heroes" (pro-slavery Americans) were in the hall, though Harriet had English enemies too. Something felt menacing. Exeter Hall could seat about three thousand, and so great was the crush of people that Charles and Harriet could not get through. Then "a police officer took charge of us," Charles recalled, "or I don't know what we should have done." Charles "saw too plainly in that deep popular excitement" that the "fires of the demonic" could be present and might easily "be roused by some spark of rage."[52]

Indeed a spark of rage landed — figuratively speaking — on Harriet's dress. It was a brown silk dress, newly made up from fabric Stowe brought along from the States. Wanting a fresh gown, she gave her measurements and the fabric to a seamstress in London. Then the London *Times* printed a letter accusing Stowe of exploiting a poor seamstress who toiled day and night for starvation wages.[53] Stowe (the article sneered) demanded justice for black slaves but ignored her poor white sisters, who were much worse off than black slaves in the South. At least Stowe was in good company, for British anti-slavery advocates were often accused of "neglecting the 'more important' claims of white Englishmen and women at home while hypocritically focusing on the condition of black slaves" in America.[54]

Deftly, Stowe brushed off the spark. She wrote to the *Times:* since that noble paper was already taking up the cause of British needlewoman, there was no need for her to do so. Now if only female cotton pickers could get their complaints published in London, Stowe said, she wouldn't have to write on *their* behalf, either. Stowe later warned "all philanthropists who may happen to want clothes when they are in London" to beware of attacks upon their character.[55]

Back in the States, Stowe's enemies continued to attack her. An unnamed writer for the *United States Review*[56] imagined Stowe riding into London in a splendid coach drawn by thirty-six horses. In her carriage rode Frederick Douglass and the Earl of Carlisle, dressed up to look like Uncle Tom. Stowe ignored Douglass and fawned over the Earl. Meanwhile the Ladies of Stafford House followed the carriage, "their faces covered with black crepe, and their horses crowned with black nodding plumes, emblematic of mourning for the wrongs of Africa." Next in the parade marched an army of coal miners covered with black dust. Overseers lashed the miners with whips, but since the miners were white Stowe ignored them. Then came the street prostitutes, at whom Stowe took offense. Passing in review were the "spinsters, knitters, and seamstresses . . . wretched, ragged and dirty." Frederick Douglass told Mrs. Stowe he never saw slaves this bad off in the States, to which Stowe replied, "Lord . . . who cares for their misery? Don't you see they are white people?" The parade continued with crippled children and throngs of starving Irish evicted from their homes, but Stowe ignored them because they were white.

These attacks were savage, but Stowe had her defenders, too. One was the popular writer Fanny Fern (a.k.a. Sarah Willis, the notorious pie thief of Hartford days). Fern made fun of Stowe's critics. In mock indignation Fern asked why "lords and ladies, and dukes and duchesses [are] paying homage" to Stowe. After all, she's "nothing but a woman — an *American* woman! And a *Beecher* at that! It is perfectly insufferable — one genius in the family is enough." Fern said, "Mrs. Tom's Cabin had no business [neglecting] her babies and her darning-needle to immortalize her name." With mock earnestness, Fern declared that women's ambition should be confined to the home. How *dare* Stowe use her husband's "inkstand for such a *dark* purpose." Tut, tut, now Mrs. Stowe must bear all the abuse from nasty editorials on her "feminine shoulders. . . . Poor *unfortunate* Mrs. Tom Cabin! Ain't you to be pitied?"[57] Fanny Fern must have chortled as she wrote this. She for one enjoyed Stowe's success, and if some men could not handle a woman's fame, let them pout!

By the end of May 1853, the American travelers prepared to go their separate ways. Calvin had to get back to his job in Andover. Charles stayed with Harriet as her traveling companion. Sarah, William, and George Jr. went off to Italy. By now Harriet was exhausted and needed to rest up before moving on to Paris. But then Lord Shaftesbury (who had been one of her patrons on this trip) invited her on a special excursion, and she could not say no. Shaftesbury wanted Stowe to see some low-income housing in London, which had been his special project. Shaftesbury was a member of Parliament, an Anglican, and an evangelical dubbed "the People's Earl"[58] because of his active compassion for the poor.

So Shaftesbury and Stowe went by carriage to visit several new housing projects for the poor. Stowe was impressed by what she saw: clean water for everyone, a modicum of privacy, and heat in winter — even a newfangled contraption for washing clothes!

Stowe saw Shaftesbury's work as one aspect of British humanitarianism. Reformers were working to improve prisons, educate the poor, put an end to drunkenness, and prevent cruel sports — and above all to end slavery. "All the modern popular movements in England," Stowe wrote, were founded on one principle: "the equal value of every human soul."[59] And all were part of "a gradual advance in religion" leading to one "pure beautiful, invisible church." A "superior spirit" was removing prejudice and seeking "conciliation and harmony."[60]

It pleased Stowe that the temperance movement brought Christians together across denominational lines. On her trip she had more invitations to women's temperance meetings than she could accept. Calvin and Charles spoke at several temperance meetings, including one in Glasgow that drew a crowd of four thousand.[61]

But the temperance movement was fighting an uphill battle. Stowe saw gin shops everywhere in London. She saw mothers carry their babies inside to buy "what turns the mother's milk to poison." She saw fathers taking money their children needed for bread and exchanging it for spirits. She saw children emerge from these shops with bottles in hand (there were no age limits for the sale of alcohol). Later Stowe said that in Paris, at least drinking was made to seem sophisticated. But in London's "gin shops men bite at the bare, barbed hook. There are no garlands, no dancing, no music, no theatricals, no pretence of social exhilaration, nothing but hogsheads of spirits, and people going in to drink."[62] Stowe could enjoy a glass of wine, but she found London's liquor-soaked poverty appalling.

Stowe's stay in London was almost over, and it was time to pack her things. Harriet's room looked like a tornado had passed through. "Books, pamphlets, dresses, letters, pictures, cameos, bracelets, brooches, combs, presents, notes, boxes, trunks, carpetbags, chambermaids," Charles wrote, all "revolved in a kind of vortex during the day, a kind of general maelstrom of goods and chattels, the center of which was Hatty's room, the vortex and outer suction, all London. Amen." On the night before their departure Harriet managed to cram everything into one trunk and one carpetbag.[63] Tomorrow she and Charles would be Americans in Paris.

CHAPTER ELEVEN

A Reformer's Pilgrimage

Early in the morning of June 4, 1853, Harriet and Charles crossed the English Channel by steamboat and took a train to Paris. For almost three weeks they stayed with an American friend who owned a fine home in the city. "Now I am released from care," Harriet wrote. "I am unknown, unknowing."[1] With the anti-slavery meetings behind her, she could have her own pilgrimage — paying homage to art, nature, and the Protestant reformers.

The next day was Sunday. Harriet and Charles attended Mass at the Madeleine, a Catholic church built in the style of a Greek temple. It was the first Catholic service Harriet had ever attended. "The strangest part of the performance" was the incense, when at certain points in the liturgy four men swung censers "with rhythmic sweep, and glitter, and vapor wreath." Charles and Harriet "felt a kind of Puritan tremor of conscience at witnessing such a theatrical pageant on the Sabbath." But while walking back to their lodgings, they saw people buying and selling, drinking and dancing, just as they did on any other day of the week. "There is no Sabbath in Paris, according to our ideas of the day,"[2] Harriet and Charles agreed.

A week or two later Stowe attended Mass at St. Germain l'Auxerrois. She felt "compassion towards these multitudes, who seemed so very earnest and solemn." The prayer books contained "much that is excellent if it were not mixed with so much that is idolatrous."[3] Here was a daughter of Lyman Beecher attending Catholic Mass; she found herself both drawn to Rome and repelled by it.

Harriet and Charles strolled along the Tuileries. They saw the Arc de Triomph and toured Notre Dame Cathedral and Versailles. A blessed anonymity allowed Harriet to buy gifts for family and friends or sit at a sidewalk café and watch the world go by.

Of all the wonders of Paris, Harriet and Charles felt nothing could compare to the Louvre — arguably the greatest art gallery in the world. While in London they visited the National Gallery, but Harriet found little to inspire her — mostly because (as she admitted later) she was too exhausted. But now the "time for examining art had really come." Harriet described herself as one who spent her previous life "in vain imaginings of what art might be." Entering the Louvre she felt "a thrill almost of awe" and vowed to answer fully the questions, "What is art? And what can it do?"[4]

Stowe did not believe in art for art's sake. Rather, she felt that art should "inspire a generous ardor, or solemn religious trust."[5] At first she wandered among the galleries searching for "any picture there great and glorious enough to seize and control my whole being," but she "looked in vain." Only when she stopped looking for "heroism, faith, love or immortality" did she begin to "enjoy very heartily" what she saw. Rembrandt reminded her of Hawthorne, the American author whose lights and shadows revealed character. Raphael had perfect technique but lacked passion, Stowe thought. Rubens was just the opposite: he "defied me to dislike him and dragged me at his chariot wheels; in spite of my protests forcing me to confess that there was no other but he."[6]

Stowe took special note of how artists portrayed women. The classical statue Venus de Milo was "missing both arms," but seemed to Harriet "a union of loveliness with intellectual and moral strength, beyond anything I have ever seen." She thought of Milton's Eve as a "glorious picture of unfallen, perfect womanhood." She was not impressed with Van Eyck's women that "resembled potato sprouts grown in a cellar." Then there was Rubens, who "made all his women seem bursting their bodices with fullness . . . Venuses with arms fit to wield the hammer of Vulcan." One of the most popular paintings was Murillo's Assumption; it showed "the Virgin . . . rising in a flood of amber light, surrounded by clouds . . . looking upward with clasped hands . . . a crescent moon beneath her feet." She decided Murillo lacked "earnestness of religious feeling."[7] Let others swoon over it; Harriet was unmoved.

Stowe yearned for art with "the emotions of GOD in it." Stowe felt that raw power in Gericault's *Raft of the Medusa* in which shipwrecked people, both living and dead, rode a raft on high seas. There Harriet saw the "suffering which underlies our whole existence in the world. To me it was a picture too mighty and too painful — whose power I confessed, but which I did not like to contemplate."[8]

After their first visit to the Louvre, Charles thought his sister "looked like one intoxicated." He asked, "Well, Hatty, have you drunk deep enough this time?" "Yes," she replied, "I have been *satisfied* for the first time."[9] They would return.

Harriet and Charles also visited the studio of Monsieur Belloc, head of the National School of Design. His wife had translated *Uncle Tom's Cabin* into French. In his studio, Belloc drew Stowe's portrait in charcoal and chalk. He posed her to have "the air of an observer."[10] As Stowe sat for her portrait, the talk turned to religion and art. "The arts that grow up out of Christianity are all tinged with sorrow," Belloc said. Stowe agreed. Christianity has enlarged the human heart, she said, and dignified our nature and deepened our capacity for sorrow. Yes, agreed Belloc, but that was no excuse for those horrid paintings of dying saints. Stowe said she had no liking for such gruesome themes, for she saw religion as "a principle of love to God that beautifies and exalts common life, and fills it with joy."[11] She felt art should show that love.

Harriet Beecher Stowe grew up a Protestant for whom faith comes by hearing. But visiting the churches and art galleries of Europe opened her eyes to the visual arts and their power to inspire religious feeling. She came to love pictures of the Virgin Mary, a subject neglected by most Protestants. Later she would decorate her home with "at least four portraits of the Madonna by the Catholic Italian Renaissance painter Raphael Sanzio." The theme of motherhood attracted Stowe to Mary, but Stowe also saw in Mary that "touch of divinity and power far beyond the limits American Protestant theology set for her."[12]

Apocalyptic Splendor

Harriet and Charles left Paris and headed for Switzerland. They took the train to Chalon-Sur-Saone and then boarded a crowded steamer to Lyons. At the landing, passenger trunks were hoisted up from the hold by rope, and loaded onto the backs of porters who carried "enough to kill a horse," Charles said. There were no claim checks, but much shouting. While trying to grab Harriet's trunk, Charles tore his trousers.

That evening, brother and sister visited the cathedral in Lyons. Twilight softened the great arches and columns. In the candlelight, "the kneeling crowds, the bells chiming vespers" all realized Harriet's "dreams of romance more perfectly than ever before," Charles told his diary. The jangle of the sexton's keys — a "signal to be gone" — broke the spell. The candles were extinguished and all the shadowy figures in the church "flitted forth" as from some enchanted cave.[13] The next day Harriet felt too ill to travel, so they rested in Lyons and Harriet tried some landscape painting with the oils she'd brought along.

When Harriet recovered, she and Charles went by stagecoach to Geneva. Even fewer people recognized them here than in Paris. They went boating on Lake Geneva and took carriage rides in and around the city, always trying to catch a glimpse of Mt. Blanc which, though forty miles distant, could be seen from Geneva on a clear day. Mist and clouds veiled the mountain for several days. Then one day during a carriage ride Harriet "sprang up suddenly as if she had lost her senses, her cheeks flushed and her eye flashing." She startled Charles half out of his wits. "There," Harriet pointed, "There he is! There's Mount Blanc." The view was partly blocked by another mountain, with Blanc glimmering beyond it. "Pooh," said Charles, "no such thing." And then he too saw and believed, like Thomas after Easter.[14]

Only sublime language could express Harriet and Charles's delight when they finally saw Mt. Blanc. In Paris they had marveled over works of art in the Louvre, but now they stood before God's own creation. Seeing the mountain was indeed a religious experience for them. They said it was like transfiguration; the glory so long hidden was now revealed. It was as though they could see God's presence shining from the mountain. Brother and sister spoke of "apocalyptic splendor," a "door opened to heaven" where "light is not of the sun nor of the moon but of the Lord God and the Lamb."[15] Lyman Beecher's children imagined "the great white throne" of John's vision. What else could they do but glorify God and enjoy him forever?

Back at the hotel they were joined by Sarah, William, and George, who had been traveling in Italy. Now the five Americans would begin their Alpine tour. They took horse and buggy to Chamonix, a village at the foot of Mt. Blanc, where they spent several days exploring the valleys, glaciers, and slopes. Hired guides showed them the best views and got them safely to various lodgings along the way. The travelers were especially thrilled by the glaciers, and Harriet liked to clamber off the beaten path to get a better view. It made their guide nervous to see Stowe "bounding through bushes, leaping and springing and climbing over rocks at such a rate." The guide seemed to think a lady "was something that must necessarily break in two, or come apart, like a German doll," Stowe recalled.[16]

In her memoir of this trip, Stowe used the glaciers as a moral object lesson. She told readers that slavery was like a glacier — a cold, cruel thing that seemed to last forever. But it must yield to the warming "presence of Jesus, whose power, so still, yet so resistless, is now being felt through all the earth." The ice of human bondage will melt away. The sun will "turn the ice of long winters into rivers of life for the new heaven and the new earth."[17]

Stowe could interpret what she saw through the language of faith. "I rejoice every hour that I am among these scenes . . . with the language of the Bible," she wrote. "In it alone can I find vocabulary and images to express what this world of wonders excites."[18] In the shadow of Mt. Blanc's raw cliffs the sunset transformed the ice fields to hues of warmest rose. She knew that some might experience only "cold, distant, unfeeling fate," or "crushing . . . power and wisdom." For Stowe, nature was the work of God:

> I beheld . . . crowned and glorified, one who had loved with our loves, suffered with our sufferings. Those shining snows were as his garments on the Mount of Transfiguration, and that serene and ineffable atmosphere of tenderness and beauty, which seemed to change these dreary deserts into worlds of heavenly light, was to me an image of the light shed by his eternal love on the sins and sorrows of time, and the dread abyss of eternity.[19]

Stowe did look over the abyss — from the back of a mule. Led by their guides, the Americans rode mules up the steep mountain trails. The mules decided when, where, and for how long their riders could gaze down the mountainside. The ornery beasts would stop at random "on the verge of some tremendous precipice, or [going] up a rocky stairway." The guide said it was all perfectly safe: nobody had gotten killed. But the travelers knew that "if a saddle should turn, or the girths break, or a bit of the crumbling edge cave away . . . all would be over with you." Harriet told herself she was in no worse danger than "in many cases where we think ourselves most secure,"[20] a thought not exactly comforting.

One day they were descending a steep road with sharp curves and sheer drops. Harriet, Sarah, and George were in a small, mule-drawn "char," or carriage, while Charles and William rode their mules on ahead. Hearing a crash and a cry, the men rode back up the trail. They saw the char, overturned by the edge of the precipice. The three passengers emerged from the wreck unharmed but shaken. Charles blamed the guide, who just before the descent had beaten and twitched the mule (twitching meant twisting a rope or chain around the mule's upper lip to force it into submission). Twitching the mules only made them skittish, and the Americans knew they had had a narrow escape that day.

Amidst the Alpine splendor Stowe saw mountain people living in poverty. Some were deformed by the goiter, a swelling of the thyroid caused by iodine deficiency. Poor children traipsed after tourists, selling strawberries and goat's milk or simply begging for coins. Even the adults were begging in some places. The locals depended on tourists to buy handmade souvenirs: wood carvings, walking sticks, skins of chamois and polished rocks. Charles and Harriet noticed how every scenic overlook had shacks where trinkets were sold. Thus "instead of falling into rapture at the sight of Mt. Blanc," wrote Stowe, "the regular routine of a Yankee is to begin a bargain for a walking stick or a snuffbox."

One very steep climb led to a spectacular view of Mt. Blanc girded by glaciers and laced by river valleys. But Harriet only felt let down. Then she realized that *getting* to the overlook brought her more joy than *being* there. "It is the greatest proof to me of the infinite nature of our minds, that we almost instantly undervalue what we have thoroughly attained." It was a good thing that the Scriptures only occasionally part the clouds and give us "flashes and gleams of something supernatural" but never fully unveil the glory of God.[21]

Having glimpsed the glories of Mt. Blanc, the travelers returned to Geneva for a few days. While there, Harriet and company visited the place where Servetus was burned at the stake in 1553. Servetus denied the Trinity and spurned infant baptism; he was therefore condemned as a heretic by Catholics and Protestants alike. Servetus seemed to court his own martyrdom, for although he was banished from Geneva and warned never to come back, he returned and made himself visible by attending Calvin's church! Historians have debated to what extent Calvin can be blamed for Servetus's death, but fairly or not, the execution of Servetus became a stain upon Calvin's legacy.

The place of execution was a green meadow when Stowe was there. She reflected deeply in that place. Many died for their beliefs during the Reformation, she knew. She felt that such violence was a blot upon Christianity. "Calvin's burning of Servetus" made Stowe think of the witch trials in New England, which were often used to discredit the Puritans.

Stowe deplored the burning of Servetus and the Salem witch trials. To her these things were tragic aberrations, not the essence of Calvinism. At that point in her life, she still strongly identified with Calvinism: "the great fundamental facts of nature are Calvinistic," Stowe said, especially the "predestination of a sovereign will . . . written over all things." Everything in nature and history moves according to God's will. Admittedly, some found this doctrine oppressive; but *she* found peace "in the thought of an overpowering will" which is "crowned with goodness."[22]

If Harriet visited John Calvin's church in Geneva (St. Peter's) she did not write about it — an odd omission, since the Geneva Reformer was a theological mentor of Puritanism. She did compare Calvin's role to that of Luther, however. "Luther was the poet of the reformation," she said, "and Calvin its philosopher. Luther fused the mass, Calvin crystallized [it]. He who fuses makes the most sensation in his day. He who crystallizes has a longer and wider power."[23] Stowe felt that Luther had ignited the Reformation, while Calvin had given it structure and system.

This Protestant Mecca

Stowe and her party traveled to Lucerne and then on to Germany to continue the Protestant pilgrimage. In Frankfurt she saw a painting that deeply affected her by Karl Friedrich Lessing, a nineteenth-century artist known for stark realism. The painting depicted the trial of Jan Huss, who was burned at the stake in 1415 after the Council of

Constance condemned his reforms of the church. Lessing painted Huss standing alone in a plain dark robe, holding an open Bible in one hand, with the other hand placed upon his heart. His face shows the "pallor" of "prison and suffering." His accusers are seated at their ease: cardinals in scarlet robes and hats, bishops resplendent in their miters — all symbols of the authority Huss offended. Stowe could imagine Huss's anguish as he asked himself, "Can it be that all the religion and respectability of the world is wrong, and I alone right?" A century later that question would torment Martin Luther, the "Saxon Huss."

Can an entire religious community be wrong? Stowe wrestled with this in her own time, when so many Christians either defended slavery or silently tolerated it, while those who fought slavery were labeled crackpots and fanatics — or, like Lovejoy, died as martyrs. In Frankfurt, as Harriet gazed upon the scene of Huss on trial, she "felt that [she] had seen an example of that true mission of art," namely, to teach us "to live and die for that which is noblest and truest." She felt that art "based on Protestant principles" could hasten the dawn of Christ's kingdom.[24]

Stowe was committed to Protestant principles, yet the art of the medieval church fascinated her. In Cologne Stowe visited the great cathedral with its high arches and noble pillars, its clouds of incense, kneeling priests, and mystical chants. The splendor made the churches back home look poor in comparison, for there "God's house [is] only a bare pen, in which a man sits to be instructed in his duties." And then she saw something deeply disturbing to her Protestant sensibilities. It was a coarse wooden shrine to the Virgin. From the shrine hung little wax figures of arms, hands, feet and legs. The little body parts betokened prayers for healing. Poor people knelt before this shrine, "praying with an earnestness" that Harriet and Charles felt "sorrowful to see" since Christ did not seem to be the object of those prayers.

The Americans proceeded on to the Basilica of St. Ursula. Ursula was a fifth-century saint whose 11,000 virgin followers were slain because they would not forsake their vows of chastity. A priest showed the Americans the relics of these virgin martyrs: bones strung on wires, skulls wearing satin caps. There was a great heap of jewelry, an ivory box full of teeth, the arrow that killed St. Ursula, a vessel containing the blood of St. Stephen, "two thorns from the crown of Christ, and a piece of the Virgin's petticoat." Charles could hardly hide his merriment. Like a naughty boy in church, he would echo the priest's words solemnly while nudging Harriet to make her burst out laughing. With difficulty she kept a straight face. Later Stowe wrote, "Here we saw, in one morning, the splendor and the rottenness of the Romish system." From the mystical chant there is "but a step down to the worship of dead men's bones and all uncleanness."[25] (Pope Paul VI suspended the cult of Ursula in 1969.)

Stowe and company passed through Berlin and on to Wittenberg, where Martin Luther ignited the Reformation in 1517. Harriet insisted on going there, though her travel companions had little interest. Charles Beecher was not impressed by Wittenberg. It was "a mean little town" where "all looks poor and low," he wrote. Luther's house (a former monastery) was shabby and dirty. And Luther's statue "stood in a filthy marketplace surrounded by dirty, stinking butchers' stalls and ugly, unwashed men and women." As for Cranach's famous portraits of Luther and Melanchthon, it gave Charles "the colic only to look at them." Yes, Luther was a titan in his own time, Charles admitted. But to him these historic sites were barren. "I am revolted," Charles said in tones like Emerson: "I turn shuddering from the place," for the altar where a great fire once burned held nothing but dust and ashes.[26]

For Harriet, however, those Reformation fires were still burning. With her novelist's imagination she could see life in the first Protestant parsonage, with Martin and Katie and their children, and she could almost hear the voices of Luther and his students and colleagues debating theology. She sensed the danger in his teaching, felt the heat of his inspired pen. But even Harriet had to admit that the Luther sites in Wittenberg were neglected and shabby, especially when compared to Shakespeare's home or the shrines of Catholic saints. What Stowe said of Wittenberg in the 1850s would still apply a century and more later: "This Protestant Mecca is left literally to the moles and the bats."[27]

Thankfully, Erfurt was in better shape. Here Stowe saw the monastery where Luther as a young monk despaired and clung to the gospel like a drowning man. Stowe imagined Luther

> buried beneath the whole weight of one of these gloomy cathedrals,
> suffocating in mortal agony, hearing above the tramp of footsteps,

the peal of organs, the triumphant surge of chants, and vainly trying to send up its cries under all this load. . . . [T]he whole pomp and
splendor of this gorgeous prison house was piled up on his breast,
and *his* struggles rent the prison for the world![28]

The last stop on the Luther tour was the Wartburg Castle at Eisenach,
where Luther translated the New Testament into German. Although
raised a Calvinist, Stowe revered Luther as the father of the Reformation and desired to walk in his footsteps. "If from the dust of the present we can recreate the past, and bring again the forms before us as
they then lived," it was worth all the effort of travel. Stowe's pilgrimage tested the patience of her fellow travelers, who were by this time
longing to go home. But Stowe felt as if she had seen "Luther,
Cranach, Melanchthon, and all the rest of them — to have talked with
them."[29]

Now the travelers turned west toward Paris. There a professional
packer was hired to help Stowe fit her dresses and bonnets, sculptures
and paintings all neatly into trunks. On the crossing to England, once
again the steamboat pitched and rolled in rough seas. Charles and
Harriet got seasick and arrived cold, wet, and miserable. Letters from
home awaited them: Calvin was lonely; one of their daughters was
sick; when was Harriet coming home? Stowe had planned a tour of
Ireland, but she canceled it.[30] Her last days in England held yet more
sightseeing and a few final events in her honor. On September 7,
1853, well-wishers lined the Mersey River to wave goodbye to Harriet
Beecher Stowe.

Home Again

Harriet had been abroad for four months. Returning to Andover she
found Calvin enjoying his work as a seminary professor, but their
older children were at an awkward phase of life. The twins Eliza and
Hattie were now seventeen years old. Thanks to their mother's success they could wear the latest fashions as they strolled around
Andover with their Italian greyhound, Giglio.[31] Henry was almost sixteen, a quiet boy studying for college and something of a mystery to
everyone. Thirteen-year-old Fred attended Phillips Andover Academy,
where he was greatly impressed by classmates who drank, smoked,

and swore prodigiously. Harriet worried more about Fred than any of the other children. Nine-year-old Georgiana attended Abbott Academy with her older sisters; she played the role of tomboy and got away with as much mischief as she could. Then there was an empty place: if Samuel Charles had lived, he would have been five years old. The caboose was little Charlie, three years old and needing constant supervision. As if their house were not full enough, the Stowes kept several dogs, one to suit every human temperament.

Harriet was glad to be back in the Stone Cabin at Andover, where she could indulge her passion for home decorating. She trained ivy to grow around the windows and kept flowers and potted plants everywhere. On the walls she hung paintings, some of her own creation and others newly acquired in Europe. She especially loved her copy of Raphael's *Sistine Madonna,* which "formed a deeper part of my consciousness than any I have yet seen."[32] To display an image of the Madonna was, to say the least, a departure from the piety of Harriet's youth. But another image of womanhood was the new portrait of Eliza Stowe, Calvin's first wife. The Stowes had found an artist who had known Eliza and could paint her likeness from memory. Every year on the anniversary of Eliza's death, Harriet and Calvin gazed at the portrait, remembering the woman whose passing brought them together.[33]

The Stone Cabin was an excellent place for Stowe to host soirees like those she'd attended in Europe. Andover faculty and their wives came for socials, musicians and singers performed in the largest parlor, and reformers gathered for meetings. Even at large events, guests could chat confidentially in the deep window seats, cushioned with pillows of velvet and satin. Neighbors dubbed the Stowe house "Uncle Tom's Cabin" — with tongue firmly in cheek, since the life there was not "life among the lowly."

Indeed, "Mrs. Stowe" was a curiosity to most folks in Andover. Never before had they seen her like. Not even Andover's learned professors were famous or well-connected to the "who's who" of Britain like Harriet Beecher Stowe. Andover was an academic town, which meant it was "a heavily masculine place." Seminary professors were "perplexed" by "a superior woman"[34] no matter how gracious and hospitable she might be.

Stowe was rumored to be a wealthy woman, thanks to her royalties and the money she received in Europe. Just how much money is unknown, but the Edinburgh offering alone was £1,000 (more than

$140,000 today). Multitudes of British readers gave to a penny offering for Stowe's own personal use, to offset the lack of royalties from British sales of *Uncle Tom's Cabin*. The penny offering totaled some $20,000,[35] a huge sum in those days. How did Stowe use this money? Critics said that Stowe had bought a mansion and was living in the lap of luxury — never mind that the Stowes were actually living in a house owned by Andover Seminary.

Stowe wrote to the committee who organized the English penny offering. She had never asked for the money to begin with, she explained; she had accepted it with the understanding that she was to be "subject to account to no one but God and my conscience." Besides, she found it "onerous" to keep accounts. She felt that the American anti-slavery movement was so divided that she could not give money to one faction without offending another one. Stowe's talent was writing, not administering funds.

To the Ladies' Anti-Slavery Society of Glasgow, Stowe wrote a letter in 1853 (published as a pamphlet to make it more widely available). There Stowe said she used the money from the Scottish National Penny Offering to purchase "one thousand copies of *Uncle Tom's Cabin* and *A Key*" for use of home missionaries. She also gave $1,000 to Miss Miner's School for African American girls in Washington, D.C. Stowe's British sponsors wrote back indicating that they were satisfied with her use of the money. "No one complained that only a third of the money had been accounted for," Stowe scholar Joan Hedrick observes; "philanthropy was a long way from being professionalized."[36]

Decades later, when compiling his mother's papers, Charles Stowe addressed the issue of how his mother used the funds from Europe. He said that she began disbursing them soon after she returned. She helped to purchase the freedom of several slaves and supported their transition to independence, and she gave money to schools for African Americans and to several anti-slavery publications, especially *Frederick Douglass' Paper.*[37] In addition she "arranged public meetings, and prepared many of the addresses" to be given at anti-slavery events. Charles Stowe may have wanted to clear up any lingering doubts about how his mother spent the money she received in Europe.[38]

Money for philanthropy was one asset Stowe brought home from Europe; another was fame. She returned from Europe an international celebrity. But how to use her fame in the American anti-slavery movement was a conundrum for Stowe. The movement was splintered into rival factions, each with its own goals, strategy, and leaders. Stowe hoped to be a unifying figure in the movement, so she never joined any particular group.

Mr. Garrison, Are You a Christian?

Stowe had crossed the Atlantic to attend anti-slavery meetings in Britain, but she would not go twenty-five miles to Boston to attend the twentieth anniversary celebration of the American Anti-Slavery Society (AASS). Its key leader was William Lloyd Garrison, editor of the *Liberator*. Stowe told Garrison that she had issues with his paper. She saw "certain tendencies of the *Liberator* and the AASS" as "erroneous, hurtful to liberty and the progress of humanity."[39] Stowe was troubled by Garrison's open contempt for "moderate clergymen and their nationally organized church denominations."[40] The "moderate clergymen" were people like Lyman Beecher who claimed to oppose slavery but did little or nothing about it.[41] Beecher's strategy was to lead from the middle and not get too far out ahead of public opinion. But Garrison's strategy was to lead from the edge and never compromise. The poet James Russell Lowell likened Garrison to Daniel Boone, who was so used to standing alone that when the world crept up to him, he went farther into the wilderness.[42]

William Lloyd Garrison launched the *Liberator* in 1831. In the first issue he thundered:

> I will be as harsh as truth, and as uncompromising as justice. On this subject [slavery] I do not wish to think, or to speak, or write, with moderation. No! No! Tell a man whose house is on fire to give a moderate alarm; tell him to moderately rescue his wife from the hands of the ravisher; tell the mother to gradually extricate her babe from the fire into which it has fallen; — but urge me not to use moderation in a cause like the present. I am in earnest — I will not equivocate — I will not excuse — I will not retreat a single inch — AND I WILL BE HEARD. The apathy of the people is enough to make every statue leap from its pedestal, and to hasten the resurrection of the dead.[43]

Jailed in Baltimore and mobbed in Boston, Garrison became one of the most hated men in America — all because he demanded abolition *and* full equality for African Americans and for women. He called on abolitionists to "secede from the government"[44] that supported slavery. He refused to vote, because political parties were corrupt. He condemned the Constitution as a "covenant with death and an agreement with hell"[45] because it protected slavery, so he celebrated the Fourth of July by burning a copy of the Constitution. He said he must raise the winds, not tinker with weather vanes.[46]

Garrison rejected organized Christianity as hopelessly corrupted by slavery. But Garrison was not an atheist. He was "spiritual and anti-institutional."[47] In the language of his time, he was "a religious come-outer." According to his biographer, Garrison "believed in redemptive love, in the power of the Christian community of souls, in the injunctions of prophets and apostles, and in the righteous power of God."[48] And like the Quakers, Garrison trusted the "inner light" instead of theology, clergy, or ceremony. He dismissed biblical authority as "absurd and pernicious" because people invoked it to defend slavery. Garrison gave the impression that abolitionists were *against* the Bible, while those who defended slavery were *for* the Bible. And defenders of slavery were quick to exploit that impression.[49]

Stowe would not endorse forms of abolition that undermined the authority of Scripture. "I am a constant reader of your paper, and an admirer of much that is in it," Stowe told Garrison. "I like its frankness, fearlessness, truthfulness, and independence. At the same time I regard with apprehension and sorrow much that is in it." She thought the *Liberator* would be fine if it "circulated only among intelligent, well-balanced minds, able to discriminate between good and evil." She personally valued the paper "as a fresh and able exposé of the ultra progressive element in our times." What then, was the issue? "What I fear is that you will take from poor Uncle Tom his Bible, and give him nothing in its place — you understand me — do you not?" Stowe told Garrison that many of his readers had "no means of investigating, no habits of reasoning." He should remember that "The Bible, as they [now] understand it, is doing them great good, and is a blessing to them and their families." But the tone of the *Liberator* was going to "lessen their respect and reverence for the Bible, without giving them anything in its place."[50]

Garrison wrote back, saying that he was not the least bit worried that radical abolition would take away Uncle Tom's Bible. Indeed, if the wicked Simon Legree "could not shake [Tom's] trust in his God and Savior, do you really think a full discussion of the merits of the Bible, pro and con, might induce" slaves to reject the Bible? Let individuals esteem the Bible as they may, said Garrison. But Scripture should be judged "in accordance with reason, truth, eternal right." He was quite willing to let people decide for themselves how much of the Bible is true. "For on Protestant ground, there is no room for papal infallibility."[51] As far as Garrison was concerned, bowing to an infallible Bible was no better than bowing to the pope in Rome.

Garrison had underestimated Stowe. She did revere the Bible, but not in the way he assumed. She did not require the Scripture to be infallible. No, the power of Scripture was the power to transform, to convert sinners and redeem relationships — to change society. Stowe believed that Jesus came to seek and save the lost; that God moves in history to bring in his Kingdom; that his Kingdom is progressive and liberating, despite the limitations even of Christians. Stowe stood her ground. She told Garrison that her "hopes of the liberties, not only of the slave, but of the whole human race" were based on the Scriptures.[52] No wonder it grieved her that persons "distinguished in the Anti-Slavery Cause should be rejecters of that Bible."

Garrison challenged Stowe. Because she was brought up believing in the "entire sanctity" of the Bible, she was "not free in spirit." What does "the cause of bleeding humanity" get from "all this veneration" of the Bible? Garrison said he got his inspiration from "the nature of man, the inherent wrongfulness of oppression, the power of truth, and the omnipotence of God."[53] Garrison could not trust Christians to interpret the Bible when it came to slavery, so he must rely upon his own conscience. Surely Stowe would not expect him to violate that, would she? Of course, Garrison did not mention that many slave holders also claimed to follow their own consciences, which by Garrison's own logic would cancel out the authority of conscience.

Stowe pushed back against Garrison's cheap shot that she was "not free in spirit." Indeed she *was* free to consider new ideas — and to reject, adapt, or adopt them as she saw fit. "Discussion of the evidence of the authenticity and inspiration of the Bible and of all theology will come more and more," she wrote, "and I rejoice that they will." She was even willing to read and consider the works of radical theologians such as Theodore Parker, the Unitarian who rejected the divinity of Jesus and the Bible.[54] Parker had a right to his views, but was she obligated to agree with him? Indeed not, for adopting Parker's views would mean for her only "death and utter despair." If she believed as Parker did "about the Bible and Jesus, I . . . could not love God. I could find no God to love. I would far rather never have been born."[55] Stowe was not about to give up on Jesus, nor to endorse the notion that to be anti-slavery one must abandon Christianity or take a scissors to the Bible.

As Calvin Stowe's wife and colleague, Harriet knew more about trends in theology and biblical studies than Garrison did. She knew there was a great gap between the theology of learned clergy and seminary professors and the faith of simple Christians. She knew that the "poor and lowly" lacked the conceptual tools to discuss the authority of Scripture. But Stowe's insider knowledge of academic theology was tempered by a deeper wisdom. She knew that intellectuals find sophisticated ways to deflect God's voice. In her fiction she often wrote scenes in which "the lowly" were closer to God than the professional religious figures. Common people found hope, dignity, and patience in Scripture. Stowe sensed that when black Christians (slave or free) heard the Bible, they heard it differently than the slaveholders — and differently than New Englanders like herself. They did not need William Lloyd Garrison to sanitize the Bible for them by choosing which texts were consistent with the anti-slavery movement.

Most churches and clergy failed to oppose slavery. On that much Stowe and Garrison agreed. But from it, they drew different conclusions. Garrison needed a pure fellowship or none at all. He chided Stowe for sitting "at the same communion table" with Christians who condoned slavery. "How marvelously inconsistent is your conduct," he scolded. But Stowe for her part would stick with the church. Not that she excused the sins of the church or of Christians when it came to slavery. In *A Key to Uncle Tom's Cabin* she confronted their moral failure in the harshest terms. And in a letter to a Glasgow anti-slavery society she lamented that the American churches were "greatly behind what they should be." She said that "the professed Christian church is pushed up to its duty by the world, rather than the world urged on by the church."[56] But Stowe was not giving up on the church. "*Our* field lies in the church as yet," she told Garrison later on. "I differ from you as to what *may* be done & hoped there."[57]

When she declined to attend the AASS meeting, Stowe invited

Garrison to her home, where the two of them could discuss their differences in private. So it was that in December 1853, Garrison came to the Stowes' house in Andover. Later, Stowe admitted being "dreadfully afraid"[58] to meet a man notorious for cutting his foes to pieces in print or on the lecture circuit. How relieved she was to find her guest instead mild-mannered and agreeable. With his high forehead, bald pate, and spectacles, he was said to have looked like a genial uncle, or perhaps a school teacher. Many who met him "commented upon the surprising contrast between the private Garrison and the public firebrand." Garrison once joked that people imagined him to be "a monster of huge and horrid proportions . . . but now finding me decently made, *without a single horn,* they take me cordially by the hand." People who knew Garrison's ferocity in print were surprised by his "ethereal mildness"[59] in person.

Garrison later wrote about his meeting with Stowe. She got right to the point: "Mr. Garrison, are you a Christian?" He replied that her question was "indefinite" (vague). "Well," Stowe pressed: "are you such a Christian as I am?" Garrison said this was even more indefinite. "Well, Mr. Garrison, do you believe in the atonement?" Stowe persisted. Garrison replied that he "did not believe that Jesus could be . . . good only for Himself. Jesus is the hope of glory and the redemptive spirit of love." That seems to have satisfied Stowe.[60] After these preliminaries, they probably discussed the anti-slavery movement, the Bible and slavery, and the role of the church in the slavery question.

On December 23, 1853, Garrison published some of their correspondence in an article in the *Liberator.* He did not use Stowe's name but referred to her as a "highly esteemed friend." They continued to write to each other and met in person several times.

Stowe wanted the anti-slavery movement to present a united front to the world, so it did not help that Garrison and Frederick Douglass were feuding in print. In the early days of the AASS the two men worked together, but some disagreements turned into "the nastiest factional quarrel the movement had ever known."[61] Stowe pleaded with them to reconcile for the sake of the movement. She chided Garrison: "You speak of him [Douglass] as an apostate. I cannot but regard this language as surprisingly severe." Why should Douglass be faulted for speaking ill of Garrison, who had also said cruel things about him? "Where is this work of excommunication to end?" she challenged. "Is there but one true anti-slavery church & all others infidels? Who shall declare which it is? I feel bound to remonstrate with this — for the same reason that I do with slavery — because I think it an injustice."[62]

There was room in the anti-slavery movement for both Garrison and Douglass and their differing strategies, Stowe felt. Douglass used to write for the *Liberator* and now had had his own paper. And Douglass (unlike Garrison) did not reject the U.S. Constitution or shun politics as a vehicle for reform. Douglass's views on these issues were developing, but what did it matter? Stowe hoped that one day the two men would "shake hands across a victorious field."[63] Stowe wondered how Garrison, who had accused *her* of narrowness, could harbor a grudge. Stowe wanted an ecumenical church and an anti-slavery movement in which people would accept their differences and work together for a common cause.

Stowe proposed to bring the various factions of the anti-slavery movement together for a lecture series in Boston in the winter of 1854. This event was to be "catholic . . . embracing such as are willing to take the ground that slavery is a sin and wrong." She meant to include many points of view from the anti-slavery movement, even a few "orthodox ministers" who had yet to state their views publicly.[64] "I am increasingly anxious," she told Garrison, "that all who hate slavery be united if not in form at least in fact — unity in difference."[65]

In Boston the abolitionists could discuss their differences, but to little effect. For out west, above the Kansas plains, an ominous cloud funneled. And in Washington City the atmosphere was charged — thanks to Illinois Senator Stephen A. Douglas, who would play with political lightning.

CHAPTER TWELVE

By Thy Wrath Are We Troubled

S tephen A. Douglas was a hard drinking, cigar smoking politician. The U.S. Senator from Illinois was also a slaveholder, having acquired by marriage a cotton plantation in Mississippi. Short of stature but politically powerful, Douglas lived up to his nickname, the "Little Giant." He used to say he did not care about slavery one way or another, as long as white men were free to do as they pleased. Douglas's cronies included railroad developers and land speculators who were panting to make a fortune developing the West. Their plans were stalled, however, while politicians argued about slavery in the West. So Douglas offered a solution: let each territory decide for itself whether to allow slavery. He called his strategy "popular sovereignty" and spelled out the details in the Kansas-Nebraska bill. If this bill passed, it would open up western territories for further development and hasten their statehood.

But there was a roadblock in the way of Douglas's scheme. The Missouri Compromise of 1820 drew a clear boundary north of which slavery could not go, and by its terms the Kansas-Nebraska territory was off-limits to slavery.[1] Northerners saw the Missouri Compromise as an almost sacred covenant that set a clear boundary for slavery. So Douglas's proposal to discard the Missouri Compromise in favor of popular sovereignty seemed, to many, like a massive betrayal. If Douglas got his way, slavery could go wherever white men voted it in. If the Kansas-Nebraska bill became law, what was to keep slavery out of the old northern states? There was fierce resistance in Congress, but Douglas was not called the "Little Giant" for nothing.

The Active Contemplative

While Congress debated the Kansas-Nebraska bill, activists rallied opposition. Harriet Beecher Stowe joined the fray with her "Appeal to the Women of Free States," which appeared in February 1854 in the *Independent,* a Congregational weekly. "I do not think there is a mother among us all," Stowe said, ". . . who could ever be made to feel it right that [her] child should be a slave. . . . I do not think there is a wife who would think it right her husband should be sold to a trader, and worked all his life without rights and without wages."[2] Women must take a stand!

Like many of her era, Stowe felt that women were naturally more religious than men since they were not corrupted by worldly pursuits. Men may be blinded by "ambition and the love of political power," Stowe wrote, but "God has given to woman a deeper knowledge" and "holier feelings . . . peculiar to womanhood." True, women had no direct political power. They were silenced, their efforts perplexed, their hands tied, Stowe said. Women were told to respect the political agreements made by men. But now the most sacred of those agreements — the Missouri Compromise — was being threatened. It was time for women to use their moral power to block the spread of slavery.

Stowe appealed to patriotism, too. Americans claim to be chosen by God "to advance the cause of liberty and religion," she wrote. But how does that claim look from a European perspective? Europeans look at America and they see slavery! Stowe told her readers that while she was in Europe she saw a "great struggle for human rights" unfolding. She saw Europeans pray fervently for America to banish slavery. How disgraceful it would be for the United States to open "all her free territories to the most unmitigated despotism." If America wanted the world's respect, Stowe said, it needed to live up to its claims to be a free, democratic country. Just as women helped the cause of freedom in the Revolutionary War, now they needed to join the cause of freedom by fighting the spread of slavery.

But how? Stowe made practical suggestions. First, women had to learn all they could about slavery *and* politics — and then educate the public. Women could make themselves heard by sending petitions to Congress. Above all, women needed to pray. "All who believe in an Almighty Guardian and Ruler of nations," Stowe wrote, must "betake themselves to his throne."[3]

Stowe wanted to get New England clergy of all denominations to sign a petition opposing the Kansas-Nebraska bill. Her scheme harked back to a time when New England clergy claimed moral leadership for the nation. Stowe must have known that clergy influence was waning; still, she would try to stir some up. She could not address clergy directly, so "Dr. Henry Martyn Dexter, the new editor of the *Congregationalist,* served as [Stowe's] public self." Dexter and other Boston clergy drew up the petition. Harriet's brother Edward spent weeks gathering signatures. Calvin Stowe helped as well, and even Lyman Beecher — now almost eighty years old — did his part. Harriet wrote privately to clergymen, urging them to sign and to get other clergy to sign.

The petition grew to be "two hundred feet long and [was] signed with 3,050 names, every one with a Reverend before it." Harriet wrote to Senator Charles Sumner of Massachusetts, predicting "an uprising of the country [such] as never has been heard of since the days of the Revolution." To William Lloyd Garrison she wrote, "We are trying to secure a universal arousing of the pulpit." Knowing Garrison's dim view of the church, she asked him to be willing to see that the church was better than he had thought. Garrison duly noted the clergy petition in the *Liberator* of April 7, 1854.

The clergy intended to present their petition to the Senate. Permission was denied, so Senator Charles Sumner received it privately. Sumner, an abolitionist, reminded the clergy delegates that in the days of the Revolution the pulpits had thundered against oppression; now "the time has come for them to thunder again."[4]

Pulpit thunder did not faze the Little Giant. He was going to get his way. As one historian wrote, Douglas cracked "the whip of party discipline" and cranked "the machinery of political patronage" in the Senate, while Alexander Stephens of Georgia (future Vice President of the Confederacy) did likewise in the House. The Kansas-Nebraska bill became law in May 1854. Now slavery could go wherever the people of a territory voted for it. Across the northern states, a howl of rage went up. Douglas later said "he could have traveled all the way home to Chicago by the light of his burning effigies,"[5] so great was the public fury. A new political party, the Republicans, arose to fight the extension of slavery in the territories. One of their leaders was a lawyer from Illinois and Douglas's political rival: Abraham Lincoln.

Stowe fought the Kansas-Nebraska scheme and tried to make

"popular sovereignty" unpopular. Alongside this protest, she also wrote a series of devotional articles on the inner life of a Christian. This series, called "Shadows on the Hebrew Mountains," was inspired by texts from the Psalms and prophets and perhaps by her travels in the Alps. In these articles, Stowe urged readers to seek "friendship and infinite union" with God, letting go of self to live in God. "The human soul is capable of this blest exchange" with God. Psalm 90 says to God, "by thy wrath are we troubled," according to our sins. But when we let God dwell within us, God's glory becomes the soul's glory, and God's "beauty, worth and excellence" the soul's very own. Although the soul "feels itself sinful" it rejoices that God "is spotless, true, and beautiful,"[6] Stowe said. Her hope was to "exchange the human for the divine" and find infinite rest in God.[7]

What did this have to do with the Kansas-Nebraska Act? Everything, for Harriet Beecher Stowe. For Stowe's spiritual writings, set alongside her activism, show her Christian life moving back and forth between prayer and action. She was both an activist and a contemplative, retreating from the world only to engage more deeply in it. In February 1854, the same month as her public "Appeal to Northern Women" appeared, one of Stowe's devotional articles called Psalm 90 "a sanctuary to retreat into."[8] But Psalm 90 ends by asking God to prosper the work of our hands. And that work, for Harriet, was her writing.

Stowe's writing did prosper. Her travel memoir, *Sunny Memories of Foreign Lands,* appeared in the summer of 1854. Armchair tourists loved it, and Americans abroad used it as a guidebook, following in Stowe's footsteps and reading her comments along the way. Europeans also bought *Sunny Memories,* which for a time was on sale at railway stations in Britain.[9] *Sunny Memories* was also a moral geography, showing the contours of religious and social reform. Finally, it had a political dimension. Contrary to those who accused Stowe of being unpatriotic for criticizing slavery while in Europe, Stowe believed that a true American patriot opposes slavery. *Sunny Memories* defended Stowe's "activities in England," writes William B. Allen, as "wholly consistent with" love of country and respectful of the freedom Americans may exercise abroad.[10]

Faith of Our Father

After her return from Europe, Stowe took on a literary project with the Beecher family. The paterfamilias, Lyman Beecher, wanted to write his memoirs. He was still strong in body, but his mind was fading and he would need help organizing his papers and writing his life story.

At this time Lyman lived with his third wife, Lydia, in Boston. He would come to Andover and stay with Harriet and Calvin in the Stone Cabin. During these visits, Harriet and other family members helped him with his memoirs. Charles Beecher was editor in chief, gathering and arranging the old man's "sermons, letters, and other manuscripts."[11] Harriet, Catharine, and other siblings would interview their father and take notes. When the old man's memory failed, his children prompted him. They also wrote their own recollections to include in the memoir, making the *Autobiography of Lyman Beecher* a family chronicle. "It is the peculiar merit of his children's record," wrote Barbara Cross, "that the mask of Christ's dauntless apostle does not conceal the homely, boisterous, passionate man."[12] In November 1854, the Stowes held a family reunion to celebrate their progress on Lyman Beecher's autobiography.

Stowe longed to have her father move to Andover so that she could see him more often. She knew he would enjoy being near a seminary campus where he could attend lectures and chapel services. She offered to have a house built for him and Lydia in Andover. Lyman wanted to accept, but Lydia said no. Lydia "never has loved or trusted us," Harriet later told Catharine; "she never wanted Father to live with us or near us and did all she could to divide us."[13] Lydia did not succeed in dividing the family, but it was not for want of trying.

Lydia gradually took control of Lyman's affairs. In 1856 she decided to move to Brooklyn, close to one of her daughters. Now at least Lyman would be living near his son Henry where he could attend worship at Plymouth Church and bask in his son's oratory. Harriet, Henry, and perhaps other siblings gave money to help support their aging father. They urged him to stop accepting monetary gifts from outside the family "because some persons" grumbled at making "contributions when Beecher had such famous children."[14]

Beecher's adult children loved him dearly, but they did not adhere to his brand of New England Calvinism. Catharine was the first to break ranks. She favored a moral religion based on free will, and declared that Pelagius, the early Christian heretic who championed free will and morals, suited her better than Augustine, the architect of western theology based on original sin and free grace. Edward was attracted to the early church father Origen and his theory of the pre-existence of souls. In 1853 Edward published *Conflict of the Ages* in which he attacked original sin and eternal punishment in favor of universalism, which held that all souls may reach heaven eventually.[15] "Edward, you've destroyed the Calvinistic barns," Lyman Beecher told his son, "but I hope you don't delude yourself that the animals are going into your little theological hencoop!"[16] The old man was right: Edward had very few followers.

Charles Beecher was one of those few. Charles found universalism much more appealing than salvation limited to God's elect. But Charles was uneasy; if Lyman's own children rejected his most basic doctrines, who would be left to carry on the old man's legacy? Charles found that compiling his father's papers was "one of the most solemn things I have attended to for a long time." Charles understood why his father preached no second chances in the afterlife. The unconverted go to hell, so there is great urgency to save souls in this life. No wonder old Beecher strove to convert sinners and prayed night and day that each of his children would experience conversion. Now, as an adult, Charles reflected on these things in a letter he wrote to Henry: "is eternal punishment a reality? Father thought so. He never doubted. Strike that idea from his mind, and his whole career would be changed, his whole influence on us modified." Charles did not believe in eternal punishment, nor did Mary and Isabella. Even "Hattie's mind I fear is shaken," Charles told Henry, but perhaps *she* would hold fast.[17]

Harriet stayed closer to her father's religion than did Edward or Catharine, but she was finding ways to assert herself. Take, for example, her Christmas tree. In her childhood, the Beechers did not have a Christmas tree or exchange gifts. Indeed most American Protestants of Lyman Beecher's day, like their parents before them, saw "Christmas as a Catholic corruption of Christianity" and did not celebrate it.[18] To follow in the footsteps of the Lord, they must forsake all pomp and display.[19] The big holidays of Harriet's childhood were Thanksgiving and the Fourth of July. These were untainted by medieval Catholicism, and spoke of God's providence in the New World. So when in December 1854 Harriet set up a Christmas tree in her home, it was a departure from her father's example. She invited Andover faculty to a party where every guest received a wrapped gift — nothing too elaborate, just some little keepsake from Stowe's travels.[20] For at least some of those professors, getting a Christmas gift would have been a novelty.

Many years later in one of her novels, Stowe wrote about her childhood Christmas (or lack thereof). One Christmas Eve, the minister's daughter sneaks out and peers through the windows of the Episcopal Church. The little girl is named Dolly, but she is Harriet as a child. Dolly is enchanted by the candles and pine boughs, the solemn creed and the heavenly music. She goes home and creeps back into bed. On Christmas Day her father (Lyman, of course) gives her some candy — not because it is Christmas, he explains, but because he loves his little daughter. He reminds her that "nobody knows when Christ was born, and there is nothing in the Bible to tell us when to keep Christmas."[21] For family devotions that morning, the minister reads aloud the story of Christ's birth. Then the children go to school, for Christmas is just another day.

"Beecher's Bibles" and the Plymouth Hymnal

Meanwhile, in 1855, far more serious and deadly matters were coming to a head. Out in Kansas, pro-slavery settlers and their opponents, often called "free-soilers" because of their insistence that the land should be free of slavery, were fighting what amounted to a guerilla war. Supporters for both sides sent "supplies" to Kansas. Among shipments of food, clothing, and farm tools, there were guns — sometimes packed in wooden crates marked "Bibles." Sharps rifles were prized, being easier to load than the old muskets and deadlier in aim. As many as one thousand Sharps rifles were sent to Kansas between 1854 and 1858[22] — some of them shipped by churches. Harriet's brother Henry Ward Beecher was one of several ministers who got his congregation to send rifles to free-soilers in Kansas, so the Sharps rifles were nicknamed "Beecher's Bibles."

Harriet's brother Henry saw nothing wrong with sending guns to Kansas. He said that Christians can use force if they have the proper mindset. The *New York Tribune* quoted Beecher as saying that when it came to slaveholders in Kansas, one rifle had more moral power than a hundred Bibles.[23] The *Liberator* reported Beecher as saying "you might just as well read the Bible to buffalos"[24] as read it to pro-slavery men in Kansas. Sometimes you just needed a gun.

Henry Ward Beecher was good at turning words into deeds. He attended a rally on behalf of anti-slavery settlers bound for Kansas at New Haven's North Church, packed from floor to gallery with professors, clergy, and other leading citizens. A Yale professor stood up and declared that the settlers must have guns, and that he would buy the first rifle. Then Beecher pledged twenty-five rifles from his congregation, *if* the crowd would raise, then and there, the money. On the spot they raised $675, enough for twenty-seven rifles. Back in Brooklyn, Beecher's church bought the twenty-five rifles. When all the supplies were gathered, the settlers marched in a torchlight parade through New Haven. Each man was "the proud owner of a Sharps rifle and a Bible embossed, courtesy of Plymouth Church, with the motto, 'Be ye steadfast and unmovable.'"[25] The group settled in northeastern Kansas in what is now Wabaunsee. For a time they were called the Beecher Bible and Rifle colony, and the church they built was "The Beecher Bible and Rifle Church."[26] To those Bibles and rifles, Beecher was soon to add hymnals.

Beecher directed the creation of a new hymnbook: *Plymouth Collection of Hymns and Tunes for the Use of Christian Congregations.* It first appeared in 1855 and was an immediate success. The hymnal project started because Henry Ward Beecher grew up in a singing family. He wanted everyone in his church to sing heartily. But Henry was bucking a trend: as American churches prospered, they bought organs, hired choir directors, and paid musicians. The folks in the pews fell into the habit of listening passively while the professionals performed.[27] Beecher would not have it. "The whole church ought to sing," Henry wrote, "because the whole church ought to worship." True worship is "voluntary and personal," including the singing.[28] Henry made Plymouth Church a singing church. It was a large, dynamic congregation; now it would be called a "destination church." People came for miles to hear the strong singing and the dynamic preaching. Plymouth Church did have professional musicians, of course. But Beecher told them to let the people sing what *they* loved to sing, not what the experts forced on them. Hymns should be memorable and singable; only then would the song of the church go out into the world.

Henry's hymnal embraced a broad range of Christian experience. It honored "the Great Humanities," Beecher said, with "hymns of

Temperance, Human Rights and Freedom, Peace and Benevolence."[29] And it included revival and camp meeting hymns, because people loved to sing them.

The *Plymouth Collection* was ecumenical for its time. In addition to the much-loved hymns of Isaac Watts, it had Moravian and Methodist songs, and even a few Unitarian hymns. Beecher raised a "storm of protest"[30] by including a few hymns by Catholic writers. But he found "much food for true piety" in Catholicism — despite what he called the "masses of darkened minds within that Church of Error."[31] Thus did Henry nod to prejudice in order to do an end run around it.

Beecher spearheaded the hymnal project, but as historian William Reynolds notes, he delegated the painstaking work to experts. Charles Beecher, a church musician, editor, and minister, was deeply involved, together with Charles Zundel, organist and choir director of Plymouth Church.

Three of Harriet's poems were set to music for the *Plymouth Collection of Hymns*. All three are in the "Christian Experience" section, under the subhead "Praise, Joy and Conflict." In Stowe's poem "Abide in Me" the soul is like a harp that needs tuning. "Dwell thou within it, tune and touch the chords till every note and string shall answer thine." To live in harmony with God, fully attuned to Christ, was Stowe's spiritual ideal. But it was "Still, Still with Thee" which became Stowe's best-known hymn, echoing Psalm 139:18, "when I awake, I am still with thee."

The *Plymouth Collection of Hymns* went through several editions and inspired similar hymnals. It popularized "Fairest Lord Jesus," "Just as I Am," and "Nearer My God to Thee," among many others. And it "changed the nature of congregational singing" by giving the people "singable tunes."[32] The *Plymouth Collection* reflected Henry's piety, and also Harriet's. It was ecumenical and socially aware, open to revivalism and yet not limited to it.

Around this time, Harriet made her sole attempt to adapt *Uncle Tom's Cabin* to the stage. She wrote "The Christian Slave," a dramatic reading for one voice. It adapted scenes and characters from the novel and called for the singing of several hymns. Stowe wrote it expressly for Mary Webb, an African American actress. Webb performed "The Christian Slave" in several northeastern cities, including Boston, where she entertained an audience of 3500.[33] Then Webb took her one-woman show to England. Stowe wrote in advance to friends there, urging them to extend their patronage to Webb. "Every new development of a talent or a prowess in this much depressed people is a new argument for us & helps the struggle in the right direction,"[34] Stowe wrote. The Duchess of Sutherland had Webb perform "The Christian Slave" at Stafford House. The work was never as profitable or popular as the fully staged "Tom shows," which were written and performed without input from Stowe. Nevertheless, "The Christian Slave" advanced the career of one woman, and showed audiences what a black artist could do with freedom and opportunity.[35]

Now that Stowe was a famous author, she refurbished some of her earlier works. The *May Flower* was reissued in 1855, with new material added (including "The Two Altars"). And her very first book, *Primary Geography,* was rewritten in light of *Uncle Tom's Cabin.*[36] According to William B. Allen, the revised *Geography* described racial characteristics in a more egalitarian way, and said slavery was bad for everyone and inconsistent with American ideals.

One day Harriet received a telegram: her beloved Aunt Esther had died. Aunt Esther had been an important figure in Harriet's life. Esther had stepped in to make things run smoothly whenever someone in the family was sick, or moving, or having babies. Harriet wrote to her son Henry, who was away at school, recalling "the great Bible out of which [Aunt Esther] used to read to me & the comfort and advice that she has given me all my life. Henry, she was a *great sufferer.* She had . . . a proud nature — great intensity of feeling — & all these had to be made subject to Christ. No nun in a convent ever lived a more self denying life & it has been a long one." Harriet then gave her aunt the highest praise: "at last everything within was conquered & before she died Christ gave her the victory & she was made perfect in love."

Aunt Esther's example "makes me feel my deficiencies," Harriet confessed. Then she promised Henry to be more faithful in showing her love for him. Perhaps Stowe felt guilty for having invested so deeply in her writing, and for being gone for months on end. She worried that "when I am gone you cannot remember so much of me" as she would remember of Aunt Esther. She assured her son Henry of her love and urged him "to choose my Redeemer — your Father's & Mother's God for your own."[37] Harriet seemed unsure of Henry's faith. Like her father, she dreaded that any child of hers might die unsaved. And it troubled her that as her children grew up, it was getting harder for her to guide them.

Even so, if being a mother of small children did not stop Stowe's pen, neither would being the mother of teenagers. Her views on slavery continued to develop after *Uncle Tom's Cabin.* And as the national mood darkened, she felt she needed to write a second anti-slavery novel.

Writing for the Times

Upon hearing of Stowe's new work, Senator Charles Sumner wrote to encourage her. He hoped her new story would "help us in our struggle for Kansas" and in the next presidential election.[38] Sumner was a fierce foe of slavery. The Massachusetts Senator made a flaming speech in the Senate, denouncing the Kansas-Nebraska Act. Its authors, he charged, took the harlot slavery as their mistress. If the harlot looked beautiful to her lovers, everyone else saw her as ugly.

That speech nearly cost Sumner his life. Two days later, on May 22, 1856, Sumner was working at his desk in the nearly deserted Senate chambers. In strode Congressman Preston Brooks of South Carolina, brandishing a gold-headed cane made of a tropical wood called gutta percha. Brooks beat Sumner nearly to death. The caning of Sumner stirred the nation. "Indignation meetings" were held across the North. But Brooks had plenty of supporters, especially in the South, and they sent him more canes.

Meanwhile out in Kansas, a pro-slavery militia attacked Lawrence, a stronghold of anti-slavery settlers. The militia smashed two printing presses, destroyed the Free State Hotel, and demolished several homes and businesses. In response to this "sack of Lawrence" — and to the caning of Sumner — an anti-slavery zealot named John Brown struck back. Brown and his followers dragged five pro-slavery settlers from their homes in Kansas and hacked them to death with broadswords.

It was in this time of rising tensions that Stowe wrote her second anti-slavery novel. She included a scene in which a slaveholder assaults an anti-slavery man with a gutta percha cane — proving the attacker's "eligibility for Congress."[39] She wrote in haste, needing to finish the book before she left for her second trip to Europe. She wrote it "in about three months," far less time than it took her to write *Uncle Tom's Cabin.*[40] She named the book *Dred: A Tale of the Great Dismal Swamp.*[41]

The story begins as a plantation romance. The young heiress Nina Gordon is a southern belle who collects marriage proposals like trophies. All of that changes when she meets Edward Clayton. Clayton was born to southern aristocracy but is troubled by slavery. Under Clayton's influence Nina blossoms into a woman of conscience and compassion. There will be no happily ever after for Clayton and Nina, for she dies abruptly and leaves him desolate.

Well into the book, Stowe introduces her character Dred, an escaped slave who lives in the swamps. Dred is the opposite of Stowe's Uncle Tom character. Tom lived and died like Christ, forgiving his enemies. But Dred is a prophet who calls down God's wrath on sinners. Tom suffered in patience, but Dred wants revenge and plots a slave revolt. However, Stowe has Dred die before he can carry out his plans. She pulled her story back from the brink, yet gave black agency and rage larger place in *Dred* than in *Uncle Tom's Cabin.* And this time, she seemed to have little hope for a peaceful end to slavery.

Stowe tried to show what it was like to be black, white, or brown in the South. The black hero is Dred, the revolutionary. The brown hero is Harry, a slave fathered by a white master. He is the half-brother of the belle Nina Gordon, but she does not know it. Harry is skillful and trustworthy, and since the old Master died it is Harry who runs the plantation. But there is no hope for a brown slave either, for Harry's wife is threatened, and he takes her to Canada rather than see her sexually exploited by a white man.

The white hero is Clayton, a southern lawyer of good family. He owns slaves but is troubled by slavery, so he treats his slaves humanely and teaches them to read — only to be attacked for his efforts. He concludes that slavery is beyond fixing and begins to see black rage as justified.

The white villain is Tom Gordon, Nina's brother and Harry's half-brother. Tom Gordon was born to wealth and power, and it has corrupted him. Stowe later said that the Tom Gordon character was her answer to the myth of southern refinement. That myth, Stowe said, was "offensively and ridiculously paraded in the face of [our] northern people for many years, & they have been content to smile in silence." The southern aristocracy played the part of "a higher and more elegant class — of being in fact the *only* class of gentlemen & ladies." But after Preston Brooks bludgeoned Sumner nearly to death, Stowe resolved "to show them as I knew them to be. . . . Tom Gordon is no caricature."[42] Stowe positioned her character Tom Gordon at the top of the plantation system, but made him the lowest of human beings.

In *A Key to Uncle Tom's Cabin,* Stowe showed how slavery corrupted the courts, the schools, and the churches. Now in the novel *Dred,* she used fiction to show the same thing. She took her readers to the courtroom and the schoolroom, to homes of rich and poor. And as for the church, Stowe said she would expose "the corruption of Christianity" and reveal slavery as a greater menace to Christianity than all the acids of modernity and every ancient heresy.[43]

Like her first anti-slavery novel, *Dred* does have its lighter moments. For example, Stowe pokes fun at her native Calvinism through her character Abijah Skinflint, a backwoods whiskey seller. Skinflint is a "particularly high Calvinist" for whom "All things is decreed! . . . it gives a fellow a kind of comfort to think on it. Things is just as they has got to be,"[44] he tells a customer. If you are destined for eternity, a little drink won't hurt. And if you are not, then you have nothing to lose, so you might as well drink! Skinflint sells whiskey at the edge of a revival meeting.

The revival is held in a clearing in the woods where wooden platforms are set up for the preachers. Beyond the clearing, tents are pitched for people to stay overnight. All manner of folk have come. Slaves enjoy a change of scene and a break from work (revivals were held after planting and before harvest). Some slaves come to the revival to soar away in the spirit, and others come to socialize with slaves from other plantations. The whites also have their reasons for attending the revival. Some find it entertaining to watch slaves leap and shout, while others hope that if they pray and sing, God might bless them too.

Off in the woods beyond the camp meeting, a slave trader has merchandise for sale. The slaves are chained together in a coffle, trudging wearily on their way to some point of sale. The trader breaks his journey for a night or two hoping to do some business around the edges of the revival. Between services he buttonholes one of the preachers: would this man of the cloth like to buy a cook who not only has housekeeping prowess, but is also "a real pious Methodist"?[45] The reverend replies that he might be interested, but the cook has a small child, and he doesn't want more children running around his place. "But consider," wheedles the trader: "the child will cost nothing to raise and might be worth a thousand dollars some day." The minister says he will think it over.

As night falls there is another service of preaching and singing. The pious mood is shattered by a loud voice booming from somewhere up in the treetops. "The Lord is against this nation," the voice intones. God "will turn your feasts into mourning, your songs into lamentation . . . a multitude of slain! There is no end to their corpses."[46] The message is clear: those who preach salvation and turn to sell souls will bring down the wrath of God!

Silence falls and everyone is afraid. The slave trader trembles. Will God punish him? He feels a pang of guilt because a slave girl in his charge is dying back there in the forest. The trader gets a preacher (Father Dickson, a rare anti-slavery man) to come and pray with the slave girl. The two men go to the place where the slaves are chained. The dying girl declares she has no will to live as a slave. The minister prays to ease her passing. Then the minister demands that the trader repent and set the slaves free then and there. But by this time the trader's fear is fading. He pleads "practical considerations." Maybe the judgment day is not coming *just* yet. The trader wants to close a deal with the slave-holding minister, who believes that since Africans bear the curse of Canaan, even a minister may safely enslave them. Thus religion is corrupted by slavery.

So much for the backwoods revival! Well, perhaps a meeting of professional clergy will give a more hopeful view of Christianity in action. Stowe takes her readers to a "Clerical Conference" of Presbyterian ministers. She reminds her readers that the Presbyterians are split along North/South lines due to certain points of theology and of course slavery. Once more Stowe lambastes Joel Parker, who had threatened to sue her for taking his name in vain in *Uncle Tom's Cabin.* This time she fictionalizes Parker as Shubael Packthread; he can twist words into a thousand shapes and believe his own lies. Stowe condemns clergy who "begin by loving institutions for God's sake" but end up letting those institutions "stand . . . in the place of God."[47] During the clergy meeting, one or two men speak against slavery, but no one listens.

What do the ministers accomplish? They pass a formal condemnation of dancing! Then they sing "Am I a Soldier of the Cross?" The hypocrisy of it all sickens one minister — the same one who comforted the dying slave girl. He warns his brethren: "The church is becoming corrupted. Ministers are drawn into connivance with deadly sin . . . in her skirts is found the blood of poor innocents . . . as God is just, I tremble for you and for us!" He leaves the assembly, but the force of his exit is blunted by another minister's blandishments: "Do come again. It is very difficult to see the path of duty in these matters."[48]

Stowe scorched pro-slavery ministers. She had Dred say, "I have found the alligators and snakes better neighbors than Christians." Dred sees the difference between religion prostituted to slavery, and Jesus Christ, who died for the sins of the world. But "the day shall come when he [Christ] shall lay down the yoke, and he will bear the sin of the world no longer. Then shall come the great judgment."[49]

Stowe's character Dred is getting angry at God. He chafes under "the toleration of that Almighty Being, who, having the power to blast and burn, so silently endures."[50] Dred demands to know why God is silent. He cannot remain silent forever! Stowe offsets Dred's rage with another black character, Milly, who still trusts in God. Stowe loosely based this character on Sojourner Truth, for Milly is dignified, strong, and deeply religious. She has suffered, yet she has never allowed hatred to possess her. Milly pleads with Dred to postpone the slave rebellion; perhaps God will intervene and put an end to slavery before it is too late.

But by the time she wrote *Dred,* Stowe was less hopeful that slavery could be ended by moral suasion alone. A drastic intervention might be needed to save the church and the nation from the cancer of slavery. She hoped slavery could end without war, but these were troubling times, and the wrath of God seemed ready to fall. *Uncle Tom's Cabin* called for an awakening of sympathy for the African race, but as Sarah Robbins says, *Dred* "anticipates and even implicitly justifies the violence of the Civil War."[51]

Dred was well received in the North and in Great Britain after its publication in 1856. But a later generation denounced it as "racist, overly long, and incoherent."[52] More recently, however, *Dred* has been called "Stowe's most honest and vulnerable fiction," because she took "risks in an effort better to understand racial difference."[53] At the very least, *Dred* shows that Stowe's views on race and slavery continued evolving.

While Harriet dramatized slavery in print, her brother Henry staged a slave auction in church. On Sunday June 1, 1856, just before the closing hymn, Beecher reminded his flock how Jesus said that "it is lawful to do good on the Sabbath." Then he told this true story: a white man from Virginia fathered a slave girl named Sarah. When she reached adolescence he decided to sell her "for what purpose you can imagine when you see her." Plymouth Church by now had a reputation for raising money to buy slaves, and the trader in charge of selling the merchandise named Sarah contacted Beecher. As a gesture of good will, the trader knocked a hundred dollars off of his asking price. Some activists had collected several hundred more dollars. So now, if the congregation would raise the rest of the money, the slave trader would sell Sarah to Plymouth Church and she would be set free.

Having told the story, Rev. Beecher asked Sarah to come forward so the congregation could see her. She was a light-skinned girl with waves of dark hair; she would no doubt bring a good price in the fancy trade. The frightened girl walked forward and sat down in the minister's chair, head bowed, hands twisting in fear or shame. "This," said Henry, "is a marketable commodity. . . . I reverence woman. For the sake of the love I bore my mother, I hold her sacred . . . and will use every means within my power for her uplifting." Henry challenged, "What will you do now? . . . Let the plates be passed, and we will see."

Soon the offering plates were piled high with coins and notes, watches, rings, and brooches. A wealthy member pledged to make up any balance remaining. Then Beecher turned to Sarah and said, "You are free now! You understand? Free!" The congregation cheered and sang a rousing hymn. They had just raised "$783, besides the jewelry," so that over and above the price of her sale, Sarah would have some money to start life as a free person.[54]

The press reported this drama at Plymouth Church. Rumors flew that a mob from the Bowery was coming to "clean out the damned abolition nest" in Brooklyn. The following Sunday police guarded the church, and several members brought canes and pistols. Some rough-looking strangers showed up and sat in the back of the church, but Beecher snubbed them, and at last they slunk away, "muttering curses against the 'abolitionists and nigger-lovers.'"[55]

In the summer of 1856, Stowe finished *Dred,* Plymouth Church "bought" Sarah, and the Republican Party, which aimed to stop slavery from spreading, held its first convention. They nominated John C. Frémont for President. The vice presidential nomination went to John McLean, a Supreme Court justice, passing over the lesser-known Abraham Lincoln. In the North, anti-slavery feeling was rising like a river in spring. Just how long it would take to reach flood stage, and what might be swept away, no one knew. But many who saw the rising water said it had been let loose by Harriet Beecher Stowe.

CHAPTER THIRTEEN

The Minister's Wooing

C alvin and Harriet sailed for Europe in the summer of 1856. With them came twenty-year-old Hattie and Eliza, eighteen-year-old Henry, and Harriet's sister Mary. This trip would be more relaxing than the first one, but there was work to do. While crossing the Atlantic Stowe had to finish *Dred,* and during her travels she was to write several travel articles for the *Independent.*

When the Stowes checked into the Adelphi Hotel in London, they worked as a team to prepare *Dred* for submission. That meant hand-copying a manuscript of several hundred pages, one copy for the London publisher and one to be sent back to Stowe's editor in the States. In the Stowes' lodgings, chapters of *Dred* lay piled in various states of readiness. Everybody had a job to do: Harriet dictated, Mary wrote, Calvin prepared the appendix, and the twins copied out the second manuscript to send home "by the *Niagara* which sails Saturday."[1] *Dred* appeared first in London (establishing the British copyright) and was released in the States while Stowe was still abroad.[2]

With *Dred* thus dispatched, Harriet and company went to Glasgow. At a train station en route they met Queen Victoria, Prince Albert, and family. The meeting was "accidental, done on purpose," Calvin said. Victoria was no friend of slavery, but she could avoid controversy by meeting Stowe informally. Calvin described Queen Victoria as "a real nice little body with exceedingly pleasant, kindly manners." The four royal children "stared their big blue eyes almost out of looking" at the author of *Uncle Tom's Cabin.*[3] Her Majesty received a signed copy of *Dred.*

After a brief stay in Scotland, Calvin returned to Andover. He wrote to Harriet that he was enjoying meals served on time and fewer broken dishes. No more old shoes, bonnets, petticoats, or cast-off dresses strewn about. No more papers, books, or "letters taped here, there and everywhere." Best of all, "no expenses except what I am consulted about beforehand & approve."[4] If Calvin enjoyed missing Harriet, she did not begrudge him the pleasure. She was enjoying her visit with the Duke and Duchess of Argyll, followed by a stay at the Sutherlands' estate in the Scottish Highlands.

Harriet reported to Calvin that *Dred* sold "one hundred thousand copies . . . in four weeks."[5] In the States it became "one of the most popular novels of the time," selling more than 200,000 copies in the nineteenth century.[6] Some of Harriet's fans told her that *Dred* surpassed even *Uncle Tom's Cabin*. And of course, *Dred* drew criticism. The *Edinburgh Review* said the book was provincial and its author was naïve.[7] Richmond's *Southern Literary Messenger* sneered that "Beecherism" was a form of "human depravity" in which the "authoress" reveled in vulgar subjects unbecoming to a lady. The *Messenger* was correct in this much: when Stowe wrote about slavery, she broke an unwritten rule necessary to maintaining the peculiar institution — namely, that women must keep silent about it. "Were [Stowe] a woman," the reviewer opined, "we should blush for the sex — luckily she is only a Beecher."[8]

Indeed the "the authoress" was a Beecher and proud of it. She was pleased that her son Henry would soon attend Dartmouth College and might carry on the Beecher family tradition of entering the ministry. They parted at Edinburgh and Henry sailed for America, followed as always by his mother's prayers. He was going to need them.

Harriet, Mary and the twins now went by train to London, and somehow their baggage got lost in a train transfer. "Confusion in the camp!" Harriet wrote to Calvin. "No baggage come, and nobody knows why! running to stations, inquiries, messages, and no baggage."[9] The ladies arrived at the elegant home of Lady Mary Labouchere — with no clean clothes to wear. What agony — especially for the twins — to be in high society and bereft of their wardrobes! At last their baggage was found, averting the tragic necessity of having to buy all new clothes in London.

By now the Queen had finished reading *Dred*. Her Majesty (Lady Labouchere reported) was "provoked" when the character Nina died, and "angry that something dreadful did not happen to [the villain]

Tom Gordon." Still, she had liked the new novel even better than *Uncle Tom's Cabin*.[10] Stowe enjoyed the royal nod. The Queen remained distant, but Harriet hobnobbed with other famous people, including the feminist Harriet Martineau and the aristocratic scholar and churchman Charles Kingsley.

One of these encounters would have long-term consequences for Stowe. She and her sister Mary were invited to stay overnight at the home of Lady Byron, something of a tragic figure. Lady Byron was wealthy and had once been a great beauty, but her marriage to the famous poet Lord Byron had ended in separation, and Lord Byron had used his poems to blame his estranged wife for his unhappiness. She had failed to appreciate his genius; she was cold and unloving; she had driven him to despair. In 1824 he went to Greece to fight for Greek independence, but died of a fever before he could fulfill his heroic passions. People said it was a tragedy that Byron had died young, depriving England of a great poet — and Lady Byron was somehow to blame. Harriet no doubt remembered how her father had reacted to the news of Byron's death all those years ago. And now a new edition of Lord Byron's works was forthcoming, and his widow braced herself for another wave of blame.

Lady Byron told Stowe the real reason her marriage had failed. It was incest: Lord Byron took his half-sister, Augusta Leigh, as a lover. Not to mention all his other lovers, one of whom famously described him as "mad, bad and dangerous to know." Stowe was not the first person to hear this, of course, but she felt burdened by it. That night Harriet spilled the story to her sister Mary, and the two sisters sat up all night agonizing over what to do. Some days later, after leaving Lady Byron's home, Stowe wrote a letter urging her new friend to remain silent — while she lived. After Lady Byron was beyond further suffering, "some discreet friends . . . shall say what was due to justice."[11] Years later, when Stowe tried to defend Lady Byron's reputation, she nearly lost her own.

After the visit with Lady Byron, Harriet and Mary took the twins to Paris. While in the city, Stowe sat for the English sculptor Susan Durant. One of the twins later described the scene at the studio. There in the "dim light, the marble dust and chippings covering the floor, the clink, clink of the chisels," was "Miss Durant, tall, handsome, and animated before the mound of clay which day by day grew into a resemblance to my mother." Later the bust "was taken to London, where I saw it, and thought it very beautiful and an excellent likeness of my mother at forty-six, — her age when it was taken."[12]

Paris and Italy

In Paris Stowe got an earful about American slavery. The French, Stowe wrote, "seem to see the truth about American slavery much plainer than people can who are in it." She thought that if American clergy and Christians could see themselves as others see them, "with what wonder, pity, and contempt they would regard their own vacillating condition!" Too many Americans had been led to believe that Scripture validated slavery. Not so in France! The French saw Scripture as the friend of freedom, Stowe observed. *Uncle Tom's Cabin* "revived the Gospel among the poor of France . . . nobody knows how many have been led to Christ by it," Harriet told Calvin. French Christians expressed "surprise and horror" that the American church[13] failed to oppose slavery.

Recent scholarship supports Stowe's impressions. Historian Mark Noll found that European Protestants and liberal Catholics had "intense religious conviction about the evils of slavery and the urgent need to end the slave system in the United States." And not "even the most theologically conservative sources" in Europe saw the Bible as legitimating slavery.[14] Europeans who admired America's freedom of religion and democratic government were deeply troubled that slavery was allowed in the U.S.

In Paris Stowe attended a gathering of French Protestants. They sang a hymn, heard an anti-slavery address, and prayed for the end of slavery in America, where "hang so many of the hopes of Protestantism."[15] At a Christmas gathering of Free Church Protestants, a French pastor told Stowe, "I grieve that any Christian should be so blinded as to *apologize* for slavery . . . but when they defend it from *the Bible* then I am indignant."[16]

Harriet and Mary went to Italy in February, leaving the twins in Paris to study French at a Protestant boarding school. Meanwhile, back in Andover, Calvin was no longer enjoying Harriet's absence. He wrote and said that *she* might be unaware of how long she was gone, but *he* was counting the days.[17] Calvin would just have to keep counting. In Rome Harriet and Mary saw the Vatican and strolled through the Roman Forum. They went down into catacombs where early Christians were buried; they saw the Coliseum by moonlight.

Proceeding on to Naples, they decided to see Mount Vesuvius, a popular excursion then as now. Tourists began their ascent in small horse-drawn carriages. When the road became too steep for the carriages, tourists rode donkeys to the summit. At the top of Vesuvius the travelers looked down into the volcano's vast, circular cone, where Harriet could see lava burning far below. Smoke and cinders drifted up, and a man stooped to light his cigar on a glowing coal.

It reminded Stowe of "Milton's descriptions of the infernal regions," and she wondered if Milton ever visited Vesuvius. Mary and Harriet also saw Pompeii and Herculaneum, which were destroyed when Vesuvius erupted in the year 79 A.D. Later Harriet used these weird landscapes in a novel. But on the day she visited Vesuvius, her immediate concern was how to get the guides to stop beating the donkeys and horses on their descent from the mountain.[18] The guides were puzzled: did the American ladies not want to get where they were going?

Harriet and Mary toured Florence, and then Venice, returning to Rome for Holy Week. *In Rome for Holy Week!* What would Lyman Beecher have said? Harriet and Mary were dyed-in-the-wool Protestants, yet they were deeply moved by the throngs gathering in Rome to remember "the death and resurrection of Jesus."[19] By early May, the sisters were back in Paris. Mary chose to stay longer on the Continent, while Harriet returned to England.

Harriet sailed for home June 6. The prospect of crossing the Atlantic filled her with "a nervous horror," she told Calvin, but "to reach you I must commit myself once more to the ocean." She comforted herself with the thought that the ocean could not carry her "beyond [God's] power and love, wherever or to whatever it bears me."[20] To her relief, the seas were calm and the voyage easy.

Early in the summer of 1857, Harriet was back in Andover. The family seemed smaller now. Hattie and Eliza were still in Paris, improving their French. Henry was at Dartmouth studying for exams; he wrote to say that he looked forward to seeing his mother soon. Frederick was home but unwell — perhaps at age seventeen he was already drinking and smoking — and his worried mother took him to a water cure establishment.

Tragedy

Harriet was at the water cure with Fred on July 9 when the telegram came: Henry was dead! Stowe rushed home "to find the house filled with [Henry's] weeping classmates, who had just come bringing his remains." Henry's body was "so calm, so placid, so peaceful," she later told a friend. Harriet could not believe that her voice, "which always had such power over him could not recall him."[21]

The tragedy had occurred when Henry went swimming in the Connecticut River with friends. Suddenly he became exhausted and cried out for help. His roommate and another young man tried to help but they were unable to save him. Henry was twenty or so yards from shore when he sank. A newspaper reported that Henry's friends could see his body lying on the bottom. By the time help arrived, Henry had been underwater for about twenty minutes. He lived only a few moments after being pulled out. "A committee of four students, one from each class," brought his remains to Andover, the report continued. "The deceased was nineteen years of age, a fine scholar, and a youth of much promise."[22]

Harriet had last seen Henry when they parted in Scotland. At that time, as far as she knew, he was unconverted. And now, if her shock and grief were not enough to bear, Harriet feared for the state of Henry's soul. Lyman Beecher always said there is no salvation for the unconverted. If that were true, and if Henry died unsaved, he must now be damned. This was no mere abstraction for Harriet; it meant deep personal anguish. Henry's salvation (or lack of it) made the difference between hope and despair. Harriet did not know if she would ever see Henry in heaven, or if he must now suffer eternal separation from Christ and all his saints.

Harriet's loss bore a strange resemblance to that of her sister Catharine years before, when her fiancé drowned unconverted. Harriet wrote to Catharine, describing herself as

> in a state of great physical weakness, most agonizing, and unable to control my thoughts. Distressing doubts as to Henry's spiritual state were rudely thrust upon my soul. It was as if a voice had said to me: "You trusted in God, did you? You believed that He loved you! You had perfect confidence that He would never take your child till the work of grace was mature! Now He has hurried him

into eternity without a moment's warning, without preparation, and where is he?"

Stowe strove to banish such thoughts as "dishonorable to God," and felt it her "duty to resist them." Over and over she told herself that "Jesus in love has taken my dear one into His bosom," and then "the Enemy" would leave her "in peace."

But not for long. The agonizing questions returned. Did God let Henry die unconverted — and then condemn him to hell? These thoughts were "an attack of the Devil, trying to separate me from Christ," Harriet said. She clung to the hope that "the mysteries of God's ways with us must be swallowed up by the greater mystery of the love of Christ." She found herself caught in an unbearable contradiction between what she was taught and what she hoped was true.

Working in the garden comforted her. She thought being a mother was like being a gardener, tending a rare exotic flower. As the plant grew, she moved it lovingly from soil to soil, from pot to pot. She counted every leaf and watched the stem grow stronger, until at last a calyx formed and a faint streak of color appeared. Just as the flower was about to open, the owner of the greenhouse came by night and took the plant away. "What then? Do I suppose he has destroyed the flower? Far from it, I know that he has taken it to his own garden. What Henry might have been I could guess better than anyone. What Henry is, is known to Jesus only."[23] Better to live with ambiguity than succumb to despair.

Everywhere Harriet saw reminders of Henry. The pictures he had loved, the presents she brought him from Europe, all pierced her heart. "I have had a dreadful faintness of sorrow come over me at times," she sighed. "I have felt so crushed, so bleeding, so helpless, that I could only call on my Savior with groaning that could not be uttered." Calvin was her companion in sorrow. "Every child that dies is for the time being an only one," Calvin lamented, one that "no time, no change, can ever replace."[24]

Two days after the funeral, Harriet and Calvin went to Dartmouth College, where they visited Henry's room and embraced his classmates. In the evening they took the forest path to the Connecticut River, where the students often went for a swim. The college rowing club kept its boats nearby, and that evening all the crews were out rowing. Henry had crewed on the *Una,* and his friends had furled its flag and trimmed it with black crepe. Watching the young men row-ing, Harriet felt a surge of love for "all of them, because they loved Henry." Not far from "where their boats were gliding in the evening light lay the bend in the river, clear, still, beautiful, fringed with over-hanging pines, from whence our boy went up to heaven," Stowe wrote. "To heaven — if earnest, manly purpose, if sincere, deliberate strife with besetting sin is accepted of God, as I firmly believe it is."[25]

Henry was buried in a graveyard on the campus of Andover Sem-inary. There Harriet planted white petunias, pansies, white immortelle, and verbenas. Harriet and Calvin would sit near the grave in the eve-nings. "I am submissive," Calvin sighed, "but not reconciled."[26] If Henry had lived, he almost certainly would have fought in the Union Army. The Stowes could not have known that soon thousands of par-ents would mourn for sons cut off in the flower of manhood.

That September, Calvin, Harriet, and nine-year-old Charley vis-ited Brunswick, Maine, to savor the memories they shared of Henry in that place. Embraced by forest on one side and ocean on the other, Harriet felt "the healing touch of Jesus of Nazareth on the deep wound of my heart, for I have golden hours of calm when I say: 'Even so, Father, for so it seemed good in thy sight.'"[27] At such times she felt sure that "the most generous love has ordered all" and she could re-sign Henry to God. These waves of serenity undulated with deep troughs of sorrow. Grief she needed to accept; despair she had to fight.

Harriet wrote to Lady Byron about her struggles. If she (Harriet) no longer believed all she learned as a child, was she still a Christian? She said she now rejected her father's doctrine of eternal punishment for the unconverted. Perhaps it sparked conversions at revivals, but to a grieving mother the doctrine was like poison. Stowe needed to hope that one day she would be reunited with Henry in heaven, that God would give Henry another chance. She was beginning to think that "probation does not end with this life, and the number of the re-deemed may therefore be infinitely greater than the world's history leads us to suppose."[28]

In November of 1857 Stowe wrote "The Mourning Veil," a medita-tion on grief. In it she sought to impart hope — to her readers and to herself — that from sorrow may grow wisdom and love. Stowe's article appeared in the very first issue of a new magazine.

It was called the *Atlantic Monthly.* The *Atlantic* was launched to "promote good literature and speak out against slavery," writes Ellery Sedgwick. It was the brainchild of Francis Underwood, who had taken Stowe to see a stage version of *Uncle Tom's Cabin*. The *Atlantic's* first editor was Harvard professor James Russell Lowell. Enlisted to contribute were famous New England authors such as Ralph Waldo Emerson, who said the *Atlantic* would "guide the age." Thomas Wentworth Higginson, abolitionist and author, saw the *Atlantic* as doing New England's duty "to guide the nation, to civilize it, to humanize it."[29] The very first issue had on its cover the image of John Winthrop, Puritan governor of Massachusetts Bay Colony. The implication was clear: the Puritans founded New England, making New England the nation's moral guardian. The literary light shone from Boston, and the darkness of slavery could extinguish it.

The *Atlantic Monthly* was run exclusively by men, in the style of the gentlemen's clubs of Boston.[30] But they needed Stowe's name to attract subscribers. As noted above, her first piece for the *Atlantic* was devotional writing — or grief counseling. In the years ahead, she would also contribute domestic sketches, social commentary, and fiction.

The Minister's Wooing

Stowe's next book, her third novel, ran as a serial in the *Atlantic* and then appeared as a book in 1859. It was set in the New England of Stowe's forebears and quaintly titled *The Minister's Wooing*. The story was a romance, but more importantly it was Stowe's day of reckoning with her father's religion. Edmund Wilson called *The Minister's Wooing* "the main key to [Stowe's] work," because there she exposed the "banishment of the spirit of Jesus from the theology and practice of Calvinist faith."[31]

The heroine of the story is Mary Scudder, a girl of high intelligence and deep faith who lives with her widowed mother. True to her name, Mary, she brings grace to others. Her childhood sweetheart, James Marvyn, has gone off to sea, and in his long absence, Mary prays for him and comes to love him more deeply.

Mary has grown into a beautiful young woman. She is noticed by a visitor in town, one Aaron Burr. Stowe's character is loosely based on the historical Aaron Burr, Vice President of the United States from

1801 to 1805, who shot Alexander Hamilton in a duel in 1804. In both history and in fiction, Burr was the grandson of Jonathan Edwards. Stowe's Burr is a cynic and a hedonist, the decadent offspring of Puritans. Burr is a predator, and the innocent Mary poses a challenge to his powers of seduction, but he fails to corrupt her.

And now another man takes an interest in Mary Scudder. He is the Rev. Dr. Samuel Hopkins, a minister who takes room and board with the Scudders. Stowe's fictional minister is loosely based on the historical Hopkins (1721-1803), a New England theologian. In fact and fiction, Hopkins taught "the theories of the Great [Jonathan] Edwards on the nature of true virtue," also called benevolence.[32] Hopkins's spiritual ideal is disinterested benevolence: a love free of self-interest, which comes only as divine gift. A truly benevolent person would be willing even to be damned for the glory of God. Mary learns from Hopkins to "walk in the high regions of abstract thought" in which true virtue and self-denial are one and the same.[33] And if Mary could learn to ignore her own feelings, she might be persuaded to marry Hopkins — and sacrifice her happiness for a theory.

Here Stowe warns her readers against making a virtue of self-denial. "The rigid theological discipline of New England," she explains, produces strength and purity, but not "enjoyment." It cannot "make a sensitive and thoughtful nature happy, however it might ennoble and exalt."[34]

Like Stowe herself, Mary senses something amiss in Hopkins's theology. How can the world be so beautiful, she wonders, when one's "next step might be into an abyss of horrors without end"? Sometimes she can feel "the walls of her faith closing round her as an iron shroud." But does Jesus really require her to wear this iron shroud? And is the love of Jesus really meant only for a few elect persons?

These questions are the deep foundations of *The Minister's Wooing*. Stowe shows her readers that a person raised in New England Puritanism can cast off that iron shroud and still be a Christian. But before Mary can do this, she must brave the icy winds of New England theology. Her trial begins when she hears that James, her childhood sweetheart, has been lost at sea and is presumed dead. And for all anyone knows, he has died unconverted — like Henry Stowe and Catharine's fiancé. According to the system of Hopkins's theology, James is doomed to hell. Mary struggles to accept this. But she finds that her heartfelt compassion for James's mother is stronger than the abstract theories she is supposed to believe. Mary feels a bond with James's mother and longs to embrace her.

Rev. Hopkins takes Mary to visit "the house of mourning" where James's parents live. But since James was not converted, Rev. Hopkins has nothing to offer the mourners — no hope, no grace, no peace. Now Stowe pauses the story line to interpret for her readers the history of New England theology. Her chapter "Views of Divine Government" is her protest against her father's religion. That protest, as Stowe scholar Joan Hedrick said, is that "men make [abstract] theological systems . . . but women must deal with the emotional reality behind them."[35]

Stowe still revered the New England mind. "Never," Stowe wrote, "was there a community where the roots of common life shot down so deeply, and were so intensely grappled around things sublime and eternal." The aim of New England theology was to reconcile the stark "facts of sin and evil" with the "Infinite Power and Benevolence" of God.[36] This was a tall order, since "only a certain decreed number of the human race can be saved." Those chosen to be saved could be known by their conversion experience, for even the most moral people were doomed if they died unconverted.

Stowe blamed this cruel system on Jonathan Edwards, the towering intellect of New England before the Revolution. His sermons were so "terrific in their refined poetry of torture" that his hearers wailed in terror. "A brother minister," wrote Stowe, once laid hold of Edwards's ministerial robe and exclaimed, "Oh! Mr. Edwards! Mr. Edwards! Is God not a God of mercy?"[37] If anything could kill one's love for God, Stowe thought, it was Edwards's theology.

After Edwards died, Stowe continued, the Americans won their freedom from England. Sovereign rulers were a thing of the past. From now on people were expected to be responsible citizens in a world of their own making. Instead of totally depraved sinners, they were "moral agents" accountable for their choices and actions. Insofar as theology mirrors anthropology, the sovereign God needed updating. The arbitrary king must become a moral governor. The system seemed to balance, but there was a hitch. Calvinists could not go so far as to let people save themselves. So they tried to have it both ways: people must *choose their own salvation,* yet they do not have the power to do so. They must get converted, but they are not able to do so. It was a "Catch-22" long before that phrase was invented.

Holding divine sovereignty together with human agency was like clutching fire and ice. Impossible! But New England preachers "never shrank from carrying an idea to its remotest logical verge." The whole system would work *if* one experienced conversion. There was no other way to be saved. Neither baptism, nor prayers, nor Christian nurture "interposed the slightest shield between the trembling spirit and Eternal justice,"[38] wrote Stowe.

So where was Jesus in all this? He could work within the system, Stowe felt. But Jesus is greater than theological systems, and is not bound by them. As Stowe was about to show, Jesus could even work through women, who had no formal religious authority. The women did not make New England theology, but they suffered emotional pain created by it. They were bound by a system not of their own making. But Jesus is greater than that system.

Stowe had come to see that she could be a Christian apart from New England theology. Indeed, the doctrinal systems of New England "differ from the New Testament as the living embrace of a friend does from his lifeless body, mapped out under the knife of the anatomical demonstrator — every nerve and muscle there, but to a sensitive spirit there is the chill of death in the analysis."[39] Stowe would rather have the living Christ.

Stowe now returned the reader to the Marvyns' house, where the bereaved mother of James is in crisis. "I can never love God!" Mrs. Marvyn cries. "I can never praise Him!" There is no hope. "Leave me alone," she shrieks, "I am a lost spirit!" This is the critical moment in the story.

Enter Candace, a black serving woman in the Marvyn household. Candace is wise and compassionate. What she knows, she knows deep in her bones. Her power is spiritual, not cerebral; her faith lives in her heart. And Stowe has this black woman preach the gospel better than the Rev. Dr. Samuel Hopkins ever could.[40]

Candace soothes the grieving mother of James. What follows is abridged from Stowe. "Now honey," Candace says, "I know our Doctor [Hopkins] is a mighty good man, and learned. He has mighty big things to say. But honey, that won't do for you now. At times like this, there is just one thing to come to, and that's Jesus. Just come right down to where poor old black Candace has to stay always. It's a good place, darling! *Look right at Jesus.* Tell you, honey, you can't live no other way now. Don't you remember how he looked on his mother, when she stood fainting and trembling under the cross, just like you? He knows all about mothers' hearts; he won't break yours. It was just because he knew we'd come into straits like this, that he went through all these things — him, the lord of Glory! Is this him you were talking about? — him you can't love? Look at him and see if you can't. Look and see what he is! Don't ask questions, and don't go to reasoning — just look at *him,* hanging there so sweet and patient, on the cross! All they could do couldn't stop his loving them, he prayed for them with all the breath he had. There's a God you can love! Candace loves him, poor, old, foolish, black, wicked Candace — and she knows he loves her."

Now Candace takes Mary aside. "Honey," she says, "don't you go troubling your mind" with James's eternal fate. "I'm clear Master James is one of the elect, and I'm clear there's considerable more of the elect than people think. Why, Jesus didn't die for nothing — all that love won't be wasted. The elect are more than you or I know, honey! There's the *Spirit,* — he'll give it to them, and if Master James *is* called and taken, depend upon it the Lord got him ready, of course he has, so don't you go to laying on your poor heart what no mortal creature can live under. Because, since we have to live in this world, it is quite clear the Lord must have fixed it so we *can,* and if things were as some folks suppose, why, we *couldn't* live, and there wouldn't be any sense in anything that goes on."[41]

Mrs. Marvyn believes the word of grace spoken by Candace. "There is but just one thing remaining," Candace tells Mary: "the cross of Christ. If God so loved us — if He died for us, — greater love hath no man than this . . . if there is a fathomless mystery of sin and sorrow, there is a deeper mystery of God's love. So Mary, try Candace's way — I look at Christ."[42]

Now comes the part of the story for which the book was named: the minister's wooing. Rev. Hopkins hopes that Mary will become his wife. Tactfully, he makes his intentions known. Mary cares for Hopkins. She respects his learning and knows him to be a man of integrity, for at the risk of offending a wealthy member of his church, Hopkins has denounced the slave trade. Mary knows that a good wife could support Hopkins in his ministry and her sense of duty tells her to accept him. Mary thinks James is dead and she can never love again, so she might as well do some good.

Mary accepts Hopkins's proposal, and the whole town plans for the wedding. But on the day of the nuptials, James returns! He was indeed shipwrecked, but he survived. James's mother receives her son as if by resurrection. Rev. Hopkins releases Mary from their engagement; he is "a good man despite, rather than because of, [his] theological system."[43] Best of all, James is now a Christian, thanks to Mary who prayed for him and sent her Bible to sea with him. Through the spiritual power of women — in this case, Candace and Mary — souls come to Jesus. Loved ones are reunited and joy triumphs over duty.

If only Stowe could have written a happy ending for her son Henry. But he would not be coming back. She would have to accept his death, but she would not, could not, believe him to be damned. As Mark Noll observes, Stowe rejected "the overwhelming compulsion of America's Reformed theologians — Presbyterian as much as Congregationalists — to figure everything out." Instead she clung to "the person and work of Christ." She found that she could reject New England theology and still be a Christian. It was "not just certain Calvinist particulars" that Stowe rejected, "but the whole way of thought that defined mainstream Calvinist debate from the 1790s onward." And yet, she treated her father's legacy with "surpassing tenderness,"[44] for she deeply loved and respected her father.

Atlantic Monthly editor James Russell Lowell hailed *The Minister's Wooing* as grand preaching — Stowe's best book yet. He saw fiction replacing sermons as the moral force in America: "An author's writing desk is something infinitely higher than a pulpit."[45] He added that no woman could be a Calvinist, since "Calvinism is logic, and no woman worth the name could ever live by syllogisms." But one critic heaped scorn on Stowe for preferring the "unintelligent faith of an amusing old negress"[46] to a sound system of theology.

The Last Trip to Europe

In August 1859, Harriet and Calvin sailed to Europe together for the third and last time, bringing their sixteen-year-old daughter Georgie. The steamer *Asia* took eleven days to make the crossing.[47] As before, Stowe obtained a British copyright for her latest novel. After a few weeks, Calvin returned to the States with Georgie. Harriet went to Paris to be with the twins, who were still studying there. She wintered in Florence with several other Americans, including some old friends from New England. Her son Frederick, who had been hiking in Italy, now joined his mother in Florence. Fred was now twenty-one years old, and Harriet was increasingly troubled by his lack of direction in life.

Fred, Harriet, and some American friends celebrated Christmas in Florence. Their lodgings were decorated for the holiday, and there was feasting and singing. This was now the second Christmas after Henry's death. Stowe hoped that it might be a bit easier to spend Christmas in a place where there were no reminders of Henry. But grief was a stowaway; it rode along in Harriet's heart.

An ocean away, Calvin continued to grieve. He wrote to Harriet of his strong feeling that Henry was somehow present. Ever since boyhood, Calvin claimed he could see and hear spirits. Now he wrote to Harriet that he distinctly heard a guitar strumming — although there was no one else in the house at the time. Harriet replied that the guitar sound was probably not made by Henry, so it must be Calvin's first wife Eliza, who had been very musical. Harriet advised Calvin to keep the guitar in his bedroom; perhaps he would hear from Eliza again.

By now Harriet and Calvin were dabbling in spiritualism.[48] It is impossible to say exactly when Stowe's interest in spiritualism started, but the void left by her son Henry's death made her more susceptible to it. On January 16, 1860, Harriet told Calvin that she felt separated "not only from [Henry] but from all spiritual communion with my God." Relief came through a spiritualist medium whom Stowe met in Florence. Stowe told Calvin that "Mrs. E." was, "without doubt . . . what the spiritualists would regard as a very powerful medium."

Mrs. E. claimed to be a devout Christian; she even worried about getting carried away by spiritualism. So Harriet told Mrs. E. "to try the spirits whether they were of God — to keep close to the Bible and prayer, and then accept whatever came." Harriet told Calvin that Mrs. E. helped her to feel close to "my Henry and other departed friends." She felt deeply comforted. Mrs. E. wanted to hear more of Calvin's experiences, since "it was so rare to hear of Christian and reliable people with such peculiarities." Mrs. E. knew her client.

Harriet told Calvin about "spirit writing," in which script appears on paper without hands or pen or pencil, communicating messages from "various historical people." She had read all about it in a book by "an old German in Paris," who combined "Pagan and Christian . . . Hindoo, Chinese, Greek and Italian literature." Harriet hedged that she did not necessarily *believe* what she read; she merely found it intriguing. Indeed, she said she saw spiritualism as a response to "the intense materialism of the present age." Back in Reformation times Martin Luther recognized a personal devil. So at the very least, Christians could "enter fully into the spiritualism of the Bible." Caution was needed, Stowe wrote, for not all spiritualism was compatible with Scripture. There were fakes who practiced "spiritual jugglery," she admitted.

Harriet could see that spiritualism involved some acting on the part of mediums, and some wishful thinking on the part of their clients. But was that all? Harriet thought there was a "real scriptural spiritualism which has fallen into disuse and must be revived." She recalled prophets and miracle workers who had "impressions of the surrounding spiritual world." Stowe failed to distinguish between supernaturalism, or the existence of spiritual powers, and spiritual*ism,* or human claims to communicate with those powers.

When Harriet met with Mrs. E. again they read the book of Revelation, and "talked of the saints and spirits of the just made perfect." As they spoke, Harriet seemed to feel Henry close by. There was a guitar hanging on the wall. No one was near it, but the bass string sounded clearly. Mrs. E. said that "if any spirit was present with us . . . it would try to touch that guitar." A little while later, they heard a sound "as if someone had drawn a hand across all the strings at once. We marveled, and I remembered the guitar at home."[49] One wonders if it occurred to Harriet that Mrs. E. somehow caused the guitar to sound because it would replicate Calvin's experience. In any event, Harriet's grief had made her more ready to believe.

To spiritualists, death was a gauzy veil, and mediums could lift that veil, or at least receive messages through it. Death was a "translation" into a higher life — not, as the apostle Paul said, "The last enemy to be destroyed" or "the wages of sin." If Harriet's son Henry had been translated into another state of being, then perhaps he was waiting, just beyond the veil, for his mother to reach out to him. In the years ahead, Harriet's interest in spiritualism would grow.

Agnes of Sorrento

At least the beauty of Italy gave Harriet some solid comfort. Late in the winter of 1860, she traveled with American friends to southern Italy.

221

The "climate of voluptuous ecstasy"[50] delighted her. In the market-place at Sorrento, Stowe saw a beautiful girl selling oranges. Stowe wanted to write about the girl, and set the story in the distant past. When bad weather made sightseeing impossible, Stowe wrote the first chapter of her story and read it to her traveling companions. The story "was voted into existence by the voices of all the party,"[51] Stowe later told her editor.

From the rugged cliffs of the Amalfi coast to the quaint villages and old churches, Stowe loved Italy. Italian artists, she wrote, used "poetry, sculpture and painting" with the same fervor as the Puritans applied to theology and morals.[52] Stowe began to wonder if medieval Catholics might have something in common with Puritans. The very idea flew in the face of all she had been taught, for New England Calvinists rejected anything that seemed Catholic. And yet, Stowe pursued, did not both groups have zeal for God, and faith in unseen things? Did they not both wage their battles for good and against evil?

Stowe called her Italian novel *Agnes of Sorrento,* and set it in the Middle Ages, when Catholicism was *the* Church. This allowed her to ask a question that compelled her: "Is there a Holy Church? Where is it?"[53] Could the true church have existed before the Reformation? Stowe knew that many of her readers, like herself, were taught to despise "the rosary, the crucifix, the shrine, the banner, the processions." And yet these things were but "catechisms and tracts invented for those who could not read." Protestants now have the "universal Press" to give the Bible to everyone, Stowe said, but they shouldn't "sneer at the homely rounds [rungs] of the ladder by which the first multitudes of the Lord's flock climbed heavenward."[54] Like a cloister garden, the medieval church was decayed — yet it lived, and had its own beauty through its very antiquity. Even now, said Stowe, healing plants grow in that cloister garden. One such "plant" was the communion of saints, a "spiritual consciousness"[55] that held the living and the dead together in Christ. The communion of saints opened death's door enough to be deeply consoling to Harriet.

Agnes of Sorrento would run as a serial in the *Atlantic* and then appear in book form in 1862. In wartime, reading a romance set in an exotic place was a good escape to someplace long ago and far away. But as usual with Stowe, there was a message: if Christianity could survive a corrupt papacy and the heresies of the medieval church, then Christianity could also survive being corrupted by slavery. Sometimes

Christians must be faithful *without* the church, or perhaps even in spite of it.

The Spirit of the Age

Stowe was abroad on October 16, 1859, when the abolitionist John Brown captured the federal arsenal at Harper's Ferry, Virginia. His failed attempt to ignite a slave insurrection sent shock waves through the nation. Brown was captured and hanged as a criminal, but many in the North saw him as a martyr in the cause of freedom. In the spring of 1860 when Stowe was in Italy, she said that John Brown did "more than any man yet for the honor of the American name."[56] Thus her voice joined the northern chorus hailing John Brown as a hero.

Harriet boarded the *Europa* on June 16, 1860, for her return voyage. She sailed with several other Americans she had spent time with in Italy,[57] including James and Annie Fields. This was to be an important connection for Stowe both personally and professionally. James Fields was a partner in Ticknor and Fields, a predecessor of modern publishers Houghton, Mifflin & Company. "By 1858 [Ticknor and Fields] was the most sought-after publishing house in the United States," and by 1860 it had become the publisher of *Uncle Tom's Cabin.*[58] Fields also became the editor of the *Atlantic Monthly.*[59] The publishing business was still very much a man's world, but James Fields tried to showcase the talents of women authors and sought to protect their interests. Annie Fields was an author in her own right; she became a close friend of Harriet's and one of her early biographers.

Shortly after Stowe returned from Europe, another shocking story broke. A U.S. Navy ship seized the *Erie,* an American slave ship off the coast of West Africa. The *Erie* was built in New York and captained by Nathaniel Gordon of Maine. Just before its capture, the *Erie* traded a cargo of rum for 897 captive Africans — half of them children. The captives had been so maltreated that thirty of them died before the U.S. Navy could deliver them to Liberia. Subsequently, two more slave ships, also built in New York and captained by Yankees, were seized. In 1862 Nathaniel Gordon was convicted and executed by hanging. Many a condemned man received Lincoln's pardon, but not Gordon. The *Erie* affair was the tip of the iceberg. Recent scholarship has confirmed that "by 1860, New York was notorious as the hub of an international illegal slave trade . . . too lucrative and too corrupt to stop." In 1859 and 1860 alone, ships from New York may have carried up to 40,000 Africans into bondage.[60]

Stowe would not keep silent. In November 1860 her article "The Church and the Slave Trade" appeared in the *Independent*. "Every week," Stowe wrote, "a slave ship leaves the port of New York . . . fitted out for this infernal traffic — to say nothing of what is done in other ports." Inspection officers, appointed by the government, are "constantly bribed" so that these "floating hells, with their living cargoes of horror and despair, are riding the waves with the connivance of" those who sit "in our churches and profess to be Christians." And what do northern church leaders say and do? Nothing!

This moral failure weakened "Christianity as a practical working force," Stowe charged. Slavery was a cancer on "the so-called Christian Church." Despite the public outcry over the *Erie,* Stowe reported, the Board of Commissioners for Foreign Missions remained silent. Stowe's father had been an early supporter of that very mission group.[61] How absurd that those who *say* they want to Christianize Africa stand silent when slave traders torch African villages, drive people in herds to the sea, and force them into the holds of ships that are floating hells, Stowe said. Stowe spoke plainly of the sweat, filth, and horrid diseases, "the daily throwing overboard of the dead" to be eaten by sharks. But all this is too "delicate" for the Board of Foreign Missions to discuss! Why pretend to send "a Gospel" to Africa, when we lack the will to prevent our own "civilized, Christianized, churchgoing people" from tolerating, or even profiting from, the slave trade? If we cannot make ourselves into Christians, Stowe challenged, what do we expect to make of the Africans?

Stowe saw the foundations of American Protestantism rotting with moral decay. It was time for new groups to take over. Christian moral power was now more likely to be found in "political speeches of the Republican Party" than in "pulpits and some so-called religious papers."

It was now the fall of 1860. And Stowe felt "a mighty force, which we call the *spirit of the age,* burning like an oven" against all injustice and cruelty. That spirit was none other than "the *Spirit of the Lord.*" If the church would not bear witness, the Spirit would work outside the churches. If need be, the Lord would raise up armies to crush slavery, that serpent from hell.[62]

CHAPTER FOURTEEN

The Galling Harness of War

Southern states threatened to secede if Lincoln won the election in November 1860, and this time they meant it. In December outgoing President James Buchanan gave a speech in which he blamed the nation's troubles on the abolitionists. It was a shame that decent southern women could not sleep in their beds at night for fear of a slave uprising, he said.

Yes, blame the North, Stowe told readers of the *Independent.* The wicked, treacherous North! Oh how *sad* that slaveholders cannot sleep in their beds at night, the poor, innocent lambs! Well, if the slaves rebel, who is to blame? Do southerners really expect slavery to last forever? In her mind's eye Stowe could see "Old Africa" rising, lifting "her poor maimed, scarred hand to heaven," crying out, "'IS GOD DEAD?'"[1] Her readers were supposed to shout a resounding "NO!" Perhaps they did, but nobody in South Carolina was listening. On December 20, 1860, the same day Stowe's article appeared, South Carolina voted to secede from the Union.

That December Stowe probably decorated her house with a Christmas tree. To make Calvin well-rounded, the daughters may have baked cookies. The family no doubt attended church services where they sang hymns and prayed for peace — or victory if war came. It must have been a very strange holiday season.

The new year brought more secession: Mississippi, Florida, Alabama, Georgia, Louisiana, and Texas left the Union. In February the Confederate States of America formed. The Confederacy began to seize federal forts and arsenals in the South. Virginia, Arkansas, Tennessee, and North Carolina joined the Confederacy. Four more slave states (Missouri, Kentucky, Maryland, and Delaware) stayed in the Union, dangling by a thread.

Lincoln gave his First Inaugural Address on March 4, 1861, pleading that North and South must not be enemies but friends. "The better angels of our nature" might yet prevail and swell the chorus of Union. Six weeks later, South Carolinians fired on Fort Sumter, and Lincoln called for 75,000 volunteers to put down the rebellion.

This was good news for Harriet's son Fred who, at twenty-three years of age, needed a cause. First he tried to enlist as an army medical officer, but was rejected; then he joined Company A of the First Massachusetts Volunteers,[2] which was then in Boston. Stowe's nephew Henry Ward Beecher Jr. was in training there too. Later, Stowe recalled that she went "every week to see them at their Armory when they first enlisted, little dreaming for what earnest and bloody work they had gone in and how few of them should ever return."[3]

One day in July, Stowe was in Brooklyn visiting family when her brother Henry rushed in, shouting that he had just seen the *Commonwealth,* with Fred's regiment aboard, sailing down the East River bound for Jersey City — a mere fourteen miles away. Harriet and several others took a carriage to Jersey City, where Fred's regiment was gathering at the railroad depot. Crowds pressed close to the locked, grated doors of the depot, straining for a glimpse of their sons and husbands and brothers inside.

Someone from Stowe's group wangled a pass. Entering the military compound, they saw a crowd of off-duty blue-clad soldiers eating, smoking, laughing, and singing. Fred saw his mother and came bounding over; Harriet's "first impulse was to wipe his face with my handkerchief before I kissed him." Fred was in high spirits, proud of his new uniform. Harriet had brought oranges, and Fred filled his haversack with them. Stowe thought both her son Fred and nephew Henry were "mysteriously changed," having "come to manhood in a day."[4] Fred and Henry would soon join thousands of Union soldiers guarding Washington City from a possible Confederate attack.

Stowe knew the war would not be easy. "We have before us a long, grave period of severe self-denial and enterprise," she told readers. The war "will task the resources, physical, mental and moral, of our Northern states." Sacrifices must be made in this "last great struggle for liberty," but Christ was coming to "save the poor and needy."[5] In a poem called "The Holy War," Stowe envisioned the Union army riding forth as if from the book of Revelation, followed by Christ clad in white raiment. This was to be a "sacred war" for freedom and justice, she told readers of the *Independent.* Stowe's millennial vision anticipated Julia Ward Howe's "Battle Hymn of the Republic," which appeared in the *Atlantic Monthly* in February 1862.

A Deafening Silence

When the war broke out, Stowe expected British reformers to support the North. Great Britain was officially neutral, for English mills needed southern cotton; and some of the British elite sympathized with southern aristocrats. Still, Harriet expected British reformers to give moral support to the Union, and their silence vexed her. What happened to the thousands of British women who signed the Appeal against slavery? What became of the cheering throngs that had welcomed Stowe in England and Scotland? Where were the British aristocrats who had opened their mansions to her? Now that the war was on, "English friends, whom we may count by millions, stood silent."[6] Stowe felt betrayed.

Nevertheless, Stowe told readers in the *Independent,* she didn't need to look across the Atlantic for inspiration when it was just outside her own front door. Across the campus of Andover and through the windows of the Stone Cabin drifted martial sounds of fife and drum. Stowe could hear the marching feet of young men whom the war diverted from ministry to the military. "The theological students" of Andover were now in uniform and drilling daily. Perhaps, Harriet told her readers, army life would save these young men from becoming "dyspeptic theologians."

In early June 1861 Andover Seminary held a flag-raising ceremony for the town. There were hymns and prayers, and Calvin Stowe preached a patriotic sermon. Local troops marched while a military band played. On the lawn facing the Stowe house, the young recruits stacked their muskets around the flag. Refreshments were served on the green. In Stowe's large home gathered local dignitaries, trustees and professors of Andover Seminary, and military officers with a company of soldiers. A speech was made about the flag bringing "liberty to the whole earth."

Weeks passed, and still England remained neutral. "Where are the voices of our former friends in England?"[7] Stowe wondered. What if Great Britain chose to recognize and give military aid to the Confederacy? It was unthinkable! Or was it?

Stowe decided to give her British friends a prod. She wrote an open letter to Lord Shaftesbury, knowing it would be printed in papers at home and in England. Stowe tried in her message to be conciliatory. If the good people of Britain did not understand what the war was really about, she would explain. The war, she said, was "the direct result" of "agitation" carried on for more than a century by anti-slavery forces *in England* and America.[8] Yes, she admitted, the stated goal for the war was to save the Union and not *officially* to end slavery. But saving the Union and ending slavery were two sides of the same coin: to save the Union, slavery must be abolished. "The very existence of a free society" hung in the balance. "This war is a great Anti-Slavery war," Stowe declared. When Lincoln won the election, the slave power could "no longer use the Union" for its own "purposes, so they resolved to destroy it." Anyone who doubted that the war was really about slavery should know that Alexander Stephens (Vice President of the Confederacy) boasted that the South had "the first Government in the history of the world based on the right to enslave the weaker races." No matter what people said, the war was about slavery. Therefore "friends in England" must now "aid us with their prayers" and stop flirting with the South. For "now, if ever, we have a country that is worth dying for, and a cause in which we count nothing too dear."

Stowe's letter ran in the *Independent* on July 21 — the day Union soldiers were defeated at Bull Run. Yankee soldiers fled in panic. (Fred Stowe, however, comported himself well at Bull Run and was promoted to the rank of sergeant.[9]) News of the southern victory reached England along with Stowe's letter, greatly weakening the force of her appeal. Stowe had said the Union army was united as one man; but at Bull Run the Union army scattered and fled. And that was not all. British reformers questioned why the North did not let blacks enlist in the army[10] and why Lincoln did not emancipate the slaves immediately.

That summer, Lydia Marie Child (writer and abolitionist) talked with Stowe at a party. Stowe said she had little faith in politicians, but she trusted God to work through events. As they talked, Child observed Stowe's "*Puritan* education," for Stowe saw "the hand of God" ordering all events, and was sure that "Pharaoh would be swamped and Israel go free."[11] Stowe looked to divine providence and God's sovereign will to bring about freedom and justice.

September found Stowe still smarting over the silence from Great Britain. "Where are the voices of our former friends in England?" she lamented. This war was for "God and liberty . . . human rights and human equality." So "with or without the help and sympathy of foreign nations, the year of Christ's redeemed has come, and . . . this war will emancipate the slave."[12]

But freedom for the slaves was slow in coming. In August 1861 the Confiscation Act "allowed the capture and liberation only of those slaves who were engaged in the Confederate military effort."[13] Thousands of slaves flocked to the Union Armies and crowded into Washington. These "contrabands of war" would not be returned to the South, which needed their labor to keep farms running, so the Confiscation Act in effect nullified the Fugitive Slave Law. The contrabands had no masters. They could earn wages, yet theirs was "an ambiguous twilight status." Many of them lived in makeshift settlements much like refugee camps.[14] They were not slaves, but they weren't really free, either.

Down in Missouri, Union General John C. Frémont invoked martial law and emancipated the slaves in that border state. Abolitionists crowed like roosters at dawn, and Stowe hailed Frémont as the man of the hour. "To give liberty to the slave" Stowe declared, makes "every heart in the nation" leap. Her September 12 *Independent* article praised Frémont's "grand and heroic" deed.[15]

The euphoria was short-lived, however, for Lincoln revoked Frémont's proclamation, relieved him of command, and transferred him "to an obscure post in western Virginia." Abolitionists seethed; William Lloyd Garrison lashed Lincoln in the *Liberator*.[16] Calvin Stowe told Salmon P. Chase (a friend from Cincinnati, now in Lincoln's Cabinet) to register "surprise, indignation, disgust, and contempt"[17] at Lincoln's actions. Harriet doubtless felt the same. Lincoln had good reasons for what he did, however. He had to keep the Border States in the Union at all costs, and Frémont's proclamation could have pushed those states toward secession. Besides, Lincoln could not permit a general in the field to make decisions that only the President should make.

This was a trying time for Stowe. Freedom for the slave seemed to be on hold, friends in England had let her down, and the lack of decisive Union victories was demoralizing. But most of all she was worried about her son Fred. Army life meant long stretches of tedium punctuated by moments of terror. Fred might be drinking to relieve boredom or to bolster his courage. Would Fred fall in battle, or succumb to the bottle? All Harriet could do for him was pray.

Who Could Write Stories?

In the middle of all of this, somehow Stowe got her Italian novel, *Agnes of Sorrento,* ready for the *Atlantic Monthly.* She was also trying to finish a story she had begun several years before — a New England novel called *The Pearl of Orr's Island,* which was slated to run as a serial in the *Independent.* However, in December 1861, Stowe wrote a notice to inform her readers that she was having trouble finishing *The Pearl of Orr's Island.* Her "health was so reduced" by "the agitations and mental excitements of the war" that the she had little time or strength to devote to writing. "Who could write stories," she said, with a son sent "to battle, with Washington beleaguered, and the whole country shaken as with an earthquake?" Indeed, "who could write fiction when fact was . . . so terrible?"

Stowe promised to resume her story for the *Independent* soon. She had intended *Pearl* to be a shorter work, but "certain spirits infesting the ink stand" made it into a full-length novel.[18] Her twin novels, *Agnes of Sorrento* and *Pearl of Orr's Island,* both appeared as books in the summer of 1862. Stowe had started writing *Pearl* back in 1852 only to shelve it in favor of *A Key to Uncle Tom's Cabin.* By the time *Pearl* was done, Stowe had made three trips to Europe, mourned her son Henry, and sent Fred off to war. Like a neglected child, *Pearl* was always waiting for the quality time that never came. If Stowe had given it her full attention, critics say, *Pearl* could have been her finest novel. Even so, John Greenleaf Whittier called it "the most charming New England idyll ever written."[19]

The *Pearl of Orr's Island* opens in tragedy. Off the coast of Maine a shipwreck causes a young wife to become a widow; she goes into labor and dies in childbirth. The baby, a girl named Mara, survives and is raised by kindly grandparents. They adopt another child — the survivor of another shipwreck — and name him Moses, for he was "drawn out of the water." Mara and Moses grow up together in a village peopled by the sort of neighbors Harriet knew as a child: the retired sea captain, the kindly minister, and the old aunts who know everything about everyone for miles around.

Mara's life is restricted because she is a girl. She is highly intelligent but cannot go away to school; she loves the sea but cannot be a sailor; she is respected by all but can never be a leader. The only path open to Mara is that of spiritual growth. Mara needs Moses to "connect" her with "the great world,"[20] and Moses relies on Mara to help him be good.

Moses goes off to sea, and Mara prays for him faithfully. After a long absence Moses returns to find Mara slowly dying from consumption. She tells Moses that her life "was all thought and feeling and the narrow little duties of this little home" while Moses "went around the world."[21] Growing up as a daughter in the Beecher household, Harriet was well aware that her brothers were allowed much more freedom than the sisters.

Yet Stowe makes Mara's world central to the reader.[22] Moses is free to roam the world, but his life lacks meaning. Only when he returns to Mara and sees her depth of soul can he be redeemed by her unselfish love. Once more, a dying person imparts blessing to those left behind. Moses marries a girl who (thanks to Mara's influence) has become a mature woman. As C. H. Foster has written, *Pearl*'s "guiding principle is 'sea change,' the transformation of death and the mystery of death [and] of all tragedy, into comedy and beauty."[23]

In Stowe's novel, Christianity it is like Maine itself — beautiful in its stark simplicity. Nature reveals the majesty of God and history (seen through eyes of faith) reveals God's providence working all things together for good, for those who love God and are called according to his purpose (Romans 8:28). Mara's life is short and hidden from the world, but as a willing instrument of God's providence[24] she accomplishes much.

The Pearl of Orr's Island has a kind of theme song that Stowe invokes three times in the course of the story.[25] The tune is called "Old China," but Stowe calls it "the old funeral psalm of New England":

Why do we mourn departing friends, or shake at death's alarms?
'Tis but the voice that Jesus sends, to call us to his arms.

Are we not tending upward too, as fast as time can move?
And should we wish the hours more slow, that bear us to our love?

Then let the last loud trumpet sound, and bid the dead arise.
Awake ye nations underground, ye saints, ascend the skies!

Stowe wanted readers to *hear* Old China it as she heard it in childhood: a "strange, wild warble, whose quaintly blended harmonies"
sounded like "moaning seas or wailing winds, so strange and grand
they rose, full of that intense pathos" as the singers invoked "something sublime and immortal."[26] Here is a primal sound, fiercely orthodox in its view of death and resurrection, yet deeply consoling, like
the sound of bagpipes from a distant hill.

Elsewhere in *Pearl,* however, Stowe articulated a view of death that
echoed spiritualism. She called death a "translation" to greater spiritual existence, from which departed spirits may bless[27] the living.
Then again, she may have echoed a sentiment of Puritan divine Cotton Mather, that "good angels *continually . . .* minister to them that are
to be the heirs of salvation."[28]

In any case, Harriet felt that saints above can somehow reach and
bless the living. And devout women were prime candidates for this
kind of sainthood. Women were supposedly more religious than men
and more sensitive to the needs of others. Stowe explored notions of
female piety in *Pearl,* but she knew this to be a two-edged sword. For if
religion made women more devoted daughters, sisters, and wives, it
could also make blacks more obedient slaves. Deeply religious people
can be exploited by those more worldly. "I love your religion," Moses
tells Mara, "because it makes you love me." It was not unusual for
men to off-load their hopes for heaven onto their wives. One of
Stowe's fictional aunts disapproves of "using up girls for the salvation
of men."[29] If women's faith was indeed a hidden treasure, a pearl of
great price, it was to be cherished, not exploited.

Near the end of *Pearl* Stowe tells readers she will give them not a
happy ending, but a bittersweet one. Success does not mean living
happily ever after, she tells her readers, for "that life is a success
which, like the life of Jesus," bears "perfect witness to the truth and
the highest form of truth."[30] Christ "speaks of himself as *bread* to be
eaten — bread, simple, humble, unpretending, vitally necessary to
human life, made by the bruising and grinding of the grain . . . having
no life or worth of its own except as it is absorbed into the life of others, and lives in them." Stowe said she wanted *Pearl* to show souls
"formed on the model of Christ." Lives lived in sacrifice may seem to

"end in darkness . . . but . . . with the eye of faith, we should see that their living and dying has been bread of life to those they left behind." Sorrow can be ennobling, she wrote. It melts "trivial ambitions and low desires" and makes a person "feel the value of love."[31] The bruising and grinding of grain was an apt metaphor for a people at war.

The war was slowly grinding on during the winter and spring of 1862. General George B. McClellan found endless reasons not to use his Union army in Virginia. General Grant used his army in southwest Tennessee at the battle of Shiloh, but both sides suffered horrific losses. At last, on April 25, Admiral David Farragut captured New Orleans — finally, a clear-cut Union victory!

I Want You to Win Laurels

Late that spring Stowe was in Brooklyn visiting family. One Sunday it rained so hard that she decided to stay home from church. Instead she wrote a long, meditative letter to her daughters. Hattie, Eliza, and Georgiana were now young women who had money, wore stylish clothes, and could travel to Europe. And Harriet was distressed that her daughters, especially the twins, seemed so frivolous and worldly.

That particular Sunday, as Stowe reminded her daughters, was Ascension Day, the ancient festival marking Christ's ascent to heaven after Easter. It was also a Communion Sunday. When "we go to the table of Christ," she reminded them, "we renew our oath of allegiance to our Heavenly King." We "pledge ourselves" to God's "great work . . . subduing all evil & wiping away all tears & bringing in the reign of perfect love." Christians belong to a world-wide body, "led by one Spirit & educated to come to this final perfection," and are called to "the most exalted ideal of life." How, then, could her daughters be so complacent?

What if a soldier joined "our army," Stowe asked, intending to get by "without effort & without sacrifice," and to avoid all discomfort and pain? That soldier would be useless! So too with Christians who "live easy." Harriet wrote that her son Fred, despite all his troubles, enlisted to fight for the Union. True, the girls could not join the army — but they could try to find some purpose! "I pray God daily that this sense of your holy calling may be given to you," she wrote. If only they would do "something *worth* all the prayers of years." Her daughters were blessed with "more than average power & energy: power of influence." Yet they seemed content "to be drones and idlers in Christ's army." Sounding very much like her father, Lyman Beecher, Stowe told her own children, "I want you to win *laurels* — such laurels as Christ gives to those who have overcome self" and have "suffered in his behalf."

In order to do so, they had to change their hearts. But how? They could start each day with this vow:

> *I am no longer of this world — as Christ is heavenly so am I. I have renounced all low aims and ambitions . . . the vanities of this wicked world. I have risen with Christ — I am baptized in his name. I have taken his vows, his ring is on my finger — his kingdom is my kingdom — his work my work — his house my house. Christ is my Lord & I am his child.*

Then Harriet got down to cases. How often she had heard her daughters indulge in mockery! It made Harriet "wonder what you laugh at in me!" Suppose that, if she and Calvin were in England hobnobbing with Lords and Duchesses and Charles Dickens, these celebrities had called Harriet "the little humpback" or mocked Calvin as "old stumpy"! But if the high-born could treat commoners with respect, then the daughters of Harriet Beecher Stowe should at least attempt to speak with refinement. How could they go to church and pray "Our Father" and in the very next breath make fun of others? Did they not know that youth and beauty are fleeting charms? That someday they, too, would be old and frumpy?

That afternoon, if the rain slackened, Harriet was planning to visit her father, who was now eighty-six years old. Father "is always delighted to see me tho he knows not who I am," she told her daughters. When she was young, the approach of his "joyful footsteps" made Harriet feel that she "had someone coming on whom I could lean all my cares." Back then, "the very touch of his hand seemed to put strength into me," but now the old man's hands trembled. His hair was pure white, and he could not call his own children by name. "My children it is a great and sacred lesson this life of man — may you learn it well. Your loving Mother."[32]

Lincoln Has Been Too Slow

Lincoln was pleading, too — for the Border States to free their slaves. He offered them financial compensation, but they refused.[33] Pleading did not work, and neither did money. It was becoming clear that an emancipation order of some kind was necessary. But Lincoln thought the Constitution did not give the President the power to issue such an order, except perhaps as a war measure. He was working on it.

That July Lincoln read a draft of the Emancipation Proclamation to his cabinet, asking for responses. Some feared that emancipation would start a race war in the South. Secretary of State William Seward pointed out that unless the Emancipation Proclamation followed a clear Union victory, it "might be viewed as the last measure of an exhausted government, a cry for help . . . our last *shriek,* on the retreat." Lincoln later said that Seward's words "struck me with very great force . . . the result was that I put the draft of the proclamation aside . . . waiting for a victory."[34] He hoped the wait would not be long. The Emancipation Proclamation was indeed a war measure to deprive the Confederacy of slave labor *and* allow black men to join the Union army. For the time being it would leave slaves in the Border States alone. That too was a war consideration. It would take a Constitutional amendment to finish the job of ending slavery. Lincoln was waiting for the right time to announce his plans for emancipation.

That summer Stowe often felt overwhelmed by the war. She would lie on her bed for hours, able only to gaze at pictures on her wall. Her favorite one depicted Christ just before his crucifixion. Stowe hung that picture where she would see it first thing upon waking and last before sleeping. Under the picture she posted these words: "Forasmuch as Christ also hath suffered for us in the flesh, arm your selves with the same mind" (1 Peter 4:1).

Stowe wrote all this to the Duchess of Argyll. "The utter failure of Christian anti-slavery England" to support the North in the war was heartbreaking to Harriet. She called London's Exeter Hall, the place where reformers rallied, "a pious humbug like the rest." And even the great Lord Shaftesbury, the so-called People's Earl, had southern sympathies. "Well — let him go — he . . . has after all the instincts of his class." She complained that the British press reported Union atrocities while "the horrible barbarities of *southern* soldiers" passed without comment. Why was "*all* expression of sympathy on the *southern* side?" Stowe sighed, "You can see I am bitter — I am."

In spite of it all, she knew one thing: "slavery will be sent out by this agony" — with or without England's support. Stowe compared the war to "the throes & ravings of the exorcism." The demon slavery was doomed, Stowe was convinced. So why did the President take so long to free the slaves? "Lincoln has been too slow," Stowe told the Duchess. "He should have done it sooner, and with an impulse, but come it must, come it will." Whether or not God was with the President or the North or the Union, Stowe knew that God "is with the slave — & with redemption will come the solution."[35]

Many others shared Stowe's impatience with Lincoln. Horace Greeley, editor of the *New York Tribune,* published an open letter to Lincoln in August 1862. The letter, entitled "The Prayer of Twenty Millions," scolded the President for his slowness to free the slaves. "Every hour of deference to Slavery is an hour of added and deepened peril to the Union," warned Greeley.[36] Lincoln should stop placating "fossil politicians" in the Border States. He should stop kowtowing to antique laws that protected slavery. Greeley scolded Lincoln as though he were some tardy schoolboy.

Within days, Lincoln sent an open letter to Greeley that was printed in the *New York Tribune.*

Washington, August 22, 1862.

Hon. Horace Greeley:
Dear Sir.
. . . As to the policy I "seem to be pursuing" as you say, I have not meant to leave any one in doubt.
I would save the Union. I would save it the shortest way under the Constitution. The sooner the national authority can be restored; the nearer the Union will be to "the Union as it was." If there be those who would not save the Union, unless they could at the same time *save* slavery, I do not agree with them. If there be those who would not save the Union unless they could at the same time *destroy* slavery, I do not agree with them. My paramount object in this struggle *is* to save the Union, and is *not* either to save or to destroy slavery. If I could save the Union without freeing *any* slave I would do it, and if I could save it by freeing *all* the slaves I would do it; and if I could

save it by freeing some and leaving others alone I would also do that. What I do about slavery, and the colored race, I do because I believe it helps to save the Union; and what I forbear, I forbear because I do *not* believe it would help to save the Union. I shall do *less* whenever I shall believe what I am doing hurts the cause, and I shall do *more* whenever I shall believe doing more will help the cause. . . . I have here stated my purpose according to my view of *official* duty; and I intend no modification of my oft-expressed *personal* wish that all men everywhere could be free.[37]

Lincoln did not reveal that the Emancipation Proclamation was slated to go into effect on January 1, 1863, or that he was waiting for an opportune time to announce it. The President may have "hoped that his letter [to Greeley] would soften the public impact of what he knew would be a controversial proclamation,"[38] writes historian Doris Kearns Goodwin.

Stowe was tired of waiting. Her article questioning Lincoln appeared in the September 11 *Independent*[39] under the odd title, "Will You Take a Pilot?" The Union, Stowe wrote, was like a ship driven by the tempest of war, and the President was not steering the ship very well. He needed a "pilot" to bring the ship safely to port. Jesus was the pilot whose mission was to "to preach deliverance to the captives . . . to set at liberty them that are bruised." But alas, the "policy of the King of kings" seemed just the opposite of Lincoln's policy.

What would Jesus say in reply to Horace Greeley's letter? Stowe parodied Lincoln's letter as she imagined Jesus saying,

My paramount object . . . is to set at liberty them that are *bruised* and *not* either to save or destroy the Union. What I do in favor of the Union, I do because it helps to free the oppressed; what I forbear, I forbear because it does not help to free the oppressed. I shall do less for the Union whenever it would hurt the cause of the slave, and more when I believe it would help the cause of the slave.[40]

Lincoln "loves the Union [but] does he believe in Christ?" Stowe pursued. If so, he must see that God wills to remove "injustice and cruelty." To allow slavery to continue a moment longer was to disobey God's will, exposing Union soldiers to the wrath of God. The Union must stop obstructing God's will, she said, and the sooner Lincoln could "take a pilot," the better. As for her readers, they too must take Jesus as their captain. "Are we ready in this dark storm to receive [Christ] into our ship?" When the will of the people "is sufficiently strong and unanimous, [Lincoln] will hesitate no more. Each individual must answer the question, 'shall Jesus of Nazareth come into our ship?'"[41]

Stowe believed that God works providentially through the events of history. Sometimes she equated God's cause with that of the North. At other times she questioned whether God's will and the northern cause might be two different things. In "Pilot" she noted that "on both sides of these armies . . . praying hands [are] uplifted for and against. Christ is for neither."[42] Christ was for the slaves, not for the North or the South. Therefore the North must try harder to be on God's side by freeing the slaves.

Lincoln's moment came in September after the battle of Antietam. Both armies suffered heavy losses (some 23,000 casualties combined), but General Lee withdrew, and a Union victory was declared. Several days later, on September 22, Lincoln told his cabinet that the time had come to announce the Emancipation Proclamation, slated to become law on January 1, 1863.

Abolitionists were wary. After all his dilly-dallying, what if Lincoln changed his mind about emancipation? Henry Ward Beecher fumed to readers of the *Independent* that Lincoln had "not a spark of genius . . . not an element for leadership. Not one particle of heroic enthusiasm." Henry at times sounded like a traitor: "the North is beaten," he wrote, and Lincoln's incompetence "is bringing us to humiliation. Be it known that the Nation wasted away by the incurable consumption of Central Imbecility."[43] Someone clipped Beecher's editorials and sent them to Lincoln, who read them while having his portrait painted. The artist, Francis Carpenter, noticed that "As Lincoln finished reading, his face flushed with indignation and he threw the packet to the floor exclaiming, 'Is thy servant a *dog*, that he should do this thing?'"[44] Then Lincoln seemed to let his anger go. Perhaps the President took Beecher's rant as an indicator that public opinion was moving toward emancipation.[45] Besides, he had more important things to worry about than Henry Ward Beecher — or his sister Harriet, for that matter.

Several of Henry's siblings tried to shush him. Thomas Beecher warned that Henry's editorials were hurting more than helping. Mary and Harriet wrote a joint letter to their brother Henry. "What possible good is to be gained," Mary chided, by destroying "all confidence in the Administration and in the commanders of our army? . . . You are doing all you can to discourage and weaken, you make every man's heart lead in his bosom." Harriet told Henry it was "hopeless" to come out in print saying Lincoln was "destitute of a single capacity for leadership."[46] He might as well tell a ship's "crew in a storm" that their captain "is drunk or imbecile." Henry's attacks on Lincoln struck Harriet as "deeply discouraging." Why, he should go to Washington and find out for himself what was happening. Go "talk with Chase and Seward and Lincoln," she said. Encourage them rather than tearing them down. "I will go if you will," she offered.

Harriet in Washington

Harriet was already planning a trip to Washington with or without her brother Henry. She had to see her son Fred, who was stationed just outside the capital. She had "heard that [Fred's] physician was prescribing whiskey for his ague. . . . God only knows what the temptations of soldiers are in so cold & comfortless a life as theirs."[47] Also, she had been invited to attend a huge Thanksgiving dinner for "contrabands" (ex-slaves) living in Washington. And of course, she must find out if the Emancipation Proclamation was a sure thing. "I am going to Washington to see the heads of departments myself," she told a friend.

At that time, Stowe was writing an open letter to British women in response to their mass petition some years before. She wanted to rally their support for the North. But to make her letter effective, she needed to be sure that emancipation was really going to happen: "I mean to have a talk with 'Father Abraham' himself, among others."[48] Lincoln's proclamation would show the world that this was a war against slavery, making the British morally obligated to support the North, Stowe reasoned. Her letter to British women was slated for the January 1863 *Atlantic Monthly* and would be picked up in the British press. The plan was for Stowe's letter to reach Great Britain at the same time as Lincoln's proclamation.

Harriet went to Washington, with her daughter Hatty (and by some accounts her son Charles and half-sister Isabella).[49] Stopping in Brooklyn for some days, Stowe again invited her brother Henry. He declined.[50] At the time Mrs. Lincoln was in New York, and Henry and Harriet arranged to meet her. In a letter to Calvin, Harriet later described Mrs. Lincoln as "a good hearted weak woman fat, & frank." But there was nothing weak about Mrs. Lincoln's opinions, for "she denounced McClellan with a will (Seward also.)" Mrs. Lincoln invited Mrs. Stowe to tea at the White House.[51]

Arriving in the capital, Harriet and Hatty set off in search of Fred. They knew he was stationed at Fort Runyon in northern Virginia, defending the Long Bridge over the Potomac into Washington. But finding him took an entire day. First Harriet and Hatty needed a permit to enter the army camp; then they were sent from one commander to another. Fred needed permission to see them and a furlough to go with them. At last all was arranged. Stowe said she was "never happier than when at last [Fred] sprang into the carriage free to go with us for forty-eight hours."[52] Harriet, Hatty, and Fred stayed in rented rooms near Fort Runyon.

Fred was "looking well," Harriet told Calvin. He had filled out some "and is as loving and affectionate as a boy can be." But garrison duty bored Fred, so Harriet pleaded with her family back home to write to him more often. "Every home letter about home things has a holy tendency" even if there was "nothing of religion specifically expressed in it,"[53] she urged. Harriet would advocate for Fred to be reassigned; while in Washington, she asked two generals about it.[54] By January Fred was "suffering in the suspense" of waiting for this new assignment, so Stowe wrote to a friend in Washington asking him to "see what the hitch is and where the thing sticks."[55] Had she known where Fred's new assignment would lead him, she might have left well enough alone.

After visiting Fred at Fort Runyon, Harriet and Hattie went back to Washington. There they attended the Thanksgiving dinner with over a thousand contrabands, roughly one-fourth of those who crowded the capital.[56] Most of these former slaves wore rags or cast-off Union uniforms, performing menial labor for the army — but they were slaves no more.

Stowe wrote scenes from this Thanksgiving dinner into her letter to the women of Great Britain. "An old blind negro" prayed over the meal, and the ex-slaves sang "Go down, Moses, Way down into Egypt's land! Tell King Pharaoh to let my people go!" As Stowe was leaving the banquet, an old black woman "came and lifted up her hands in blessing."[57]

Stowe sent her letter off to the *Atlantic Monthly,* assuring her editor, James Fields, "it seems to be the opinion here that the president will stand up to his Proclamation . . . a glorious expectancy." According to Joan Hedrick, Stowe dated and mailed her letter a week *before* meeting with Lincoln in the White House.[58] Thanks to her contacts in Washington, including Senators and at least one cabinet member, Stowe was sure that Lincoln would follow through with emancipation.

On Monday, December 1, young Hatty (perhaps accompanied by her mother) "had the pleasure . . . of seeing Congress open and hearing the President's message read."[59] "In giving freedom to the slave, we assure freedom to the free," Lincoln wrote. ". . . We shall nobly save, or meanly lose, the last best hope of earth."[60]

On the evening of December 2, Stowe and her daughter Hatty (and perhaps sister Isabella and son Charles) went to the White House, accompanied by Senator Henry Wilson of Massachusetts and his wife. Wilson introduced the Stowes to Lincoln.[61] As the story goes, Lincoln quipped, "So you are the little woman who made this big war."[62] The comment, if indeed it was made, had a touch of wry humor, for it was common knowledge that slaveholders blamed the war on abolitionists generally and on *Uncle Tom's Cabin* in particular. And Harriet was indeed "little" in stature compared to the tall, gaunt Lincoln. He must have had to bend low just to shake her hand.

"It was a very droll time that we had in the White House," Hatty wrote home to her twin sister, Eliza. Hatty said she and her mother were "ready to explode with laughter all the while our backs were almost broken trying to keep it in." Somehow they suppressed their mirth, but as soon as they got back to their rooms, Hatty said, "we perfectly screamed and held our sides while we relieved ourselves of the pent up laughter that had almost been the cause of death." What was so funny? Maybe it was a release of tension; maybe Lincoln's sense of humor tickled them; or perhaps Stowe's daughter Hatty was amused by Lincoln's gangly appearance and his Illinois twang.[63]

Lincoln, for his part, may have found his New England visitors equally amusing. Harriet was devout; Hatty was vain; and Isabella (if she was there) was so *very* sincere. Perhaps Lincoln enjoyed poking fun and watching the New Englanders try to maintain decorum. One wonders what Stowe and Lincoln talked about — her letter to the women of England perhaps, or the Emancipation Proclamation. But when Harriet wrote to Calvin, she said only, "I had a real funny interview with the President . . . the particulars of which I will tell you."[64]

Except for the laughter, no particulars of that meeting have survived. Several years later, Stowe recalled Lincoln's sense of humor. Lincoln could laugh at times "when crying could do no good," she said. "His jests and stories helped off many a sorry hour," and nerved the weary "for another pull in the galling harness."[65] And the harness of war was indeed galling in December 1862, when southern forces slaughtered Union soldiers at Fredericksburg.

When Stowe returned home from Washington, she could easily have written an article about her evening in the White House. Instead she told readers in the *Independent* of a surprise visit by a black preacher. "There came a black man to our house a few days ago," Stowe said, "who had spent five years at hard labor in a Maryland penitentiary for the crime of having a copy of *Uncle Tom's Cabin* in his house." He was sentenced to ten years, but abolitionists demanded his release. Finally this was granted — if the man would go to Canada and never return to Maryland. He agreed to these terms. On his way north, the released prisoner stopped in Andover to meet the author whose book had cost him so much. He had lost everything he owned in this world, Stowe said, and had nothing but "an infirmity of the limbs which he had caught from prison labor." He did not complain, but bore it in patience like the innocent man who helped to carry Jesus' cross. Stowe's guest said his jailers confiscated his copy of *Uncle Tom's Cabin.* Would she spare him a copy so he could finish reading it? She was glad to oblige.[66]

CHAPTER FIFTEEN

A Real and Living Power

January 1, 1863, was a New Year's Day like no other. Lincoln was going to sign the Emancipation Proclamation, and receptions were held throughout Washington City in anticipation. At the White House visitors lined up to congratulate Lincoln, who looked, according to one reporter, grizzled and stooped. But he greeted each person with "a smile and a kind remark,"[1] and kept his "old pump handle" busy, shaking hands without letup.

That afternoon Lincoln returned to his office to sign the proclamation. A White House aide saw him dip his pen in ink and move his hand as if to sign. Then Lincoln stopped and laid the pen down. "I never, in my life, felt more certain that I was doing right, than I do in signing this paper . . . my whole soul is in it," Lincoln said. But his hand and arm ached, and he did not want his signature to express hesitation. He paused, picked up the pen, and signed his name "slowly and carefully." Lincoln's signature was "unusually bold, clear, and firm, even for him," recalled the aide.[2]

Like thousands of people across the North, Stowe awaited news that Lincoln had signed. The day grew late, and no telegram came. *Had Lincoln changed his mind?* At Boston's Tremont Temple a crowd of some three thousand waited for "the first flash of the electric wires," Frederick Douglass recalled, and messengers stood ready to run from the telegraph office with the news.[3] That night Stowe was in Boston too, at Music Hall, where literati such as Emerson, Longfellow, and Whittier waited for news of Lincoln's signing, passing the time with music, prayers, and poetry readings.

Around 10:00 that night, runners from the telegraph office sped through the crowds, shouting, "It is coming! It is on the wires!" Stowe was in the gallery at Music Hall when a man ran onto the stage shouting, "Lincoln has signed!" The hall erupted with cheering, weeping, hugging, and kissing. A cry went up for Harriet Beecher Stowe, and the crowd began to chant her name. Amid thunderous applause she came to the balcony and stood clutching the railing, her dress rumpled and her "bonnet awry"[4] as tears spilled down her cheeks.

If only Lyman Beecher could have seen his daughter in that moment. He could have said, "she has won laurels." But Harriet's father was slipping away. For the last two weeks of his life he lay unconscious, unable even to recognize his own children. He rallied once "to tell those around him that he'd been assured of his resurrection."[5] When he died on January 10, at the age of eighty-seven, it was to his family like the fall of a great oak tree.

Lyman Beecher lived believing "that the millennium was at hand." He always felt "that he had a great work to do for God and man, which must be done at once — not a minute to be lost."[6] His slow decline into feebleness was heartbreaking; death came, finally, as a release. Harriet "never felt more joyful" than at the funeral. "My father was restored to me," she wrote. "I felt his love, it seemed as if I could touch his glorious harp and feel the joy of his reunion with my mother, Aunt Esther and all the many friends gone before." At the funeral Harriet felt that the very air was filled with spirits bright, "who *live* now more truly than we do." But when the funeral was over and the family left the church, winter and war once more closed in.[7]

Meanwhile, news of the Emancipation Proclamation crossed the Atlantic. And so did Stowe's "A Reply [to] . . . Women of Great Britain and Ireland,"[8] in response to the anti-slavery letter from British women written nearly a decade ago. All these years Stowe had waited to respond until that time when American slavery would come to an end. Stowe's "Reply" appeared in the January 1863 issue of *Atlantic Monthly.* It ran in British papers at about the same time they printed news that Lincoln had signed the Emancipation Proclamation. Stowe's "Reply" sounded much like her father, for it proclaimed that in God's moral government, nations prosper only by seeking justice. She warned that for Britain to support the South would unleash "all the curses that God has written against oppression." Northern women sent their brothers and husbands and sons to battle against slavery, but where did the women of Great Britain stand? "Sisters, what have you done [for the cause of freedom] and what do you mean to do?" She asked them to pray and to get the men of Great Britain to support the North.

Since so few British women had a public voice, it is hard to know what effect Stowe's letter had. Scholar Wendy Hamand cites British editorials (written by men) that oozed contempt for Stowe and women generally. "Only a woman," said one critic, could have written this "monstrously annoying" letter. Another wrote, "I will never be angry with anything a woman does until she is unnatural enough to attempt to think." But now that emancipation was real, Great Britain could not "aid the south without appearing to support the forces of slavery." The British remained neutral and never formally recognized the Confederacy.

Back in 1852, when Stowe mailed those first copies of *Uncle Tom's Cabin* across the Atlantic, she had tried to rally British support for the American anti-slavery movement. By the time the Civil War broke out, Stowe's anti-slavery writings had "helped to establish the moral superiority of the Union cause in the eyes of many English readers." When a Confederate diplomat in London failed to win formal British support for the South, he "told Jefferson Davis that too many Britons had read *Uncle Tom's Cabin*."[9] Stowe's "Reply" was her last attempt to rally British support to end slavery in America.

She now turned to family matters. Late in the winter of 1863 Stowe went to Brooklyn to work with her brother Henry on preparing Lyman's memoirs for publication. But even as Harriet honored her father's legacy she was reaching beyond it to more catholic traditions. For example, while in Brooklyn she wrote to her adult daughters about the holy season of Lent.

As a child Harriet did not observe Lent or the seasons of the liturgical year. Instead, her family marked sacred time by keeping the Sabbath and by holding revivals. But now at midlife and in wartime, Harriet found solace in Lent, the penitential season leading up to Easter. Lent is a time for "looking away from ourselves to Christ," she wrote to her daughters. It is a time to cultivate "earnestness of feeling" for Jesus' "self-sacrifice on our behalf."

Stowe sent her daughters an essay she wrote, entitled "Lent." Lent was not a medieval Catholic corruption, she explained. It had roots in Apostolic times, beginning with the "friends of Jesus who knew him personally." Lent is a holy season, "not a myth — not a romance & fable" but "a standing witness" to the actual events of Christ's life. "So the Christian church with her system of feasts and fasts & her whole internal arrangement [is] founded on events of Christ's life." Lyman Beecher saw Christianity, at least in part, as a system of doctrines and morals to which individuals converted. But Harriet was coming to see Christianity as a faith to be practiced communally, in rituals observed down through the long centuries of time.

New England Calvinism had discarded Lent and many other Christian traditions, in an attempt to observe only that which was mandated by the Bible. Now Harriet saw this as a minority report. Lent was omitted "only by that portion of the Christian church which sprang from the influence of the Puritans," she wrote. In contrast, the "nominal" churches "all unite" in observing Lent. (*Nominal,* "in name only," was a term used by conversion-centered Christians to describe churches that do not require conversion.) But Stowe had come to see that the "nominal churches" had water in their wells that conversion-based Christians lacked. "When we join the great majority of . . . Christians in celebrating" Lent, she wrote, we "draw nearer to Christ & make him a more vivid reality." Stowe longed to drink deeply from this well.

In the spring of 1863 Calvin retired from his professorship at Andover. The family moved to Hartford, Connecticut, where Harriet's sisters Mary and Isabella lived with their families. Harriet fondly recalled her days as a young teacher at the Hartford Female Seminary, when she roamed the countryside. She had found a lovely grove of trees near the Park River[10] and dreamed of one day building a house there. And now the Stowes bought this very property and hired an architect[11] to build Harriet's dream house. She oversaw every aspect of the construction.[12] "My house with eight gables is growing wonderfully," she told a friend. "I go over every day to see it. I am busy with drains, sewers, sinks, digging, trenching, and above all, with manure" for her gardens. She would grow roses and grapes and pears, and name the place Oakholm.

Calvin's retirement left Harriet the sole breadwinner. The Stowes had some investments and income from ongoing sales of Harriet's books, but to maintain their way of life, Harriet had to continue writing. By now it was clear that twins Hattie and Eliza would neither marry nor live independently. "You cannot make money," Harriet told them, "but you can set my mind free to make it for you." Having the twins run the household would keep their operating costs down, but they would still need some domestic help. Stowe proposed finding a twelve-year-old girl — an orphan, perhaps — to work as an indentured servant. The Stowes could provide a home for the girl and train her to become reliable help, and then she would be paid wages when she came of age.[13]

In the Front Ranks of Battle

But the war overshadowed these domestic plans. On June 1, 1863, Harriet noted her "constant . . . bleeding away of strength in these national agonies." Sometimes "neuralgic attacks" kept her from writing, and every day she feared that Fred had died. "I look for it in every battle and wonder as yet that amid the perfect rain of shells & that in a recent battle my boy as yet lives to say 'Mother I prefer death to dishonor & I shall see the cause thru or go underground.'" Adding to her worries — if also to her Beecher family pride — were several of Stowe's nephews "in the front ranks of battle."[14]

Harriet's son Fred was under the command of General Mead in the Battle of Gettysburg, where three days of fighting left 50,000 Americans dead or wounded. Fred was at "the very central point of the battle where fifty two shells a minute exploded around them," Harriet wrote later. Fighting alongside Fred was his cousin Robert Beecher, William's son. When Fred was struck by a bullet, Robert helped him "into a private home at Gettysburg where a widow and her daughter nursed him."[15] The Union won the battle, but Lee's army escaped to fight on.

Harriet and Calvin did not know if Fred was dead or alive. About a week after the battle, they received a letter from a chaplain: Captain Stowe was "struck by a fragment of a shell, which entered his right ear" and he was "anxious that [his family] should hear from him as soon as possible." The Stowes rejoiced that Fred was alive and prayed he would recover from his wound. Calvin set off by train for Gettysburg, but he was robbed at a railroad station and returned to Hartford. Fred was cared for in several military hospitals before he was sent home. He was not mortally wounded, but the shell fragment that lodged in his ear produced ringing, buzzing, and throbbing. Surgery for such a wound was impossible.

The North rejoiced that Vicksburg, Mississippi, fell to General Grant on July 4. "The Father of Waters now flows un-vexed to the sea," Lincoln said. But the Union was vexed as draft riots swept over New York City. The rioters were mostly working-class whites, angry that men who had three hundred dollars to spare could buy their way out of the draft.[16] Many of the rioters were recent Irish immigrants who wanted nothing to do with a war to free slaves.

The violence started at an office building where men were being conscripted into the army. Protesters shattered windows, burned buildings, and attacked the police, who were sent out to suppress the riot. Blaming "the negro," rioters destroyed an orphanage for African American children and lynched, beat, shot, or stabbed to death an unknown number of innocent blacks.[17] Lincoln sent several thousand federal troops to put down the riot. Some came straight from the battle of Gettysburg; Harriet feared that her son Fred would be among them, but he was not.

Harriet's nephew Fred Perkins, however, was there. This Fred was the son of Mary Beecher Perkins. Harriet wrote to her brother Henry, then in Europe, to tell him that Fred was a hero: he held off "the mob with his fist while a trembling negro escape[d]." Apparently Fred Perkins punched one rioter right between the eyes and felled him. Just thinking of it gave Harriet "new vigor" whenever her spirits drooped. "I am converted to pugilism," Harriet joked to Henry. Of course, she preferred to strike a blow with art. She joked that she would like to commission John Rogers (a sculptor famed for his group action scenes) to capture that moment when Fred Perkins punched the rioter and a black man escaped. "When the deeds of our family are perpetuated in my new Cathedral," Stowe intoned, this new work of art would be there. Stowe was teasing, of course, but in her heart she enshrined all the brave deeds of her family.

Harriet thought the draft riots would achieve nothing, except to disgrace the rioters. She hoped the whole sorry episode would cause the anti-war northerners, called copperheads, to lose credibility. In classic Beecher-speak Harriet said that the "wrath of man is beginning to praise God. This riot will sink the copperhead vessel lower than ever plummet sounded." Unfortunately, these copperheads could swim, and would live to cause more trouble in the North.

Meanwhile, there were battles to fight on other fronts. Parishioners were charging their pastor, Charles Beecher, with heresy. Harriet told Henry that "Twenty-seven members" of their brother Charles's church "signed a petition declaring" that Charles's teachings did not meet standards of orthodoxy.[18] They put him on trial for heresy and tried to force him out of the ministry. It was yet one more church fight in the war between the Old and New School Calvinists.

For Henry's edification, Harriet listed the charges against their brother Charles. He taught the pre-existence of souls and an intermediate state where souls remained until the judgment; he had universalist tendencies; he did not believe in real fire and torture in hell; he did not believe God would withhold forgiveness from the lost; he did not assume that all heathen were damned; he did not insist that belief in the Trinity was required for salvation. Harriet also wrote to Yale professor Leonard Bacon. Her brother Charles, she explained, was "full of imagination and loves to plunge and explore and revel in the celestial statistics and geography in years before the world was. . . . Now certain moles and bats pick up fragments of these things and pore over them as heresies."[19]

When a Beecher was on trial, the family rallied. Edward Beecher traveled from Illinois to Georgetown, Massachusetts, to support his younger brother — after all, Charles was in trouble for believing *Edward's* theories. Harriet also went to witness part of the proceedings. She could see the toll it was taking on Charles; he was "thin & pale & his voice is hollow — he has been badgered and baited by these ugly Christians till little is left of him."[20]

Even during the Battle of Gettysburg, the heresy trial ground on. When word came that Charles's son Fredrick Beecher was wounded at Gettysburg, Charles did not go to him, lest he appear to be ducking his trial. Instead his wife Sarah went and found their son "in a barn with an abscess forming above the [wounded] knee & another below."[21] Sarah nursed her son until he was strong enough to be moved.

Finally the heresy trial concluded. The ministers found Charles's teachings "fundamentally erroneous" and recommended that his church send him packing. But Charles's allies in the congregation rallied around their pastor, and his accusers withdrew. "A few years later, another conference of Congregational ministers . . . restored [Charles] to good standing."[22] It was all in the life of a Beecher.

A Great Day to Be Living In

The heresy trial of a Beecher was hardly noteworthy except to the Beechers, for great events were unfolding in the Civil War. Lincoln's Emancipation Proclamation made it possible for black soldiers to join the Union Army to fight for their freedom. One of the first official black units was 54th Massachusetts, commanded by Colonel Robert Shaw. Stowe had seen Shaw's regiment in Boston in May 1863. "Thursday this week," Stowe told a friend, "the first negro regiment left Boston amid waving banners & the cheers of the whole population. I went out the other day to visit them in their camp and was at dress parade. No regiment has left Boston better drilled with a more true soldierly bearing — they are full blacks, most of them fugitive slaves, and as they moved with a sturdy strong tramp in [heavy] columns marching & wheeling they seemed grand & solemn. They have a gallant Colonel from one of the oldest Boston families." Stowe called the enlistment of blacks into the army "the most important [step] for the negro of any that has been taken." This was their "chance for heroism — honor & glory." Despite her fears for her son Fred, and her nephews, the black soldiers moved Stowe to say, "This is a great day to be living in — is it not?"

On July 18, 1863, the 54th Massachusetts Brigade stormed Fort Wagner in South Carolina. The 54th lost the battle but proved the valor of black troops. The white commander, Colonel Shaw, died with his men. Confederate victors stripped Shaw's body and dumped it into a mass grave with the slain black soldiers. "You have heard how Col. Shaw fell & was buried with his brave negroes," Harriet told her brother Henry. Shaw's "Father, Mother, sisters & young wife all bear it like martyrs. His mother's first remark on hearing it was 'Well — it was what I educated him to do.' Oh Henry — the race of heroes is not dead among us — we smile in our pain and triumph in our agony! Who will give us back such young men — sons of such mothers?"[23] The fate of Colonel Shaw and the 54th Massachusetts hit the Beecher family close to home, for James Beecher, Harriet's half-brother, was also commanding black troops in the South.

James Beecher was Lyman's youngest son. As a young man, James went to China as a missionary, and then returned to New England and become a minister. When the Civil War broke out he became an army chaplain. For years James fought depression while his wife, Annie, battled alcoholism.

In the spring of 1863, Harriet had a strange vision about her sister-in-law Annie. One night she lay awake thinking about her son Fred in the army, and she had a vivid sensation that someone close to her was dying. She roused her daughter Georgiana and they said prayers for the dying from the *Book of Common Prayer.* Stowe sensed that the dying person was Annie. If Christ could cast seven devils out of Mary Magdalene, Harriet thought, surely he could save Annie's soul. Somehow Harriet saw herself standing before the cross and raising Annie up in her arms as though giving her to Jesus. She heard herself say Jesus' words of exorcism: "I charge you to come out of her and vex her no more." Then Harriet saw Annie sitting at the feet of Christ "clothed and in her right mind" like the demoniac Jesus healed (Luke 8:35). The next day the telegram came: Annie Beecher was dead. Harriet wrote to James describing how she and Georgiana had prayed as if they were at Annie's deathbed. Stowe felt that "their prayers had prevailed to help heal her soul."[24]

Meanwhile James had been sent to New Bern, North Carolina, to recruit black men, mostly former slaves, into the army. Of his early experiences he wrote,

> Had services at 6 P.M. before dress parade. I formed the battalion into close column by division; then, having no chaplain, gave out "My Country, 'tis of thee." We have some sweet singers among the officers and many of the men sing too. Then I read the 34th Psalm and they seemed to feel its import. "The Lord is nigh unto all them that are of a broken heart. . . . This poor man cried and the Lord heard him." Then I prayed with them . . . they knelt down and bowed their heads — near seven hundred men in United States uniform. It affected me beyond measure. . . . When I spoke of their past lives — of their having been bought and sold like brutes, of their wives and children not their own, of their sorrow and degradation, many wept like children.[25]

Harriet herself designed the banner for James's regiment; former slave women of New Bern collected small change to pay for the materials. In a letter to her brother Henry, Stowe sketched the banner she had designed. The word LIBERTY arched "in crimson & black letters" above a sun rising in rays of "gilding & glory," she explained. Below the sun ran the motto, "The Lord is our Sun & Shield." Stowe told

Henry, "Fancy one of us Beechers with a brigade of blacks planting this banner within view" of Charleston. Stowe recalled how a black man named Denmark Vesey plotted a slave rebellion back in 1822. Vesey was hanged along with thirty-four others in Charleston, but now Harriet fancied that the spirits of these insurrectionists were "invisibly wing[ing] the bombs and shots"[26] at southern troops.

That summer Henry Ward Beecher was vacationing in Europe. He declined numerous invitations for public speaking until near the end of his trip, when he was invited to speak on the British response to the American Civil War. He asked to give several speeches in manufacturing towns where anti-Union sentiment ran high because the war cut off cotton shipments from the South, causing British textile mills to close. Jobs had vanished, families were going hungry, and many people blamed the North for their hardship.

Henry accepted what proved to be his toughest gig so far. Every audience Henry faced was hostile; some were seething. But like his father, Henry rose to the occasion, and his lightning repartee won the respect of the crowds. His goal was always to show that Britain's interests lay with a United States free from slavery. Later he said that making this case was like "giving orders to a mutinous crew in the midst of a tropical thunder-storm."[27] But everywhere he spoke, he brought the ship into port. His speeches were printed and read by thousands throughout Britain and North America. When Beecher came home, crowds gave him a hero's welcome. People said that Henry's oratory stopped Britain from helping the South! Henry knew this was an overstatement, but the adulation was welcome. He had become an unofficial diplomat whose advice was sought after by high officials in Washington. Despite Henry's earlier anti-Lincoln screeds, he is said to have met the President on more than one occasion.[28]

Later that fall Lincoln went to Gettysburg for the dedication of the battlefield as a national cemetery on November 19. His Gettysburg Address gave meaning to the suffering of soldiers who had died to give the nation a new birth of freedom. The President called on the people to finish the work the soldiers had begun, and to "care for 'him who has borne the battle.'"

Fred Stowe had borne the battle at Gettysburg. For the rest of his life he would have a bullet lodged deep in his ear. It was the worst kind of wound: enough to ruin his life, yet not enough to get a discharge from the army. After a period of convalescence, some of it at Oakholm, Fred returned to active military duty. Late in November, Harriet was in Brooklyn visiting her brother Henry when Fred had a short leave and arranged to see his mother there. She was alarmed to see him suffering from the "constant deep pain in his wound & violent headaches." Beside herself with worry, Harriet wanted Fred to see a doctor and get a medical evaluation, which she hoped would result in Fred's permanent discharge.[29] She would also write to Secretary of War Stanton to plead for it.

Christmas was coming, but Stowe felt she must stay in Brooklyn. "Fred is not in a state for me to leave him alone at Uncle Henrys in this uncertainty," she told her daughter Hatty. "Uncle Henry is gone to Washington & [has] promised to see Stanton on Fred's affairs." Harriet found some needed distraction in shopping. She bought "each of my little girls [fabric for] a new dress — it may be foolish but Mammas *are* foolish about their little girls."[30]

By January 1864 Fred's discharge was still pending. Then he received orders "to report at Indianapolis" and Stowe was "very anxious" for him. At least "he has used no tobacco" lately, she told Hatty (tobacco was a euphemism for alcohol). Stowe hoped and prayed that "this time he may succeed" in breaking his addiction, yet she knew that Fred was badly damaged.

Of Calvin and Harriet's two surviving sons, only Charlie, the youngest, seemed to have a future. But Charlie had a habit of lying. Having tried and failed to break this habit, Harriet and Calvin sent Charlie to a boarding school in Connecticut, where strict rules might help him.

The school was called "The Gunnery," after its owner, Mr. Gunn. The boys wore uniforms and had "military drill twice a day,"[31] imitating their older brothers in the army. Mr. Gunn sternly punished miscreants. Charlie stood it as long as he could, but eventually he ran away to Bridgeport and signed onto a ship's crew. Charlie wrote a farewell letter to his parents — this time he told them the truth — thinking the letter would reach them after he had sailed. Alas for Charlie, the mail moved faster than expected and his parents rushed to Bridgeport, found Charlie just in time, and dragged him back to Hartford.

Harriet and Calvin told Charlie he was too good to be a common sailor. If he really wanted to go to sea, they felt he should prepare himself to be a ship captain. If he would study accordingly, Harriet and Calvin "would use [their] influence to get him a good ship and let him try the sea." But Charlie did not want more schooling. He kept "pining for the sea like a schoolgirl for her horse."[32] Eventually Harriet and Calvin gave their permission for Charlie to join the crew of a ship "bound for Spain and Italy."[33] Charlie was fourteen — too young for the army. But he was certainly capable of lying about his age, as so many boys did. Harriet and Calvin had lost two sons already, and Fred was severely damaged. Given a choice, the Stowes would rather have Charlie sail away from the war than march straight into it. These were the times when General Ulysses Grant was hurling his legions against Lee's dwindling army at the Wilderness and Spotsylvania. Then, at Cold Harbor, Federal troops assaulted Confederate defenses and were mowed down like ripe wheat. Grant marched his army about twenty miles south of Richmond and dug in around Petersburg for nine months of trench warfare.

On the Home Front

Harriet could distract herself from these weighty matters by doing something she enjoyed: putting the finishing touches on Oakholm, her new house in Hartford. Built in the Gothic Revival style, Oakholm boasted eight gables trimmed with lacy-cut verge boards, or gingerbread.[34] Bay windows let in the sunlight, and arched windows evoked memories of Italy. The huge front porch offered a pleasing prospect of oak trees and gardens, a conservatory and a fountain. Inside, the house was richly decorated with marble fireplaces, oak paneling, lush drapery, and thick carpets. Both Calvin and Harriet had their own study. Downstairs was ample space to display Stowe's beloved statues and paintings, and to receive guests — invited or uninvited, for many sought to meet the famous author.

The Stowes moved in before the house was finished. Harriet wrote to a friend about workmen coming and going at all hours, making noise and leaving piles of dirt, sawdust, and building debris. "One parlor and my library have thus risen piecemeal by fits and convulsions," she wrote. When finally the last box of books was unpacked, Stowe was exhausted. "In a month more, perhaps, I shall get my brains right side up."[35] Even when major construction was done, something always needed fixing — especially the plumbing. One winter night some pipes burst in their bedroom ceiling, soaking Calvin in his nightshirt. "O yes, all the modern conveniences!" he groaned: "shower baths while you sleep."[36]

Around this time, Stowe joined the Episcopal Church. Calvin's retirement and Lyman's death freed her to do so. She had been impressed with what she saw of the Church of England and now turned to its American version. It had been her mother's church, and Stowe cherished that connection.

In Harriet's lifetime many Anglican and Episcopal churches were seeking to restore older Christian practices rejected by the Reformation. (This was called the Oxford Movement.) So Harriet could have her cake and eat it too; she could partake of ancient and medieval traditions without becoming a *Roman* Catholic.[37] In 1864 she officially joined St. John's Episcopal Church in Hartford.[38] Stowe did not like everything about the Episcopal Church. For example, it claimed to have the only valid ministry — the historic episcopacy. Harriet could not agree to that claim, for her father, husband, and brothers all were ministers outside the historic episcopate. Also, Episcopal preaching was often tepid compared to the moral urgency and biblical zeal she had grown up with. And like many older denominations, the Episcopal Church failed to oppose slavery. But Stowe found food for her spirit in the rituals of the Episcopal Church and its embrace of the arts. She would make a home there. Calvin stayed in the tradition of New England Calvinism, but he understood Harriet's choice.

Several members of Harriet's family preceded her into the Episcopal fold. Hattie and Eliza joined sometime during the war. Stowe went to church with them sometimes, especially to receive Holy Communion in a sacramental service "more beneficial to me than ours."[39] Fred Stowe used the Episcopal prayer book, seeking spiritual strength in his struggle with alcohol; he joined the Episcopal Church in January 1864.[40]

Catharine Beecher did not wait for their father to die before joining the Episcopalians. She preferred a church that infants could enter through baptism, believing that baptism erases "the evil done by Adam's sin, so that the child can be successfully *trained* by a *religious growth*." In other words, conversion was not needed. Catharine told a friend to "go into the Episcopal Church and you will be free — more free than in any other denomination."[41] Most likely, Catharine said the same thing to Harriet.

And Harriet did feel free in the Episcopal Church: free from mandatory conversion, free from iconoclasm, yet also free to keep all that she found to be life-giving. As for the rest, she would fold it up and store it away, like a child's clothing outgrown but rich in memory. No longer did Stowe think of Episcopalians as "nominal" Christians. Later in her life, she wrote that "souls of great earnestness" who seek "definite faith with wide charity" find a happy combination in the Episcopal Church. Christians there may differ on doctrine but join together in the "beautiful, ancient, devout, liturgy." In the Episcopal Church, "abstract dogmas" yield to "the emotions of the heart of the practical aims of life."[42]

Harriet's practical aims always included writing. During the war she wrote a series of domestic articles for the *Atlantic Monthly*. Stowe told an editor that she did not "feel that the public mind is just now in a state for a story. It is troubled, unsettled, burdened with the war. The home nest is everywhere disturbed, and the birds consequently flutter around that. . . . Home is the thing we must strike for now, for it is here we must strengthen the things that remain."[43]

For this new series of articles, Stowe used the pseudonym Christopher Crowfield. Everyone knew that Stowe was the author, but the pseudonym signaled her attempt to write, sometimes playfully, from a man's point of view. What would a modern, enlightened man have to say about the home and women's contribution to society? "Crowfield" praised women's work as honorable and necessary. Only in America could a woman do the work of her own household and still be considered a lady. There was dignity and freedom in the most menial task if it supported the home, for the home was the basis for a just and moral society. In another article "Crowfield" challenged women to show their patriotism by purchasing American goods whenever possible. If northern women would buy more American products, "we shall come out of our great contest not bedraggled and ragged and poverty-stricken, but developed, instructed, and rich."[44]

Another "Crowfield" piece dealt with practices of mourning. In wartime every family was in mourning or knew someone who was. Why make grief harder to bear by following morose rituals? What was the use of draping windows in black, covering mirrors and pictures in white gauze, and wearing black for months on end? Rather than making homes look "spectral," it would be better to make every home "so religiously cheerful, so penetrated by the life of love and hope and Christian faith, that the other world may be made real by it." The home "should be a type of the higher life . . . it shall not be sacrilegious to think of heaven as a higher form of the same thing."[45]

In "Home Religion," "Crowfield" urged families to hold regular devotions in the home and faithfully attend public worship. Everyone has an obligation to support the church, she said. It carries the values of the Christian home to the wider society.

That was all well and good, but by 1864 northern resolve seemed weak. Some northerners wanted to give up the fight, recognize southern independence, and even let slavery continue. Others vowed to see the war through to Union victory. It was a presidential election year, and politics accentuated these divisions. If the northern Democrats won, perhaps they would let the South go. But Grant besieged Petersburg and Richmond, and Sherman marched through Georgia leaving smoking ruins behind. With Union victory getting closer, Lincoln was reelected on November 8, 1864.

Several days later, Stowe wrote from Brooklyn to her daughters in Hartford. Stowe asked her daughters to refrain from snide comments and "evil speaking" about their brother Fred. She found her daughters' hardheartedness toward Fred distressing. Stowe did not claim to be without fault, referring to herself as a sinner in need of forgiveness. But if Hattie, Eliza, and Georgiana could not overcome their own sins, which seemed so trifling, how in heaven's name did they expect Fred to overcome problems so profound? "Christ rejects all sin alike," she said. "He thinks a hard spirit & harsh judgment as bad as a profane oath or as drunkenness." Stowe said that "*despising* another human being" is worse in Christ's sight than other sins. Christ's "tender pity" should be their feeling for Fred.

Harriet's heart went out to "poor Fred," whose "brain & nerves are so shattered that it is difficult for him to steady himself at all." Stowe thought it "hard providence" that her son Henry, "who would have been our pride & reliance," had died before the war, while Fred, "for whom we fear, for whom we suffer," yet lived. Stowe hoped that bearing with Fred would make the family "gentler, more Christ like"; but for that to happen, they must all "bear this anguish together" and "unite their hearts in love." They should all be writing to Fred once a week and praying for him every day.

Harriet told her daughters that she prayed for Fred "the first thing when I kneel in church" and throughout each day. No prayer is ever lost. Did her daughters not know how to pray for Fred? Then they should consult the *Book of Common Prayer.* In the section on "Prayers for the Sick" they would find "A Prayer for a Person Troubled in Mind and Conscience." Fred had said that that very prayer described his case. It began in lament, and then asked for God's help against temptation. Then it asked for mercy, healing, and peace.[46] Perhaps this prayer would help Harriet's daughters to change their hearts.

At least Harriet could be proud of Colonel James Beecher. Her half-brother was still in command of the 35th Regiment United States Colored Troops, which fought in "several engagements in South Carolina and Florida until the end of the war."[47] On November 30, 1864, Beecher led his men in the Battle of Honey Hill, in an attempt to "break the enemy's line on the Charleston and Savannah Railroad."[48] Col. Beecher was wounded but recovered and returned to his command. When his men had opportunity in camp, they worked hard to learn basic reading and writing. This too was part of their fight for freedom.

As Christmas of 1864 approached, everyone wondered where Sherman and his army were. For several weeks he was out of communication, living off the land and destroying everything in a wide swath from Atlanta to Savannah. At last Sherman sent a telegram to Lincoln, presenting him as a Christmas present the city of Savannah, because it was too beautiful to be burned. Such were the times when the Stowes celebrated their first Christmas at Oakholm.

War's End

Harriet's first *Atlantic* article for 1865 began with a cozy fireside scene. But then, like Charles Dickens switching scenes in *A Christmas Carol,* Stowe took her readers to an army encampment in winter and then to the homes where families mourned their men. What could these stricken families expect in the new year? They might at least hope for compassion from their fellow citizens. They might hope that their sacrifice would somehow bless the nation. Grief must be accepted and borne patiently, Stowe counseled her readers. Sorrow can break a person but it can also ennoble; it all depends on how people respond to it. Even those who mourn, if they walk with Christ, can impart a blessing to others.

Christianity offers no easy escape from grief, Stowe said. Our faith is "a worship and doctrine of sorrow" because the cross "made [Christ] perfect as a Savior." In the cross of Christ Stowe found hope for her family and for her bleeding country. "War shatters everything," and yet the whole society must soon begin "rebuilding and binding up and strengthening anew." After death comes new life; Americans needed to believe this. "We, as individuals, as a nation, need to have faith in that AFTERWARDS,"[49] lest we be overwhelmed.

Harriet wondered what would become of all the orphans and widows. How would society care for all these "helpless and dependent" ones? There would be more single women than ever, and it was "urgent and imperative"[50] that they find ways to support themselves. She hoped that society would open more ways for women to earn a decent living. As it was, too many women — and girls — were turning to prostitution, because it was better than starvation. Stowe did not blame the women, but the society that gave women so few ways to make money. The war should open a better future for blacks and for women, she urged. Stowe prayed that the nation would "come forth from this long agony, redeemed and regenerated, then God himself shall return and dwell with us, and the Lord God shall wipe away all tears from all faces, and the rebuke of his people shall be utterly taken away."[51]

By late winter of 1865, the Confederacy appeared to be melting. The South could not replace its dead and wounded soldiers. Deserters went home to see what, if anything, was left of their farms. A few southern leaders considered dissolving their armies and carrying on guerilla warfare, while others said it was time to enlist slaves in the southern army, in exchange for freedom. But it was too late.[52]

Columbia, South Carolina, fell into Union hands in February; Charleston fell in March. James Beecher with his black troops "command[ed] the upper half of Charleston." They were quartered in the Citadel,[53] an elite military academy. In the largest church in Charleston, Beecher preached to a huge congregation of freedmen. Laying down his sword and taking up his Bible, he read from Galatians, "the freedom for which Christ made us free." Many of his troops wept for joy.[54] Around this time, James Beecher attained the rank of brigadier general.

Early that April, Lee's army at last abandoned Petersburg, leaving the nearby Confederate capital of Richmond undefended. Southern officials fled westward by train, while Richmond locals destroyed anything in town that might be of value to the Yankees. Whiskey flowed through the streets. Warehouses full of tobacco went up in flames. Stockpiles of ordnance exploded in deafening blasts. Richmond was a smoking ruin by the time the Yankees marched in. Lincoln came to Richmond and was greeted by throngs of freed slaves. Lee marched his starving troops westward, hoping to join up with other Confederate forces — but his way was blocked. Lee surrendered on April 8.

In Charleston harbor a grand celebration was planned, in which the Union flag would be raised once more over Fort Sumter. Military bands would play, and Henry Ward Beecher was to be the main orator. He came down from Brooklyn aboard a steamship that carried William Lloyd Garrison, some Union generals, and other dignitaries. Arriving in Charleston harbor, they were greeted by news of Lee's surrender.

Nearly four thousand people gathered inside the ruined fort, while out in the harbor boats were decked with flags and bunting. Harriet was not present, but her thoughts must have been there with Henry. James was there with the 35th Regiment U.S. Colored Infantry — perhaps carrying the banner Stowe designed.

The great symbolic moment came when Major General Anderson (who four years earlier had lowered the flag to surrender the fort) now raised that same flag to the top of the pole. Guns fired and "cannons boomed from every ship and every barricade in the harbor."[55]

Then Henry Ward Beecher stood to address the crowd. He usually spoke without notes, but this time he had a prepared speech that lasted for over an hour. Struggling to make himself heard over the gusting sea winds, Beecher blamed southern leaders for deceiving their people and leading them into disastrous war. The elite few should be punished for their crimes. But as for the vast majority of southerners, "the moment their willing hand drops the musket and they return to their allegiance," the North should embrace them, he said.[56] After the ceremony, boats ferried the crowds from Fort Sumter across the bay into the city, where celebrations at the Charleston Hotel went on into the wee hours of night.

That night in Washington, Abraham Lincoln was celebrating, too. He took his wife Mary to see a play at Ford's Theater. And there John Wilkes Booth was waiting with a .44 caliber Derringer. The night Lincoln was shot, a second assassin stabbed Secretary of State William Seward almost to death. A third conspirator failed to carry out a planned attack on Vice President Andrew Johnson.

The North reeled from shock. Lincoln was dead! Suddenly everyone was wearing black, and donning mourning badges. It seemed that every window was hung in black, Stowe wrote later. No one had to be told what to do; all seemed to obey "the same spontaneous impulse. . . . It seemed almost as if the funeral bells tolled of themselves and without hands."[57] People grieved as though for a close family member.

Shortly after Lincoln's death, Confederate general Joe Johnston surrendered his army to Sherman. But no victory could ease the heartbreak caused by Lincoln's death. "The kind, hard hand, that held the helm so steadily in the . . . storm [was] stricken down just as we entered port," Stowe wrote. Earlier in the war, Lincoln's slowness to free the slaves had exasperated Stowe. But in hindsight she came to see him as holding "first [place] among that noble army of martyrs who have given their blood to the cause of human freedom."[58]

Somehow life went on. Stowe's daughter Georgiana, now twenty-two years old, planned to get married in August, but sent her mother into a tizzy by moving the date up to June. The nuptials were to take place at Oakholm — which was still a work in progress. Harriet had to get the house and grounds ready and oversee the making of the wedding dress for the bride and clothes for Calvin, Fred, Charley, and herself. The wedding took place on June 14 as thousands of soldiers were mustering out of the armies. Nine days later the last Confederate general, a Cherokee chief, surrendered his troops in Indian Territory.[59]

Revelations about the war were still coming out. Stowe was outraged by reports on the conditions at Andersonville Prison in Georgia, where captured Union soldiers died of disease and starvation. Her August article for the *Atlantic* called for vengeance upon the men responsible at Andersonville. "Peace has come," she wrote, ". . . but if we look, we shall see on every blessing a bloody cross."[60] She could forgive the rank-and-file Confederates who simply obeyed orders. But any talk of "mercy and magnanimity" toward top rebel leaders was "weak and ill-advised." She wanted Robert E. Lee, Jefferson Davis, and others punished — not from "personal vengeance," but from "a sense of the eternal fitness of things." Stowe doubtless expressed the views of many in the North, "caught up in the blind fury over Lincoln's death."[61] Later, her attitude toward the South softened.

Stowe wrote to her friend the Duchess of Sutherland in the fall of 1865. The war years, she said, "weighed upon us all with a weight so heavy — such a steady pressure of emotion — that we could not write of what we were feeling." The war was not over for Harriet, since "My son Capt. Stowe has come thro the war with life, but a severe wound at Gettysburg makes him an invalid and a source of great anxiety to me."[62] By the year's end, she could rejoice that the Thirteenth Amendment was ratified, forever outlawing slavery in the United States.

Late in that first winter of peace, Stowe looked back in awe. Somehow an impassable range of mountains had been crossed, but at a cost no one could count. "I am lost in amazement," Stowe told the Duchess of Argyll, "when I think of what has been done these last few years." For Stowe and for countless Americans, *Uncle Tom's Cabin* had brought them to the foothills of those impassable mountains. And so in February 1866, Harriet read her book once more, as a way to ponder "the magnitude of the changes wrought by the war." *Uncle Tom's Cabin* had been written in hopes of ending slavery without war. But now it was "scarred and seared and burned into with the memories of anguish and horror that can never be forgotten." She could hardly believe that the war and slavery were "all over now, all past." From now on, "no private or individual sorrow" could leave her comfortless. "If my faith in God's presence and real, living power in the affairs of men ever grows dim," the end of slavery "makes it impossible to doubt."[63]

CHAPTER SIXTEEN

The Queen Bee of That Hive

S towe had high hopes for the postwar South. Within one or two generations blacks would exercise their full rights as citizens, she thought, and the South would become "a true democracy." Reconstruction would bring the former Confederate states back into the Union, but just *how* this was to be done without Lincoln's guiding hand was fiercely debated in the North. Radical Republicans like Charles Sumner demanded full equality for ex-slaves — and no concessions made to southern whites. But moderate Republicans like Henry Ward Beecher thought it "unwise" to "force negro suffrage at the point of the bayonet," lest "an immediate war of the races" result.[1]

Harriet agreed with her brother Henry, but she told him to leave off politics. "As to our party, the Republicans," she advised her brother, "let them alone. God after all is in the vox populi. *You* have other work, Christ's work, and who can stop you there? Can the South resist our love if we love them? If we go down with food for their widows and orphans, with schools for their children and sympathy for their distresses, will they refuse us?" The southern people needed immediate, practical relief, and northern churches could help to provide it.

In the long run, Stowe saw education as the key to the South's future. Blacks needed education and so did whites, though for different reasons. Southern whites needed to *un*-learn their deeply embedded sense of racial superiority. "The only way to save the negro is to educate the white," Stowe declared, by teaching them to treat blacks as free people with rights. Missionary teachers who went south after the war were "women baptized from above," Stowe said, worthy of the "primitive [apostolic] age."[2] Harriet herself would help to found a

263

mission school and church in Florida. But she might never have gone there if not for her son Fred.

Fred and Florida

The war never ended for Frederick Stowe. The bullet lodged in his ear still plagued him, and for relief he drank. One day in Hartford — perhaps in a bar — Fred met two Union veterans. While serving the Union in Florida, these men thought they saw a fortune waiting to be made, what with abandoned farms, ex-slaves needing work, and cotton fetching high prices. After the war these two ex-soldiers rented Laurel Grove, a cotton plantation on the St. Johns River near Jacksonville. Now they were back in their native Connecticut seeking investors. Might Fred be interested?

He was. He had time, and his parents had money. Harriet and Calvin were so eager for Fred to have a fresh start that they invested $10,000 in the venture. Lest her son be alone among strangers, Harriet persuaded one of Fred's cousins, Spencer Foote, to go along. Fred and Spencer left for Florida in the fall of 1866.[3]

Weeks passed, and Harriet wondered how Fred was getting along. She was also eager to see something of the postwar South. In February 1867 she left Hartford for Florida, accompanied by her brother Charles and Spencer Foote's wife and baby. The travelers took a steamship down the Atlantic coast through water so rough that Stowe got seasick. Relief came as they reached calm seas and warm air. From Jacksonville, a smaller boat took the travelers up the St. Johns River to Laurel Grove. Harriet's hopes soared when she saw her son Fred looking tan and healthy. Once in her guestroom, Stowe cast off the wool clothes of her "winter captivity" and donned a light cotton dress. Feeling "quite young and frisky," she put a flower in her hair. The warm, gentle breeze coming through the window made her feel like she had fooled old man winter.[4]

Soon she was busy sprucing up the dilapidated farmhouse that had once belonged to the slave trader Zephania Kingsley (1765-1843), who, even after the transatlantic slave trade was illegal,[5] continued trafficking in human beings from Africa. (Later, Stowe wrote a story about a haunted house on the St. Johns River. It was cursed by ghosts of Africans who drowned when a slave trader, pursued by lawmen on the river, threw the chained slaves overboard. For many years, those passing by on the river saw that house and said that there must be a hell to punish slave traders.)[6]

How very strange that on the old Kingsley place her son Fred was the boss of a hundred ex-slaves! Stowe felt sure, however, that Fred and his partners were not just perpetuating slavery by another name. No indeed, for these northern men aimed to "to put [the ex-slaves] at once on the ground of free white men and women, and to make their labor profitable to their employers." The workers had contracts "all drawn up in writing and explained" and "the fruits of their labors constantly in hand" either as "rations or wages."[7] Stowe felt sure that a transition to better times was happening before her very eyes.

One day Fred took his mother by boat to the little hamlet of Mandarin on the St. Johns, where the mail was delivered twice weekly. There on the river bluff they saw a cottage surrounded by huge live oak trees, with an orange grove, five date palms, and an olive tree.[8] The thirty-acre parcel of land was for sale.

Harriet wrote to Calvin: he *must* get $5,000 to buy this property. Let him sell some stock or take out a loan on their house in Hartford; she didn't care how he got the money. Now Harriet brimmed with plans for other family members: Fred and Spencer could manage the orange grove . . . Charles Beecher could buy a share of the cottage and, if her brother would only switch denominations and become an Episcopal priest, he could establish "a line of churches along the St. John's River."[9] Harriet would write to the Bishop of Florida about it! (Charles did move to Florida, but not on Harriet's terms.) Late in the spring Stowe returned to Hartford, thrilled by all she had seen.

Some weeks later her bubble burst when Fred showed up in Hartford. Laurel Grove was a failure, he said. After all that work and money, the plantation yielded only two bales of cotton — which were destroyed by mildew. Cotton worms, bad weather, high overhead, poor farming methods — all took a toll. Worst of all, Fred was drinking again. At Laurel Grove he would show up late to direct the farm workers, or leave them to shift for themselves while he was on a binge in Jacksonville.[10]

What was to become of Fred? He agreed with his parents that it was time to take more drastic measures in his quest for recovery. He checked into a mental institution in Binghamton, New York, where he was locked in a room for "the initial stages of withdrawal from nicotine and alcohol." The doctor blamed Fred's troubles on his war wound and hoped that Fred might yet recover. Fred wrote home to his sisters that it was better for him to be institutionalized than to "be out in the world disgracing the name you bear."[11] He knew his sisters were ashamed of him, and being the son of Harriet Beecher Stowe only made him feel like more of a failure.

In the summer of 1868, after Fred's treatment had run its course, Calvin took him on a Mediterranean voyage. Calvin hoped that the fresh sea air (and no alcohol) would solidify Fred's recovery. Once back on land, however, Fred was drinking again. Eventually he returned to Florida, where he was supposed to manage the Stowes' orange grove. He would stay sober for a week or two, only to slink off and drink himself into a stupor. Harriet, Calvin, and the twins were in Florida in the winter of 1869-70 and saw Fred at his worst.

My Rabbi

During this long struggle with Fred, Calvin had one great satisfaction: the book he had worked on for years was finally published in 1867. Without Harriet's intervention it might never have happened. Harriet saw that her perfectionist husband might never finish his book and so, according to one family story, she told Calvin's editor to inform him that the book was going to press, and that he must submit whatever he had ready and finish the rest as quickly as possible.[12] (Calvin complied with the first order, though not the second. His projected volume on the Old Testament was never finished.) Calvin's book was called *Origin and History of the Books of the New Testament, Both the Canonical and the Apocryphal, Designed to Show What the Bible Is Not, What It Is, and How to Use It.*

Calvin's scholarship informed Harriet's view of the Bible. Calvin saw the Bible as a book about God's ways with human beings. Sin broke humanity's relationship with God, but *God acted* to restore the relationship. Facts and theories cannot restore people to God, nor can science, biblical scholarship, or doctrine. Not even conversion can heal the breach, if conversion is a requirement people must meet. No, Calvin insisted, "God saves us by His Word and by His Spirit, neither without the other . . . but usually by both together in harmonious and inseparable co-operation."[13]

Since Calvin believed that God's Word and Spirit are working to save sinners, modern methods of study, such as linguistic and historical analysis, posed no threat. For him, the authority of Scripture was its power to change people. Therefore, he felt no need to defend Scripture against evolution or other scientific theories. He kept up with scholarly trends and almost certainly discussed them with Harriet. At the same time, he held himself accountable to the Bible's testimony about the life, death, and resurrection of Jesus.

The Stowes lived in times of intellectual ferment. Charles Lyell's *Principles of Geology* (1830-33) showed the earth to be much older than people deduced from the biblical record. Charles Darwin's *Origin of Species* (1859) argued that life evolved gradually through natural selection — and this challenged traditional belief in divine, instantaneous creation. Evolution intrigued the Stowes and did not threaten their faith, because their understanding of biblical authority did not assume a particular time frame for creation.

Other new ideas were more troubling. In 1846 the English translation of David Strauss's *The Life of Jesus, Critically Examined* appeared; Strauss denied miracles and presented Jesus as merely human. And the English translation of Ludwig Feuerbach's *The Essence of Christianity* appeared in 1854, saying that God did not create people, but people created God.

America's reckoning with nineteenth-century European thought was delayed by the all-consuming conflicts over slavery, culminating in the Civil War. As General Sherman famously said, "war is all hell." And that grim truth posed a greater challenge to faith in a loving God than all the ideas of European scholars put together.

Through it all Calvin Stowe maintained a scholarly devotion to the Scriptures. He was aware of European scholarship, and he respected critical inquiry. Yet — perhaps influenced by Harriet — he saw that while scholars need theories, sinners need grace. So he dedicated his book "to those who with me believe and love and trust the Bible."

Calvin addressed some troubling questions in his book. Take for example, the unity of Scripture. How can a book — written by many authors in various times, places, and languages — be anything but a hodgepodge? Calvin explained that "the unity of Scripture is not an external, it is an internal, a spiritual unity, the unity of one grand idea running through the whole, the idea of reuniting the human soul to God, from whom it has been so sadly broken off by sin." Then Calvin (sounding like Harriet) used an analogy. From the outside looking in, "the Bible is like some of those grand old rural dwellings in England, a congeries of different buildings in every variety of style, the disconnected work of many successive generations." From the inside, however, the Bible is "a perfect harmony . . . all proceeding on one idea."[14]

What was that one idea? It was God's love. Calvin pointed to John 3 ("For God so loved the world that he gave his only Son") and Romans 8 ("there is no condemnation for those who are in Christ Jesus"). If the rest of the Bible were to be lost and only John 3 and Romans 8 remained, and "if we could be assured of their truth . . . [these would] guide us safely through all the darkness and sorrow of this life, and bring us to the haven of light and peace above."[15] The unity of the Scripture was its message of divine grace.

Calvin also tackled the question of inspiration. How can the Bible be divinely inspired, and still contain factual errors or internal contradictions? All depends, Calvin said, on what is meant by *divine inspiration.* Calvin did not think that God dictated scriptures word for word. No, "the writers of the Bible [were] 'God's penmen, and not God's pens.' . . . It is not the words of the Bible that were inspired, it is not the thoughts of the Bible that were inspired; it is the men who wrote the Bible that were inspired."[16]

Related to inspiration, a deeper problem was the charge that the Bible contained things unworthy of God, such as hatred, murder, or slavery. Calvin answered that just because something is *in* the Bible does not mean God approves of it. We do not like or approve of everything in the newspaper, but we want to know what is happening in the world. Yes, there are offensive things in the Bible. That is the world we live in, that is the world God loves. Biblical inspiration does not mean that God likes everything in the Bible! It means that God works through (and sometimes in spite of) sinful human beings in the real world. The human fingerprints all over the Bible and human failings it records point to God's mercy and patience for this fallen world.

But what if the Bible did not conform to advances in science? Calvin told readers not to look in the Bible "for what God never put in it." The Bible was not about "mathematics or mechanics . . . metaphysical distinctions or the abstruse sciences." What we should look for in the Bible is "the way of spiritual life and salvation." Seek that in the Bible, "and you will find enough, an abundance for all your spiritual needs."[17] The Bible tells believers to abide in Christ, as a branch abides in the vine and bears much fruit (John 15:5).

Calvin's book bore much fruit, earning $10,000 — a hefty sum in those days. This was the capstone to Calvin's career. Harriet used to call him "my rabbi," and he looked the part. Now sixty-seven and portly, he often wore a black skull cap, and his kindly face was fringed by his long white hair and beard. Professor Stowe was a meticulous scholar who toiled for years on a single work.

Harriet was just the opposite. She often wrote in haste, juggling several projects at once. In 1865 her Christopher Crowfield essays from the *Atlantic Monthly* were published in a book called *House and Home Papers.* After the war she published two collections of children's stories — *The Daisy's First Winter* and *Queer Little People* — and a volume of religious poems. With her sister Catharine she produced a volume of domestic advice, *The American Woman's Home.* She wrote for the *Atlantic.* She contributed to *Men of Our Times,* a collection of short biographies.

It irritated Stowe that editors and printers seemed to earn more from her labors than she did herself, and with far less time invested, notes scholar Joan Hedrick.[18] Stowe promised her editors many small jobs that got in the way of her most important new work, a novel set in New England.

Deadlines do not go away, but in Florida Harriet could more easily ignore them. Besides, she found that fixing up the cottage and working in her garden was the perfect balance for writing. "I found a hut," she told a friend, "built close to a great live oak tree . . . with overarching boughs eighty feet up in the air, spreading like a firmament, all swaying with mossy festoons." The "hut" was really a cottage with gables. The main living area was outdoors — a wide verandah encircling the great live oak. Here Calvin would sit with his books, gradually moving his chair with the shade. Inside the Stowes added "a large parlor to be used as a dining room and a place of worship" as well as bedrooms for guests. The house was like a tree "throwing out new branches, till our cottage is like nobody else's."[19]

The Woman Question

Meanwhile the feminist movement was putting forth new growth, too. On January 1, 1868, Susan B. Anthony and Elizabeth Cady Stanton[20] published the first issue of *The Revolution* proclaiming "The true republic — men, their rights and nothing more; women, their rights and nothing less." With slavery abolished, it was time to advance the rights of women.

Stowe agreed, but *The Revolution* was too radical for her. So at the end of 1868 she helped to launch a new periodical called *Hearth and Home*. It was to be "emphatically a family paper," Stowe told readers, devoted to "farm, garden and fireside." Stowe's work on *Hearth and Home* was brief but significant, for there she tackled "the woman question."

Stowe spoke her mind in the very first issue. She saw no need to free women *from* the home. But she did see an urgent need for society to prize women's work *in* the home more highly. "Domestic and family duties," Stowe insisted, are not "degrading and unworthy of [woman's] powers," nor is domestic life "forced upon her by the tyranny of man." Far from it! "We hold that . . . there is nothing as sacred as . . . the time honored institutions of the HEARTH AND HOME."

Stowe supported women's rights. She thought "a larger sphere for [women] is both possible and probable." She saw no reason why women should not vote. Furthermore, she told her readers, women could do all kinds of work just as well as men, even public speaking. She pointed out the financial value of the unpaid work of women.[21] She just didn't want to be lumped together with the radical feminists who seemed to see men as the enemy.

Stowe's views on women's rights continued developing. Her sister Isabella gave her a copy of John Stuart Mill's *The Subjection of Women* (1869), in which Mill argued that women have the same natural rights as men. Stowe read the book and declared that Mill "has wholly converted me — I was only right in *spots* before [but] now I am all clear." She added, "Yes I do believe in Female Suffrage. The more I think of it the more absurd this whole government of men over women looks."[22]

Stowe summarized Mill's argument in *Hearth and Home*. Married women have no rights to property, to their children, or even their own bodies. A woman's legal position is "similar to that of the negro slave," Stowe wrote. But what about those lucky women whose husbands treat them well? They might brush off the question of women's rights, saying "I am sure *I* have all the rights I want." Well, said Stowe, "perhaps *you* have, but is it generous of you, because *you* have safety, protection, and a happy home, not to care what becomes of women" who are less fortunate? Even women whose husbands treat them as equals know that "many men . . . [are] quite unfit to be trusted with such absolute power."

All great social changes pass through three stages: ridicule, discussion, and acceptance, according to Mill. Stowe agreed that challengers of male authority were "often ridiculed as the Women's Rights party." Stowe hoped that the ridicule stage was passing and that Americans were getting ready for serious discussion of women's rights.

She encouraged that discussion. In *Hearth and Home* she wrote a piece called "What is and What is Not the Point in the Woman Question?" The point, Stowe said, is *the right to vote.* "Have women the same right to suffrage that men have?"[23] Women pay taxes, so they should vote. Stowe agreed with Mill that natural rights apply to women as well as men.

What about the Bible and women's rights? Does Scripture decree male superiority and female subjugation, or is that interpretation being imposed on Scripture? Stowe happened to know a biblical scholar who could address these questions. Professor Calvin Stowe wrote on "The Woman Question and the Apostle Paul" for *Hearth and Home.* Paul was reluctant to violate "established customs of society," wrote Calvin. But that did not mean he approved of "despotic government, slavery," and the subjugation of women. Indeed, Paul preached "general principles whose growth would gradually change" those institutions. This was Paul's general principle: "In Christ is neither Greek nor Jew, neither bond nor free, neither male nor female — but all are one" (Galatians 3:28). Paul preached and trusted the Holy Spirit to work this out in history.

For those who wanted proof of women's equality in Bible times, not in some distant future, Calvin pointed to Deborah and Hulda in the Old Testament. They were judges, chosen by God just like the male judges. The Hebrew people revered these women as divinely appointed leaders. What about the New Testament? Calvin said "it was a customary thing for women to speak under prophetic inspiration in Christian assemblies."[24] Calvin concluded that both in its general principles and specific examples the Bible supported women's rights.

Harriet wanted to get Ralph Waldo Emerson to write for *Hearth and Home.*[25] He was a known friend of the women's movement, having signed Stanton's "Declaration of Principles" at the 1850 National Women's Rights Convention. Stowe asked him to write "specifically [on] the question of Female Suffrage." She wanted him to give "a little *well timed advice* to the zealous, earnest leaders of this movement." He might advise them not to shock "the public taste" with "extreme views" but use "respectful and delicate consideration." Stowe offered fifty dollars, but Emerson never wrote the article.

Stowe had a deep ambivalence about the "woman question." On the one hand, she thought women should have the vote. She thought women could do the professional jobs heretofore reserved for men. All her life she stood for women's education and the intellectual equality of the sexes. On the other hand, she saw home and motherhood as sacred, and believed that women had special moral and spiritual powers.

She also saw that women could exploit men, especially through the use of "feminine wiles." Women of wealth or beauty could feign weakness and ignorance in order to manipulate men. Stowe had no patience for the games females play, and she thought that both women and men needed to be liberated. So she wrote a novel called *Pink and White Tyranny.* Her hero is a good, decent man who "in a fit of poetical romance" marries a "pretty pink & white doll." She quickly takes control of him. But when the pink and white doll dies of an illness, the hero is free to marry a strong, sensible woman.

Stowe meant to "offset" the notion that men are always the "oppressors" and women the "sufferers" in domestic life, she told her editor. She described herself as "to some extent a woman's rights woman" and "to some extent something of almost everything that goes," and thus she had "a right to say a word or two on the other side." She disliked both frilly femininity *and* strident feminism, for, in her view, the "right kind of woman [was] neither a tyrant nor a martyr."[26]

In Stowe's day there were different kinds of feminism, as there are today. Two of the most powerful feminists, Susan B. Anthony and Elizabeth Cady Stanton, wanted Stowe to move a step closer to their kind of feminism. They hoped she could do for the women's movement what she did for the anti-slavery movement — namely, write something to help a "radical" cause go mainstream.

So Anthony and Stanton asked Stowe to become the new editor of *The Revolution*[27] alongside her sister Isabella Beecher Hooker. Harriet was more traditional than Isabella, but the name of Harriet

Beecher Stowe would draw legions of readers. And Isabella Beecher Hooker was already a leader in the National Woman's Suffrage Association. With her lawyer-husband, Isabella was working to change Connecticut law to give women the same property rights as men.[28] Stowe was proud of her sister's efforts; she told a friend that *"the absolute equality of women in the marriage relation"*[29] was coming. (The law was passed in 1871.)

In time, Stanton hoped, Stowe would run *The Revolution* and Hooker would be president of the National Woman's Suffrage Association. "No one would rejoice more than I,"[30] wrote Stanton, if the Beecher sisters would take on this work, freeing Stanton to do the writing she felt was needed to lay a foundation for American feminism.

But Stowe declined to play the part Anthony and Stanton offered her. She told Anthony she "was not quite ready to *join the Woman's* Rights *Church.*" Anthony hoped Stowe might change her mind; she wrote to Isabella that when "[Harriet] is ready — and when she does enter it [the Woman's Rights Church] — I can tell you there will be *rejoicing* in our heaven not less than that we read about." When literary women "one & all, *believe* in our Gospel," wrote Anthony, "[we] wait only the revival forces to bring them into line of actual numbers."[31]

The use of religious language — and particularly the language of revivalism — is striking. *Woman's Rights Church,* our *Gospel, rejoicing in our heaven,* and *revival forces* — even if all this was a bit tongue-in-cheek, the women's rights movement was a religion for many. It required a conversion to a new point of view. It had its own forms of sin (oppression) and salvation (equality). Its devotees needed faith to work for a future yet unseen and suffer for the cause. For those who gave it their all, the women's rights movement was their mission in life. But Stowe already had a driving faith in her life. That was why she could support women's rights and yet not join the women's rights "church." And as an author, Stowe wanted to set her own priorities.

In August 1869 Anthony and Stanton met personally with Stowe and Hooker to discuss *The Revolution.*[32] Harriet and Isabella found the magazine's name too radical, and suggested *True Republic* instead. Stanton insisted on *The Revolution.* Also, the sisters wanted to be paid for their work, although Stanton and Anthony "were not paid themselves and the paper was almost broke."[33] Anthony wanted to do whatever it would take. She told a friend that of all the literary women, Harriet Beecher Stowe is the *Queen Bee* in that hive — And if she will do so much for *The Rev.* we can at once set it on its own *splendid feet* — And if *Cash will bring Mrs. Stowe* to *The Rev.* with her *deepest holiest Woman, Wife & Mother Soul struggle* — clothed in her *inimitable story garb,* then it is *cash that must be* — *Mrs. Stowe* . . . has never yet *given to the world her very best* — for she nor any other woman can, until she *writes direct out of her own souls experiences.*[34]

In the end, Harriet and Isabella agreed to write for *The Revolution* but declined "any formal relationship."[35] Isabella followed through; Harriet did not. *The Revolution* folded in 1872, and Susan B. Anthony nobly paid its debts with money she earned over several years on the lecture circuit.

Oldtown Folks

The queen bee had her own hive to tend. She was busy with a new novel, *Oldtown Folks,* which she saw as her literary masterpiece. Unlike so many of her other novels, this one would not run as a magazine serial; it would appear only as a book, giving Stowe the freedom to go back and revise — and (Stowe hoped) producing stronger book sales.

Oldtown Folks was set in Calvin's hometown of Natick, Massachusetts. The narrator, Horace Holyoke, represents Calvin in his youth. Stowe peopled her story with characters from Calvin's past, like Sam Lawson. Sam was a lazy handyman who did odd jobs for others while his own farm fell into neglect. Children followed Sam, begging for ghost stories and Indian lore. Sam could stretch out any task long enough to be invited for pie and cider. He could predict the weather. Sam was a keen observer of human nature and knew all the local gossip.

He knew theology too, having heard sermons all his life. At one point in the story, Sam comments on a sermon he has heard. "Parson Simpson's a smart man," Sam allowed, but his preaching was so discouraging! The parson said the human condition is like that of a man who fell down into a deep well, with nothing around but glare ice. We were obliged to get out "'cause we was free, voluntary agents. But nobody ever had got out, and nobody would, unless the Lord reached down and took 'em." Not one in ten thousand would be saved, and "it was all sovereignty." Sam didn't see much point in it all, so he "kind o' ris up and come out." He felt like going "round by South Pond [to] inquire about Aunt Sally Morse's toothache."[36] Better a real toothache than a theological headache.

Like Sam, Harriet "ris up" and went out from her father's church. As Charles Foster observed, Stowe respected "the way of life which had shaped her," but her own experience called her father's theology into question.[37] Finally she found she could unhook from New England theology, yet still embrace Christianity. "Nothing has ever moved me more powerfully and deeply"[38] than my work on *Oldtown Folks,* she told her editor.

Like the biblical character Jacob, Stowe wrestled with angels and vowed, "I will not let you go until you bless me." That wrestling match may be seen in *Oldtown Folks* in the chapter called "My Grandmother's Blue Book." The "Blue Book" title was shorthand for Joseph Bellamy's 1750 *True Religion Delineated and Distinguished from all Counterfeits,* a primer on theology.

Stowe entertained readers with many a charming scene in *Oldtown Folks.* But she also had some heavy lifting to do. So at the start of "My Grandmother's Blue Book" she warned: "Reader, this is to be a serious chapter." She advised "people who want to go through the world without giving five minutes' consecutive thought to any subject to skip it." It would not be entertaining, she said, and it would demand about a half-hour of serious thought. "Who knows what may happen to [one's] brains, from so unusual an exercise?"[39]

Stowe's "exercise" was to show that New England theology was something people had constructed. But who? Stowe said it was Jonathan Edwards (1703-1758), the theologian of the Great Awakening, and his disciples. And how did this theology affect those who believed it? It made religion into a barbed hook: the more one tried to work it loose, the more damage it did. In *Oldtown Folks* Stowe tried to clip the barb so that being a Christian need not hurt so much.

She explained to her readers how the trouble got started. By about 1700, according to Stowe, New England Puritanism was relaxing, becoming more at home in the world. As it aged it looked more like its mother, the Church of England. Stowe wished this mellowing had been allowed to continue. But Jonathan Edwards came along and forced a return to old standards, which required conversion. Edwards's congregation balked under his demands and dismissed him. Edwards continued his brilliant writings and eventually became President of the College of New Jersey (now Princeton). He died at age fifty-five, but his disciples codified his teachings and set the hook — mandatory conversion — deeply in the souls of the faithful. And the proof of conversion was pure unselfish benevolence.

The trouble was that no one could meet that standard without divine grace. Conversion imparts that grace, so we must have it. Yet God alone chooses who is saved and who is damned. We are required to do what we cannot do, and then punished for not doing it. No wonder some people learned to hate religion, Stowe said.

Yes, Edwards was a "*poet* in the intensity of his conceptions." But "some of his sermons are more terrible than Dante's Hell." Stowe told her son Charles that Edwards distorted the gospel — "his God was not a Father."[40] And Edwards's disciples only made things worse by codifying a theological system that brought "mental anguish . . . helplessness . . . [and] the most torturing sense of responsibility."[41] No wonder Sam Lawson, the local handyman, would rather sit with someone who had a toothache than sit through sermons on divine sovereignty. At least the toothache could be fixed by pulling the tooth out!

Why then, Stowe asked, did people accept this theology for so long? Perhaps because faithful church people "never expected to find truth agreeable," and the harsher the sermon, the more likely it was to be true. But others came to see "religion, and everything connected with it, as the most disagreeable of all subjects," to be avoided like the plague.[42] That was a tragedy. For Edwards's theology was *one* type of Calvinism, which in turn was *one* branch of Christianity — which meant that one did not have to swallow a barbed hook to be a Christian.

The Bible endures forever and reveals the mind of God, wrote Stowe. But theology is "the outgrowth of the human mind, and therefore must spring from the movement of society." Theologians *make* theology. And "nothing is more common than for [theology] to come up point-blank in opposition to the simplest declarations of Christ."[43]

Well, said Stowe, of course the theologians who made this theology were all men. It was men who made "thinking . . . a disease" in New England. And when only men made theology, women were sure to suffer.

> The great subject of thought was, of course, theology; and woman's nature has never been consulted in theology. Theologic[al] systems

... have, as yet, been the work of man alone. They have had their origin ... with men who were utterly ignorant of moral and intellectual companionship with women, looking on her only in her animal nature as a temptation and a snare. Consequently . . . it was the women who found it hardest [to live with this theology,] and many a delicate and sensitive nature was utterly wrecked in the struggle.[44]

Stowe has her narrator conclude that he would be better off with the "simple Gospel which my mother taught me." Yes, that gospel was taught by *a mother* who said Jesus Christ is the Friend, the Lord and Savior, of "every human soul on this earth." There is a redeeming power in being beloved, wrote Stowe, but many human beings "have never known what it is to be beloved." Theology should not alienate people from God. It should help them experience God's love. And to know oneself as beloved by God is to be saved.[45]

Within three months[46] *Oldtown Folks* sold 25,000 copies, and it still holds its place among Stowe's best works. After the novel was published, Stowe told her brother Henry, "I have all my life but especially lately gone with a gospel burning in my bosom, which I longed to preach but could not because I was a woman."[47] In *Oldtown Folks,* she was finally able to deliver the message.

Defending Lady Byron

In the summer of 1869 Stowe went to Canada to get a British copyright for *Oldtown Folks.* On her trip she read something that greatly disturbed her, in a British journal called *Blackwood.* It was a favorable review of a memoir by Countess Guiccioli, Lord Byron's last mistress. *My Recollections of Lord Byron, and Those of Eye-Witnesses of His Life,* portrayed Lady Byron as the cold wife who broke her genius-poet-husband's heart. Stowe was thankful that Lady Byron, having died in 1860, could no longer be hurt by these slanders.

Years ago, Stowe had warned Lady Byron not to defend herself in public. Now Stowe decided the time was right to tell the world the truth about Lord Byron — that his marriage ended because he was an adulterer who committed incest — and that *Lady* Byron was innocent.

Stowe's family and her *Atlantic* editor tried to talk her out of it. They thought nothing good would come from this campaign to vindicate Lady Byron. But Stowe had made up her mind. She must write "The True Story of Lady Byron" out of her deep "reverence for pure womanhood" — a sentiment she thought all Americans shared.[48]

In September of 1869 the *Atlantic* ran "The True Story of Lady Byron's Life." Readers were horrified. So many subscriptions were canceled that the *Atlantic* nearly sank. In Britain and America Stowe was attacked in the press. Stowe was a scandal-monger, they said, and as a piece of literature her Byron piece was a failure. Stowe replied that her defense of Lady Byron was not a "literary effort." She demanded to know if "the cries of the oppressed, the gasps of the dying, the last prayers of mothers," or "*any* words wrung like drops of blood from the human heart" should "be judged as literary efforts."[49]

One of Stowe's defenders was Elizabeth Cady Stanton. The "howls" from the "male press," Stanton wrote, merely showed that men are *not* women's protectors but the guardians of their own privilege. Stanton hoped that Stowe's article would inspire "thinking people" to "reexamine the position of women," writes Barbara White.[50] But it was much easier to blame the messenger. One political cartoonist drew Stowe as a hag clambering up a statue of Byron, leaving dirty footprints all over his pristine marble image.[51] In a way the cartoonist was right: Stowe had defaced an idol.

It was something Stowe knew how to do. Slavery, the great idol of the century, was sometimes called "Moloch" after an ancient god that demanded human sacrifice. Stowe attacked slavery with her pen and mortally wounded it. But what did the sex life of a dead poet have to do with slavery? Stowe saw a connection: in both cases, the powerful were abusing the powerless. Lord Byron was an abuser, Lady Byron the abused. Just as Tom refused to obey Legree by beating other slaves, so Lady Byron refused "to be the cloak and the accomplice of [her husband's] infamy."[52] Lady Byron was a person of privilege, so it seems far-fetched to compare her to a slave. But Stowe saw an injustice and she felt honor-bound to expose it.

When her *Atlantic* article backfired, Stowe decided she must prove that the charges against Lord Byron were true. With the help of her sister Isabella, Harriet compiled a book of testimonies and commentary in which she cited some of Byron's own poems as evidence of his emotional cruelty toward his wife. *Lady Byron Vindicated* came out in 1870, and Stowe hoped it would "free a dead sister's name from grossest insults."[53]

Stowe saw Lord Byron as an abuser who inflicted pain on his wife — spiritually, emotionally, and perhaps physically. At the root of it all lay his abuse of words. The poet used words to seduce women — and readers — into sinful thoughts and actions. He used words to convince people that his debauchery was a mark of true genius. Lady Byron once called her husband "the absolute monarch of words" who used words "as Bonaparte used lives: for conquest." Byron had no regard for the true meaning of words.[54] This offended Harriet, who from infancy was taught to revere the word, written or spoken. Words should be used to judge and to heal, to comfort and to liberate — and above all, to praise God. Lord Byron's use of a divine gift for unholy purposes made him, like Lucifer, a fallen angel.

Stowe cared deeply about words. But the reading public cared that Stowe had attacked a Great Poet. Stowe broke a taboo by outing the poet's incest and adultery. Everyone knew, but no woman was supposed to say, that men had more sexual freedom than women. Women were supposed to bear men's infidelities in silence. Stowe was ridiculed in the press for breaking that silence. The sexual double standard remained in place, and so did Lord Byron's status as a Romantic hero. What suffered was Stowe's reputation.

Mission in Florida

Harriet sought relief from her troubles in the Swedish movement cure — a new therapy that combined massage and exercise. But Florida was the best medicine. It sheltered Harriet from critics and bathed her in warm breezes. The Stowes were now spending almost half of each year in the Sunshine State, and their migrations back and forth were big productions. Silverware, china, and linens had to be carefully packed. Furniture was dismantled and crated for reassembly in Florida. The Stowes brought pictures for the walls, a portable organ, and various pets. Stowe also needed her paints and brushes, and of course her garden tools, along with roots, bulbs, and seeds. Calvin required at least a small working library, and Harriet needed her writing desk and materials for various writing projects. Hattie and Eliza did much of the packing and unpacking for the trip to Florida and back to Hartford each year.

It was worth the effort, for Harriet thrived in Florida. She spent as much time outdoors as possible — gardening, fishing, tramping through the woods in search of wildflowers. She loved to paint pictures of orange blossoms and other flowers. Playfully she wondered what Florida would look like as a living person. Florida must be "a brunette, dark but comely . . . with a sort of jolly untidiness, free, easy, and joyous."[55]

The Stowes sought more in Florida than a personal escape from winter. They wanted to help build a new South after slavery. So they worked hard over a span of several years to found a church and a school in their adopted community of Mandarin.

Calvin began by visiting all the families within a seven-mile radius of their property. He found some "fifty black families and perhaps a dozen homes owned by whites."[56] Many were Christians of various backgrounds, while others had little knowledge of the faith. All were invited to the Stowes' cottage for Christian fellowship. Professor Stowe gave Bible studies — a combination of preaching and teaching. Harriet and the twins led the singing. When the gatherings got too large for the Stowes' house, they decided to build a simple structure that would house both a church and a school. It was to be used by everyone, black or white. The Stowes donated land for the building site and the Freedmen's Bureau granted $1,500 to build the structure.

Stowe wanted the new church to be Episcopalian. With its practice of "sacramental baptism,"[57] the Episcopal Church did not demand conversion. Neither did it expect its members to be literate. Thus former slaves and poor whites, the converted and the unconverted, would all be welcome. "I long to be at this work," Harriet told her brother Charles, "and cannot think of it without my heart burning within me."[58]

When the new building was ready, Stowe hired a northern woman to conduct the school. Both black and white children were to be taught by the same teacher in the same room — but not at the same time. "The white school moved into the new building to-day," Stowe wrote a friend; "the colored school is not yet organized." The decision to have separate schools in the same building may have reflected several factors: black children often worked in the fields during regular school hours; white parents may have resisted having their children taught alongside blacks; white children were more likely to have some education already, while black children likely had none; too much integration, too soon, might bring reprisals from whites who resisted Reconstruction.

Worship at the Mandarin Church was also divided along racial lines. "Yesterday we had [worship] service in our mission church for the first time," Stowe wrote to a friend. The new building could hold up to three hundred people. "Mr. Stowe preached. He is going to hold service for the colored folks in the morning."[59] During Reconstruction independent black churches were springing up everywhere, run by former slaves exercising freedom of worship for the first time.[60] This may also have been true of the community church in Mandarin. There Harriet "conducted Sunday-school, sewing classes, singing classes, and various other gatherings for instruction and amusement, all of which were well attended and highly appreciated by both the white and colored residents of the neighborhood," Charles Beecher later recalled.[61]

But after only two years in use, the community building burned down. The fire destroyed everything — even the portable organ the Stowes had brought from Hartford. Harriet assumed the fire was accidental, although new schools or churches started by Yankees and blacks were targets for arson in those days.

Whether the fire was an accident or a crime, the people of Mandarin were not about to give up. They held church and school sessions in private homes — or outside, weather permitting — while the Stowes and others raised money for a new building. Completed in 1873, the building stands today as the Mandarin Community Club.[62]

For five or six months each year, Calvin volunteered his services as the minister of the church at Mandarin. He preached and taught, baptized and conducted funerals; and Harriet continued her community-building work. The Stowes were part of a wider movement of Yankees who planted their culture in postwar Florida.[63] In the decades that followed, northerners flocked to Florida and gave it a distinctive profile in the South.

Harriet and Calvin still cherished their New England roots. The birth of their first grandchild in 1870 brought new joy to the time they spent in the North. Harriet was in Stockbridge, Massachusetts, to be with her daughter Georgie at the birth. Since Georgie was married to an Episcopal clergyman, the baptism followed the Book of Common Prayer. Calvin took part in the ceremony and spoke his lines "as if he had been born & brought up" in the Episcopal Church, Stowe said proudly.[64] The baptismal gown and other finery were handmade by women in the family, and Harriet herself arranged green ferns around the baptismal font. The baby boy was named Freeman, in honor of emancipation.

Yet even as Harriet and Calvin gained a grandson, they lost their son Fred. So great was his despair over the pain in his ear and his alcoholism that Fred even considered suicide: "I know that you and all the family would feel the disgrace such an end would bring upon you and the talk and the scandal it would give rise to." In 1871 Fred joined the crew of a merchant ship sailing around the horn of South America, and was last seen in San Francisco. For years the Stowes tried to contact their son. They continued to pray for him and to wait for some word from him. "Where is my poor Fred?" Harriet lamented. "I never forget my boy."[65]

CHAPTER SEVENTEEN

Moonshiny Mazes

Harriet was proud of her brother Henry Ward Beecher. He was the most successful of Lyman Beecher's sons, a famous preacher, a popular lecturer and author. With several income streams, Henry could afford two homes — one in the country and one in town — which he filled with fine furniture and objects of art from Europe. Henry loved beautiful things; he kept loose gemstones in his pocket for the sheer pleasure of holding them in his hand. Admirers sent him flowers; he often received several deliveries on the same day. Beecher was a passionate man, and it was whispered that some of his female parishioners would do anything for him. But Henry's wife, Eunice, resented sharing her husband with the world; she was so cold and forbidding that her Beecher in-laws called her "the griffin" behind her back.

If Henry did not find warmth in his own home, for several years he found it in the home of his parishioners Theodore and Elizabeth Tilton. Theodore was Henry's protégé; the two men collaborated on the *Independent* (for which Stowe wrote many articles). Theodore became a journalist well connected to writers, artists, and social reformers. His wife, "Lib" Tilton, was beautiful, cultured, and emotionally fragile. When one of the Tiltons' children died, Henry comforted Lib and visited when her husband was away on business. Tilton may have encouraged Beecher's visits because Lib was depressed and lonely.[1]

Theodore was frequently away and may have been unfaithful to Lib. As the marriage began to fall apart, Lib turned to Henry for support. Their friendship deepened, and whether or not there was a physical affair, there was almost certainly an emotional one. Lib wrote a strange sort of confession to Theodore, who assumed this meant Henry had become Lib's lover; but when confronted, Henry denied any wrongdoing. By this time Henry had become "a cultural icon" and "the most trusted man in America,"[2] so he had a great deal to lose from a scandal. He pleaded for silence, for the sake of all of their reputations but especially his own.

While Beecher suffered in solitude, the Tiltons shared their misery with friends, some of whom were leading feminists. One night Elizabeth Cady Stanton was at the Tiltons' house when a distraught Lib poured out her story of an unhappy marriage and of her relationship with Beecher. Stanton told a few of her feminist colleagues, including Victoria Woodhull.[3] And that proved fateful.

The Woodhull

Victoria Woodhull was a flamboyant feminist who shocked Victorian society by promoting free love. Better love without marriage than marriage without love, she used to say. Woodhull accused married people of moral cowardice, because she said many were having affairs while pretending to keep their marriage vows. If these hypocrites dared to make their words match their deeds, free love would become socially acceptable. This appalled Harriet Beecher Stowe. She wanted women to have more rights, but feared that Woodhull would alienate the public and cause a backlash against women's rights.

Stowe had reasons to be nervous about "the Woodhull," as detractors called her. The woman had had a checkered career. She had been a practitioner of magnetic healing. In the course of her life she married several times. Her sister Tennessee Claflin was rumored to have been a prostitute. The two sisters were spiritualist mediums; they found favor with the tycoon Cornelius Vanderbilt, who set them up in the first female stockbrokerage on Wall Street. Victoria and Tennessee also ran *Woodhull & Claflin's Weekly,* a paper so radical that it became the first to print the "Communist Manifesto" in English. Woodhull was elected president of the American Association of Spiritualists in 1871; then she ran for President of the United States, representing the Equal Rights Party.

Woodhull's feminist colleagues had to watch her closely for, although she had personal charisma and was very articulate, she was unpredictable. Once when Woodhull was about to give a speech to the National Woman's Suffrage Association, Susan B. Anthony found out that Woodhull was going to take advantage of the platform to promote her candidacy for President. Anthony had the gas lights turned off, effectively canceling Woodhull's speech.[4]

Stowe wanted Woodhull silenced, period. On June 9, 1870, Stowe wrote a letter to the *Woman's Journal*[5] warning readers away from free love — and by implication, Victoria Woodhull. There was a personal concern too: Harriet's sister Isabella was a close colleague of Woodhull's in the woman's movement, and seemed to be coming under her influence.

Stowe satirized Woodhull in her 1871 novel, *My Wife and I,* under the fictional name "Audacia Dangyereyes." Audacia's paper, *The Emancipated Woman,* touted "the wildest principles of French Communism" and maligned "Christianity, marriage, the family state, and all human laws and standing order, whatever." Audacia was a vulgar hussy with no respect for the virtue and purity of women. All who wanted progress for women should shun her.

In *My Wife and I* Stowe also sent a warning to her sister Isabella: stay away from Woodhull. Stowe's fictional Isabella was named "Miss Cerulean" — true blue, but naïve. The gullible Miss Cerulean could see no evil in Audacia. Miss Cerulean should shun Audacia and "introduce into politics that superior delicacy and purity, which women manifest in family life."[6] Neither Isabella nor Victoria took kindly to this treatment in *My Wife and I,* but Harriet did not expect consequences. At the time she knew nothing of Henry's troubles.

So when Woodhull heard the rumor of Henry's affair with Lib Tilton, she was filled with glee. If she could be the one to expose Beecher, she could strike a blow for free love *and* pay Stowe back for insulting her in print. What fun it would be to make those sanctimonious Beechers writhe. (Too bad about Isabella Beecher Hooker, Woodhull's comrade in the women's movement; Isabella would just have to roll with the punches.) Woodhull would blackmail Beecher and Tilton[7] and then break the scandal to the press. How profitable it would be, and how amusing![8]

Meanwhile Isabella had heard (from Stanton or from Woodhull) about the alleged affair between Henry and Lib Tilton. She personally felt that Henry was guilty, but did not want Victoria to hurt her family. "Miss Cerulean" thought she could get everyone to be friends.

Isabella arranged for Woodhull to meet Catharine Beecher in New York City in February 1871. For privacy's sake the two women conversed while taking a carriage ride in Central Park. It seems that Catharine lectured Victoria against free love. Then Victoria revealed that *Catharine's own brother Henry* had taken Lib Tilton as his lover. What a pity Henry lacked the courage to admit that he was practicing free love, Victoria observed. Catharine vowed, "I will strike you dead."

Catharine lost no time in telling her sisters Harriet and Mary. Together the three Beecher women mounted "a steady stream of public and private attacks"[9] on Woodhull. If they could not silence her, they could at least discredit her, so that when she tried to break the scandal no one would believe her. The three older sisters also pressured Isabella to renounce Woodhull and to affirm Henry's innocence.

On May 22, 1871, the *New York World* ran a "card" (public notice) from Woodhull. "I know of a man," she wrote, "a public teacher of eminence, who lives in concubinage with the wife of another public teacher of almost equal eminence." Woodhull then made a personal visit to Theodore Tilton, perhaps to extort money from him. She also wrote to Henry that two of his sisters went out of their way to attack her in published works and in private letters. Woodhull now warned that she had the "power to strike back" devastatingly against Henry.[10] She would wait until she had gotten what money she could from the protagonists, but not long enough for someone else to be the first to break the story.

In September 1872 Woodhull addressed a convention of spiritualists. She told them that a stronger power moved her to reveal that Beecher was Lib Tilton's lover. Newspapers ignored the story as unfit to print. So be it; Woodhull would print the story herself. On November 2, 1872, *Woodhull & Claflin's Weekly* published "THE BEECHER-TILTON SCANDAL CASE: The Detailed Statement of the Whole Matter by Mrs. Woodhull." She described Beecher as a man of "immense physical potency" who craved the intimacy of cultured women. What a pity he lacked the moral courage to admit his own practice of free love![11] Woodhull and Claflin were arrested for sending obscene material through the mails; the sisters were in and out of various jails before being released on a technicality.[12]

Undaunted, Woodhull planned to give a public lecture in Boston on the Beecher-Tilton affair. Stowe used her connections to stop the lecture, calling on well-positioned friends to silence Woodhull. The upshot was that the mayor of Boston denied Woodhull a license to lecture in Boston's Music Hall.[13] Stowe told a friend that Woodhull belonged "in the Penitentiary." But Stowe saw Henry as a model of Christian charity — "forgiving, healing, restoring, returning good for evil & blessing for cursing & God help him he will carry it through." Poor Isabella remained under the "spell" of that "vile harpy" Woodhull.[14] Soon Isabella was off to Europe, where Harriet hoped her younger sister would come to her senses.

Isabella was sure her brother Henry was guilty of infidelity, and she wanted to help him come clean. She told him that if he would write a letter of confession, she, Isabella, would read it publicly to his congregation. *She* would be the agent of his redemption and help him to be an honest man once more. Henry declined the offer, but Harriet feared that Isabella would show up at Henry's church and make some shocking testimony. So for several Sundays, Harriet attended Plymouth Church and sat in the front pew — ready to stop Isabella by force if necessary. But Isabella never came. Perhaps she realized that if she spoke out, she herself might be accused of promoting free love.[15]

Edward and William Beecher, the two oldest brothers, thought that Isabella was insane; they may have contemplated having her committed to an asylum.[16] Isabella's sisters called her "monomaniacal." They pleaded with John Hooker, Isabella's husband, to rein in his wife. But John agreed with Isabella that Henry was guilty.

It was an immense relief to the family when Isabella left for Europe, where she would stay until the scandal had passed. In her hotel room in Paris she had the vivid impression that her deceased mother (Lyman's second wife, Harriet Porter Beecher) appeared and spoke to her — not just once but several times. She heard the visitor say that Isabella "would become president of the United States and, by effort and example, spread the concept of matriarchal government around the world as a prelude to the coming of Christ's kingdom."[17] Someday when her family saw the light, Isabella would forgive them.

Three Trials

Meanwhile back in Brooklyn, Plymouth Church was in an uproar. In October 1873 a special committee of Plymouth Church investigated charges of adultery brought by Tilton against Beecher. They found

Beecher innocent, charged Theodore Tilton with slander, and excommunicated him. On June 21, 1874, Tilton told his side of the story to several New York editors (who now saw the story as fit to print). "The battle still rages," Stowe told a friend; "the skies rain stinking pitch."[18]

Plymouth Church held a second investigation in the summer of 1874. The new accuser was Frank Moulton, a mutual friend of Tilton and Beecher. During the cover-up phase of the scandal, Henry had given a sheaf of sensitive letters to Moulton "for safe keeping." Moulton read those letters and, now convinced that Beecher was guilty, decided to use Beecher's own letters against him. Plymouth Church then asked Henry to defend himself — without being allowed to review his own letters. As deliberations drew to a close, crowds waited outside Plymouth Church to hear the verdict. Reporters waited for the latest news of the scandal and police positioned themselves around the church, bracing for a riot. But when Beecher was cleared of all charges, the crowd roared its approval, and Moulton was hustled into a carriage and taken away under police protection.[19] Harriet praised Plymouth Church as a "great organization of three thousand men & women whom [Henry] has centered around him." Stowe saw the attack on Henry's character as a "national event" on par with the "assassination of Lincoln."[20]

Harriet stayed with Henry and Eunice Beecher in Brooklyn for about three weeks in the summer of 1874, during the second church trial. Harriet was there to give moral support to her brother Henry. However, "the griffin" found her sister-in-law to be a nuisance. Eunice had her own method of dealing with reporters and curiosity seekers who came to her door: she sent them packing. But Harriet tried to speak to those unwanted visitors, determined to persuade all comers that Henry was innocent. Eunice told her daughter that "Aunt Hattie Stowe" was going to "make a mess of things" just like in the Byron affair. "I wish she'd go home," Eunice sighed, "but she is father's sister."[21] Eunice must have been relieved when Harriet returned to Hartford.

Writing to a friend at about this time, Stowe let her imagination run wild. She feared that Henry's letters had been read over by "Mrs. Stanton & the free love roost of harpies generally." Stowe imagined them cackling "over the scrape [Henry] was being drawn into." This free love crowd meant to "coerce [Henry] into favoring their unclean theories [free love] & unclean leader [Woodhull]."[22] *They* were trying to destroy Henry. *They* had put Isabella under an evil spell. Harriet would believe anything before she would consider that Henry might have sinned.

Winter came, and the Stowes migrated to Florida. Harriet knew that staying in the North would not help Henry, and besides, she felt responsible for the little church at Mandarin. "When I consider that Mr. Stowe is pastor and preacher, and that the Sunday services, Sunday-school, and all, depend on us, I feel it would be a mere yielding to my feelings to leave our few poor sheep in the wilderness."[23] But Harriet prayed for Henry and wrote letters defending him. Twice a week a boat brought mail and newspapers to Mandarin so that Harriet could keep abreast of the scandal.

The next act in the drama was a civil trial. In Brooklyn's City Court Tilton sued Beecher for alienating his wife's affections. The trial began in January 1875 and lasted six months. Reporters and celebrities vied for places in the packed courtroom, while newspapers across the nation covered the proceedings. The Beecher-Tilton scandal was a sensation, taking up "more space in newspapers than any event since the Civil War."[24] Not for nothing was it called "the scandal of the century."

After six days' deliberation and fifty-two ballots, the jury voted nine to three in Beecher's favor. Plymouth Church retained Beecher as their minister and raised $100,000 to defray his legal expenses.[25] Theodore Tilton fled to Paris, where he stayed for the rest of his life. Woodhull and her sister Tennessee went to England and eventually married wealthy men. Three years after the trial, Lib Tilton confessed that she had indeed committed adultery with Beecher.[26]

So what really happened? Historian Richard Fox says that "what 'really happened' . . . was that stories were created by the principals and by the assorted friends, enemies, lawyers and onlookers."[27] Harriet Beecher Stowe created stories, which she no doubt believed, to defend her brother. Her version: Henry was attacked by people who wished to destroy his character.

The scandal shook Harriet to the core. Even after the trial, Stowe kept on defending Henry in her private correspondence. There was "nothing impure in [Henry's] relation to any woman," she insisted.[28] The only fault Harriet could see in Henry was his "inability to believe evil." Henry was "hopelessly generous and confiding," and left himself open to attack. Harriet saw many reasons why people would hate Henry: his politics, his theology, and most of all his popularity. Henry was "overwhelmed" with "love, worship, idolatry," Harriet wrote. That such idolatry can tempt the idolized away from virtue was not something she was ready to consider.

Back in 1844, long before the scandal, Henry wrote to Harriet about several ministers who were disgraced for patronizing prostitutes. Harriet in turn wrote to Calvin about it; if he proved unfaithful, she would be devastated. She told Calvin she trusted him but had a "'horrible presentiment' that one or more of her clergymen brothers would someday fall." At the time she was certain "that Henry would not be one of them."[29]

Harriet had always been close to Henry — so close that she seemed unable to differentiate herself from him. The scandal, she sighed, "has drawn on my life — my heart's blood — he [Henry] is *myself*—yes — ... I felt a blow at him more than at myself. I *know* his purity, honor, delicacy — know that he has been from childhood of an *ideal* purity." To defend Henry was to defend herself, Harriet felt. Their bond was one of both blood and faith: "[Henry] and I are Christ worshippers adoring Him in the Image of the Invisible God & all that comes from believing this." Harriet implied that to attack Henry was tantamount to attacking Christ.

The scandal plunged Harriet into spiritual warfare. She told her son Charles how during that time she struggled to rise above "lower states" of weariness and disgust "into that region where is the eternal God who is our Refuge."[30] One Sunday during the scandal Harriet was too weary even to go to church. So she lay down to rest — "like a pig in the mud," she told Charles. At that low point, she was given "a clairvoyant view of a passage of Scripture." The twenty-third Psalm "rose up luminous" before her, "embracing the whole *ALL* of life for an individual ... above the uncontrollable inexplicable laws of matter & time."[31] These visionary moments sustained her in one of her darkest hours.

Woman in Sacred History

And so did her work. Harriet needed to write, and her family needed the income. Like many Americans, the Stowes lost money in the financial panic of 1873, which lasted for several years. In 1873 Stowe published *Woman in Sacred History: A Celebration of Women in the Bible.* This collection of essays on biblical women was illustrated in color, using the new technique of chromolithography, with art Stowe herself chose or commissioned.

Harriet consulted Calvin while writing *Woman in Sacred History.* "I studied faithfully under your Father's [Calvin's] direction and he read all I wrote," she told their son Charles. She said that she saw Scripture as "a system of education, and gradual revelation, unfolding from age to age . . . appearing visibly when there are important steps to be taken in the world history."[32] The concept of development informed Stowe's view of women in the Bible.

That development, Stowe told readers, took place "UNDER DIVINE CULTURE."[33] Bible women were forerunners to "that high ideal of woman which we find in modern Christian cultures." Stowe saw "a *system* progressively developing from age to age," in which society moves toward greater freedom and integrity for all. But women of the Bible can inspire modern readers through their shared humanity.

On a personal level Stowe had "some fear, for myself & my faith" as she began her research on Old Testament women. She knew she would find violence, polygamy, and a God who seemed unpredictable. Yet she tried to suspend judgment and enter into the stories in a "filial" empathetic spirit, praying over "every difficulty."[34]

One difficulty she sidestepped: Eve did not get a place in *Woman in Sacred History.* Eve had long been blamed for bringing sin into the world, and all manner of female "weaknesses" were ascribed to her.[35] Besides, Eve belonged to pre-history. Stowe would rather begin with Sarah, the mother of Israel. And Stowe chose not the old, barren Sarah, but the young woman whose beauty attracted powerful men and put Abraham at risk.

The story of Hagar also intrigued Stowe. Hagar was Sarah's servant who bore Abraham a son when Sarah was unable to conceive. It was Sarah's idea for Hagar to be a proxy mother, yet Sarah became jealous, and caused Hagar to be cast out into the desert to die with her son Ishmael. God took pity on Hagar and gave her water to drink. Ishmael is traditionally considered an ancestor of Muslims, and Stowe told her son Charles that she saw in the story of Hagar and Ishmael "a wide field of hope for nations we have been in the habit of dismissing." She felt that the children of Ishmael share in "the paternal care of God," whose promise to Abraham to bless the world through his offspring included descendants of Isaac *and* Ishmael: Muslims as well as Christians and Jews.

Stowe gave Mary the mother of Jesus not one but *two* chapters in *Woman in Sacred History*. "Mary the Mythical Madonna" includes a history of Mariolatry written by the Anglo-Catholic Edward Pusey. Then, in "Mary the Mother of Jesus," Stowe explores what the Bible actually says about Mary. For inspiration Stowe directed her readers to Mary as Mother, not Mary as Virgin. "Mary's palpable experience of womanhood"[36] drew Stowe in. As a mother, Mary had the sacred duty of forming Jesus' character. She could do this because her personality was free of all "self-seeking"; pure benevolence was "the crowning perfection of Mary's character." By releasing Mary from Catholic doctrine and endowing her with Puritan virtue and enlightened motherhood, Stowe reclaimed her for Protestants: "We may not adore, but we may love her."[37]

Messages from the Other Side

Stowe did not confine her spiritual quest to Christianity. Spiritualism — which claimed to open up communication between the living and the dead — fascinated her. Calvin encouraged Harriet's interest in the supernatural. As a child Calvin believed that he saw ghosts, fairies, and spirits, not just once, but repeatedly, and Calvin later wrote down these spectral scenes for the Semi-Colon Club.[38] Harriet said Calvin was "over head and ears in diablerie."[39] According to their son Charles, Calvin's "exceptional experiences" in his "early life" made spiritualism an "unfailing interest" for both his parents. Calvin made an "elaborate and valuable collection of the literature on the subject," from which both he and Harriet read deeply. Spiritualism was "prominent" in the conversation of both his parents, Charles recalled. After their son Henry's tragic death in 1857, spiritualism became more than a passing interest, for it offered hope of contact with their lost son. All three of the Stowes' daughters dabbled in spiritualism as well.

It was more than dabbling for some of Harriet's siblings. The Beechers were drawn to spiritualism for religious reasons, writes Marie Caskey. "They saw it as a much-needed force" to offset "scientific materialism and religious indifference." It seemed to support "supernaturalism in general, and, specifically . . . the belief in angels and demons."[40] Spiritualism might help skeptical modern people take seriously the miraculous element of Christianity.

On the lighter side, many people of that era embraced spiritualism as a form of entertainment. Families who owned a checker board or a chess set might also have an Ouija (spirit) board with letters and numbers to spell messages from the spirit world. These letters were "chosen" by means of a small heart-shaped device called a planchette. When placed lightly under one's fingertips the planchette moved over the board, resting on letters or numbers to spell out messages. Anyone could use the planchette, but someone with a good imagination, a flair for drama, and some family secrets could "get" convincing messages from the "other side." The messages might be funny, mysterious, or scary depending on the desired effect.

Stowe recalled a parlor game that took place at Oakholm after her daughter Georgie was married (1865). Georgie was "making experiments" with a "toy planchette," Stowe told a friend. It was "merely as a frolic." Georgie was moving the planchette on a large sheet of paper, probably an improvised Ouija board. Stowe told Georgie this was "foolish" and "trifling" — a silly waste of time. Then the planchette spelled out "I do not trifle & I love those who believe." It began to write about past events, finishing with a prediction so "sinister and menacing" that Georgie "got up and broke the planchette and resolved never to use it again."[41] But of course she did use it again, as did the twins, Hattie and Eliza.

Many devotees of spiritualism started out with parlor games and went on from there. Those who were serious about contacting someone from beyond the grave could consult a professional medium. The medium might go into a trance state and speak the message from the other side in an altered voice. This required some acting skills and sensitivity to what the client wanted — or dreaded — to hear. Advance research into the client's family could be quite useful. Some mediums produced "phenomena," or, in today's parlance, "special effects." We have already encountered guitars that seemed to play themselves. There were also strange noises and lights, images in mirrors, pens that wrote by themselves, flying objects, furniture moving or levitating. To be effective, these phenomena must seem to occur without help from the medium; many mediums had assistants behind the scenes or hidden devices to produce effects. Some mediums toured and gave public exhibitions, charging admission.

Some people saw spiritualism as a new form of science. After all, if unseen forces like electricity, magnetic fields, and radio waves were being harnessed, why not try to understand and use unseen forces in the spirit world? Some thought of séances as scientific experiments that might ultimately benefit society. In séances, methods of contact could be tried and repeated, the data gathered and interpreted. Catharine Beecher thought spiritualism had scientific potential.[42] And Harriet sometimes spoke of spiritualism in this way. She told a friend, "I regard them [spiritualist manifestations] simply as I do the phenomena of the Aurora Borealis, or Darwin's studies on natural selection, as curious studies into nature. Besides, I think someday we shall find a law by which all these facts will fit into their places. . . . I wish it were all brought into the daylight of inquiry."[43]

In Harriet's day, social reform and spiritualism overlapped. William Lloyd Garrison was drawn to spiritualism, as was the progressive editor Horace Greeley. Reformers often spoke at spiritualist conventions.[44] Spiritualism attracted those who desired "rapport with more sublime levels of reality . . . without the mediation of clergy or church organization."[45] Historian Ann Braude shows that many early feminists were drawn to spiritualism in part because it did not exclude women from leadership.[46] Alternative medicine, including water cures, attracted spiritualists. When Stowe suffered stress over the Lady Byron affair, she sought relief in a new therapy called the Swedish Movement Cure, and it just so happened that her therapist, Dr. Taylor, hosted séances in his home.

Spiritualism was becoming a religion in its own right with its own leaders, publications, societies, and rituals. Theologically it resonated with Universalism[47] — the notion that all people will ultimately be saved, that this life and the afterlife are states of probation for perfecting the spirit. Death is not the end, but only a "translation" into another state for further refinement. In spiritualism, death is a gauzy veil through which messages can pass, making the presence of departed loved ones felt here and now.

The spiritualist craze started before the Civil War and grew because of it. So many families never found out how or when their soldiers died and never got to say goodbye. Grieving people sought assurance that the afterlife is not to be feared. They wanted consolation that their loved one was somehow present. Some people used spiritualism as a substitute for Christianity; others blended the two.

Testing the Spirits

Just what was the relationship of Christianity and spiritualism? One of Harriet's friends, Oliver Wendell Holmes Sr., compared spiritualism to a "a fog upon the landscape" that softened "the sharp angles of Calvinist belief."[48] That softening clearly appealed to Harriet Beecher Stowe. Yet at her father's knee, Harriet had learned that Jesus Christ is the one and only mediator between God and human beings. Did that rule out spiritualism? After all, spiritualists did not claim to get messages from God, but only from deceased mortals. Christianity pointed to a world beyond this one, and the Bible told of supernatural events. Stowe seems to have felt that Christians *may* practice spiritualism, but most would be better off not to. At any rate, Stowe felt *she* could be a Christian and practice spiritualism at the same time.

When it came to spiritualism, there was tension between what Stowe told her readers and what she practiced herself. She told readers to get their spiritual needs met through Christianity, not spiritualism. Yet she herself read spiritualist literature, attended séances, and used the planchette. Perhaps she saw herself as so deeply anchored in Christianity that spiritualism posed no threat to her faith. And the more she pulled away from Lyman Beecher's belief in eternal punishment for the unconverted, the more she saw as necessary some probationary state after death. She must have known that spiritualism, followed to its logical conclusions, challenged the need for Jesus and the cross. Harriet would not go that far, however. She insisted that the Bible's revelation was superior to anything that might come from spiritualism.[49]

In the fall of 1870 Stowe wrote a series of articles on spiritualism for *The Christian Union,* presenting spiritualism as a religious movement in its own right.[50] Its main attraction was its promise to relieve sorrow by restoring contact between the living and the dead. Now the Church, Stowe said, has the power to comfort those who mourn. That power lies in "the communion of saints," an article of faith since ancient times.[51] It unites souls in heaven with souls on earth, joined in the body of Christ. Christ's victory over death makes it possible for saints in heaven and on earth to intercede for one another. Alas, in medieval times the communion of saints became "a monstrous system of bargain and sale of prayers for the dead." But Protestants went too far when they rejected the communion of saints instead of merely reforming it.

After the Reformation, "modern rationalistic religion" came in, Stowe explained. Christians began to doubt everything supernatural. As a result, "the pastures of the Church" have "become bare and barren of one species of food which the sheep crave," namely, supernatural comfort for those who mourn. So the sheep "break out of the enclosure and rush, unguided, searching for [food] among poisonous plants which closely resemble it — but whose taste is deadly."[52] If people thought the Church could not help them, they turned to spiritualism.

What Christians needed was to lay hold of "the strong and splendid supernaturalism of the Bible." Above all they should look to Christ: "He once died himself, and has risen again to new and immortal life, so that the whole of that mysterious, dreaded experience has been fully proved by him."[53] More than a year later, in January 1872, Stowe told *Christian Union* readers not to seek comfort in spiritualism, since Christianity has much more to offer.[54]

She did not take her own advice. Her correspondence with George Eliot (pen name of the British author Mary Anne Evans) is particularly revealing. In 1872 she told Eliot about a séance in which a medium called up the spirit of Charlotte Bronte (d. 1855). The deceased author was in a chatty mood, speaking through the planchette for two whole hours, Harriet said. How remarkable that the medium ("Mrs. K") just *happened* to call up one of Harriet's favorite authors! Stowe told Eliot that despite some doubts, "I cannot get over the impression that I have had a conversation with Charlotte Bronte."[55] Three months later Stowe was still thinking about that séance, in which "Bronte" described the future state as one of "eternal peace . . . calm, improvement, order, usefulness."[56] Mrs. K. (the medium) made several visits to Harriet's home, bringing her planchette and conducting sessions for Stowe and the twins. When the planchette made subtle puns in French — and even wrote poetry — Mrs. K's clients were convinced that the spirit of Charlotte Bronte was speaking, since Mrs. K could not have made up such things herself.

George Eliot, though, was not impressed. Bluntly the British author told Harriet that she found spiritualism "enormously improbable. . . . I must frankly confess that I have but a feeble interest in these doings." Elsewhere Eliot told Stowe that spiritualism "appeared to me either as degrading folly, imbecile in the estimate of evidence, or else as impudent imposture." Eliot preferred a religion that cared "less . . .

for personal consolation" and more for a "sense of responsibility to man."[57] Harriet did not take the hint.

Stowe wrote to Eliot about a séance led by Katie Fox, one of the most famous mediums of the day. In 1848 Katie and her sister Margaret heard mysterious "rappings" or knockings in their home in Hydesville, New York. Rumors spread that the house was haunted. Curious neighbors came to watch as the sisters, seated at a table, received and translated "rappings" purported to come from a murdered peddler who lay buried beneath the house. The Hydesville rappings contributed to a nationwide craze in spiritualism. Some forty years later, at least one of the Fox sisters confessed that the rapping sounds were produced by the cracking of their own toe joints (hidden by their long skirts as they sat at the table).

But by the time Stowe met Katie Fox, at the home of Dr. Taylor in New York, the medium was much more sophisticated. Stowe did not give the date of the séance, but listed those in attendance: "Katie, Myself & husband, Dr. & Mrs. Taylor, my sister & brother" (probably Charles and Catharine). Stowe told Eliot, "We had her [Katie Fox] between us holding her hands." Holding hands in a circle allowed psychic power to flow through the participants. (It also kept the medium's hands from causing special effects, though it could not prevent the activity of some hidden helper.) Stowe said she saw "phosponic [*sic*] lights" that "rose and floated about us — they were like clear lights of a glow worm . . . one of them struck the table with a loud report like the firing of a pistol." One of these globes had a hand in it, which took paper & pencil and wrote a message. "A guitar was raised up over our heads and played on. My husband who is a very stout man weighing two hundred was moved back from the table five feet to the wall chair & all & then placed again at the table."[58]

It was a good show, but Stowe doubted Katie Fox's integrity. She wondered if the "moral deficiency" of a medium discredited "the phenomena." If a medium was not a trustworthy person, could one still credit as genuine things that happened in a séance? Stowe pondered this for some time. She told Eliot it was "a disadvantage and an embarrassment" that "the phenomena come mostly through morally diseased and incapable" people. Stowe shared Eliot's "disgust" at such mediums. However, Stowe pitied Katie Fox as an "unfortunate." If the results of scientific experiments can be independent of the scientist's moral character, the same may hold true in supernatural experiments: perhaps supernatural "phenomena are quite independent of these [moral] considerations."[59] Even if the medium is a shyster, spiritualism itself might still be valid.

When it came to spiritualism, Stowe was of two minds. "I have had every confidence of an invisible, intelligent spirit — other than that of the medium," she told Eliot. Still, she was "by no means certain" that she had really looked into the beyond. She believed spirits had communicated with her, but were those spirits what they professed to be? She had her doubts, but still she did not "despise . . . those who have seen more" than she saw. She could only "wait and hope for some clearer light."[60] Stowe described herself as "a believer in the Bible and Christianity" and told Eliot that spiritualism and its phenomena "are not likely to be a religion to me."[61] Stowe knew that some mediums were fakes, but could not give up the hope of communicating with the world beyond the grave.

Stowe's friend and early biographer, Annie Fields, presented spiritualism as a passing interest for Stowe — something that Stowe dabbled in and then rejected. In her *Life and Letters of Harriet Beecher Stowe,* Fields quoted at length from a letter Stowe wrote about spiritualism. There Stowe said that grieving people are vulnerable to spiritualism. That is understandable. But if our loved ones are in heaven, Stowe asked why we would

> wish them to return . . . to juggle, and rap, and squeak, and perform mountebank tricks with tables and chairs; to recite over in weary sameness harmless truisms, which we were wise enough to say for ourselves; to trifle, and banter, and jest, or to lead us through endless moonshiny mazes? . . . [I]f this be communion with the dead, we had rather be without it . . . if the future life is so weary, stale, flat, and unprofitable . . . one would have reason to deplore an immortality from which no suicide could give an outlet. To be condemned to such eternal prosing would be worse than annihilation. . . .

Jesus shed real tears over the grave of Lazarus, Stowe preached. He knows our sorrows. If we cannot speak with departed loved ones, we can pray to Christ who is intimately present "with them as with us. He is the true bond of union between the spirit world and our souls." His love surpasses all knowing, and "is better than all those incoherent, vain, dreamy glimpses with which longing hearts are cheated." Those who long for "communion with spirits" should draw near to Christ. He has promised, "'I will not leave you comfortless. I will come to you.'"[62]

This letter expressed Stowe's "mature views" on spiritualism, Fields said. Harriet's son Charles also reprinted this letter in Harriet's memoir, calling it "the mature reflection of many years." But neither Fields nor Charles mentions that the letter was written in 1868 — after which Stowe attended séances, consulted the Ouija board, and wrote letters about her paranormal experiences. Again in 1872 Stowe firmly advised readers "whose souls are weakened by loss of friends . . . *not to seek comfort*" in spiritualism but in "the old Bible."[63] But she did not follow her own advice.

It would be easy to charge Stowe with hypocrisy, but it is probably more accurate to see this as a painful struggle for her. She described that struggle in an essay about the witch of Endor,[64] a figure she included in *Woman in Sacred History.* Since this story is from the Bible, Stowe said, it may be possible for a medium to summon spirits of the dead. But mediums cannot be trusted to impart guidance or comfort. They cannot take the place of true "communion with God." Mediums have a "constant tendency to place themselves before our minds as our refuge and confidence rather than God," Stowe warned. She herself had seen "the very best and most remarkable phenomena" in spiritualism. Even if some of these were genuine, they led to a "restless hunger of mind, an appetite forever growing and never satisfied." Spiritualism was like an undertow, relentlessly pulling the Christian away from Jesus, the true "Comforter, Guide, Teacher, Friend," who promises to dwell with all who believe in him.[65]

Writing to Oliver Wendell Holmes in 1876, Stowe said she had "long since concluded" that the phenomena of spiritualism were natural ones. Someday they would be explained scientifically. She had "no faith whatsoever in mediums who practice for money." She thought "the Law of Moses, that forbade consulting those who dealt with 'familiar spirits' a very wise one."[66]

But she could not give spiritualism up entirely. As late as 1883 in a letter to Isabella, Stowe mentioned receiving a message from her lost son Fred through a medium — then she commended Fred to the care of Christ. And when Isabella claimed to have received a message from Fred, Harriet asked her to copy and send it.[67] Sometimes Stowe saw clearly the difference between Christianity and the occult; at other times, tears blurred her vision.

Other Writings

Late in her career Stowe published three "society novels," including the already-mentioned *My Wife and I* and *Pink and White Tyranny.* The third society novel, *We and Our Neighbors,* appeared in 1875. All three novels were set in the post-war urban North; all three were serialized in the *Christian Union* before appearing as books.

The society novels have been dismissed as sentimental and frivolous.[68] They lacked the passion of *Uncle Tom's Cabin* and fell short of the literary standards of Stowe's New England novels. But they allowed her to comment on many things, including religion in postwar America. Stowe saw Christianity losing its power to shape public opinion; it seemed that the press had replaced the pulpit. No longer did people rely on preachers to tell them the news or make meaning of it. For that they relied on newspapers and magazines — which spewed more information than readers could absorb. Information overload, it seems, is not new.

In *My Wife and I* Stowe said Christians have nothing to fear from modern science and biblical criticism. Yes, "man-made theologies and creeds" were being challenged. Very well then, let the old theology "drop away just as the blossom does when the fruit forms." In the end what really matters is Christ within and a life well lived. Stowe assured her readers that "Christ's religion will be just the same as ever — his words will not pass away."[69]

Stowe felt Christianity could adjust to modernity without losing its essence. To her the *practice* of faith was far more important than a *system* of belief. In *My Wife and I,* Stowe praised the ancient liturgy as a stabilizing force for modern times. She praised Catholics and Episcopalians for bringing the children of the Puritans back to the customs of the ancient church.[70] The ancient liturgy and the communion of saints soothed her soul.

And so did Florida. There she found joy and solace — and much to write about. Her essays and letters about Florida were published in 1873 as *Palmetto Leaves.*[71] Florida was then an obscure and exotic place to most northerners, but Stowe helped to change that. She wrote of fishing on the St. Johns River, gathering exotic flowers, and watching colorful birds. She touted Florida's healthful climate, and told how to grow cucumbers in January.

Florida was a society being re-born after slavery, she told readers.

She saw black Floridians working hard and enjoying their freedom. And she heard their voices. One night, sitting outside a cabin where black Christians worshipped, Stowe heard a preacher say, "Gabriel, Gabriel, blow your trump: take it cool and easy, cool and easy, Gabriel: dey's all bound for to come." In black worship Stowe felt "a reaching and longing for . . . God and immortality, and a future beyond this earth."[72] She felt inspired by black worship, and seeing former slaves become independent farmers gave her hope.

Palmetto Leaves sold well and attracted many northern tourists to Florida; Stowe herself paid a price for that when curious tourists invaded her privacy in Mandarin. Boats would slow their progress on the St. Johns River so that passengers could gawk at Stowe's cottage up on the bluff. Sometimes people even got off the excursion boats and climbed the hill to peer through the windows.

Calvin Stowe would sometimes oblige these visitors by telling stories. But when provoked, Calvin could be fierce. One tourist reached up and broke off "a large branch covered with orange blossoms which hung right in front of the veranda." Calvin banged his cane down on the porch. "You ruthless little varlet," he growled, "drop that branch and get off this place as fast as you can travel." The offender protested, *was this not Harriet Beecher Stowe's place?* "So it is," Calvin roared, "and I'll have you know that I am the proprietor of Harriet Beecher Stowe and of this place — now git!"[73]

Vandalism of Stowe's orange trees was part of a general disregard for nature. In *Palmetto Leaves,* Stowe told of excursion boats whose passengers toted guns and shot at anything that moved in trees, water, or sky. The alligators were a favorite target, for when hit they thrashed their tails and performed barrel rolls in the water. On some of these tour boats a "constant firing [was] kept up by that class of men who think the chief end of man is to shoot something," Stowe wrote. Stowe saw nothing wrong with hunting for food, and she loved a meal of fresh-caught fish. But shooting animals just to watch them die was wrong. "The tiger kills for food, man for amusement,"[74] she observed.

Stowe was an advocate for animals. In an article called "The Rights of Dumb Animals" (1869) Stowe passed along to readers some facts gathered by the Society for the Prevention of Cruelty to Animals. Her readers needed to know that livestock were shipped to market in freezing airless train cars; that turkeys were plucked alive; that horses were whipped and dogs abandoned; that animals were tortured for sport and nature was "wounded" by over-hunting. These things should not be, Stowe said. The animals are the "Creator's handiwork" and we are accountable for how we treat them. Do we owe anything to the animals we use, or own, or eat? What if God feels and suffers for the animals as well as for human beings? "If there be any oppressed class that ought to have a convention" and demand better treatment, it should be the poor creatures of the earth.[75]

Stowe sounded the alarm against the over-hunting of Florida's birds. In *The Semi-Tropical* in 1877 she said that bird trappers were robbing Florida of "one of its chief attractions. . . . Who will get a protection law passed that will secure to us the song, beauty and usefulness of these charming fellow citizens of our lovely Florida?"[76] According to Olav Thulesius, a proposal to protect the birds failed to pass the Florida legislature, despite Stowe's plea. In those days feathers were used to decorate ladies' hats: plumes of the snowy egret were especially prized, and the Carolina parakeet — the only parrot species in the eastern U.S. — was hunted to extinction. In *Palmetto Leaves* Stowe warned that a "war of extermination" was being "waged in our forests."[77]

On the Lecture Circuit

Like the birds she loved, Harriet migrated with the seasons. In 1873 she feathered a new nest in her northern habitat. That year the Stowes sold Oakholm and moved into a smaller, more practical house on Forest Street. It was built in Greek revival[78] style with a steep roof, porches, and bay windows. Downstairs were two parlors, a dining room, and a modern kitchen. Just across Stowe's back yard there arose an ornate red brick mansion, and in 1874 Mark Twain and his family moved in. The Stowes and Twains were on friendly terms. Once when Twain's wife scolded him for calling on the Stowes without a necktie, he repented by sending to the Stowe house a silver tray bearing a necktie.

Mark Twain and other authors of the day made good money on the lecture circuit, reading from their published works. Stowe was intrigued. She was the breadwinner for her family, supporting two homes in uncertain financial times. By the 1870s more women were speaking in public, and Harriet joked that she would love to do it, hate to do it, and wished she didn't want to do it.

She did it. *Atlantic* editor James Fields found an agent to book Stowe's tour of New England for the fall of 1872 — forty stops in all. Her first lecture was in Springfield; it was well attended, but Harriet did not know how to project her voice or keep the crowd's attention. She dreaded her next engagement — at Boston's Tremont Temple, where the literati were sure to gather. In Boston, Stowe stayed with James and Annie Fields. On the day of the performance, Harriet called Annie into the guest bedroom. Looking into the mirror, Harriet brushed her short gray curls straight up in mock imitation of her father. "Look here, my dear," Harriet told Annie, "now I am exactly like my father, Dr. Lyman Beecher, when he was going to preach," and she held up her forefinger "warningly." Annie knew that this time Stowe would hold her audience.

An hour later at Tremont Temple, Annie sat with Harriet in the anteroom off-stage. "I could feel the power surging up within her," Annie recalled. "I knew she was armed for a good fight." This time Stowe did not just read from her works. She acted out the characters of *Uncle Tom's Cabin* and more recent works. Stowe's voice was still hard to hear at times. But the audience stood and leaned forward to catch every word. A reporter described Stowe as "small in stature . . . and with the merriest twinkle in her eye, betokening a reservoir of fun and mirth sufficient to explode a funeral assembly with laughter."

With a successful Boston reading under her belt, Stowe continued her tour with confidence. Along the way she met children named after her, or named for characters in *Uncle Tom's Cabin.* One woman declared that it was better to meet Harriet Beecher Stowe than Queen Victoria! Yet Stowe often felt lonely and travel-weary. She longed to sit beside Calvin and sing their old favorite songs. She missed Calvin, but told him "I have never felt the near, kind presence of our Heavenly Father so much as in this." God gives strength to the weary, she wrote; "I have found this true all my life." She decided that lecturing was "as easy a way of making money as I have ever tried, though no way of making money is perfectly easy." Stowe finished the tour in time to spend the entire winter in Florida.[79]

She made a second lecture tour the following fall, this time in the Midwest. For company she brought her daughter Hattie, and they hired a young man to assist with luggage and other practical needs.

The first stop was Reading, Pennsylvania. Then they went to Cleveland, Detroit, Louisville, St. Louis, and Chicago, where Stowe gave two readings. From there the train trip east to Cincinnati was an ordeal: thirteen hours in a crowded, overheated car. In Cincinnati they stayed with George Beecher, Harriet's nephew. The Cincinnati audience loved seeing Harriet Beecher Stowe in person — to think that she had lived obscurely in their town for eighteen years! George Beecher took his aunt Harriet to see Walnut Hills above the town of Cincinnati. There was Lane Seminary and the house where Lyman Beecher had lived with his family; she saw the places where she and Calvin began their married life and where all but one of her children were born. If she visited the grave of little Charlie who died from cholera all those years ago, she kept that memory private. From Cincinnati she went east by train, stopping for speaking engagements along the way.

At the age of sixty-two, Stowe was tired of traveling. Calvin needed her and she wanted to be with him. Early in December 1873, Stowe began her journey to Florida, where she would meet her family. In Washington, D.C., she stopped to give her last public reading.[80] She had lived to see the day when it was no longer shocking for women to speak in public. She had tried it and succeeded, and was now content to leave it to others.

CHAPTER EIGHTEEN

Resolved into Love

Before the Civil War, many in the South saw Harriet Beecher Stowe as an enemy. But in 1874, she was invited by the governor of Florida to a reception honoring northerners who helped Florida to rise after the war. Stowe deserved the honor: not only did her writings draw tourists and settlers to Florida, but she helped start a school and a church, and her orchard helped to promote oranges as Florida's new cash crop. Harriet's brother Charles also made a contribution, serving for two years as Florida's superintendent for public schools and establishing a successful farm in Newport on Florida's panhandle, where Harriet visited from time to time.[1]

After the governor's reception in Tallahassee, Stowe went by train to New Orleans. Crowds of black people gathered at train stations along her route to catch a glimpse of the author whose book helped to end slavery.[2] But that was long ago. Harriet's children were grown up and gone, and her writing career was winding down.

In her winter home in Mandarin, Harriet loved to paint pictures of orange blossoms or putter in her garden. Excursions on the St. Johns River offered excellent bird-watching. More and more, Harriet would go with friends or with her twins and leave Calvin to sit in the shade of the live oak trees. He was growing feeble, and they both knew that the time would come to leave Florida for the last time. Harriet felt like someone "playing and picnicking on the shores of life & waked from a dream late in the afternoon to find that everybody — almost — has gone over to the Beyond & the rest are sorting their things and packing their trunks & waiting for the boat to come and take them."[3]

But it was no dream one day on the river when Harriet saw a boat with captives chained to the deck. They were Cheyenne and Kiowa warriors being transported to St. Augustine, there to be incarcerated at Fort Marion. These Indians were said to be the "wildest, the most dangerous, the most untamable of the tribes," Stowe wrote later. They wore skins and blankets, their faces were "painted in weird colors," and they wore feathers and scalps in their long hair. Folks living along the St. Johns feared that the prisoners might escape and ravage the countryside. Stowe wrote, perhaps sarcastically, that "the conscience and Christianity of our century" did not allow these warriors to be "shot down like so many captured tigers." Instead they were sent to Florida to be "kept out of mischief"[4] while the United States army established control of the western plains.

Some two years later Stowe toured Fort Marion. There she saw no "savages" — only eager pupils and willing workers. The Indians were now wearing government-issue clothing and learning to speak English. Someone told Stowe that in just one year these captive Plains Indians earned five thousand dollars from handcrafts they made and sold to tourists. Stowe also attended a prayer meeting at Fort Marion. Everyone had a copy of "the little Moody and Sankey hymn-book," and the service began with the singing of "Just as I Am." A chief named Eagle's Head prayed in the Cheyenne language. Harriet didn't understand a word, but the chief's fervor impressed her. She concluded that these Indians were not heathens; they were "theists" who believed in a "Great Good Spirit" much as white folk believed in "the Supreme."

"We have tried fighting and killing the Indians" and it did not work, Stowe told readers of the *Christian Union.* "We have tried feeding them as paupers" on reservations, only to have "dishonest contractors" cheat the government and starve the Indians. Stowe thought it was pointless to spend money on "armies, forts, and frontiers." Instead, she thought the government should educate the Indians and teach them to "live like civilized beings."[5] Today that attitude seems condescending at best. Yet in Stowe's own time, her approach toward the Indians was progressive. Her two-part piece on "The Indians of St. Augustine" appeared in 1877, less than a year after Custer's defeat at Little Bighorn, when many whites were so outraged that they called for the Plains Indians to be slaughtered like the buffalo. Not Harriet Beecher Stowe. She said that the Plains Indians deserved a chance to be part of the country that had forced them off their lands. However patronizing her views appear in hindsight, she did see the prisoners of war at Fort Marion as fellow human beings. Perhaps she recalled how, as a young teacher at the Hartford Female Seminary, she worked to halt the removal of Cherokee from their lands.

Sisters

And now it was within her own tribe — the Beechers — that Harriet needed to make peace. She was still estranged from her sister Isabella, who had believed their brother Henry to be guilty of adultery. Isabella was back from Europe, her finances depleted. She had grandiose ideas about her psychic powers, held séances in her Hartford home, and alienated friends and family with her weird predictions. Harriet had a high tolerance for spiritualism, but she could not forgive Isabella for taking sides against Henry. Since Harriet and Isabella lived in the same neighborhood in Hartford, their estrangement was painful indeed.

It was the oldest sister, Catharine, who helped Harriet and Isabella to reconcile. One summer when Catharine was staying in Hartford with Harriet and Calvin, she invited Isabella to play croquet, an outdoor game that would not violate the ban on Isabella entering Harriet's house. Isabella told Catharine of her dire financial condition; later, Catharine told Harriet. Harriet felt sorry for Isabella, and sent her a cash gift via Catharine.[6] This was the olive branch signaling that it was time to make peace. Perhaps the sisters agreed to disagree about Henry; in any case, they resumed their relationship, and Isabella remained a faithful friend for the rest of Harriet's life.

Catharine Beecher never married or had a home of her own. In the old tradition of maiden aunts, she moved around from one relative to the next, staying for weeks or months at a time. Now well into her seventies, Catharine suffered from sciatica, nerve pain in the leg and lower back, and she needed to settle down. Harriet was probably her closest sibling, but the Stowes' annual migration to Florida did not appeal to Catharine.

Finally Catharine chose to settle with her younger half-brother, Thomas Beecher. Thomas lived with his wife Julia in Elmira, New York. Elmira had a women's college and a water cure where Catharine could mix with like-minded people. Harriet was relieved. "Too many years have passed over your head," she told Catharine, "for you to be wandering around like a trunk without a label." But Catharine settled too late, and now her health was failing. Thomas said that Catharine was like a fractured mirror: all disconnected pieces. In a final burst of energy, she was trying to do everything at once: writing, sewing, playing the piano, and studying "metaphysics." On May 12, 1878, she died in her sleep, probably from a stroke.[7]

Stowe was in Florida, and slow travel made it impossible for her to attend the funeral. But she felt Catharine's death deeply. Apart from Lyman Beecher himself, no one did more than Catharine to shape Harriet's life. After their mother Roxana died, Catharine was like a mother to Harriet. Then she became Harriet's mentor at Hartford Female Seminary. When the family moved to Ohio, Catharine was Harriet's senior partner at the Western Female Institute. Catharine demanded much from Harriet, but she also gave back. Catharine gave of her time so that Harriet could write *Uncle Tom's Cabin;* Catharine and Harriet co-authored *The American Woman's Home* (1869). To be sure, Catharine was bossy and easier to love at a distance. But she was a true Beecher, a force to be reckoned with. Harriet would later write a tribute to Catharine as a pioneer of female education for the 1884 volume *Our Famous Women.*

The Only Son

As Harriet reached and passed midlife, she invested much in her youngest son Charles. Of the Stowes' four sons, Charles alone survived to carry on the family torch by becoming a minister. Yet Charles (whom the family also called Charley or Charlie) was slow to accept his destiny. As a child he made mischief by telling lies, got into trouble at boarding school, and tried to run away to sea, hoping some day to become the captain of his own ship.

At long last Charley returned to land, resumed contact with his parents, and eventually told them he would go into the ministry. "I cannot describe to you the ardor," Harriet wrote, "with which I desire & pray that you may become a minister after Christ's own heart."[8] She reminded him of his "peculiar history" as Lyman Beecher's grandson and Calvin Stowe's son. Surely the ministry was "bequeathed" to him as a "sacred trust by their prayers and consecration."[9] Charley had always loved the sea. But now the church would be his ship, the pulpit his tiller, and the congregation his crew.

Charles went to Yale to prepare for the ministry. But instead of finishing his course there, he went abroad and studied theology in a German university. Returning to the States, he took a position in a Congregational church in Saco, Maine. He married Susan Munroe, and they had two children, Lyman Beecher Stowe and Leslie Stowe. Harriet and Calvin supplemented Charley's low salary so that he could get a piano and other things the young clergyman could not afford. Harriet visited Charley and Susie in Maine several times and attended their church.

The church in Saco went through some rough seas, and the crew nearly mutinied. Today the online congregational history says, "A segment of the congregation resisted [Charles Stowe's] views which they considered too liberal." Lay leaders warned their young minister to "be silent on matters of doubtful concern and preach the pure simple truths of Salvation by Faith and Obedience."[10] Harriet repeatedly advised her son to avoid doctrinal controversies and preach a "personal Almighty Savior." That was the tack, she said, that helped Lyman Beecher and his sons prevail despite headwinds.[11]

Although he was a compassionate and faithful minister, Charles Stowe could be high-handed. One Communion Sunday he served wine instead of the usual grape juice. The church was "in an uproar." On the next Communion Sunday, the young Rev. Stowe said that since he could not in good conscience administer the Supper as the people demanded, he would not serve it at all! Later he relented, but the damage was done.

In letter after letter, Harriet urged Charley to stay the course in Saco. He must avoid needless controversy and preach only the life of Christ. She did her motherly duty and prayed for him often. Conflicts in the congregation were not unusual, she reminded him. So many clergy in the family had weathered these storms. What worried Harriet was that Charley seemed weak in his own faith. He harbored doubts about Christianity and indulged in skepticism. His mother urged him to look at *Christ the person,* not a set of doctrines *about* Christ. "For Christ is Christianity & to see & Know *Him* is the best way to believe," she wrote.

One of Charley's letters hit a raw nerve when he vented his disgust at the "liberal orthodoxy" of his Uncle Henry Ward Beecher. Charles said he hated the "slovenly inconsistencies" and "dishonesty" of his famous uncle. It was wrong, Charley felt, for Henry Ward Beecher to remain a Congregational clergyman while disbelieving certain tenets of that denomination. To Charley, this reeked of hypocrisy.

Well, Harriet replied, what *if* Henry — or she herself for that matter — did not believe everything the church taught? What if they did not believe that Adam fell because he took a bite from the apple? What of it? What matters is knowing that we are sinners, and repenting from that sin. It was the relationship that mattered, not the details of ancient stories. But no, Charley thought a minister should be consistent. Either you believe the teachings of your denomination or you don't. Harriet disagreed. She did not want to be defined by doctrine; she cared about spiritual practice and living in relationship with Jesus. Here she had found peace, so why must Charley make things difficult?

But Charley only wanted to be consistent. He doubted Christianity's supernatural claims, and thought perhaps he should join the Unitarians. When Harriet read this, she was horrified. "I protest with all the energy of my heart & soul against your joining the camp of the Unitarians," she declared. Oh, to be sure, there were "good soldiers & servants of Christ" among the Unitarians. Harriet said she had friends who were Unitarians *and* sincere Christians. But as for Unitarian*ism,* she saw it as sterile and lifeless. It had no mystery, no miracle, and had severed its ties with the communion of the saints.

Harriet had come to experience Christianity as a rich banquet with Christ himself presiding at the table. It was a very large table, laden with a great variety of food. As a child, Harriet sat with Christians who ate only plain, solid food: a diet of Scripture (preached, read, and prayed) and water from the well of hymns. But as an adult, Stowe acquired a taste for sacraments, for holy days and seasons, and even a festival here and there. She had moved to a place at the table where wine was served, where she could feast on sacred art; she could drink in the ancient chants and sample new songs. She had even come to love Mary, who sat quite far away from the Puritans at the table of the Lord. Stowe had spent a lifetime exploring this banquet table. And if she had strayed from it, she always came back. And now here was her son, her only remaining son, who would starve himself on the stale bread of rationalism! If he *must* live on crumbs, could he not at least remain at the Lord's Table?[12]

Harriet was exasperated. "I *always regretted*" (here she underlined heavily) "that you did not finish your studies at Yale." So what if studying in Germany had made him a better scholar; could this offset his "lack of faith"? She didn't think so. She said that "rationalist doubts" filled Charley's head, flapping like "bats wings," whenever he tried to walk the "simple old paths of childlike trust." So it would be "peculiarly bad" for him to "go into a denomination of skeptics and rationalists" who agree on nothing except what they do *not* believe. Didn't Charley notice that Unitarians often quit attending church because "it had nothing to offer"? On the last page of the letter, Harriet announced that Calvin agreed with her; Calvin warned their son against hasty decisions. And in case Charley hadn't gotten the message, Harriet repeated it. "Going over to the Unitarians" would be the worst move he could make. The Unitarians were not liberal, she felt, but actually far too narrow.

Tempers cooled. Charley did not become a Unitarian. Stowe later wrote to reassure him that she trusted his "good sense & manly feeling." She hoped that he would outgrow his hyper-sensitivity to criticism, whether from his parents or his parishioners. She empathized with him, saying that in her younger days criticism had hurt her deeply. But "I have outlived it & now do not suffer tho [I am] abundantly & often criticized." She had learned to rest in Christ, "resigned to the imperfection of our mortal state — to the thousand shortcomings & mistakes & infelicities in myself that I see. My Lord knows what I aim at, & how I try & why I fail as I so often do & He will make it all right."[13]

A Wideness in God's Mercy

As Harriet aged, she cared less and less what people said about her. She also cared less and less about doctrine. Indeed, one scholar said that Stowe became "loosed from all strictures of logic."[14] Surely she was loosed from the strictures of Calvinist logic. Like others in her generation, she stepped out of the harness of Calvinist logic based on divine sovereignty and sought a kinder, gentler form of Christianity. This can be seen in her correspondence with Oliver Wendell Holmes Sr., who like Harriet had a Calvinist minister for a father. As an adult, Holmes rejected Calvinism in favor of a more tolerant, forgiving religion. In January 1879 Stowe wrote to Holmes, saying that "all your theology . . . I subscribe to with both hands."[15]

Just what was Stowe subscribing to? Perhaps to a God who is all-forgiving and a heaven with doors wide open. In her letter to Holmes, Stowe quotes Revelation 21:4, which promises that God will wipe away all tears, and death, mourning, crying, and pain will be no more. Stowe stopped short of a nearby verse where the wicked are cast into "the lake that burns with fire." The wrath of God that she had preached at the end of *Uncle Tom's Cabin* had cooled off quite a bit.

At sixty-eight years of age, Stowe inhabited a different theological world[16] than the one of her anti-slavery days.[17] When she was in her early forties she burned with righteous indignation at slavery. Her spirituality then expressed conflict and vindication: in the battle between righteousness and sin, God sides with the oppressed. God will triumph when the powerful are brought low and the lowly are raised up. Conflict and vindication was the theological world of Lyman Beecher and of New England Calvinism generally.

All her life Stowe cared deeply for "the lowly" or oppressed. But her personal quest shifted with the death of her son Henry, who drowned in 1857. That tragic loss made the problem of separation, rather than injustice, paramount. What Harriet suffered with Henry was a double separation: that of the living from the dead, and the saved from the unsaved. She longed to overcome those separations, and thus became fascinated with spiritualism. At the same time she mined Christianity for strength to face separation and ultimately to overcome it. She found Christian hope through the communion of saints in this life and the promise of resurrection in eternity.

Just as Harriet cultivated her gardens, she tended Christian hope, keeping the holy seasons and festivals of the church year. Harriet wrote to her son Charley about Holy Week and Easter in the little church in Mandarin, Florida, where her spiritual practice was "hands on." She gathered flowers and arranged them in the church: "a cross of blood red phlox over the pulpit — a cross of fair white roses & other flowers in front & a bower of palmetto leaves & various flowers" at the lectern. By using flowers devotionally, Stowe merged nature and faith. She also baked the communion bread for Holy Week, brought the wine into the church, and polished "the sacred vessels & set the table." Doing these things, she told Charley, gave her a "sacred feeling" of nearness to God in the "little humble school room church."[18] As

John Gatta observed, "a response to beauty was integral to [Stowe's] religious experience."[19]

An aging Harriet bought a small crucifix to use for meditation. "As long as we are in the body we want something . . . that we can grasp with the hand or touch by the sense," she told her son in 1881. She said that for the first time in her life, she had some fear of dying. But holding the crucifix reminded her that Jesus "in his own person [walked] every step of the dark way which any child of his may be called to tread."[20] She said she could see why a dying person would find strength in clinging to the crucifix.

Belonging to a faith community was essential. Harriet told Charley that the individual Christian is gradually shaped into the image of Christ in the company of other believers. When Charles told his mother that many people avoid church because it places constraints on them, Harriet replied that the church is a school for sinners. A school cannot function without rules. And like good medicine, some constraints are life-giving. Harriet asked Charley why he kept throwing obstacles in the way of a simple path to God. He made simple things complicated, and then complained about the complications! Very well then, she would boil it all down for her rationalist son. This is what the church asks us to do: "1st repent of all wrong; 2nd believe with the heart on the Son Jesus Christ as your Master Lord & Savior; 3rd openly profess this belief." Do these things and you belong to "Christ's school where those who wish to learn of him put themselves under his teaching."[21]

God asks very little of us, she reminded him, when we consider all that God has done for us. "The Divine Love," Harriet told Charley, "is forever atoning forever giving itself to & for the unworthy — Christ was slain from the foundation of the world." But only on Calvary was divine suffering made so clear that human nature "could appreciate it." The cross revealed "a love that had always been there — always yearning — always devoting itself — forever seeking the wandering and the lost." People are "oftentimes wounded discouraged & beaten down by suffering," Harriet wrote. "But God gave us a captain whom suffering made perfect . . . Christ who was God's son — his innermost heart — his *beloved* his *only* one became one of us [and] identified himself so with us that our sins weighed upon him as a man's own sins."[22]

After all the storms of life, Stowe's faith remained anchored in Jesus. The same had been true of her father's faith. But the rope binding

Stowe to this anchor was long, and by the time she reached old age, Stowe could circle beyond her father's views and still feel secure in Christ.

This range can be seen in Stowe's last two major works. In 1877 Stowe published *Footsteps of the Master,* a collection of meditations on the life of Christ. The book followed the life of Christ through the liturgical seasons of Advent, Christmas, Epiphany, Lent, Easter, and Ascension. This was a marked contrast from Stowe's childhood. Now, as an older woman, she embraced the old church year as a form of devotion, connecting her to the wider church down through the ages. Yet she was very much in tune with her own times, for in one meditation, "The Attractiveness of Jesus,"[23] Stowe made Jesus sound like the ideal nineteenth-century mother — compassionate, tender, and wise.

Each chapter of *Footsteps* developed a scene from Jesus' life and ended with a hymn or poem for meditation. Many of the verses Stowe chose were written by Anglicans, some of whom were leaders in the Oxford movement (Anglo-Catholicism), reflecting the direction of her own piety. Take for example the F. W. Faber hymn, "There's a Wideness in God's Mercy." God's love is much broader than the narrow limits we place on it, Faber wrote, for "the heart of the Eternal is most wonderfully kind."[24] This became an anthem of mainline American Protestants well into the twentieth century.

This was the faith Stowe embraced. "The infinite tolerance of our Lord," she said, includes doubters and skeptics who help their fellow human beings but without embracing a creed. Perhaps with her son Charles in mind, Stowe in *Footsteps* commended the "true-hearted doubter" to the love of Christ. If we would win others to Christ, Stowe said, we must live for others by becoming a "soul-friend — a consoler, a teacher, and enlightener."[25]

Devotional writing was deeply satisfying for Stowe. She would like to do more of it, she told Charley. But since people demanded stories, why not write them?[26]

Her last important story appeared in 1879. It was a New England novel called *Poganuc People: Their Loves and Lives.* In contrast to *Footsteps,* which showed Stowe's mature spirituality, *Poganuc People* revisited her childhood and said a last farewell to her father's world. "Poganuc" is a fictional name for Litchfield, Connecticut; the girl named "Dolly" is Harriet, and Dolly's father, "Dr. Cushing," is Lyman Beecher.

The novel lingers lovingly over a New England that was now gone. *Poganuc People* tells the stories of young people growing up, and explores religious questions. Is there more than one way to be a Christian? Dolly's father was the Congregational minister in town. If Dolly's father was right about everything — and Dolly wanted him to be — then why was there also an Episcopal church in town? Dolly wanted to know what her father thought about those other Christians who were not in his church. Dr. Cushing admitted, "there can be truth and goodness in both forms of worship." Dolly was allowed to attend the Episcopal church when she visited relatives in Boston. With a touch of gentle humor, Dr. Cushing said that Episcopalians *could* be Christian and their articles of faith were "mostly acceptable."[27]

The Puritans, Stowe told her readers, put an ocean between themselves and all "scenic presentations of the religious life." They renounced every aid to the senses "to face the solemn questions of destiny in their simple nakedness, without drapery or accessories." Theirs was a noble quest. But the Puritan Way was not, and is not, the only way to be Christian. For "the true church is invisible to human eyes — one in spirit though separated by creeds . . . united in the prayer, 'thy kingdom come, thy will be done.'" Stowe defined Christianity as "The religion of Christ [which] owes its peculiar power to its revealing a Divine Lover, the Only Fair, the Altogether Beautiful, who can love the unlovely back into perfectness."[28]

With her last novel done, Stowe now planned to write her memoir. But her letters and papers were in such disarray! Just to organize her things so others might know "where and what they were" was a job in itself. And when she read these old letters she felt like one going "into the world of spirits," for most of her old correspondents were dead. And the things they wrote about now seemed faded and forgotten. What, if anything, had endured? Only "the intense unwavering sense of Christ's educating, guiding presence and care . . . is *all* that remains now . . . 'the beginning and end of all is Christ.'"[29]

The Garden Party

On June 14, 1882, Stowe's publisher, Houghton, Mifflin & Co., gave a garden party in honor of her seventy-first birthday.[30] The party was held at the country home of the former governor of Massachusetts, whose wife was a close friend of Harriet's. About two hundred guests attended. Among them were authors and clergy, doctors and judges, the president of Wellesley College, the mayor of Boston, feminist Lucy Stone, and several former leaders of the anti-slavery movement. William Lloyd Garrison was no longer living, but his son and namesake was there. Beecher and Stowe family members turned out in force.

It was a lovely summer day, and guests had ample time to socialize in the gardens and parlors and porches on the estate. On the lawn a large tent was set up for a program to be given in Stowe's honor. Mr. Houghton himself gave the opening address. *Uncle Tom's Cabin* "began by being a prophecy, and is now history," he said. Houghton recalled how Stowe received her vision of Tom's death "at the communion table," as she pondered Christ giving "himself for the redemption of humanity." And now "our own beloved country is redeemed" from slavery and its evils. Although Stowe went on to write many fine books, Houghton saw *Uncle Tom's Cabin* in a class by itself, because it had dealt a death blow to slavery.

Then Henry Ward Beecher spoke — as usual, about himself. Henry said that when *Uncle Tom's Cabin* first appeared, many people assumed that *he* was the author. Alas, that notion was dispelled when Henry's own novel, *Norwood,* came out and showed the world that he could not have written *Uncle Tom's Cabin.* Speaking of the Beecher family, Henry said, "My mother is to me what the Virgin Mary is to a devout Catholic."[31] This may have echoed Harriet's feelings.

In the tributes that followed, several speakers noted that *Uncle Tom's Cabin* was written by a woman — for example, the last stanza of "The Cabin," by J. T. Trowbridge.

> Woman, they say, must yield, obey;
> Rear children, dance cotillions;
> While this one wrote, she cast the vote
> Of un-enfranchised millions![32]

Stowe thanked the guests for honoring her. Then she turned their attention to "what God has done." The end of slavery, Stowe said, was the greatest event of their lives. It had given courage and hope to everyone. Whatever personal doubts, sorrows, or pains might come, nothing could dim this one great truth, that slavery was no more. Of course, Stowe added, everyone wondered what the future of the freed slaves would be. She told a few anecdotes about her black neighbors in Florida, how they worked, prospered, and enjoyed their freedom.

But on that summer evening in 1882, night was falling on hopes for racial equality in the South. Reconstruction — and the liberty it promised blacks — had ended in 1877. Federal troops were withdrawn from the South; laws protecting black people were quickly dismantled and replaced by "Jim Crow" laws enforcing white control. Not until the Civil Rights movement of the 1950s and 1960s would the nation address the unfinished business of the Civil War.

Frederick Douglass knew that Stowe had her limits in understanding the experience of black people; still, he knew that her novel was a turning point in the struggle against slavery. Douglass was invited to Stowe's party but could not attend, so he wrote a tribute to her for the occasion. In it he said that no one else was able to "move so many minds and hearts" for the slaves as Mrs. Stowe. "Hers was the word for the hour," said Douglass, "and it was given with skill, force and effect."[33] Douglass thought Stowe deserved to be honored by her own and future generations.

Farewells

The following year, something else happened that gave the Stowes deep satisfaction. The little church in Florida that Harriet and Calvin had nurtured all these years moved out of the school house. It now had a real church building, newly built on a bluff overlooking the St. Johns River. The Church of Our Savior could now afford to call its own pastor, so Calvin could retire from his volunteer ministry. Harriet wanted to have a stained glass window installed in the church to commemorate the Stowes' work there. Eventually the window was made by the great stained glass artist Louis Comfort Tiffany. It depicted "two oak trees of the Stowe river front against the river and sunset sky." Some church members thought it lacked "religious significance but [the window] was admired and beloved by most,"[34] according to the church's website.

Stowe did not live to see the Tiffany window, but Florida's natural beauty was more than enough. "This glorious, budding, blossoming spring," she wrote, brings "days when merely to breathe and be is to be blessed. I love to have a day of mere existence." She declared that she never wanted to "go back North, nor do anything with the toiling snarling world again." Her days of striving past, she was studying "nothing but Christ's life," which gave her needed strength as she suffered "more pain, more weariness and weakness, than ever in my life before," she told her friend Annie Fields.

The winter and spring of 1884 was the Stowes' last season in Florida. Indeed, if not for their twin daughters, who did the housekeeping and managed the packing and moving, Harriet and Calvin would have had to leave Florida much sooner. But now Calvin's health was failing. He needed to stay year-round in Hartford, Harriet told a friend, with "such conveniences as an invalid needs." She prayed to outlive Calvin so that she could make him comfortable and happy. This was her "appointed work," and she hoped "to do it faithfully."[35]

Back in Hartford to stay, Harriet wrote often to her remaining siblings. "I think more of my brothers and sisters than I ever have done before," she told Isabella, "and have written to all and get replies from all but Henry."[36] As usual, the twins managed the household. Harriet wrote that her daughter Hattie rationed out some good sherry "at dinnertime at tea time & again at bed time . . . & if I fell on my knees to her I could not get it at any other time."[37]

Around this time Charles Stowe and his family left Saco, Maine, and moved to Hartford. Charles was now the minister of the Windsor Avenue Church (Congregational). Harriet and Calvin gave their son money from the sale of their Florida property so he could buy a house in Hartford. Charles now did all he could to help his aging parents.[38]

And Harriet did all she could for Calvin. His mind was still sharp, but he suffered from a kidney ailment called Bright's disease (nephritis). As Harriet discreetly put it, Calvin required "the personal attentions that only a wife ought to render." Charley, Hattie, and Eliza wanted to hire a nurse, but Harriet resisted until she grew so weary that she had no choice. By the end Calvin had nursing care around the clock. The family gathered around Calvin's deathbed to pray and sing hymns. Calvin's last words were "Peace with God! Peace with God!"[39] He died on August 6, 1886, at the age of eighty-four, and was buried at Andover in the chapel cemetery next to the grave of their son Henry.

"*Why* am I spared?" Harriet wondered. "Is there anything yet for me to do?"[40] She missed Calvin terribly. She had relied on him to keep her abreast of "all that was going on in the world."[41] She felt increasingly isolated.

As her world got smaller, so did her circle of family members. Harriet's half-brother James died in 1886. For years he'd suffered from depression, only to rise like a phoenix to lead black troops during the war. Later he served churches in upstate New York, and depression once more engulfed him. He died from a gunshot to the head, much like his brother George had in 1843. This time, however, no one called it an accident.

Henry Ward Beecher was next. On March 8, 1887, he had a stroke and died. Henry's wife Eunice never forgave Isabella for believing Henry was unfaithful, so "the griffin" barred Isabella from attending the private family service. Throughout Brooklyn, bells tolled and businesses closed. In front of Plymouth Church, people stood in line for hours to file past the flower-covered casket inside. After the solemn funeral in the church Henry had made famous, a huge procession followed the casket to the graveyard. But Henry's half-brother Thomas refused to get into the family carriage: "I'm not going to traipse all over Brooklyn behind a corpse," he declared.[42]

Five months later, Stowe's daughter Georgiana died. She was only forty-four years old, but she had battled illnesses of body and mind for most of her adult life. In those days, doctors often prescribed morphine as a pain reliever, and Georgiana became addicted. Over the years she tried one cure after another. She would improve for a time, only to sink down again. Stowe kept vigil at the deathbed, where she sought comfort in copying out a poem she had written years before. It was called "The Other World," and it ended with the words: "Your joy be the reality/Our suffering life the dream." She inscribed the date and place: "August 5, 1887, the daughter's room."[43] The Stowe family remembered Georgie as "the most brilliant and gifted" of all Harriet and Calvin's children, "the only one who could be truly said to have inherited real genius."[44] Now only three of the Stowe children were living: Hattie, Eliza, and Charles.

Not long after Georgiana died, the temperance leader Frances Willard visited Harriet in her home. To Willard, the Stowe house felt like a museum filled with mementos of a bygone time. Stowe was a "little woman, decidedly under-size, and weighing less than a hundred pounds." She wore a basic dress of "black-and-white check, with linen collar and small brooch, her hair, which had once been brown, hung fluffily upon a broad brow and was bound by a black ribbon. . . . Her nose is long and straight, eyes dimmed by years, mouth large and with the long Beecher lip, full of the pathos of humanity's mystical estate." This, mused Willard, "is what time has left of the immortal Harriet Beecher Stowe."[45]

In That Bright Morning

Harriet had one more thing left to do. With her son Charles's help, she had to complete her memoir. It was taking a long time. Charles found it a daunting task to organize his mother's letters and papers, which lay scattered about the house or tossed into trunks and boxes. And Calvin had pasted some of the most important letters into scrapbooks, obliterating the pasted sides! But Charles assembled his mother's papers in order as best he could. He would read them aloud to her, prompting her memory and writing down her comments, much as she had done years before for her father.

The *Life of Harriet Beecher Stowe: Compiled from Her Letters and Journals* was published in 1890. Stowe wrote a letter of introduction.

> . . . If these pages shall lead those who read them to a firmer trust in God & a deeper sense of His fatherly goodness throughout the days of our earthly pilgrimage I can say with Valiant for Truth in the Pilgrim's Progress, "I am going to my Father's & tho with great difficulty I am got hither, yet now, I do not repent me of all the troubles I have been at, to arrive where I am.
>
> "My sword I give to him that shall succeed me in my pilgrimage & my courage & skill to him that can get it."
>
> Hartford September 30, 1889 Harriet Beecher Stowe.[46]

Harriet then went to Long Island for some rest. She had always loved the sea. While there, she suffered a health crisis, probably a stroke. She was brought back to Hartford, where her family thought she would soon die. She rallied, but her mind had become childlike. She would sit for hours petting Bosco, her tortoiseshell cat. She wandered the neighborhood picking flowers from neighbors' yards, sometimes drifting into the Twains' house to play the piano or pick flowers in the conservatory. She would proudly present the flowers to Twain's wife, Livy, who graciously thanked Stowe and pretended that the blossoms had come from Harriet's own garden. "If you didn't know Mrs. Stowe was in your house," said Mark Twain, "she could slip up behind a person who was deep in dreams and musings and fetch a war whoop that would jump that person out of his clothes."[47]

Harriet did have her lucid moments. Edward Bok, editor of *Ladies Home Journal,* visited Stowe several months after the stroke and found her alert.[48] Charles Stowe accompanied Bok, warning beforehand that his mother might not recognize Bok even though she had met him before. As the two men walked up the steps and rang at the front door, two fat old pugs, Punch and Missy, barked furiously to announce the visitors. Hatty and Eliza opened the door, and then Stowe herself appeared. A light of recognition flickered over Harriet's face, but then she grasped Bok's hand and peered into his eyes, trying to decide just who he was.

The interview lasted about twenty minutes. Bok or Charles mentioned a southern school for blacks in which the white teachers ate in a separate dining room. And Bok saw "the old fire" come into Stowe's eyes. "Shameful!" she said. "Can such things be at this time!" She could imagine "such a distinction twenty-five years ago, but now, it is dastardly and unworthy of our times." Charles asked his mother if she would "be willing to eat at the same table with colored people." "Would I be willing! Charlie, I am surprised you should ask me such a question! Of course I would, and gladly! Why should I not! Are they not the children of God the same as we!"

Bok asked Stowe if she recalled the furor over *Uncle Tom's Cabin.* "I suffered much in my day from things that invaded my personality," she replied. But "words don't kill or I should have been dead long ago." She said she held no grudges. "I am resolved into love. I love everybody, even the dirtiest beggar upon the street." Of her health, she said "Well, Old Time has a grudge against me. He has hit me a whack and I fear I shall never get over it." Asked if she believed in the resurrection, she replied, "do I believe in the resurrection? Why, of course, I do! If the past is a dream to me, the future is not."

On another occasion, Edward Bok was sitting in the parlor at Mark Twain's house, waiting for Twain to return from a walk. Through the open windows he heard a low, tremulous voice singing hymns. Looking outside, Bok saw Harriet sitting on a bench in the flower-house. She swayed gently and beat time with one finger while she sang "Jesus, Lover of My Soul" and "Nearer, My God, to Thee." Another time, Bok was walking in the neighborhood when Stowe spotted him. She called out, "young man, young man, you have been leaning against something white." She approached him and began to brush the sleeve of his coat. When Bok spoke her name, she replied, "That is my name, young man. I live on this street. Are you going to have me arrested for stopping you?" Then she gathered up her skirts and ran away, looking over her shoulder to make sure she was not being pursued.[49]

Harriet's children hired a nurse to be always at their mother's side, but Stowe made a game of eluding her keeper. Once in a while, one of the twins saw flashes of Harriet's "old self that come and go like falling stars."

Stowe had changed the world with her pen. Now she rarely wrote, except to send a brief note to a friend, or to copy Lyman Beecher's motto, "Trust in the Lord and do good"[50] (Psalm 37:3). One day in February 1893 a letter came from Oliver Wendell Holmes Sr., asking Harriet about her health and happiness. She managed a reply. After her "alarming illness" four years past, her body was well but her mind was "nomadic." She enjoyed roaming the neighborhood, greeting neighbors and picking flowers. Harriet described herself as almost always happy. Looking at picture books brought her great enjoyment, and she could never get enough music. She said she made no mental effort of any sort, because her brain was tired out. "It was a womans brain & not a mans & finally from sheer fatigue & exhaustion in the march & strife of life, gave out before the end was reached. And now I rest me, like a moored boat, rising & falling on the water with loosened cordage & flapping sail."[51] Even as the end was nearing, she could still turn a phrase.

Stowe's copyright on *Uncle Tom's Cabin* expired in May 1893. Once it entered the public domain, her great protest novel could be published by anyone with no royalties paid out. Fortunately her editors at Houghton, Mifflin had seen this coming. Before the copyright expired they published new editions of *Uncle Tom's Cabin* from which Stowe earned royalties. But by the end of her life Stowe's income had slowed to a trickle, barely enough to support her household.[52]

Stowe was no longer aware of money. Indeed she scarcely thought of herself as an author. One day in her garden she was hailed by an old sea captain who lived nearby. The man said he would be deeply honored to shake the hand that wrote *Uncle Tom's Cabin.* Stowe obliged and shook his hand. "I did not write it," she informed him. "God wrote it. I merely did his dictation."[53]

A second stroke left Harriet partially paralyzed. She rallied briefly, and then began to sink. One night she awoke and told her nurse, "O I have had such a beautiful dream!" When the nurse gave her some medicine, Harriet spoke her last words: "I love you." On July 1, 1896, Harriet Beecher Stowe "passed peacefully away, as though into a deep sleep." Present at her deathbed were Hattie and Eliza, Harriet's sister Isabella and her husband John Hooker, and Harriet's attending physician, her nephew Edward Hooker.[54]

The following afternoon, relatives and friends gathered at the Stowe house for a simple funeral of prayers, Scripture readings, and hymns. Three clergymen (in addition to Charles Stowe) were present. A male quartet sang "Nearer, My God, to Thee," and "The Other World," the poem Harriet had copied at her daughter Georgie's deathbed. Harriet's casket was "covered with silver-gray broadcloth, which rested in a bank of ferns and flowers."[55]

On July 3, Stowe's casket was taken by train to Andover, where family members and "a large number of friends" followed the funeral cortege to the cemetery. Nearby stood the house where the Stowes lived when Harriet was finishing *Uncle Tom's Cabin;* the Stone Cabin was "draped with an American flag" and "festooned with black." Harriet's remains would be laid to rest alongside those of her husband Calvin and son Henry, whose graves were strewn with flowers, as though in welcome.

Later, Harriet's three surviving children placed an obelisk of rose-colored granite on the grave. The base bears the inscription, "her children rise up and call her blessed." The obelisk gracefully rises into the shape of a cross in the fleur-de-lis style, calling to mind the Trinity and the beauty of the lilies.

> So shall it be at last, in that bright morning
> When the soul waketh and life's shadows flee;
> O in that hour, fairer than daylight dawning,
> Shall rise the glorious thought, *I am with Thee!*
>
> *Harriet Beecher Stowe*[56]

Epilogue

The year after Stowe died, Leo Tolstoy called *Uncle Tom's Cabin* "the highest art," and ranked it alongside the best works of Dickens, Hugo, Eliot, and Dostoyevsky.[1] Great literature, he said, evoked "positive feelings of love of God and one's neighbor, and negative feelings of indignation and horror at the violation of love." Similar observations were made by an African American writer in Topeka, Kansas. Stowe's "reflective turn of mind . . . [her] kind, generous and sympathetic nature," recoiled from slavery and her book, *Uncle Tom's Cabin,* did more than anything else to end it. And with Stowe's passing "the Negro race" had lost "one of its greatest benefactors." The writer called *Uncle Tom's Cabin* "the greatest production in American literature"[2] because of its noble aim and the results it produced.

Stowe's Tom was a Christ figure who died so that others might live. That was noble, and it was also troubling. William Lloyd Garrison asked if Stowe intended that *only* blacks were supposed to turn the other cheek, and that *only* blacks were to lay down their lives without striking back. And Frederick Douglass, speaking to black soldiers in 1865, praised them for *not* being sheepish like Uncle Tom, for *not* being willing to be "whipped by anyone who wanted to whip [them]."[3]

The image of Tom as subservient and cowardly was spread by staged versions of *Uncle Tom's Cabin.* These so-called "Tom shows" began as early as 1853 and ran for decades after Stowe's death, becoming the most popular play in the history of American theater. Stowe had no editorial control over what happened to her plot and characters; she got no profits from ticket sales. Some productions were anti-slavery plays in keeping with Stowe's wishes. But to sell tickets, many theater managers told their script writers to do "anything to cover up the real drift of the play."[4] In those days white actors donned blackface to play the black characters, and exploited racial stereotypes to entertain white audiences. Touring "Tom troupes" danced and sang and made slavery look almost jolly. And Tom became a shuffling old darkie. A reviewer of an 1853 production in New York described the Uncle Tom character (played by a white man) as "a meek, pious, and subdued old negro . . . [a] pathetic" man.[5]

This bugaboo of "Uncle Tom" lives on in the American consciousness. African American author James Baldwin famously attacked Stowe and *Uncle Tom's Cabin* in a landmark essay entitled "Everybody's Protest Novel" in 1949. Stowe, said Baldwin, "robbed [Tom] of his humanity and divested him of his sex."[6] And in 1963 Black Muslim leader Malcolm X called Martin Luther King Jr. an "Uncle Tom" because King preached nonviolence.[7]

Whites also attacked Stowe's masterwork, albeit for opposite reasons. F. Hopkinson Smith, the architect for the base of the Statue of Liberty, blamed Stowe for precipitating the war. Her incendiary fiction made "the North believe nothing but the worst of the South . . . it was an outrage . . . an appalling, awful, and criminal mistake."[8] Smith was a northerner, and his views were published in the *Chicago Tribune*. Historian David Reynolds shows that in some parts of the South, theatrical versions of *Uncle Tom's Cabin* were banned well into the twentieth century. Despite the racial prejudice that so often attached itself to these shows, the deep current of the story was anti-slavery. And so, long after Stowe died, her work provoked "anti-Tom literature." For example, Thomas Dixon, a Southern Baptist minister, upon seeing a "Tom show," wrote his own play, *The Clansmen*. That in turn became the basis for D. W. Griffith's 1915 silent film *Birth of a Nation,* touting the Ku Klux Klan as the defender of white female virtue and southern honor.[9]

Around the time of Stowe's death, new standards in literature demanded art for art's sake, and Stowe's work was dismissed as sentimental, moralistic, and preachy. But in recent decades, many scholars have reclaimed Stowe's writings as literature with power to reform society. In a now-famous essay from 1985, Jane Tompkins said that Stowe's "critique of American society [was] far more devastating" than any offered by the so-called literary giants, and the huge popularity of her work was reason enough to take *Uncle Tom's Cabin* seriously. Tompkins underscored the "spiritual power" of Stowe's novel, in which religious conversion is necessary "for sweeping social change."[10] Stowe's moral urgency and "sentimental power" — the power to engage emotions and motivate actions — were strengths, not weaknesses.

The cultural stereotype of Uncle Tom is still around, but it need not prevent serious engagement with Stowe. William B. Allen, a political scientist, devoted years of his life to the study of Stowe's works. In *Re-Thinking Uncle Tom,* Allen sees Stowe as a political philosopher who believed the United States was "founded on natural rights and Christianity." Seeing that slavery contradicted this belief, Stowe became "the *only* great American author to address *frontally*" the moral issue of slavery. Allen also sees Stowe as "a preacher" whose use of fiction as a form of "moral persuasion" enjoyed spectacular success. As for the character of Tom, Stowe meant him to be "a human model of surpassing excellence as a democratic standard."[11]

The legacy of Harriet Beecher Stowe as a positive force for social change and as a great author in her own right continues to be lifted up. When the Library of Congress announced its list of eighty-eight "Books that Shaped America," three of the titles were Stowe's: *Uncle Tom's Cabin, A Key to Uncle Tom's Cabin,* and *The American Woman's Home* (co-authored with Catharine Beecher). When we reached the 150th anniversary of the Emancipation Proclamation, PBS marked the occasion with a new series, *The Abolitionists,* in which Harriet Beecher Stowe is one of the featured leaders in the fight against slavery.

She deserves to be remembered for this. But, more broadly, it was her humanity and her skill in describing human nature that made her a great author. She saw human nature by the light of grace, and longed to make things better. Her humanity — at once ordinary and visionary — still shines through the pages she wrote.

Abbreviations

AF, *Life and Letters*	Annie Fields, *Life and Letters of Harriet Beecher Stowe* (London: Sampson Low, 1898)
BL	Yale University, New Haven, Conn. The Beecher Family Papers, American Literature Collection, Beinecke Rare Book and Manuscript Library
BPL	Boston Public Library, Special Collections
CES, *Life*	Charles Edward Stowe, *Life of Harriet Beecher Stowe: Compiled from Her Letters and Journals* (1890; reprint, Honolulu: University Press of the Pacific, 2004)
CHS	Cincinnati Historical Society, Special Collections
HB	Harriet Beecher
HBS	Harriet Beecher Stowe
HPL	Hayes Presidential Library, Fremont, Ohio
JH, *HBS: A Life*	Joan Hedrick, *Harriet Beecher Stowe: A Life* (New York: Oxford University Press, 1994)
LB 1, LB 2	*The Autobiography of Lyman Beecher,* ed. Barbara Cross, 2 vols. (Cambridge: Belknap Press, 1961)
NYPL	New York Public Library, Berg Collection
SchL	Arthur E. and Eliza Schlesinger Library on the History of Women in America, Harvard University, Cambridge, Massachusetts, Beecher-Stowe Family Papers, 1798-1956
SD	Stowe Day Center, Hartford, Conn.
SML	Sterling Memorial Library, Yale University, HBS Correspondence 1828-1885
UTC	*Uncle Tom's Cabin,* in *Harriet Beecher Stowe: Three Novels* (New York: Library of America, 1982)
UVa	University of Virginia Library, Charlottesville, Papers of HBS, Clifton Walter Barrett Library of American Literature Special Collections

Notes

Note to the Introduction

1. Doris Kearns Goodwin, *Team of Rivals: The Political Genius of Abraham Lincoln* (New York: Simon & Schuster, 2005), 689; see also 500 for description of January 1, 1863.

Notes to Chapter 1

1. HBS, *Poganuc People: Their Loves and Lives* (Boston: Houghton Mifflin, 1906), 8.
2. HBS, *Men of our Times, or Leading Patriots of the Day* (Hartford Publishing Co., 1868), 506.
3. LB 1, 46.
4. AF, *Life and Letters*, 10.
5. Vincent Harding, *A Certain Magnificence: Lyman Beecher and the Transformation of American Protestantism, 1775-1863* (Chicago Studies in the History of American Religion, 1991), 21.
6. LB 1, 57, 71.
7. Harding, *Magnificence*, 31.
8. LB 1, 97.
9. Lyman Beecher Stowe, *Saints, Sinners and Beechers* (New York: Bobbs-Merrill, 1934), 75.
10. HBS et. al, *Our Famous Women. An Authorized Record of the Lives and Deeds of Distinguished American Women of our Times* (Freeport, N.Y.: Books for Libraries Press, 1883), 76.
11. LB 1, 117. (The revival took place in 1807; the synod meeting was in 1808.)
12. LB 1, 127.
13. AF, *Life and Letters*, 7.
14. L. B. Stowe, *Saints, Sinners and Beechers*, 37.

15. Milton Rugoff, *The Beechers: An American Family in the Nineteenth Century* (New York: Harper & Row, 1981), 25.

16. Descriptions of Litchfield are from LB 1, 154; and L. B. Stowe, *Saints, Sinners and Beechers,* 38.

17. LB 1, 94.

18. LB 1, 168.

19. HBS, *Poganuc People,* 144-46.

20. HBS, *Men of our Times,* 508.

21. HBS, *Poganuc People,* 124, 125.

22. Tuberculosis is a bacterial infection, most commonly attacking the lungs but also capable of destroying the central nervous system and other vital bodily functions. Many nineteenth-century novels featured a character slowly dying of consumption, for example, "Little Eva" in *Uncle Tom's Cabin.*

23. LB 1, 205, hymn words by Isaac Watts.

24. Stuart Henry, *Unvanquished Puritan: A Portrait of Lyman Beecher* (Grand Rapids: Eerdmans, 1973), 92.

25. LB 1, 179-80.

26. Stephen Snyder, *Lyman Beecher and His Children* (Brooklyn: Carlson Publishing, Inc., 1991), 25.

27. HBS, *Poganuc People,* 157.

28. Lynne Templeton Brickley, "Sarah Pierce's Litchfield Female Academy," in *To Ornament Their Minds: Sarah Pierce's Litchfield Female Academy 1792-1833* (Litchfield, Conn.: Litchfield Historical Society, 1993), 39.

29. AF, *Life and Letters,* 41.

30. LB 1, 392, 395.

31. Hugh McGraw, ed., *The Sacred Harp* (Carrollton, Ga.: Sacred Harp Publishing Company, Inc., 1991), "Saint's Delight," 114; "Jordan," 66; "Florida," 203; and "Gainsville," 70.

32. George Marsden, *The Evangelical Mind and the New School Experience* (New Haven and London: Yale University Press, 1970), 21.

33. Marsden, *The Evangelical Mind,* 22. Marsden quotes Lyman Beecher, "The Bible, a Code of Laws."

34. Marsden, *The Evangelical Mind,* 56.

35. Mark Noll, *America's God: From Jonathan Edwards to Abraham Lincoln* (New York: Oxford University Press, 2005), 280-81.

36. HBS, *My Wife and I* (New York: J. B. Ford, 1871), 6.

37. LB 1, 215.

38. CES, *Life,* 4.

39. LB 1, 217.

40. AF, *Life and Letters,* 13.

41. CES, *Life,* 4.

42. LB 1, 224-25; 221-22, 59.

43. AF, *Life and Letters,* 14.

44. LB 1, 228, 233.

45. AF, *Life and Letters,* 21, 16, 22.

46. LB 1, 40.

47. AF, *Life and Letters,* 18.

48. LB 1, 229-30; AF, *Life and Letters,* 23.

49. LB, 231, 233.

50. Snyder, *Lyman Beecher,* 32.

51. Henry, *Unvanquished Puritan,* 77.

52. LB 1, 239.

53. Henry, *Unvanquished Puritan,* 23.

54. Rugoff, *The Beechers,* 35.

55. LB 1, 262.

56. LB 1, 266.

57. LB 1, 266-68.

58. HBS, *Men of our Times,* 507.

Notes to Chapter 2

1. LB 1, 301, 313.

2. Mary Kelley, *Learning to Stand and Speak: Women, Education and Public Life in America's Republic* (Chapel Hill: University of North Carolina Press, 2008), 157. Kelley quotes a 1787 issue of *Columbian Magazine.*

3. HBS, *Men of our Times,* 507.

4. CES, *Life,* 10, 9; LB 1, 391.

5. HBS, *Poganuc People,* 122-23.

6. Dorothy Baker, "Puritan Providences in Stowe's *The Pearl of Orr's Island:* The Legacy of Cotton Mather," *Studies in American Fiction* 22:1 (March 1994): 62.

7. HBS to Mr. Wood, Andover, January 10, 1863, Sara Parton Papers, Sophia Smith Collection, Smith College Library, Northampton, Mass.

8. Forrest Wilson, *Crusader in Crinoline* (Philadelphia: Lippincott, 1941), 58. Wilson links the presence of Scott's novels in the Beecher household with Catharine's inheritance of Professor Fisher's books in 1823, when Harriet was about 12 years old.

9. LB 1, 390-91.

10. LB 1, 393.

11. HBS, *Our Famous Women,* 584.

12. LB 1, 393.

13. LB 1, 104.

14. HBS, *Our Famous Women,* 80.

15. HBS, *Poganuc People,* 144-46.

16. LB 1, 352. Feb. 1822 letter of Catharine Beecher to Harriet Beecher.

17. HBS, *Poganuc People,* 144-46.

18. LB 1, 388-89; 390-91.

19. Lyman Beecher to George Foote, Jan. 24, 1819, quoted in JH, *HBS: A Life,* 29.

20. Information on the churches of Litchfield is from Catherine Keene Fields, Director Litchfield Historical Society, June 19, 2008.

21. LB 1, 151-52 for the interior description of Beecher's church. Lynne Templeton Brickley, "Sarah Pierce's Litchfield Female Academy," in *To Ornament Their*

Minds: Sarah Pierce's Litchfield Female Academy 1792-1833 (Litchfield Historical Society), 57, for a sketch of the exterior of Beecher's church.

22. LB 1, 53.

23. *The Sacred Harp,* 48f.

24. LB 1, 46.

25. LB 1, 394; AF, 39.

26. Henry, *Unvanquished Puritan,* 76.

27. Albert Van Dusen, "The Constitution of 1818," Connecticut's Heritage Gateway, http://www.ctheritage.org/encyclopedia/ct1763_1818/constitution1818.htm (accessed May 1, 2012).

28. LB 1, 252, 345; see also 336-37, 339.

29. HBS, *Poganuc People,* 126.

30. LB 1, 252.

31. Noll, *America's God,* 176.

32. LB 1, 253.

33. Kelley, *Stand and Speak,* 67.

34. Sally Schwager, "'All United Like Sisters': The Legacy of the Early Female Academies," in *To Ornament Their Minds,* 12-13.

35. Sources differ on exactly when Harriet Beecher first attended Litchfield Academy. In *To Ornament Their Minds,* the appendix (p. 115) gives the date as 1817.

36. Martha Tomhave Blauvelt, *The Work of the Heart: Young Women and Emotion, 1780-1830* (Charlottesville and London: University of Virginia Press, 2007), 52.

37. Brickley, "Litchfield Female Academy," 36.

38. In 1833 Oberlin became the first college to admit a female student. Vassar, Wellesley, and Smith opened in 1865, 1873, and 1875, respectively. Mt. Holyoke began as a female seminary in 1837, when Harriet was twenty-six years old.

39. Brickley, "Litchfield Female Academy," 69.

40. Blauvelt, *Work of the Heart,* 52-53.

41. Brickley, "Litchfield Female Academy," 23, 25.

42. Brickley, "Litchfield Female Academy," 24.

43. LB 1, 165.

44. Kelley, *Stand and Speak,* 39. Hannah More was an English devotional writer; Maria Edgeworth was an English novelist.

45. HBS to [Sarah Pierce], n.d., Miscellaneous Manuscripts, Litchfield Historical Society, Litchfield, Connecticut. (Sarah Pierce died in 1852.)

46. LB 1, 397.

47. Brickley, "Litchfield Female Academy," 35.

48. Brickley, "Litchfield Female Academy," 50.

49. HBS, *Oldtown Folks,* in *Harriet Beecher Stowe: Three Novels* (New York: The Library of America, 1982), 1291.

50. LB 1, 165.

51. Brickley, "Litchfield Female Academy," 42; see also Blauvelt, *Work of the Heart,* 56.

52. CES, *Life,* 13.

53. Kelley, *Stand and Speak,* 96.

54. LB 1, 399.

55. CES, *Life,* 20.

56. LB 1, 398-99.

57. CES, *Life,* 14-15; Kelley, *Stand and Speak,* 97.

58. Brickley, "Litchfield Female Academy," 56-60.

59. Blauvelt, *Work of the Heart,* 153.

60. Brickley, "Litchfield Female Academy," 36.

61. Blauvelt, *Work of the Heart,* 150.

62. Brickley, "Litchfield Female Academy," 58, 60.

63. LB 1, 396.

64. Kathryn Kish Sklar, *Catharine Beecher: A Study in American Domesticity* (New York: Norton, 1976), 28-29.

65. HBS, *Our Famous Women,* 86.

66. HBS, *Our Famous Women,* 76.

67. Sklar, *Catharine Beecher,* 38, 41.

68. LB 1, 360, 377.

69. Sklar, *Catharine Beecher,* 49.

70. LB 1, 378, 384.

Notes to Chapter 3

1. Rugoff, *The Beechers,* 53.

2. CES, *Life,* 32, 69.

3. John Wilkinson, introduction to Richard Baxter, *The Saints' Everlasting Rest* (London: Epworth Press, 1962), 8. Baxter's book inspired John Wesley (founder of Methodism) and William Wilberforce (who fought the British slave trade).

4. CES, *Life,* 32.

5. Harding, *Magnificence,* 202.

6. CES, *Life,* 33-34.

7. Catharine Beecher to Edward Beecher, March 26, 1825, in Jeanne Boydston, Mary Kelley, and Anne Margolis, eds., *The Limits of Sisterhood: The Beecher Sisters on Women's Rights and Woman's Sphere* (Chapel Hill and London: University of North Carolina Press, 1988), 38.

8. LB 2, 27, 30-31. William Beecher studied briefly at Andover; Edward and George attended Yale; Henry went to Amherst; Charles went to Bowdoin; Thomas went to Illinois College while Edward was president there; James went to Dartmouth.

9. Noll, *America's God,* 286-87.

10. LB 2, 35.

11. Harding, *Magnificence,* 201.

12. Sklar, *Catharine Beecher,* 66, 67.

13. LB 2, 82.

14. CES, *Life,* 34.

15. LB 2, 32.

16. Debby Applegate, *The Most Famous Man in America: The Biography of Henry Ward Beecher* (New York: Doubleday, 2006), 53.

17. LB 2, 83, 81.

18. Harding, *Magnificence,* 216-18.

19. LB 2, 84.

20. "Lyman Beecher, An American Family: The Beecher Tradition," Newman Library, Baruch College, City University of New York, http://newman.baruch.cuny.edu/digital/2001/beecher/lyman.htm (accessed May 1, 2012).

21. Harding, *Magnificence,* 216.

22. LB 2, 87.

23. Edward Alexander Lawrence and Theodore Dwight Woolsey, *Life of Rev. Joel Hawes, D.D.* (Harvard University, 1881), 106. Electronic version http://archive.org/details/liferevjoelhaweoowoolgoog (accessed July 11, 2008).

24. CES, 36, 39-40.

25. Sklar, *Catharine Beecher,* 68.

26. HBS to Sarah Ann Terry [1826]. KS Day Collection, Stowe Day Center, Hartford, CT (hereafter cited as SD).

27. HBS, "Earthly Care a Heavenly Discipline" (Cincinnati: American Reform Book and Tract Society, 1852), online version by Steven Railton, Uncle Tom's Cabin in American Culture, http://utc.iath.virginia.edu/christn/chfihbsat.html (accessed May 1, 2012).

28. Catharine Beecher, "To Those who profess or have the hope of Piety in Miss Beecher's School," abridged in Boydston et al., eds., *The Limits of Sisterhood,* 40-41.

29. Sklar, *Catharine Beecher,* 69, 70.

30. Lawrence and Woolsey, *Life of Rev. Joel Hawes, D.D.,* 359.

31. Catharine Beecher to Edward Beecher, in *The Limits of Sisterhood,* 39.

32. CES, *Life,* 49.

33. CES, *Life,* 37-38.

34. Charles Edward Stowe and Lyman Beecher Stowe, *Harriet Beecher Stowe: The Story of Her Life* (Boston and New York: Houghton Mifflin, 1911), 55.

35. Harding, *Magnificence,* 308-9; Noll, *America's God,* 295-96.

36. Rugoff, *The Beechers,* 88.

37. Marie Caskey, *Chariot of Fire: Religion and the Beecher Family* (New Haven and London: Yale University Press, 1978), 128.

38. CES, *Life,* 46, 40. Edward's views may echo German theologian Friedrich Schleiermacher (1768-1834).

39. CES, *Life,* 43, 42.

40. Catharine Beecher, *Educational Reminiscences and Suggestions* (New York: J. B. Ford & Co., 1872), 31.

41. Sklar, *Catharine Beecher,* 72; see also Catharine Beecher, *Reminiscences,* 33.

42. HBS, *Our Famous Women,* 87.

43. Catharine Beecher, *Reminiscences,* 34, 49.

44. Catharine Beecher, *Reminiscences,* 55.

45. Harriet Beecher, "Modern Uses of Language," in Joan Hedrick, ed., *The Oxford Harriet Beecher Stowe Reader* (New York: Oxford, 1999), 23. Hedrick notes that "Modern Uses of Language" was later published in the March 1833 issue of *Western Monthly Magazine.*

46. Beecher, "Modern Uses of Language."

47. JH, *HBS: A Life,* 53-54.

48. HBS to James Parton, n.d., Parton Papers, Smith College Library, Northampton, MA.

49. CES, *Life,* 45.

50. CES, *Life,* 47-49.

51. Daniel Walker Howe, *What Hath God Wrought: The Transformation of America 1815-1848* (Oxford University Press, 2009), 349; see also John A. Andrew III, *From Revivals to Removal* (Athens: University of Georgia Press, 1992), 205.

52. Howe, *What Hath God Wrought,* 349.

53. Catharine Beecher, *Reminiscences,* 62-63.

54. Howe, *What Hath God Wrought,* 349-51.

55. Eric Foner and John Garraty, eds., *The Reader's Companion to American History* (Boston: Houghton Mifflin, 1991), 160, 1081 (henceforth *RCAH*).

56. Sklar, *Catharine Beecher,* 92.

57. HBS, *Our Famous Women,* 87.

58. Sklar, *Catharine Beecher,* 90.

59. Catharine Beecher, *Reminiscences,* 65-67, 69-72.

60. Marsden, *Evangelical Mind,* 9.

61. LB 1, 181, 184.

62. LB 1, 167-68.

63. LB 1, 201.

Notes to Chapter 4

1. William Beecher was pastor of a church in Rhode Island. Edward Beecher was already in the West, serving as president of Illinois College. Mary Beecher Perkins was married and living in Hartford.

2. LB 2, 208.

3. "Jubilee," *The Sacred Harp,* 144.

4. LB 2, 209.

5. Harding, *Magnificence,* 326.

6. C & H Beecher, *Primary Geography for Children,* 5th edition (Cincinnati: Corey & Fairbank, 1833), 105-6.

7. Forrest Wilson, *Crusader in Crinoline* (Philadelphia: J. B. Lippincott Co., 1941), 105-6.

8. HBS, *Men of our Times,* 250-51.

9. William Cheek and Amy Cheek, "John Mercer Langston and the Cincinnati Riot of 1841," in Henry Louis Taylor, ed., *Race and the City* (University of Illinois Press, 1993), 32, 36.

10. CES, *Life,* 63-64.

11. LB 2, 229, 231.

12. JH, *HBS: A Life,* 70, 72.

13. Wilson, *Crusader,* 114.

14. Kelley, *Stand and Speak,* 78, 80; Brickley, "Litchfield Female Academy," 46.

15. C & H Beecher, *Primary Geography,* 53, 54.

16. Wilson, *Crusader,* 112, 116.

17. CES, *Life,* 72.

18. Sklar, *Catharine Beecher,* 111.

19. CES, *Life,* 72, 67.

20. Louis Tucker, "The Semi-Colon Club of Cincinnati," *Ohio History* 73 (1964): 15-17.

21. JH, *HBS: A Life,* 82.

22. Tucker, "Semi-Colon," 20-21.

23. Quoted in Thomas Gossett, *Uncle Tom's Cabin and American Culture* (Dallas: Southern Methodist University Press, 1985), 40.

24. Wilson, *Crusader,* 124.

25. E. Bruce Kirkham, *The Building of Uncle Tom's Cabin* (Knoxville: University of Tennessee Press, 1977), 43.

26. Tucker, "Semi-Colon," 24.

27. Wilson, *Crusader,* 121.

28. HBS, *Men of our Times,* 534.

29. LB 2, 216-18, abridged by the author.

30. Kirkham, *Building,* 28, 86.

31. CES, *Life,* 72.

32. CES, *Life,* 5.

33. Applegate, *Most Famous Man,* 107-8.

34. JH, *HBS: A Life,* 95-96. Hedrick quotes a letter from Harriet Porter Beecher to Lyman Beecher, August 12, 1834.

35. LB 2, 241.

36. Harding, *Magnificence,* 348.

37. LB 2, 243.

38. Harding, *Magnificence,* 350-51.

39. Gilbert Barnes, *The Anti-Slavery Impulse 1830-1844* (American Historical Association, 1933), 73. For the views of Beecher's children on slavery see Barnes, 230 n. 21.

40. Harding, *Magnificence,* 352.

41. Henry, *Unvanquished Puritan,* 194.

42. Harding, *Magnificence,* 353-54.

43. Chris Padgett, "Evangelicals Divided: Abolition and the Plan of Union's Demise in Ohio's Western Reserve," chapter in *Religion and the Antebellum Debate over Slavery,* ed. John McKivigan and Mitchell Snay (Athens: University of Georgia Press, 1998), 261-62.

44. Barnes, *Anti-Slavery Impulse,* 229-30. Note 17 follows Lyman Beecher's movements from May to October. There are several different variations on Lyman Beecher's whereabouts during the Lane crisis arising from inconsistencies in the historical record. However, Beecher was in Cincinnati during the actual debates and then went east.

45. Harding, *Magnificence,* 369.

46. Henry, *Unvanquished Puritan,* 197.

47. LB 2, 245.

48. Harding, *Magnificence,* 372. Apparently there was a preparatory school where students could gain academic competency before beginning seminary.

49. Quoted in Wilson, *Crusader,* 149.

50. Mrs. Wm. Beecher (Katharine Edes) to Mr. and Mrs. Thomas (Mary Beecher) Perkins, November 3, 1834, Cincinnati Historical Society.

51. Harding, *Magnificence,* 392.

52. LB 2, 261-62.

53. Harding, *Magnificence,* 389.

54. Wendell Phillips, "Explanation and Defense," *National Anti-Slavery Standard,* March 23, 1853.

55. HBS, *Men of our Times,* 252.

56. Rugoff, *The Beechers,* 224; Kirkham, *Building,* 28.

57. John Rankin, *The Life of Rev. John Rankin Written by himself in his 80th year c1872* (Ripley: Rankin House National Historic Landmark, 2004), 36.

Notes to Chapter 5

1. CES, *Life,* 76.

2. Rugoff, *The Beechers,* 226.

3. Wilson, *Crusader,* 167.

4. Calvin Ellis Stowe, "A brief account of his professional life," n.d., written in HBS's hand, perhaps dictated by Calvin. Beecher-Stowe Family Papers, 1798-1956, folder 309, microfilm version, SchL.

5. CES, *Life,* 420-21.

6. HBS, *Men of our Times,* 538.

7. Rugoff, *The Beechers,* 220, 222; CES, *Life,* 421-35.

8. CES, *Life,* 78.

9. Calvin's *Report on Elementary Public Instruction in Europe* was published in 1838.

10. CES, *Life,* 80-81.

11. Harding, *Magnificence,* 417-19.

12. Wilson, *Crusader,* 181.

13. Rugoff, *The Beechers,* 230.

14. CES, *Life,* 82.

15. Kelley, *Stand and Speak,* 102.

16. [HBS], "To the Editor of the *Cincinnati Journal and Luminary,"* in Hedrick, ed., *Oxford Reader,* 49-51.

17. Doris Kearns Goodwin, *Team of Rivals* (New York: Simon & Schuster, 2005), 109.

18. CES, *Life,* 86.

19. Ohio History Central: an Online Encyclopedia of Ohio History, "James Birney," Ohio Historical Society, http://www.ohiohistorycentral.org/entry.php?rec =37 (accessed October 26, 2006). See also Wilson, *Crusader,* 182-89; Rugoff, *The Beechers,* 229-31; and JH, *HBS: A Life,* 105-8.

20. CES, *Life,* 84.

21. JH, *HBS: A Life,* 111.

22. Rugoff, *The Beechers,* 232; JH, *HBS: A Life,* 112; Wilson, *Crusader,* 195.

23. JH, *HBS: A Life,* 112.

24. "Panic of 1837," Wikipedia, http://en.wikipedia.org/wiki/Panic_of_1837 (accessed November 1, 2006).

25. JH, *HBS: A Life,* 113-14, 421.

26. Tucker, "Semi-Colon," 16, 26. For Tappan and Lyman Beecher's salary see LB 2, 307, and Rugoff, *The Beechers,* 232.

27. JH, *HBS: A Life,* 113.

28. JH, *HBS: A Life,* 129-30.

29. HBS to Mary Dutton, Dec. 1838, BL, Folder Za Stowe ll.

30. HBS to "Dear Friends All," [April 16,] 1837, in Boydston, ed., *Limits of Sisterhood,* 64.

31. JH, *HBS: A Life,* 115.

32. Rugoff, *The Beechers,* 237, 613.

33. CES, *Life,* 91-92.

34. CES, *Life,* 87-88.

35. Sidney Ahlstrom, *A Religious History of the American People* (New Haven: Yale University Press, 1973), 468.

36. CES, *Life,* 88.

37. LB 2, 323.

38. Marsden, *Evangelical Mind,* 101.

39. Wilson, *Crusader,* 199.

40. Paul Simon, *Freedom's Champion: Elijah Lovejoy* (Carbondale: Southern Illinois University Press, 1994), 32.

41. Simon, *Freedom's Champion,* 103, 112.

42. Rugoff, *The Beechers,* 198-200.

43. Edward Beecher, "Narrative of Riots at Alton," in Stephen Railton, "*Uncle Tom's Cabin* & American Culture," University of Virginia, http://www.iath.virginia .edu/utc/christn/cheseba11f.html (accessed on January 8, 2009).

44. Sklar, *Catharine Beecher,* 123.

45. Catharine E. Beecher, *An Essay on Slavery and Abolitionism, with Reference to the Duty of American Females* (Freeport, N.Y.: Books for Libraries Press, 1970), 102-3.

46. Sklar, *Catharine Beecher,* 131; see also 116-17, 139.

47. Sklar, *Catharine Beecher,* 300.

48. HBS to Mary Dutton, Dec. 1838, BL.

49. HBS to Mrs. [D. H.] Allen, Dec. 31, n.y., Papers of Harriet Beecher Stowe 6318, UVa.

50. Harding, *Magnificence,* 441, 443.

51. HBS to Mary Dutton, Dec. 1838, BL.

52. LB 2, 307.

53. LB 2, 307-8. Lane Seminary survived until 1932, when it was absorbed by McCormick Theological Seminary in Chicago.

54. CES, *Life,* 93.

55. HBS, *Men of our Times,* 259, states that Van Zandt "figured in *Uncle Tom's Cabin* under the name of Van Tromp." See also Kirkham, *Building,* 111-12.

56. Rugoff, *The Beechers,* 237-38. HBS, *Men of our Times,* 259-62, describes Salmon P. Chase's defense of van Zandt and the outcome of the trial. See also L. B.

Stowe, *Saints, Sinners and Beechers,* 175-76. Concerning the Stowes' black worker, accounts vary as to what year this incident took place, whether the servant was legally free when the Stowes hired her, whether or not she had a child with her, and which of the Beecher brothers accompanied Calvin to the home of Van Zandt.

57. CES, *Life,* 201, 202.

58. CES, *Life,* 101.

59. William Cheek and Amy Cheek, "John Mercer Langston and the Cincinnati Riot of 1841," in Henry Louis Taylor, ed., *Race and the City* (University of Illinois Press, 1993), 32, 42-43.

Notes to Chapter 6

1. HBS to Harriet Foote, Jan. 5, 1841, quoted in JH, *HBS: A Life,* 131.

2. HBS, "The Drunkard Reclaimed," *New York Evangelist,* November 30, 1839; continued December 7, 1839.

3. HBS, "Literary epidemics — No. 2," *New York Evangelist,* July 13, 1843.

4. HBS, "Uncle Sam's Emancipation," JH, ed., *Oxford Reader,* 52-56. Originally published as "Immediate Emancipation" in *New York Evangelist,* January 2, 1845.

5. Sklar, *Catharine Beecher,* 140.

6. Kelley, *Stand and Speak,* 216.

7. Calvin Stowe to HBS, April 30, 1842, Acquisitions, SD.

8. Boydston et al., eds., *Limits of Sisterhood,* 68-69.

9. CES, *Life,* 105, 103.

10. HBS to Calvin Stowe, September 4 [1842], SchL, folder 67.

11. JH, *HBS: A Life,* 150-51.

12. JH, *HBS: A Life,* 174.

13. HBS, *The May Flower* (Boston: Phillips, Sampson, and Company, 1855), 4.

14. Gordon Thomas, "The Millerite Movement in Ohio," *Ohio History* 81 (Spring 1972): 95.

15. C. E. (Calvin Ellis) Stowe, *A letter to R. D. Mussey, M.D. on the utter groundlessness of all the millennial arithmetic* (Cincinnati: J. B. Wilson, 1843). Princeton Seminary Special Collections.

16. Rugoff, *The Beechers,* 200-203.

17. Caskey, *Chariot,* 214. For a description of Charles Finney's Oberlin perfectionism see Charles Hambrick-Stowe, *Charles Finney* (Grand Rapids: Eerdmans, 1983), 181-88, 197.

18. LB 2, 312.

19. CES, *Life,* 108.

20. Applegate, *Most Famous Man,* 180.

21. LB 2, 345-46.

22. Henry Ward Beecher to Sarah Beecher, August 19, 1843, CHS.

23. LB 2, 346-47.

24. CES, *Life,* 110.

25. HBS, "The Interior Life: Or, Primitive Christian Experience," *New York Evangelist,* June 19, 1845.

26. HBS to Thomas Beecher, June 2, 1845, in LB 2, 367.

27. LB 2, 369.

28. CES, *Life,* 111-12.

29. LB 2, 377.

30. Wilson, *Crusader,* 220.

31. CES, *Life,* 113.

32. Rugoff, *The Beechers,* 220.

33. Susan Cayleff, *Wash and Be Healed: The Water-Cure Movement and Women's Health* (Philadelphia: Temple University Press, 1987), 2.

34. Cayleff, *Wash and Be Healed,* 38.

35. Jane B. Donegan, "Hydropathic Highway to Health: Women and Water-Cure in Antebellum America," *Contributions in Medical Studies* 17 (New York: Greenwood Press, 1986), 10.

36. Sklar, *Catharine Beecher,* 318.

37. CES, *Life,* 116; Sklar, *Catharine Beecher,* 185.

38. Cayleff, *Wash and Be Healed,* 117.

39. Cayleff, *Wash and Be Healed,* 49-50, 17-18.

40. Ann Braude, *Radical Spirits: Spiritualism and Women's Rights in Nineteenth-Century America* (Bloomington and Indianapolis: Indiana University Press, 2001), 155.

41. HBS to Charley Stowe, October 3, 1877, SchL.

42. Cayleff, *Wash and Be Healed,* 143.

43. Braude, *Radical Spirits,* 155.

44. CES, *Life,* 114.

45. CES, *Life,* 116-18.

46. HBS to Calvin Stowe, January 7 [1847], SchL.

47. HBS to Charley Stowe, October 3, 1877, SchL, folder 192.

48. CES, *Life,* 119.

49. Wilson, *Crusader,* 224, 226; CES, 118.

50. Dr. E. W. Mitchell, typewritten extract of an article on the cholera epidemic from *Ohio Arch. & Hist. Quarterly,* Oct. 1942, CHS. Theodore W. Eversole, University of Cincinnati, unpublished paper, "The Cincinnati Cholera Epidemics of 1832 and 1849: A Case for Revision," CHS.

51. CES, *Life,* 120-25.

52. Wilson, *Crusader,* 227.

53. CES, *Life,* 122.

54. CES, *Life,* 124.

55. Mitchell, extract, CHS. In CES, *Life,* 128, Calvin Stowe estimated that the death toll exceeded 9,000.

Notes to Chapter 7

1. Foner and Garraty, eds., "Compromise of 1850," *RCAH,* 209-10. The Compromise included many other trade-offs. For example, slave auctions were banned from the nation's capital, but not slavery itself.

2. Foner and Garraty, eds., "Fugitive Slave Law," *RCAH,* 432-33. Federal commissioners would be able to "issue warrants, gather posses, and force citizens to help catch runaway slaves under penalty of fine or imprisonment. Captured blacks would be denied a jury trial and could not testify on their own behalf. They could be sent to the South on the basis of a supposed owner's affidavit." Commissioners deciding these cases would be paid "ten dollars for returning the fugitive to the claimant, five dollars if they freed the person." Any federal marshal or other official who did not arrest an accused fugitive slave could be fined $1,000.

3. Gregg D. Crane, *Race, Citizenship and Law in American Literature* (Cambridge University Press, 2002), 12-13.

4. Crane, *Race, Citizenship and Law in American Literature,* 12-15. Crane explains that the concept of Higher Law was not invented by Seward or by abolitionists. It had multiple roots in philosophy, politics, and religion, and especially in justifications for the American Revolution — which involved massive disobedience of English law.

5. Esther Beecher to Isabella Beecher Hooker, March 30, 1850, quoted in JH, *HBS: A Life,* 193.

6. CES, *Life,* 131-33.

7. HBS to Calvin Stowe, May 1850, SchL.

8. Wilson, *Crusader,* 242.

9. HBS to Calvin Stowe, May 1850, SchL.

10. Susan Belasco Smith, "Serialization and Uncle Tom's Cabin," in Kenneth Price and Susan Belasco Smith, eds., *Periodical Literature in Nineteenth-Century America* (Charlottesville and London: University Press of VA, 1995), 78.

11. Stanley Harrold, *Gamaliel Bailey and Antislavery Union* (Kent, Ohio: Kent State University Press, 1986), 88. See also Chapter 7, "The *National Era,*" 81-93.

12. Smith, "Serialization," 79.

13. HBS, "The Freeman's Dream," *National Era,* August 1, 1850.

14. From daughter Harriet and HBS to Calvin Stowe, December 29, 1850. HBS wrote, "I wrote to Mr. Bailey to continue to send the *Era* & either you or I would send the subscription soon. I wish you would do it for I have forty other ways to spend dollars just now." SD.

15. Sklar, *Catharine Beecher,* 233.

16. Kirkham, *Building,* 77.

17. CES, *Life,* 139.

18. CES, *Life,* 145.

19. Son Henry Stowe and HBS to Calvin Stowe, Dec. 1850, SD.

20. Harriet Stowe (daughter) and HBS to Calvin Stowe, Dec. 22, 1850, SD.

21. Harriet (daughter) and HBS to Calvin Stowe, Dec. 29, 1850, SD.

22. CES, *Life,* 144.

23. HBS to George Eliot, March 18, 1876, Berg Collection, New York Public Library (henceforth NYPL). See also Kirkham, *Building,* 65, for Harriet's many accounts of Henry's midnight visit.

24. CES, *Life,* 152.

25. HBS, "The Two Altars; Or, Two Pictures in One," Anti-Slavery tracts No. 13 (Boston: John Jewett & Co., 1852). The work originally appeared as two articles in the *Independent,* June 12 and 19, 1851. In *The Building of Uncle Tom's Cabin* (p. 70), Kirk-

ham says that the two installments in the *Independent* formed a "diptych": one side showing sacrifices for the American Revolution, the other side showing sacrifices (of the slave) that held the Union together.

26. HBS to Isabella Beecher [Edward's wife], 1852, HBS Correspondence 1828-1885, Microfilm Collection HM #63, Reel 1 of 1, SML.

27. Henry Mayer, *All on Fire: William Lloyd Garrison and the Abolition of Slavery* (New York: St. Martin's Press, 1998), 412.

28. CES, *Life*, 148.

29. HBS to Gamaliel Bailey, 1851, transcribed from a typescript in Boston Public Library. Electronic version in Stephen Railton, *"Uncle Tom's Cabin* & American Culture," http://utc.iath.virginia.edu/uncletom/utlthbsht.html (accessed March 7, 2010).

30. Kirkham, *Building*, 67.

31. CES, *Life*, 148. Compare Gossett, *Uncle Tom's Cabin and American Culture*, 91-92, for how Stowe wrote the death of Uncle Tom.

32. Kirkham, *Building*, 72-75.

33. Kirkham, *Building*, 72-73. Kirkham is quoting HBS, "Introduction," to 1879 edition of *Uncle Tom's Cabin*.

34. For a fuller discussion of Stowe's sources see David S. Reynolds, *Mightier Than the Sword: Uncle Tom's Cabin and the Battle for America* (New York and London: W. W. Norton and Co., 2011), 87-116; and Kirkham, *Building*, 61-103.

35. Kirkham, *Building*, 102.

36. Reynolds, *Mightier Than the Sword*, 103.

37. Robin Winks, introduction to *Autobiography of Josiah Henson: An Inspiration for Harriet Beecher Stowe's Uncle Tom* (Mincola, N.Y.: Dover Publications, Inc., 1969), xx.

38. Kirkham, *Building*, 98.

39. JH, *HBS: A Life*, 437. Hedrick credits the term "romantic racialism" to George M. Frederickson, *The Black Image in the White Mind: The Debate on Afro-American Character and Destiny, 1817-1914* (New York: Harper & Row, 1971), 104-5, 110.

40. Robert Levine, "Introduction to Harriet Beecher Stowe," in *Dred: A Tale of the Great Dismal Swamp* (New York: Penguin Books, 2000), xix.

41. Sarah Robbins, *The Cambridge Introduction to Harriet Beecher Stowe* (Cambridge University Press, 2007), 43, 44. Robbins uses the phrase "racial essentialism" to describe Stowe's approach to race. See also Arthur Riss, "Racial Essentialism and Family Values in *Uncle Tom's Cabin*," *American Quarterly* 46 (Dec. 1994): 513-44.

42. HBS, *Uncle Tom's Cabin*, in *Harriet Beecher Stowe: Three Novels* (New York: Library of America, 1982), 270 (henceforth *UTC*).

43. Marva Banks, "Uncle Tom's Cabin and the Antebellum Response," in *A Routledge Literary Sourcebook on Harriet Beecher Stowe's Uncle Tom's Cabin*, ed. Debra J. Rosenthal (New York and London: Routledge, 2004), 37.

44. Charles Dickens to HBS, July 17, 1852. In Rosenthal, ed., *A Routledge Sourcebook*, 33, 34.

45. *UTC*, 212-13.

46. Quoted in Smith, "Serialization," 70.

47. Kirkham, *Building,* 75, 113, 129, 130.

48. Kirkham, *Building,* 155, 140. For a thorough description of Stowe's revisions, see 165-94.

49. "Absorbed in Her Story: Mrs Stowe Couldn't Take Care of Her Family While Writing Uncle Tom. The Interesting Reminiscences of an Old Resident of Brunswick-Town." No author, n.d., newspaper clipping of unnamed newspaper, Bowdoin College, special collections.

50. HBS to "Father & Henry," September 19, 1851, SML.

51. Sklar, *Catharine Beecher,* 323.

52. CES, *Life,* 145.

53. Kirkham, *Building,* 135.

54. JH, *HBS: A Life,* 222.

55. Rugoff, *The Beechers,* 207.

56. Wilson, *Crusader,* 218.

57. Caskey, *Chariot,* 164.

58. Rugoff, *The Beechers,* 408, notes that Charles's sermon was published in New York by J. A. Gray, 1851.

59. Andover Seminary was founded in 1808 to train Congregational clergy after Harvard became Unitarian.

60. Wilson, *Crusader,* 244.

61. HBS to Calvin Stowe, Jan. 1851, typed transcript, SD.

Notes to Chapter 8

1. Unsigned advertisement, *National Era* (April 15, 1852), on Railton website, http://utc.iath.virginia.edu/notices/noaro1ft.html (accessed February 25, 2012).

2. *UTC,* 12.

3. Reynolds, *Mightier Than the Sword,* 37.

4. *UTC,* 169, 170.

5. *UTC,* 232.

6. *UTC,* 516-17. Here Stowe is critical of colonization.

7. *UTC,* 34.

8. *UTC,* 475.

9. *UTC,* 240.

10. *UTC,* 217, 219.

11. *UTC,* 307.

12. Jane Tompkins, "Sentimental Power: *Uncle Tom's Cabin* and the Politics of Literary History," in *Routledge Sourcebook,* 45-46.

13. *UTC,* 387.

14. *UTC,* 405-6.

15. *UTC,* 415.

16. *UTC,* 419-20.

17. *UTC,* 455.

18. *UTC,* 442.

19. *UTC,* 462-63.

20. *UTC,* 482.

21. *UTC,* 480.

22. Eugene Genovese, *Roll, Jordan, Roll: The World the Slaves Made* (New York: Random House, 1976), 242, 253.

23. Jane Tompkins, "Sentimental Power," 46-47; CES, *Life,* 154.

24. *UTC,* 9.

25. HBS to Gamaliel Bailey, 1851: Railton website, http://utc.iath.virginia.edu/uncletom/utlthbsht.html (accessed March 7, 2010).

26. HBS, "The Author's Introduction," *Uncle Tom's Cabin,* Riverside Edition (Boston & New York: Houghton, Mifflin & Co., 1895, 1896), lx.

27. Gossett, *Uncle Tom's Cabin and American Culture,* 98.

28. Ann Douglas, *The Feminization of American Culture* (New York: Doubleday, 1988), 241.

29. HBS, preface to 1852 French edition of *UTC,* digital version on Railton website, http://utc.iath.virginia.edu/uncletom/uteshbsgt.html (accessed March 7, 2012).

30. *UTC,* 41-42.

31. Genovese, *Roll, Jordan, Roll,* 248, 249.

32. *UTC,* 42.

33. *UTC,* 43.

34. Genovese, *Roll, Jordan, Roll,* 245-46, 249.

35. Genovese, *Roll, Jordan, Roll,* 249, quoting W. E. B. Du Bois, *Souls of Black Folk.*

36. Genovese, *Roll, Jordan, Roll,* 241.

37. *UTC,* 214.

38. *UTC,* 457.

39. Mark Noll, *The Civil War as a Theological Crisis* (Chapel Hill: University of North Carolina Press, 2006). See also Noll, *God and Race in American Politics: A Short History* (Princeton University Press, 2008).

40. Abraham Lincoln, Second Inaugural Address, March 4, 1865. "Meditation on the Divine Will," September 1862, "Abraham Lincoln Online Speeches & Writings," http://showcase.netins.net/web/creative/lincoln/speeches/meditat.htm (accessed March 26, 2012).

41. *UTC,* 151-53. See also p. 48, where Mrs. Shelby complains about a minister who defends slavery. Clergy do not come off very well in *Uncle Tom's Cabin.* No major characters are clergy.

42. *UTC,* 218.

43. *UTC,* 322-23.

44. *UTC,* 101.

45. *UTC,* 110; Michael Gilmore, "Uncle Tom's Cabin and the American Renaissance," in *Cambridge Companion to Harriet Beecher Stowe,* ed. Cindy Weinstein (Cambridge: Cambridge University Press, 2004), 60-64.

46. Gilmore, "Uncle Tom's Cabin and the American Renaissance: The Sacramental Aesthetic of Harriet Beecher Stowe," in *Cambridge Companion,* 61.

47. *UTC,* 101.

48. John Gatta, "The Anglican Aspect of Harriet Beecher Stowe," *New England*

Quarterly 73 (September 2000): 433. Jonathan Edwards, *The Nature of True Virtue* (1765), is chiefly responsible for translating the concept of benevolence from British moral philosophy into Calvinist theology.

49. Noll, *God and Race in American Politics,* 27.

50. *UTC,* 302.

51. *UTC,* 363.

52. *UTC,* 415.

53. Railton, "The Bible & The Novel," http://utc.iath.virginia.edu/christn/kjb_utc.html (accessed January 1, 2012).

54. *UTC,* 519. See also p. 362, where Stowe quotes Matthew 25:31-46, a parable of the last judgment.

Notes to Chapter 9

1. Kirkham, *Building,* 141.

2. Quoted in JH, *HBS: A Life,* 223, from a review in the *New York Daily Times,* September 18, 1852; Kirkham, *Building,* 190, gives the amount of Stowe's earnings as $10,300.

3. HBS to Jewett, undated draft of a letter protesting the handling of the contract for *Uncle Tom's Cabin,* SchL.

4. Michael Winship, "'The Greatest Book of Its Kind': A Publishing History of *Uncle Tom's Cabin," Proceedings of the American Antiquarian Society* 102 (1999): 320. Winship is quoting a letter of Isabella Hooker to John Hooker.

5. HBS to Edward Beecher, n.d., SchL.

6. Barbara A. White, *The Beecher Sisters* (New Haven and London: Yale University Press, 2003), 56.

7. Gamaliel Bailey, *National Era,* April 15, 1852, Railton website, http://www.iath.virginia.edu/utc/reviews/rere01czt.html (accessed May 10, 2012).

8. *Christian Inquirer,* April 10, 1852, Railton website, http://www.iath.virginia.edu/utc/reviews/rere115at.html (accessed May 10, 2012).

9. *Southern Literary Messenger,* October 1852, Railton website, http://www.iath.virginia.edu/utc/reviews/rere24at.html (accessed May 10, 2012).

10. *New York Daily Times,* June 22, 1853, Railton website, http://www.iath.virginia.edu/utc/reviews/rere05bt.html (accessed May 10, 2012).

11. *Boston Morning Post,* May 3, 1852, Railton website, http://www.iath.virginia.edu/utc/reviews/rere50at.html (accessed May 10, 2012).

12. Elizabeth Fox-Genovese and Eugene Genovese, *The Mind of the Master Class: History and Faith in the Southern Slaveholder's Worldview* (Cambridge University Press, 2005), 387.

13. William Lloyd Garrison, *The Liberator,* March 26, 1852, Railton website, http://www.iath.virginia.edu/utc/reviews/rere02at.html (accessed May 10, 2012).

14. CES, *Life,* 161.

15. William G. Allen, letter to *Frederick Douglass' Paper,* May 20, 1852, quoted in Henry Louis Gates Jr. and Hollis Robbins, eds., "Harriet Beecher Stowe and 'The Man That Was a Thing,'" unsigned introduction to *The Annotated Uncle Tom's Cabin*

(New York and London: W. W. Norton, 2006), xxxvii. For the controversy over colonization in *Uncle Tom's Cabin,* see Sarah Robbins, *Cambridge Introduction,* 41.

16. C.V.S., "George Harris," in *Provincial Freeman,* July 22, 1854, Railton website, http://utc.iath.virginia.edu/africam/pfhp.html (accessed February 17, 2012). Instead of [alas] the original read, "save the mark."

17. Gossett, *Uncle Tom's Cabin and American Culture,* 213. See also Stephen Railton's extensive website, "*Uncle Tom's Cabin* & American Culture: A Multi-Media Archive," http://www.iath.virginia.edu/utc/ for full texts of primary sources related to *Uncle Tom's Cabin,* including several "anti-Tom" novels.

18. Joy Jordan-Lake, *Whitewashing Uncle Tom's Cabin: Nineteenth-Century Women Novelists Respond to Stowe* (Nashville: Vanderbilt University Press, 2005), 127.

19. Unsigned editorial, "Rev. Joel Parker, D.D. vs. Mrs. Harriet Beecher Stowe," *The Independent* 4 (November 1852): 182.

20. Letter of HBS to the Rev. Joel Parker, May 22, 1852, in Joan Hedrick, ed., *The Oxford Harriet Beecher Stowe Reader* (New York and Oxford: Oxford University Press, 1999), 68. See also Kirkham, *Building,* 190.

21. Applegate, *Most Famous Man,* 263.

22. Quoted in Sklar, *Catharine Beecher,* 326. Sklar refers to a May 1852 letter in the *New York Observer.*

23. HBS to Henry Ward Beecher, November 1, 1852, SML.

24. HBS to Editor, *New York Observer* [May 1852], SML.

25. JH, *HBS: A Life,* 230.

26. HBS to Henry Ward Beecher, November 1, 1852, SML.

27. HBS to Mrs. Follen, February 16, 1853, in CES, *Life,* 203.

28. Weinstein, "Uncle Tom's Cabin and the South," in *Cambridge Companion,* 53.

29. HBS, *Key to Uncle Tom's Cabin* (New York: Arno Press, 1968), 153 (henceforth, *Key*).

30. *Key,* 242.

31. *Key,* 133.

32. Samuel Otter, "Stowe and Race," in *Cambridge Companion,* 29.

33. *Key,* 384-85.

34. *Key,* 388.

35. *Key,* 407-8.

36. *Key,* 481.

37. *Key,* 491, 496, 494.

38. *Key,* 503-4.

39. Gossett, *Uncle Tom's Cabin and American Culture,* 190-91.

40. Wilson, *Crusader,* 370; Rugoff, *The Beechers,* 331.

41. Frederick Douglass, *Frederick Douglass' Paper,* April 29, 1853, Railton website, http://utc.iath.virginia.edu/africam/afaro3nt.html (accessed February 15, 2011).

42. CES, *Life,* 203.

43. Francis Underwood, [Stowe at a Performance of *Uncle Tom's Cabin,* 1853], in Susan Belasco, ed., *Stowe in Her Own Time: A Biographical Chronicle of Her life, Drawn from Recollections, Interviews, and Memoirs by Family, Friends, and Associates* (Iowa City: University of Iowa Press, 2009), 75.

44. Four or five years before *UTC* was published, Mr. Edmondson (a free black man) sought Henry Ward Beecher's help to ransom two daughters. Mary was thirteen years old, her sister Emily fifteen; they were being held in a slave warehouse, soon to be shipped to New Orleans for sale. Because of their light skin, they would bring a high price in the "fancy trade" as sex slaves and breeders. Mary and Emily had been part of a failed escape attempt: seventy-seven slaves from Washington, D.C., tried to escape aboard the schooner *Pearl.* The ship's captain planned to sail down the Potomac and then north up the Atlantic coast, releasing the fugitives on free soil. But an informer betrayed them and the *Pearl* was caught. Irate masters sold off the newly captured slaves to a large slave-trading firm, which would sell the whole lot in New Orleans. Mr. Edmondson was given an option to buy his own daughters for the sum of $2500, *if* he could raise the money *before* the girls were shipped to New Orleans. The father could never hope to earn a sum exceeding $70,000 in today's money. Mr. Edmondson went north to seek help from abolitionists. Someone from the New York anti-slavery society sent him to Henry Ward Beecher. Moved by the father's tears, Beecher agreed to help. Beecher held a meeting in the large Broadway Tabernacle; he dramatized the story to the crowd, role-playing the stricken parents, the calculating slave trader, and the poor innocent girls. Finally, Henry staged a mock auction and worked the crowd until they bid up the entire amount needed to buy the Edmondson girls' freedom. The two girls were ransomed, but when Harriet first met Mrs. Edmondson she was still a slave, and several more of her children were still enslaved. *Key,* 306-30.

45. CES, *Life,* 180-81; see also JH, *HBS: A Life,* 248-49.

46. Jean Fagan Yellin, *Harriet Jacobs: A Life* (Cambridge, Mass.: Basic Civitas Books, 2004), 121.

47. Belasco, ed., "Harriet Jacobs," in *Stowe in Her Own Time,* 95.

48. Yellin, *Harriet Jacobs,* 220.

49. Thanks are due to Claudia Egelhoff for her comments on this section.

50. Frederick Douglass, "First Meeting with Stowe," 1853, in *Stowe in Her Own Time,* 86-94. Douglass's idea for an industrial school for blacks preceded Tuskegee Institute by twenty-eight years.

51. Douglass, in *Stowe in Her Own Time,* 94.

52. Douglass, in *Stowe in Her Own Time,* 94; see also JH, *HBS: A Life,* 247.

53. Nell Irvin Painter, *Sojourner Truth: A Life, A Symbol* (New York: W. W. Norton & Co., 1996), 130-31.

54. Carleton Maybee, *Sojourner Truth: Slave, Prophet, Legend* (New York University Press, 1993), 112-13.

55. HBS, "The Libyan Sibyl," *Atlantic Monthly,* April 1863, 476-77.

56. CES, *Life,* 170, 173-74. JH, *HBS: A Life,* 236, identifies two female anti-slavery groups that invited Stowe: the Glasgow Ladies Anti-Slavery Society and the Glasgow Female New Association for the Abolition of Slavery.

57. Hedrick, *Oxford Reader,* 451-52.

58. CES, *Life,* 197-204.

59. CES, *Life,* 190.

60. Audrey Fisch, "Uncle Tom and Harriet Beecher Stowe in England," in Cindy

Weinstein, ed., *Cambridge Companion,* 101. Fisch cites the *Nonconformist* and *The Eclectic Review.*

61. Fisch, "Stowe in England," 99.

62. Fisch, "Stowe in England," 97.

63. David Brion Davis, *Inhuman Bondage: The Rise and Fall of Slavery in the New World* (New York: Oxford University Press, 2008), 246.

64. Anne Farrow, Joel Lang, and Jenifer Frank, *Complicity: How the North Promoted, Prolonged, and Profited from Slavery* (New York: Ballantine Books, 2008), 124.

65. Fisch, "Stowe in England," 105; see also 97, 107, 110.

Notes to Chapter 10

1. Charles Beecher, *Harriet Beecher Stowe in Europe: The Journal of Charles Beecher,* ed. Joseph VanWhy and Earl French (Stamford, Conn.: The Stowe Day Foundation, 1986), xvii (henceforth Beecher, *Journal*).

2. HBS, *Sunny Memories of Foreign Lands,* vol. 1 (New York: Bibliobazaar, 2007), 1, 84-86 (henceforth HBS, *SM* 1).

3. HBS, *SM* 1, 96.

4. Beecher, *Journal,* 27.

5. HBS, *SM* 1, 97.

6. Beecher, *Journal,* 27.

7. Beecher, *Journal,* 136-37.

8. JH, *HBS: A Life,* 238.

9. Beecher, *Journal,* 36-37.

10. Mark Noll, *Civil War as Theological Crisis,* 102-3.

11. HBS, *SM* 1, 125-26.

12. HBS, *SM* 1, 141.

13. Beecher, *Journal,* 45.

14. Beecher, *Journal,* 51-52.

15. Wilson, *Crusader,* 357.

16. William B. Allen, *Rethinking Uncle Tom: The Political Philosophy of Harriet Beecher Stowe* (New York: Rowman and Littlefield, 2009), 257. Allen is quoting Calvin Stowe.

17. Beecher, *Journal,* 42.

18. HBS, *SM* 1, 186.

19. HBS, *SM* 1, 202.

20. HBS, *SM* 1, 209-10.

21. HBS, *SM* 1, 226.

22. HBS, *SM* 1, 161.

23. HBS, *SM* 1, 268.

24. Beecher, *Journal,* 58-60.

25. Beecher, *Journal,* 63.

26. HBS, *SM* 1, 245.

27. HBS, *SM* 1, 276-77.

28. HBS, *SM* 1, 279.

29. Gossett, *Uncle Tom's Cabin and American Culture,* 250-51. Gossett describes a review of *UTC* that Dickens co-wrote with Henry Morely for *Household Words* (September 18, 1852). See also Wilson, *Crusader,* 328, for the "noble but defective" quote. Dickens thought Stowe portrayed slavery too harshly. And as noted earlier, he thought she praised Africa and Africans too highly.

30. HBS, *SM* 1, 282.

31. HBS, *SM* 1, 284.

32. Unsigned editorial, [from] The Foreign News, *Richmond Daily Dispatch,* May 17, 1853, Railton website, http://utc.iath.virginia.edu/proslav/prar170aqt.html (accessed May 13, 2007).

33. HBS, *SM* 1, 283.

34. Wikipedia, "Lancaster House," http://en.wikipedia.org/wiki/Stafford_House (accessed July 30, 2007).

35. Beecher, *Journal,* 82.

36. Beecher, *Journal,* editor's n. 114, 362: Stowe knew the contents of the address, since it was already in print. The volumes of signatures had already been sent to America.

37. Beecher, *Journal,* 85.

38. Beecher, *Journal,* 89.

39. HBS, *SM* 1, 323. Stowe also helped Greenfield make a connection with Sir George Smart, "the head of the queen's musical establishment" (297).

40. Beecher, *Journal,* 120.

41. Unsigned editorial, June 23, 1853, [from] The Foreign News, *Richmond Daily Dispatch,* Railton website, http://utc.iath.virginia.edu/proslav/prar170ayt.html (accessed September 12, 2007).

42. Harriet Beecher Stowe, *Sunny Memories of Foreign Lands,* vol. 2 (Whitefish, MT: Kessinger Publishing Reprints, 2004), 96 (henceforth HBS, *SM* 2).

43. New Schaff-Herzog Encyclopedia Online, s.v. "Noel, Baptist Wriothesley." http://www.ccel.org/ccel/schaff/encyc08/Page_186.html (accessed June 20, 2009).

44. HBS, *SM* 1, 319-20.

45. HBS, *SM* 2, 38.

46. HBS, *SM* 1, 320.

47. HBS, *SM* 1, 298.

48. HBS, *SM* 2, 51.

49. Wikipedia, s.v. "Thomas Clarkson," http://en.wikipedia.org/wiki/Thomas_Clarkson (accessed June 27, 2009).

50. Beecher, *Journal,* 115; HBS, *SM* 2, 58.

51. HBS, *SM* 2, 74.

52. Beecher, *Journal,* 122.

53. Wilson, *Crusader,* 382-83.

54. Audrey Fisch, "Uncle Tom and Harriet Beecher Stowe in England," in Weinstein, ed., *Cambridge Companion,* 103.

55. HBS, *SM* 2, 59-60; 63-68.

56. Unsigned Notice, May 1853, "Reception of Mrs. Beecher Stowe in London," *The United States Review,* Railton website, http://utc.iath.virginia.edu/notices/noar124at.html (accessed September 11, 2007).

57. Fanny Fern [Stowe and *Uncle Tom's Cabin*, 1853] in Belasco, ed., *Stowe in Her Own Time*, 70-72.

58. Susie Steinbach, *Women in England 1760-1914: A Social History* (New York: Palgrave Macmillan, 2004), 168.

59. HBS, *SM* 2, 85.

60. HBS, *SM* 2, 91.

61. HBS, *SM* 1, 211.

62. HBS, *SM* 1, 287.

63. Beecher, *Journal,* 41-42.

Notes to Chapter 11

1. David McCullough, "'I Have Come into a Dreamland': Harriet Beecher Stowe Seeks Refuge in Paris from the Notoriety of *Uncle Tom's Cabin*," *American History* (August 2011): 54.

2. HBS, *SM* 2, 101; Beecher, *Journal,* 148-49.

3. Beecher, *Journal,* 181.

4. HBS, *SM* 2, 108-9.

5. HBS, *SM* 1, 96.

6. HBS, *SM* 2, 110.

7. HBS, *SM* 2, 116, 111.

8. HBS, *SM* 2, 114.

9. Beecher, *Journal,* 152.

10. Beecher, *Journal,* 163.

11. HBS, *SM* 2, 119.

12. Carla Rineer, "Stowe and Religious Iconography," in Denise Kohn, Sarah Meer, and Emily Todd, eds., *Transatlantic Stowe: Harriet Beecher Stowe and European Culture* (Iowa City: University of Iowa Press, 2006), 194.

13. Beecher, *Journal,* 191.

14. Beecher, *Journal,* 200.

15. Beecher, *Journal,* 201.

16. HBS, *SM* 2, 164; Beecher, *Journal,* 262.

17. HBS, *SM* 2, 163.

18. HBS, *SM* 2, 149; see also 215.

19. HBS, *SM* 2, 148.

20. HBS, *SM* 2, 152-53.

21. HBS, *SM* 2, 177, 154-56.

22. HBS, *SM* 2, 188.

23. HBS, *SM* 2, 188.

24. HBS, *SM* 2, 216, 234.

25. HBS, *SM* 2, 222.

26. Beecher, *Journal,* 302-3.

27. HBS, *SM* 2, 245.

28. HBS, *SM* 2, 250.

29. HBS, *SM* 2, 253.

30. JH, *HBS: A Life,* 250.

31. Wilson, *Crusader,* 397; JH, *HBS: A Life,* 253-54.

32. John Gatta, "Calvinism Feminized: Divine Matriarchy in Harriet Beecher Stowe," in Gatta, *Images of the Divine Woman in Literary Culture* (New York: Oxford University Press, 1997), 54.

33. L. B. Stowe, *Saints, Sinners and Beechers,* 163.

34. Elizabeth Stuart Phelps, Recollections of Stowe at Andover, in Belasco, ed., *Stowe in Her Own Time,* 126.

35. Beecher, *Journal,* 45, 47; Fisch, "Stowe in England," in Weinstein, ed., *Cambridge Companion,* 109.

36. JH, *HBS: A Life,* 248.

37. CES, *Life,* 250.

38. Wilson, *Crusader,* 371-72.

39. Louis Ruchames, ed., *Letters of William Lloyd Garrison,* vol. 4 (Cambridge & London: Belknap Press of Harvard University, 1975), 286. HBS to William Lloyd Garrison, November 1853, BPL.

40. Mayer, *All on Fire,* 214.

41. Mayer, *All on Fire,* 226. In 1836, when Beecher supported the exclusion of abolitionist speakers from Congregational parishes in Connecticut and Massachusetts, Garrison criticized him in print.

42. Mayer, *All on Fire,* 328.

43. William Lloyd Garrison, "To the Public," from the Inaugural Editorial in the *Liberator,* January 1, 1831.

44. Mayer, *All on Fire,* 239, 327.

45. Louis Menand, *The Metaphysical Club: A Story of Ideas in America* (New York: Farrar, Straus and Giroux, 2002), 14.

46. Mayer, *All on Fire,* 276.

47. Menand, *Metaphysical Club,* 13. For Garrison's own vision of his prophetic call to abolition, see Mayer, *All on Fire,* 149-50.

48. Mayer, *All on Fire,* 465, 214, 223.

49. Noll, *Civil War as a Theological Crisis,* 31, 72.

50. CES, *Life,* 263.

51. Ruchames, ed., *Letters of Garrison,* vol. 4, 283.

52. Ruchames, ed., *Letters of Garrison,* vol. 4, 284.

53. Ruchames, ed., *Letters of Garrison,* vol. 4, 284.

54. Ahlstrom, *Religious History,* 606.

55. CES, *Life,* 264.

56. CES, *Life,* 254.

57. HBS to William Lloyd Garrison, February 18, 1854, BPL.

58. Ruchames, ed., *Letters of Garrison,* vol. 4, 287. JH, *HBS: A Life,* 251-52, notes that Stowe requested a meeting with Garrison; in 422 n. 15 Hedrick cites indirect evidence that Garrison and Stowe met for the first time *before* her trip to England. Wilson, *Crusader,* 395, has Garrison an overnight guest at the Stone Cabin. Mayer, *All on Fire,* 421, reports that Stowe and Garrison met in person.

59. Mayer, *All on Fire,* 213, see also 119, 141.

60. Mayer, *All on Fire,* 465.

61. Mayer, *All on Fire,* 432.
62. HBS to William Lloyd Garrison, December 19, 1853, BPL.
63. HBS to William Lloyd Garrison, December 19, 1853, BPL.
64. HBS to William Lloyd Garrison, December 22, 1853, BPL.
65. HBS to William Lloyd Garrison, February 18, 1854, BPL.

Notes to Chapter 12

1. Technically, slavery was prohibited north of the parallel 36° 30′ north, except within the state of Missouri.
2. HBS, "An Appeal to Women of the Free States of America, on the Present Crisis in Our Country," in Hedrick, ed., *Oxford Reader,* 453.
3. HBS, "An Appeal to Women," 456.
4. The account of the clergy petition relies on Wilson, *Crusader,* 401-2.
5. Mayer, *All on Fire,* 436-37.
6. HBS, "Shadows on the Hebrew Mountains," *Independent* 3 (January 26, 1854): 1.
7. HBS, "Shadows," 1.
8. HBS, "Shadows," *Independent* 4 (February 23, 1854): 1.
9. JH, *HBS: A Life,* 266, 269.
10. Allen, *Rethinking Uncle Tom,* 258.
11. Harding, *Magnificence,* 466.
12. Cross, ed., Introduction to LB 1, xi.
13. HBS to Catharine Beecher, August 27, 1858, SchL.
14. Harding, *Magnificence,* 465-67. I am following Harding's account of Lyman Beecher's old age.
15. Peter Thuesen, "The 'African Enslavement of Anglo-Saxon Minds': The Beechers on Augustine," *Church History* 72 (September 2003): 580, 585.
16. L. B. Stowe, *Saints, Sinners and Beechers,* 70.
17. Sklar, *Catharine Beecher,* 231.
18. Howe, *What Hath God Wrought,* 39.
19. HBS, "The First Christmas of New England," in *The First Christmas of New England and Other Tales* (Hollywood, Calif.: Aegypan Press, 2006), 99. (First published as *Betty's Bright Idea,*1875.)
20. Wilson, *Crusader,* 407.
21. HBS, *Poganuc People,* 35.
22. "Beecher Bibles," Kansas State Historical Society, http://www.kshs.org/portraits/beecher_bibles.htm (accessed February 27, 2008).
23. Applegate, *Most Famous Man,* 281.
24. Mayer, *All on Fire,* 448.
25. Applegate, *Most Famous Man,* 281-82.
26. William Reynolds, "Henry Ward Beecher's Significant Hymnal," *The Hymn* (April 2001): 22-23.
27. Reynolds, "Hymnal," 17.
28. Reynolds, "Hymnal," 18; Reynolds is quoting Beecher's 1874 Yale Lectures.

29. Henry Ward Beecher, *Plymouth Collection of Hymns and Tunes for the Use of Christian Congregations* (New York: A. S. Barnes & Co., 1857), iv.

30. Reynolds, "Hymnal," 20.

31. H. W. Beecher, *Plymouth Collection,* v.

32. Reynolds, "Hymnal," 20, 22.

33. F. J. Webb, "Biographical Sketch [of Mary Webb]," in Railton website, http://www.iath.virginia.edu/utc/uncletom/xianslav/xsesfjwat.html (accessed May 16, 2012).

34. HBS to Lady Hatherton, May 24, 1856, in Railton website, http://www.iath.virginia.edu/utc/uncletom/xianslav/xsmshbsat.html (accessed May 16, 2012).

35. Stowe's "The Christian Slave" was published by Philips, Samson and Company in 1855. See Robbins, *Cambridge Introduction,* 73-76.

36. Allen, *Rethinking Uncle Tom's Cabin,* 437-40.

37. HBS to son Henry Stowe, 1855, SchL.

38. Wilson, *Crusader,* 409.

39. HBS, *Dred: A Tale of the Great Dismal Swamp* (Cambridge, Mass.: Riverside Press, 1884), 519. First published in 1856 by Philips, Sampson & Co.

40. JH, *HBS: A Life,* 260.

41. Stowe did *not* name her novel after Dred Scott, a slave who sought legal freedom on the grounds of having lived for years in free states or territories, and whose case came before the Supreme Court in 1856 and was decided, negatively, in 1857. Stowe named her book and its black hero Dred after one of the conspirators in the slave uprising led by Nat Turner in 1831. The dismal swamp was home to escaped slaves ("maroons") who hid there. The "dismal swamp" may also have implied a nation mired in slavery and sinking into war.

42. HBS to Lady Byron, October 16, 1856, SchL.

43. CES, *Life,* 266.

44. HBS, *Dred,* 268.

45. HBS, *Dred,* 270.

46. HBS, *Dred,* 276.

47. HBS, *Dred,* 441.

48. HBS, *Dred,* 455-56.

49. HBS, *Dred,* 290-91.

50. HBS, *Dred,* 288.

51. Robbins, *Cambridge Introduction,* 71.

52. Robert S. Levine, "Introduction," *Dred: A Tale of the Great Dismal Swamp* (New York and London: Penguin Books, 2000), v.

53. Levine, "Introduction," x; see also xix.

54. Wilson, *Crusader,* 412-13; Applegate, *Most Famous Man,* 284.

55. Applegate, *Most Famous Man,* 285.

Notes to Chapter 13

1. JH, *HBS: A Life,* 262.

2. JH, *HBS: A Life,* 263.

3. CES, *Life,* 271.

4. JH, *HBS: A Life,* 449.

5. CES, *Life,* 273, 278.

6. CES, *Life,* 279, for British sales of *Dred.* Levine, "Introduction" to *Dred,* ix, states that this book sold more than 200,000 copies in the U.S. during the nineteenth century.

7. JH, *HBS: A Life,* 262-63.

8. Unsigned, "Mrs. Stowe and *Dred," Southern Literary Messenger,* October 1858. Railton website, http://utc.iath.virginia.edu/redirect.php (accessed September 7, 2009).

9. CES, *Life,* 282-83.

10. CES, *Life,* 285.

11. Wilson, *Crusader,* 428-29.

12. AF, *Life and Letters,* 207.

13. CES, *Life,* 291-92.

14. Noll, *Civil War as Theological Crisis,* 7.

15. CES, *Life,* 292.

16. HBS, *Independent,* January 29, 1857.

17. JH, *HBS: A Life,* 270.

18. CES, *Life,* 301, 303.

19. CES, *Life,* 306.

20. CES, *Life,* 307.

21. CES, *Life,* 316.

22. "The Death of Young Stowe," August 13, 1857, *New York Times* online archive, http://query.nytimes.com/mem/archive-free/pdf?_r=1&res=9D02EEDE163 CEE34BC4B52DFB166838C649FDE&oref=slogin (accessed March 1, 2008).

23. CES, *Life,* 321, 322.

24. CES, *Life,* 319.

25. CES, *Life,* 320.

26. CES, *Life,* 324.

27. CES, *Life,* 326.

28. CES, *Life,* 339-40.

29. Ellery Sedgwick, "The Atlantic Monthly," in Edward Chielens, ed., *American Literary Magazines* (New York: Greenwood Press, 1986), 50-52. See also Cullen Murphy, "A History of the Atlantic Monthly," http://www.theatlantic.com/about/ atlhistf.htm (accessed April 5, 2008).

30. JH, *HBS: A Life,* 289.

31. Edmund Wilson, *Patriotic Gore: Studies in Literature of the American Civil War* (Richmond, Va.: Hogarth Press, 1987), 39-40.

32. HBS, *The Minister's Wooing,* in Sklar, ed., *Stowe: Three Novels,* 539 (henceforth, *MW*).

33. *MW,* 542.

34. *MW,* 540.

35. Joan Hedrick, "'Peaceable Fruits': The Ministry of Harriet Beecher Stowe," *American Quarterly* (Spring 1988): 320.

36. *MW,* 727-28.

37. *MW,* 730.

38. *MW,* 732.

39. *MW,* 731.

40. Candace was the name both of the Ethiopian queen in the book of Acts and also of the servant who comforted a very young Harriet Beecher when her mother died. See John Gatta, *Images of the Divine Woman,* 64, and Wilson, *Patriotic Gore,* 40.

41. *MW,* 636-37. The author has slightly abridged and updated this passage.

42. *MW,* 742.

43. Gatta, *Images of the Divine Woman,* 64.

44. Noll, *America's God,* 325-26.

45. CES, *Life,* 335.

46. "Theology and Morality of the Minister's Wooing," unsigned editorial, *Independent,* February 9, 1860.

47. CES, *Life,* 345-55.

48. Stowe's contact with spiritualism dates back at least to 1853 and her first trip to Europe. Charles Beecher's *Journal,* 149, mentions a séance they attended in Paris. Charles noted several factual errors in messages purported to be from dead relatives. "The rappings and tippings are spreading here [in Europe] I judge" wrote Charles. See also 163, 179. Charles was skeptical about spiritualism, but later took it seriously.

49. CES, *Life,* 349-52.

50. HBS, *Agnes of Sorrento* (London: Elibrion Classics, 2005), 156 (henceforth, *Agnes*).

51. HBS to Mr. Fields, quoted in Annie Fields, "Days with Mrs. Stowe," in Belasco, ed., *Stowe in Her Own Time,* 140.

52. *Agnes,* 241.

53. *Agnes,* 137.

54. *Agnes,* 90.

55. *Agnes,* 232.

56. Reynolds, *Mightier Than the Sword,* 163-64, 303. Reynolds cites an article by Stowe for the *Independent,* February 16, 1860, p. 1; and a letter from HBS to John Brown Paton, March 2, 1860, E. Bruce Kirkham Collection, SD, for Stowe's quotes on John Brown.

57. Jennifer Harris, "It's a Family Affair: Harriet Beecher Stowe and Annie and James T. Fields," in Earl Yarington and Mary De Jong, eds., *Popular Nineteenth-Century American Women Writers and the Literary Marketplace* (Cambridge: Scholars Publishing, 2007), 322.

58. Winship, "Publishing History of *Uncle Tom's Cabin,*" 324.

59. Harris, "Family Affair," 324.

60. Anne Farrow, Joel Lang, and Jenifer Frank, *Complicity: How the North Promoted, Prolonged and Profited from Slavery* (New York: Ballantine Books, 2005), 121-22.

61. Harding, *Magnificence,* 73, 216.

62. See Noll, *Civil War as Theological Crisis,* 50.

Notes to Chapter 14

1. HBS, "The President's Message, *Independent* 12 (December 20, 1860): 1. The "old Africa" part may refer to a speech by Sojourner Truth. See Maybee, *Sojourner Truth,* 83.

2. Rugoff, *The Beechers,* 352; CES, *Life,* 364.

3. HBS to Charles Sumner, quoted in Wilson, *Crusader,* 479.

4. CES, *Life,* 366.

5. HBS, "Getting Ready for a Gale," *Independent* 13 (April 25, 1861): 1; "The Holy War" (May 9, 1861): 1.

6. HBS, "Letter from Andover: The Times, the British People, the Havelock Grays, the Andover Company," *Independent* 13 (June 20, 1861): 1.

7. HBS, "Letter from Andover," 1.

8. HBS, "Letter to Lord Shaftesbury," *Independent* 13 (July 21, 1861): 1. Emphasis added.

9. Wilson, *Crusader,* 43.

10. Wendy Hamand, "'No Voice From England': Mrs. Stowe, Mr. Lincoln, and the British in the Civil War," *New England Quarterly* 31 (March 1988): 10-11.

11. Lydia Marie Child, "[An Evening with Stowe in 1861]," in Belasco, ed., *Stowe in Her Own Time,* 143.

12. HBS, "Letter from Andover," *Independent* 13 (September 12, 1861): 1.

13. Hamand, "No Voice," 13n.26.

14. Mayer, *All on Fire,* 526.

15. HBS, "Letter from Andover," 1.

16. Mayer, *All on Fire,* 527.

17. Wilson, *Crusader,* 475.

18. HBS, "A Card by Mrs. Harriet Beecher Stowe," *Independent* 13 (December 5, 1861).

19. Wilson, *Crusader,* 465.

20. HBS, *The Pearl of Orr's Island* (Hartford: Stowe-Day Foundation, 1990), 252 (henceforth, *Pearl*).

21. HBS, *Pearl,* 423.

22. Dorothy Baker, "Puritan Providences in Stowe's *The Pearl of Orr's Island:* The Legacy of Cotton Mather," *Studies in American Fiction* 22, no. 1 (March 1994): 69.

23. Charles H. Foster, *The Rungless Ladder: Harriet Beecher Stowe and New England Puritanism* (Durham, N.C.: Duke University Press, 1954), 151.

24. Baker, "Puritan Providences," 60-79.

25. HBS, *Pearl,* 15, 375, 430.

26. HBS, *Pearl,* 15.

27. HBS, *Pearl,* 399, 424.

28. Baker, "Puritan Providences," 65.

29. HBS, *Pearl,* 348; see also 269, 347.

30. HBS, *Pearl,* 396.

31. HBS, *Pearl,* 414.

32. HBS to "My Dear Girls," Ascension Sunday, June 1, 1862, SchL.

33. Doris Kearns Goodwin, *Team of Rivals: The Political Genius of Abraham Lincoln* (New York: Simon & Schuster, 2005), 459.

34. Goodwin, *Team of Rivals,* 468.

35. HBS to Duchess of Argyll, July 31, 1862, UVa.

36. Horace Greeley, "The Prayer of Twenty Millions," Lincoln Studies: Abraham Lincoln and the Civil War, http://www.lincolnstudies.com/archives/80 (accessed May 18, 2012).

37. Don E. Fehrenbacher, ed., *Abraham Lincoln: Speeches and Writings,* vol. 2 (New York: Library of America, 1989), 357-58.

38. Goodwin, *Team of Rivals,* 471.

39. HBS, "Will You Take a Pilot?" in Hedrick, ed., *Oxford Reader,* 471.

40. HBS, "Will You Take a Pilot?" 473.

41. HBS, "Will You Take a Pilot?" 475.

42. HBS, "Will You Take a Pilot?" 473.

43. Rugoff, *The Beechers,* 391, 390.

44. 2 Kings 8:13.

45. Applegate, *Most Famous Man,* 339.

46. Typescript of letter from Mary Beecher Perkins and Harriet Beecher Stowe, to Henry Ward Beecher, Nov. 2, 1862, SML.

47. JH, *HBS: A Life,* 304-5.

48. AF, *Life and Letters,* 262.

49. Some versions of the story have Stowe's son Charles accompanying her (see Hamand, "No Voice," 15, and L. B. Stowe, *Saints, Sinners and Beechers,* 205).

50. JH, *HBS: A Life,* 305.

51. Hamand, "No Voice," 14.

52. CES, 366-67.

53. HBS to Eliza Stowe, last page of a letter from Hatty Stowe to Eliza Stowe, Washington, December 3, 1862, SchL.

54. JH, *HBS: A Life,* 305; see also CES, *Life,* 367. The two generals were Steinwahr and Buckingham.

55. HBS to Mr. Wood, Andover, Jan. 10, 1863, Sara Parton Papers, Sophia Smith Collection, Smith College (henceforth SC).

56. "Contrabands and Freedmen, Mister Lincoln and Freedom," Lehrman Institute, Lincoln Institute, http://www.mrlincolnandfreedom.org/inside.asp?ID=30 &subjectID=3 (accessed December 28, 2009).

57. HBS, "Address to the Women of Great Britain," in AF, *Life and Letters,* 266.

58. JH, *HBS: A Life,* 305.

59. Hatty Stowe to Eliza Stowe, Washington, Dec. 3, 1862, SchL.

60. Abraham Lincoln, "Annual Message to Congress," in Fehrenbacher, ed., *Lincoln: Speeches and Writings,* 414-15.

61. JH, *HBS: A Life,* 306.

62. L. B. Stowe, *Saints, Sinners and Beechers,* 205. There are variations on this quote, which has never been verified but seems plausible.

63. Hatty Stowe to Eliza Stowe, Washington, December 3, 1862, SchL. For a version of this meeting that has Charles, rather than Hatty, present, see Wilson, *Crusader,* 484-85. In L. B. Stowe, *Saints, Sinners and Beechers,* 206, twelve-year-old Charles Stowe

asks his mother about Lincoln's quaint grammar. In Rugoff, *The Beechers,* 356, Stowe's son Charley sees "the President rubbing his hands before an open fire" and hears him say, "I do love a fire in a room. I suppose it's because I always had one to home." Afterward Charley asked his mother why Lincoln said "to home" instead of "at home." Stowe is said to have quoted 2 Corinthians 11:6: "Though I be rude in speech but not in knowledge; but we have been thoroughly made manifest among you in all things.'" These are apocryphal reports.

64. JH, *HBS: A Life,* 306. If Stowe ever wrote more about her meeting with Lincoln, the account has not survived.

65. HBS, *Men of our Times,* 74. On Lincoln's use of humor, see Joshua Wolf Shenk, *Lincoln's Melancholy: How Depression Challenged a President and Fueled His Greatness* (Boston and New York: Houghton Mifflin, 2005), 133-38.

66. HBS, "Simon the Cyrenian," *Independent* 14, quoted in Diana Butler Bass, *A People's History of Christianity: The Other Side of the Story* (New York: HarperCollins, 2009), 258-60.

Notes to Chapter 15

1. Goodwin, *Team of Rivals,* 498.

2. Goodwin, *Team of Rivals,* 499.

3. Goodwin, *Team of Rivals,* 500.

4. L. B. Stowe, *Saints, Sinners and Beechers,* 207.

5. Harding, *Magnificence,* 472.

6. LB 2, 432.

7. HBS to Hatty Stowe, January 17, 1863, SchL.

8. HBS, "A Reply of Many Thousands of Women of Great Britain and Ireland, to Their Sisters, the Women of the United States of America," *Atlantic Monthly,* January 1863, 133.

9. Hamand, "No Voice," 18, 20, 22.

10. AF, *Life and Letters,* 294.

11. Rugoff, *The Beechers,* 357.

12. Robbins, *Cambridge Introduction,* 10.

13. JH, *HBS: A Life,* 311.

14. HBS to Duchess of Argyll, June 1, 1863, UVa.

15. HBS to Henry Ward Beecher, August 20, 1863, SML.

16. On March 3, 1863, Congress passed the Conscription Act authorizing the President to draft men for military service. But an exemption could be bought for three hundred dollars.

17. Foner and Garraty, eds., *RCAH,* s.v. "Draft Riots," 295.

18. Rugoff, *The Beechers,* 412.

19. Rugoff, *The Beechers,* 412.

20. HBS to H. W. Beecher, August 20, 1863, SML.

21. HBS to H. W. Beecher, September 11, 1863, SML.

22. Rugoff, *The Beechers,* 413.

23. HBS to H. W. Beecher, September 11, 1863, SML.

24. Caskey, *Chariot,* 314-15. Caskey quotes a letter from HBS to James Beecher, April 28, 1863.

25. L. B. Stowe, *Saints, Sinners and Beechers,* 386.

26. HBS to Henry Ward Beecher, September 11, 1863, SML.

27. L. B. Stowe, *Saints, Sinners and Beechers,* 291.

28. Rugoff, *The Beechers,* 392-394.

29. HBS to Hatty Stowe, November 27, 1863, SchL.

30. HBS to Hatty Stowe, December 13, 1863, SchL.

31. JH, *HBS: A Life,* 308.

32. HBS to Mr. Gunn, June 6, 1864, SML.

33. JH, *HBS: A Life,* 309.

34. Rugoff, *The Beechers,* 358.

35. AF, *Life and Letters,* 296.

36. Rugoff, *The Beechers,* 359.

37. Theusen, "African Enslavement," 589.

38. Gatta, "Anglican Aspect," 425.

39. Gatta, "Anglican Aspect," 423.

40. Gatta, "Anglican Aspect," 424; JH, *HBS: A Life,* 324.

41. Sklar, *Catharine Beecher,* 260.

42. HBS, *Our Famous Women,* 654.

43. Wilson, *Crusader,* 502.

44. Harriet Beecher Stowe, *House and Home Papers,* googlebooks, http://books
.google.com/books?id=xlcLAAAAIAAJ&printsec=frontcover&dq=House+and+Home
+Papers&cd=1#v=onepage&q=&f=false, 162 (accessed May 21, 2012).

45. HBS, *House and Home Papers,* 333.

46. The 1662 *Book of Common Prayer,* http://www.eskimo.com/˜lhowell/bcp
1662/occasion/sick_visit.html (accessed May 21, 2012).

47. Rugoff, *The Beechers,* 457.

48. L. B. Stowe, *Saints, Sinners and Beechers,* 386.

49. HBS, *Household Papers and Stories* (Boston & New York: Houghton Mifflin &
Co., 1896), 433, 429, originally published as "The New Year," *Atlantic Monthly,* January 1865.

50. HBS, *Household Papers and Stories,* 434.

51. HBS, *Household Papers and Stories,* 437.

52. Jay Winik, *April 1865: The Month That Saved America* (New York: Harper,
2001), 48-62.

53. L. B. Stowe, *Saints, Sinners and Beechers,* 387.

54. Rugoff, *The Beechers,* 460. According to Rugoff, James Beecher continued
working in the Charleston area after the war, seeking fair wages for black laborers.
Beecher was relieved of his command when the 35th United States Colored Troops
was mustered out of service in June 1866.

55. Applegate, *Most Famous Man,* 9-10.

56. L. B. Stowe, *Saints, Sinners and Beechers,* 296.

57. HBS, *Men of our Times,* 96.

58. Stowe, "The Noble Army of Martyrs," *Atlantic Monthly,* August 1865, 233.

59. Winik, *April 1865,* 323.

60. Stowe, "Noble Army," 237.
61. Winik, *April 1865,* 299.
62. HBS to the Duchess of Sutherland, September 1865, UVa.
63. CES, *Life,* 397.

Notes to Chapter 16

1. CES, *Life,* 397.
2. HBS to Henry Ward Beecher, October 8, 1866. Typed transcript, SML.
3. Olav Thulesius, *Harriet Beecher Stowe in Florida, 1867-1884* (Jefferson, N.C.: McFarland and Co., 2001), 32.
4. Susan Eaker, "Gender in Paradise: Harriet Beecher Stowe and Postbellum Prose on Florida," *Journal of Southern History* 99:3 (1998): 495, quoting a letter from HBS to Calvin Stowe and children, March 10, 1867.
5. Thulesius, *Stowe in Florida,* 33-34.
6. HBS, "The Captain's Story," *Our Continent* (December 27, 1882): 790.
7. Thulesius, *Stowe in Florida,* 38-39.
8. Thulesius, *Stowe in Florida,* 51-52.
9. CES, *Life,* 401-2.
10. Thulesius, *Stowe in Florida,* 39.
11. JH, *HBS: A Life,* 336.
12. L. B. Stowe, *Saints, Sinners and Beechers,* 230. See JH, *HBS: A Life,* 327, for a critical view of the family anecdote on how Calvin's book was published.
13. Calvin Stowe, *Origin and History of the Books of the New Testament, Both the Canonical and the Apocryphal, Designed to Show What the Bible Is Not, What It Is, and How to Use It* (Hartford: Hartford Publishing Co., 1867), 37.
14. Stowe, *Origin and History,* 13-14.
15. Stowe, *Origin and History,* 32-33.
16. Stowe, *Origin and History,* 18-19.
17. Stowe, *Origin and History,* 32.
18. JH, *HBS: A Life,* 337.
19. Thulesius, *Stowe in Florida,* 69-71.
20. The first phase of feminism was closely tied to the anti-slavery movement. Many reformers hoped that women could get the vote along with freedmen after the war. In 1866 the American Equal Rights Association was formed to push for the enfranchising of blacks *and* women. Hopes for women's suffrage were dashed when the Fifteenth Amendment granted voting rights to black males but not to women. Moderate reformers supported the Fifteenth Amendment, preferring gradual progress for women to none at all. But radical reformers felt betrayed. Rejecting the idea that black males deserved the vote more than any women, black or white, these feminists were dubbed "irreconcilables." Led by Susan B. Anthony and Elizabeth Cady Stanton, they formed the Boston-based National Woman's Suffrage Association (NWSA) in 1869. Then a moderate group, led by Lucy Stone and others, formed the American Woman Suffrage Association (AWSA), headquartered in New York, with

Henry Ward Beecher as president. The two groups had different principles, styles, and strategies, as did the factions of the anti-slavery movement before the war.

21. HBS, "Greeting from Mrs. Stowe," *Hearth and Home,* December 26, 1868, 8. For Stowe on the value of women's unpaid labor, see Stowe, "Who Earned that Money," *Hearth and Home,* October 9, 1869, 665.

22. HBS to Fanny Fern, quoted in White, *Sisters,* 146.

23. HBS, "What Is and What Is Not the Point of the Woman Question?" *Hearth and Home,* August 28, 1869, 568.

24. Calvin Stowe, "The Woman Question and the Apostle Paul," *Hearth and Home,* September 11, 1869, 600-601.

25. HBS to Ralph Waldo Emerson, [n.d.]. Photocopy viewed at SD; original in Houghton Library of Harvard University.

26. HBS to Edward Everett Hale, April 14, 1869, SD.

27. White, *Sisters,* 149.

28. White, *Sisters,* 145.

29. HBS to George Eliot, May 1 and 2, 1869, NYPL.

30. White, *Sisters,* 150.

31. Susan B. Anthony to Isabella Beecher Hooker, August 9 and 10, 1869, SD.

32. They met in the New York home of Paulina Wright Davis, another leading feminist.

33. White, *Sisters,* 149.

34. JH, *HBS: A Life,* 357.

35. White, *Sisters,* 152.

36. HBS, *Oldtown Folks,* in *Harriet Beecher Stowe: Three Novels,* ed. Kathryn Kish Sklar (New York: Library of America, 1982), 954-55.

37. Foster, *Rungless Ladder,* 172.

38. Wilson, *Crusader,* 530-31.

39. HBS, *Oldtown Folks,* 1237.

40. HBS to Charles Stowe, May 4, 1874, SchL.

41. HBS, *Oldtown Folks,* 1249.

42. HBS, *Oldtown Folks,* 1238, 1255.

43. HBS, *Oldtown Folks,* 1244, 1247.

44. HBS, *Oldtown Folks,* 1305.

45. HBS, *Oldtown Folks,* 1458.

46. JH, *HBS: A Life,* 345, 347.

47. White, *Sisters,* 153.

48. HBS, "True Story of Lady Byron's Life," in Hedrick, ed., *Oxford Reader,* 558.

49. HBS, *Lady Byron Vindicated* (Fairford, England: Echo Library, 2006), 1-2.

50. White, *Sisters,* 152.

51. "Stowe It!" cartoon in *Fun Magazine,* Sept. 1869, 17, in Belasco, ed., *Stowe in Her Own Time,* 183.

52. HBS, "The True Story of Lady Byron's Life," in Hedrick, ed., *Oxford Reader,* 545.

53. HBS, *Lady Byron Vindicated,* 1, 2.

54. HBS, *Lady Byron Vindicated,* 180.

55. HBS, *Palmetto Leaves* (Gainesville: University Press of Florida, 1999), 36.

56. John T. Foster Jr. and Sarah Whitmer Foster, *Beechers, Stowes, and Yankee Strangers: The Transformation of Florida* (Gainesville: University Press of Florida, 1999), 74.

57. Gatta, "Anglican Aspect," 412-13, 415.

58. CES, *Life,* 402.

59. AF, *Life and Letters,* 329.

60. Thulesius, *Stowe in Florida,* 80-81.

61. CES, *Life,* 404-5.

62. Thulesius, *Stowe in Florida,* 82.

63. See Foster and Foster, *Beechers, Stowes, and Yankee Strangers,* 4.

64. I have relied on JH, *HBS: A Life,* 381, for details about the baptism of Freeman Allen.

65. Thulesius, *Stowe in Florida,* 76.

Notes to Chapter 17

1. Richard Wightman Fox, *Trials of Intimacy: Love and Loss in the Beecher-Tilton Scandal* (University of Chicago Press, 1999), 210.

2. Fox, *Trials,* 2-3.

3. White, *Sisters,* 205. As in all scandals, there are different versions of who said what to whom and when.

4. Ann Braude, *Radical Spirits: Spiritualism and Women's Rights in Nineteenth Century America* (Bloomington and Indianapolis: Indiana University Press, 2001), 171.

5. JH, *HBS: A Life,* 373. The *Woman's Journal* was the organ of the American Woman's Suffrage Association, the conservative rival to Stanton's National Woman's Suffrage Association.

6. Harriet Beecher Stowe, *My Wife and I* (New York: J. B. Ford & Co., 1871), 257, 269.

7. Samuel Schreiner, *The Passionate Beechers: A Family Saga of Sanctity and Scandal That Changed America* (Hoboken: Wiley, 2003), 265, 270.

8. JH, *HBS: A Life,* 373-74.

9. Applegate, *Most Famous Man,* 413.

10. Fox, *Trials,* 155.

11. Schreiner, *Passionate Beechers,* 272; Fox, *Trials,* 294-95.

12. Fox, *Trials,* 157.

13. JH, *HBS: A Life,* 376.

14. HBS to Mrs. Claflin, December 24, 1872, Claflin Collection, HPL. Mrs. Claflin was the wife of William Claflin, governor of Massachusetts, and a distant relative of Victoria Woodhull and her sister Tennessee Claflin.

15. Rugoff, *The Beechers,* 572.

16. White, *Sisters,* 211-12.

17. Schreiner, *Passionate Beechers,* 305.

18. HBS to Mrs. Claflin, July 27, 1874, HPL.

19. Applegate, *Most Famous Man,* 431-32; 441.

20. HBS to George Eliot, August 20, 1874, NYPL.

21. Applegate, *Most Famous Man,* 438; Fox, *Trials,* 69.

22. HBS to Mrs. Claflin, July 27, 1874, HPL.

23. AF, *Life and Letters,* 357.

24. Rugoff, *The Beechers,* 496.

25. Schreiner, *Passionate Beechers,* 293-94.

26. Fox, *Trials,* 39.

27. Fox, *Trials,* 5.

28. HBS to George Eliot, March 18, 1876, NYPL.

29. Reynolds, *Mightier Than the Sword,* 61.

30. HBS to Charles Stowe, May 25, 1875, SchL.

31. HBS to Charles Stowe, September 20, 1873, SchL.

32. HBS to Charles Stowe, September 27, 1874, SchL.

33. HBS, *Woman in Sacred History: A Celebration of Women in the Bible* (New York: Portland House, 1990), 11.

34. HBS to Charles Stowe, September 27, 1874, SchL.

35. Rineer, "Stowe and Religious Iconography," in *Transatlantic Stowe,* 188.

36. Gatta, *Divine Woman,* 55-58.

37. HBS, *Woman in Sacred History,* 198.

38. See CES, *Life,* 421-36, for Calvin's account of his paranormal experiences.

39. CES, *Life,* 484. "Diablerie" is black magic or sorcery, or in a lighter sense, mischief.

40. Caskey, "Spiritualism," *Chariot,* 287-331. Caskey devotes an entire chapter to showing spiritualism as "pervasive and compelling . . . in the lives of the Beechers."

41. HBS to George Eliot, May 11, 1872, NYPL.

42. Schreiner, in *Passionate Beechers,* 306, says that Catharine Beecher consulted with Katie Fox. Catharine reported that Fox claimed to "see" Lyman Beecher "kneeling before Catharine and presenting her a rose as a sign of her purity." Catharine dismissed that as nonsense, for her father never praised Catharine, except that "he used to say I was the best boy he had."

43. CES, *Life,* 466. See also HBS, "The Debatable Land," *Christian Union,* January 24, 1872. There Stowe said, "The phenomena of spiritualism are proper subjects for scientific research . . . [but] the science of that realm is yet in its infancy, and the facts are too incomplete to build a system upon."

44. Braude, *Radical Spirits,* 73.

45. Mayer, *All on Fire,* 465.

46. Braude, *Radical Spirits,* xxi.

47. John Buescher, *The Other Side of Salvation: Spiritualism and the Nineteenth-Century Experience* (Boston: Skinner House Books, 2004), 127-28.

48. AF, *Life and Letters,* 370.

49. Caskey, *Chariot,* 298, 302, 328.

50. HBS, "Spiritualism," *Christian Union,* September 3, 1870, 129.

51. HBS, "Spiritualism," *Christian Union,* September 10, 1870, 145.

52. HBS, "Spiritualism," *Christian Union,* October 1, 1870, 177-78.

53. HBS, "A Look Beyond the Veil," *Christian Union,* November 5, 1870, 277.

54. HBS, "Debatable Land," January 24, 1872, n.p.

55. HBS to George Eliot, February 8, 1872, NYPL. This letter was written two years after Stowe's *Christian Union* articles. However, the experiences Stowe relates in the letter are not dated.

56. HBS to George Eliot, May 11, 1872, NYPL.

57. Gordon S. Haight, ed., *The George Eliot Letters,* vol. 5 (New Haven: Yale University Press, 1955). George Eliot to HBS [24] June 1872, 281; George Eliot to HBS July 1869, 48-49; George Eliot to HBS May 8, 1869, 31.

58. HBS to George Eliot, February 8, 1872, NYPL.

59. HBS to George Eliot, May 11, 1872, NYPL.

60. HBS to George Eliot, May 11, 1872, NYPL.

61. CES, *Life,* 466.

62. AF, *Life and Letters,* 307-10; also CES, *Life,* 484-88. On May 2, 2011, Beth Burgess, Collections Manager of the Harriet Beecher Stowe Center in Hartford, Connecticut, accessed the Kirkham Collection notes on Stowe's "mature views" letter. Kirkham dates this letter to c. 1868.

63. HBS, "Debatable Land," n.p.

64. In 1 Samuel 28:3-25 King Saul commands a medium to call up the spirit of the dead prophet Samuel. Saul sees Samuel's ghost and hears his own defeat and death predicted.

65. HBS, *Woman in Sacred History,* 129-30.

66. CES, *Life,* 413.

67. JH, *HBS: A Life,* 391; 471, n. 69; Caskey, *Chariot,* 412.

68. Douglas, *Feminization of American Culture,* 244, 247, 253.

69. HBS, *My Wife and I, Or, Harry Henderson's History* (New York: L. B. Ford & Co., 1871), 90.

70. Gatta, "Anglican Aspect," 421.

71. *Palmetto Leaves* was compiled from earlier sketches first published in *Christian Union.* See Susan Eaker, "Gender in Paradise: Harriet Beecher Stowe and Postbellum Prose on Florida," *The Journal of Southern History* 64:3 (August 1998): 498.

72. HBS, *Palmetto Leaves* (Gainesville: University Press of Florida, 1999), 293, 295.

73. Thulesius, *Stowe in Florida,* 96.

74. HBS, *Palmetto Leaves,* 258-61.

75. HBS, "The Rights of Dumb Animals," *Hearth and Home* 1 (January 2, 1869): 24.

76. Mary B. Graff, *Mandarin on the St. Johns* (St. Augustine: University of Florida Press, 1953), 63.

77. Thulesius, *Stowe in Florida,* 114.

78. "Harriet Beecher Stowe House," Harriet Beecher Stowe Center website, Hartford, CT, http://www.harrietbeecherstowecenter.org/visit/hbs_house.shtml (accessed May 24, 2012).

79. AF, *Life and Letters,* 344, 346-48.

80. Wilson, *Crusader,* 587.

Notes to Chapter 18

1. Thulesius, *Stowe in Florida,* 128.

2. Thulesius, *Stowe in Florida,* 133.

3. HBS to George Eliot, March 1876, NYPL.

4. HBS, "The Indians at St. Augustine," *Christian Union* (April 18 and 25): 345, 372.

5. HBS, "The Indians at St. Augustine," 345, 372.

6. Schreiner, *Passionate Beechers,* 306.

7. Sklar, *Catharine Beecher,* 272-73.

8. HBS to Charles Stowe, September 27, 1874, SchL.

9. HBS to Charles Stowe, October 3, 1877, SchL.

10. First Parish, Saco, Maine, "Our History," http://firstparishsaco.org/cgi-bin/menu.pl?churchid=church3343 (accessed July 8, 2011).

11. HBS to Charles Stowe, April [?] 1879, SchL.

12. HBS to Charles Stowe, February 4, 1881, SchL. The banquet table analogy is the author's interpretation.

13. HBS to Charley, n.d., SchL.

14. Gatta, *Divine Woman,* 53.

15. CES, *Life,* 415. Stowe was responding to Holmes's 1861 novel *Elsie Venner,* which criticized basic tenets of Calvinism. See Foster, *Rungless Ladder,* 131-35.

16. W. Paul Jones, *Theological Worlds: Understanding the Alternative Rhythms of Christian Belief* (Nashville: Abingdon, 1989). The paradigms "conflict and vindication" and "separation and reunion" are adapted from Jones.

17. Gatta, "Anglican Aspect," 416.

18. HBS to Charley, April 9, 1877, SchL.

19. Gatta, "Anglican Aspect," 420.

20. HBS to Charley, n.d. (probably 1881).

21. HBS to Charley, undated fragment, SchL.

22. HBS to Charley, October 1877, SchL.

23. HBS, *Footsteps of the Master* (London: Sampson, Low and others, 1877). See chapter entitled "The Attractiveness of Jesus," 172-83.

24. HBS, *Footsteps of the Master,* 189-90.

25. HBS, *Footsteps of the Master,* 186-88.

26. Robbins, *Cambridge Introduction,* 93.

27. HBS, *Poganuc People,* 248, 250,

28. HBS, *Poganuc People,* 215, 73, 219.

29. CES, *Life,* 507.

30. Anonymous, "The Birthday Garden Party to Harriet Beecher Stowe," 1882, in Belasco, ed., *Stowe in Her Own Time,* 193.

31. "Birthday Garden Party," 202.

32. "Birthday Garden Party," 212.

33. "Birthday Garden Party," 220.

34. "The History of the Church of Our Savior," official website of Episcopal Church of Our Savior, http://www.coos.org/ (accessed April 26, 2011). In 1964, Hurricane Dora destroyed most of the church building, including the Tiffany window. A new church was built on that location and the congregation remains active.

35. AF, *Life and Letters,* 386-89.

36. Boydston, Kelley, Margolis, eds., *Sisterhood,* 355.

37. JH, *HBS: A Life,* 396.

38. Charles Stowe left his church in Hartford in 1891 to serve the Congregational Church in nearby Simsbury, Connecticut.

39. Stowe and Stowe, *Story of Her Life,* 297.

40. CES, *Life,* 512.

41. [Edward] William J. Bok, "Mrs. Stowe Talks: Probably the Last Interview With the Great Authoress" [1889]. Clipping of several columns, from an unidentified publication, in HPL.

42. Applegate, *Most Famous Man,* 467-68.

43. JH, *HBS: A Life,* 397; and HBS, "The Other World," in *Religious Studies, Sketches and Poems, The Writings of Harriet Beecher Stowe,* vol. 15 (Boston and New York: Houghton, Mifflin and Co., 1896), 312-13.

44. Stowe and Stowe, *Story of Her Life,* 297.

45. Wilson, *Crusader,* 628.

46. CES, *Life,* n.p.

47. Thulesius, *Stowe in Florida,* 138.

48. Bok, "Mrs. Stowe Talks," n.p.

49. Edward Bok, *The Americanization of Edward Bok* (New York: C. Scribner's Sons, 1920), Google Books, http://books.google.com/books?id=Z5ZZAAAAMAAJ&dq =Stowe%2C+Bok&q=Stowe#v=snippet&q=Stowe&f=false (accessed June 27, 2011), 96.

50. JH, *HBS: A Life,* 397.

51. Exchange between Harriet Beecher Stowe and Oliver Wendell Holmes in 1893, in Belasco, ed., *Stowe in Her Own Time,* 245.

52. JH, *HBS: A Life,* 398.

53. AF, *Life and Letters,* 377.

54. Stowe and Stowe, *Story of Her Life,* 301.

55. New York Times Online, "On This Day July 2, 1896, Obituary Harriet Beecher Stowe," http://www.nytimes.com/learning/general/onthisday/bday/0614.html (accessed June 2, 2011).

56. HBS, "When I Awake I Am Still with Thee," *Religious Studies, Sketches and Poems,* 357.

Notes to the Epilogue

1. Tolstoy, *What Is Art?* trans. Alymer Maude (New York: Thomas Y. Crowell & Co., 1898), 145. Google Books, http://books.google.com/books?output=html&id =0SYVAAAAYAAJ&jtp=145 (accessed December 31, 2012).

2. *The Weekly Call,* unsigned piece, Topeka, July 3, 1896. http://utc.iath .virginia.edu/africam/afar58at.html (accessed December 31, 2012).

3. David S. Reynolds, *Mightier Than the Sword: Uncle Tom's Cabin and the Battle for America* (New York: W. W. Norton & Co., 2011), 256.

4. Thomas Gossett, *Uncle Tom's Cabin and American Culture* (Dallas: Southern Methodist University Press, 1985), 277.

5. Gossett, *Uncle Tom's Cabin and American Culture,* 279.

6. Jane Tompkins, "Sentimental Power: *Uncle Tom's Cabin* and the Politics of Literary History," in *A Routledge Literary Sourcebook on Harriet Beecher Stowe's Uncle Tom's Cabin,* ed. Debra Rosenthal (New York: Routledge, 2004), 41.

7. "A Summing up: Louis Lomax Interviews Malcolm X," 1963, transcription of interview, http://teachingamericanhistory.org/library/index.asp?document=539 (accessed December 31, 2012).

8. Stephen Prothero, *The American Bible: How Our Words Unite, Divide, and Define a Nation* (New York: Harper Collins, 2012), 177.

9. Reynolds, *Mightier Than the Sword,* 210.

10. Tompkins, "Sentimental Power," in Rosenthal, ed., *Routledge Literary Sourcebook,* 43, 46.

11. William B. Allen, *Rethinking Uncle Tom: The Political Philosophy of Harriet Beecher Stowe* (New York: Rowman & Littlefield Publishers, Inc., 2009), 233, 244.

Index